The Chaco Mission Frontier

The Chaco Mission Frontier

The Guaycuruan Experience

JAMES SCHOFIELD SAEGER

THE UNIVERSITY OF ARIZONA PRESS

TUCSON

The University of Arizona Press
www.uapress.arizona.edu

 Published 2000
First paperback edition 2016

Printed in the United States of America
21 20 19 18 17 16 7 6 5 4 3 2

ISBN-13: 978-0-8165-2017-6 (cloth)
ISBN-13: 978-0-8165-3359-6 (paper)

Design and composition by Wilsted & Taylor Publishing Services

Cover designed by Wilsted & Taylor Publishing Services
Cover image: A Mocobi chief with his wife and son. [From Florian Paucke, *Hacia allá y para acá (una estada entre los indios Mocobíes, 1749–1767)*, vol. 2]

Library of Congress Cataloging-in-Publication
Saeger, James Schofield.
The Chaco Mission Frontier : the Guaycuruan experience / James Schofield Saeger.
p. cm.
Includes bibliographical references and index.
ISBN 0-8165-2017-8 (acid-free paper)
1. Guaycuruan Indians—Missions. 2. Guaycuruan Indians—History.
3. Missions—Gran Chaco. I. Title.
F2230.2.G78 S34 2000
982'.3—dc21
00-008254

British Library Cataloguing-in-Publication Data
A catalogue record for this book is available from the British Library.

♾ This paper meets the requirements of ANSI/NISO Z39.48-1992 (Permanence of Paper).

To my sons,
Jamey and Ted

CONTENTS

FIGURES

PREFACE

Catholic missions were institutions by which Spanish and Portuguese societies represented themselves to others. They are thus important measures of the Iberian empires. In *The Chaco Mission Frontier*, I consider the effectiveness of Catholic missions in Spanish America by examining how Guaycuruan peoples of the Gran Chaco adapted to them in the 1700s. What follows differs from many other accounts of the institution. Guaycuruan reductions began with Jesuit missionaries, but this book is not an addition to the voluminous literature about Jesuits.[1] The experience of Guaycuruans is instructive, especially that of the Abipones, Mbayás, Mocobis, and Toba, four linguistically related culture groups of the Gran Chaco of South America who accepted missions. In the following chapters, they are at center stage.

Guaycuruans stood apart from many other Native Americans who accepted missionization. Unlike semisedentary peoples who brought prior agricultural experience to reductions in Paraguay, Moxos, northern Mexico, and later the southwestern United States, Guaycuruans—including Abipones, Mocobis, Mbayás, the Toba, Pilagá, and others—were nonsedentary (or semi-nomadic) hunters and gatherers. Not true nomads, because they traveled in circumscribed areas, they nevertheless wandered frequently in search of game and plant foods. They usually moved within territories that they claimed exclusive rights to exploit, although private ownership of land had no meaning for them before missionization. Guaycuruans were not, at first glance, good candidates for Catholic reductions.[2] Being warrior peoples, they believed that hunting and war made life worthwhile. They scorned peoples like their neighbors the Guaranis of central Paraguay and those natives in the Jesuit reductions who grew crop foods. Because Guaycuruans lacked experience with, and regard for, the agricultural traditions that missionaries saw as necessary to reduction life, their attitudes and behaviors can tell us much about the impact of missions on native peoples.

In a spirited essay, "The Ibero-American Frontier Mission in Native American History," David Sweet synthesizes the process of how Catholic missions in Latin America damaged indigenous peoples. He challenges other historians to answer his assertions that reductions promoted population decline and alienation from nature, and the present study of Guaycuruans is partly a response to his bold, critical account of the fundamental impact of missions on the peoples of the Amazon basin, of California, and many other locations. His generalizations are most accurate where missions were a prelude or an adjunct to Spanish and Portuguese conquests of Native Americans. The Guaycuruan experiment with missions, however, diverged from the pattern that Sweet delineates, and I will show how it differed in the following chapters. In the conclusion I examine Sweet's argument and explicitly contrast the Guaycuruan experience with his model.

This book owes a great intellectual debt to Paraguayan anthropologist Branislava Susnik. Her multivolume works, including *El indio colonial del Paraguay, Los aborígenes del Paraguay,* and *El rol de los indígenas en la formación y en la vivencia del Paraguay,*[3] provide essential insights into the nature of Guaycuruan, as well as Guarani, society in the colonial era. Nevertheless, her dismissal of the importance of the missions for which Guaycuruans pleaded is very different from my understanding. Susnik's failure to recognize the importance of Guaycuruan missions arises in part from her declining interest in Native Americans as they move closer to Hispanic societies, an attitude once common among North American anthropologists.[4] I am also indebted to three remarkable Jesuit missionaries who in their European exile wrote detailed chronicles of Guaycuruan life: Martin Dobrizhoffer on the Abipones, Florian Paucke on the Mocobis, and José Sánchez Labrador on the Mbayás. Without their multivolume accounts, this book would not have been possible. It is rumored that a similar examination of Toba ways, possibly written by José de Solís (Jolís), once existed. If so, it has been lost or remains buried in some European archive.

Although I am not unmindful of the important connections that were established at the outset of the colonial era between such Guaycuruan groups as the Abipones, Mocobis, Mbayás, Toba, and Payaguá on the one hand and Spanish and Portuguese societies in South America on the other, I have tried to focus as tightly as possible on the Guaycuruans themselves. Such early historians of missions as Herbert Eugene Bolton and his students in the first half of the twentieth century wrote mostly about the activities of priests, often Jesuits, and colonial policy. These topics are still worthy of research, but they are secondary to the major concerns of this book. Hoping to put the Guaycuruans in sharp focus, I have tried to hear their voices, which call faintly to us through Spanish documents. While it would be arrogant folly to suppose that anyone could recapture *the* Guaycuruan point of view, or even to assume that there was any one Guaycuruan point of view, I have attempted to discover Guaycuruan viewpoints when I could, and to elevate them above the more accessible perspectives of missionaries and bureaucrats.

The absence of a written Guaycuruan language imposes constraints on the historian. As Robert Muchembled says of the popular classes of France, "we have to ask repression to recount the history of what it is repressing. It follows that an exhaustive and totally objective understanding of the matter is not yet possible, and may never be so."[5] But we must nevertheless make the effort. For Mexico James Lockhart and his students have studied indigenous peoples in the colonial era through Nahua language sources.[6] They have enlarged significantly our understanding of the popular classes of Mexico. For the Gran Chaco, however, I have been forced to rely on missionary accounts and archival documents from Argentina, Paraguay, and Spain. Only a handful of clearly Guaycuruan documents appear in the archives—most notably a "Memorial" by Abipon Cacique and Corregidor Miguel Jerónimo Benavides and a few letters from Mocobi Cacique Domingo Nevedagnac, housed in the Archivo General de la Nación, Buenos Aires, Argentina. Thus, the Guaycuruan story must be gleaned almost entirely from records left by their enemies and tutors. For the most part I have assumed that Guaycuruans spoke most clearly through their behavior.

In chapter 1 I trace Guaycuruan history from contact in the 1500s to the coming of missions in the 1740s and investigate Guaycuruan relationships with the Spanish world, especially power. In chapter 2 I explain how the Guaycuruan mission system developed in the Gran Chaco, from the founding of the first missions in the 1740s to the overthrow of the Spanish Empire, when independence struggles overcame the reductions. Chapters 3 to 6 deal with Guaycuruan economics, society, politics, and religion and form the core of the book. In the first part of each of these chapters, I explain social, economic, political, and religious life on the eve of missions; then I analyze the changes and continuities with the past resulting from missionization. Guaycuruan life was indigenous but not aboriginal by the early 1700s. The penetration of European influences already had forced many innovations. Abipones, Mocobis, the Toba, and Mbayás had lived adjacent to Spanish societies for almost two centuries before they settled in missions. Long before, they encountered devastating European diseases and material influences of European origin such as iron and horses and cattle. Plagues, tools, and animals brought profound alterations. Additionally, Guaycuruan bands incorporated women and children from Hispanic communities beginning in the 1500s, and they lost many of their own women and children to Spanish armies. Some Guaycuruans over the years moved to the enemy's settlements because Spanish militias dragged them there, and a few returned to their original bands. Other Guaycuruans took up residence in Spanish centers voluntarily. Most Guaycuruans reconstructed trading networks with Spanish communities in the 1600s to replace the Native American networks that had been destroyed by the European invasion in the 1500s. Thus, many ties connected Guaycuruan and Spanish communities before the coming of the eighteenth-century missions, but both cultures only reluctantly acknowledged the magnitude of the relationship.

Over the two centuries after the Spanish conquered Peru and shattered the economies of the Guaycuruans' Andean trading partners, the Chaco peoples constructed new connections with other Native Americans and with Spanish communities. They sold the livestock and human prizes that they had seized for profit to Spanish and part-Spanish buyers. They also sold honey, wax, salt, furs, and other Chaco products in Spanish markets. Thus the Guaycuruan ways that I describe in the first sections of chapters 3 to 6 were indigenous but no longer aboriginal. Although Spaniards altered Guaycuruan destinies, explanation of the clerical and civil policies toward Guaycuruan missions must await future works. Chapter 7 outlines Guaycuruan history in the nineteenth and twentieth centuries, and the conclusion offers an assessment of what Catholic missions meant to Guaycuruans.

I should explain how and why I use the names, terms, and spellings I have employed, especially those of the Guaycuruan peoples. I have generally accepted the form most common in the historical or anthropological literature in English. The Abipones, the Mocobis, the Mbayás, the Toba, the Payaguá, and the Pilagá were the most prominent Guaycuruans in the eighteenth century. They spoke similar languages, which modern scholars have called Guaycuruan. The designations I use came, as did so many terms in the upper Plata region, from the Guaranis, who called these groups Guaycurú. Except for the riverain Payaguá, Guaycurú referred to a similarity in housing styles; it also implied customs and languages that had roughly the same degree of commonality as the Romance languages of Europe and the societies that they represented. Guaycuruan cultures were similar but not identical. In the colonial era Guaycuruans lived in or just beyond the Gran Chaco of the northern Río de la Plata region, now mostly in Argentina but also extending into the current republics of Paraguay, Bolivia, and Brazil. Few colonial Guaycuruans knew themselves by the names under which they appear in this book—Abipones, Mocobis, etc.—but those in missions did. Following current fashion, I have tried to avoid using the word *Indian;* but like others I found that impossible. When looking at events from their vantage point, I usually call Guaycuruans and others *Native Americans* when necessary. When my subject shifts to clerical or government policy, I have used the term *Indian,* as the priests or bureaucrats would have done.

ACKNOWLEDGMENTS

I would like to thank the following people and institutions for their encouragement, helpful criticism, and financial assistance along the way.

My friends at the Lehigh University Libraries were unfailingly cooperative and courteous. The library personnel at the University of Pittsburgh and the University of Arizona were also kind and generous with their time and assistance. The directors and personnel of the Archivo General de Indias, Seville, Spain; the Archivo General de la Nación, Buenos Aires, Argentina; the Archivo General de la Provincia de Santa Fe, Santa Fe, Argentina; the Archivo Histórico de Jujuy, Jujuy, Argentina; the Archivo Nacional de Asunción, Asunción, Paraguay (especially Luis G. Benítez and many years ago Hipólito Sánchez Quell); and the Archivo Nacional de Chile were unfailingly supportive.

Many individuals in Spain and Latin America rendered me assistance. In Paraguay my family and I lived for nine months in the home of the late Julio César Chaves, an outstanding historian and a great gentleman. He and Señora de Chaves opened many doors. Their good friend and the then director of the national archive, Hipólito Sánchez Quell, relaxed the rules so that I could begin my work when his institution was officially closed. In Buenos Aires Eduardo Saguier was regularly able to direct me to the manuscripts I sought. Rolando Costa Picasso and Oscar Rizzo helped in innumerable ways, as did Marta Babuglia. Señorita Sandra Sánchez made it possible for me to work in Jujuy in a collegial environment. In Santa Fe Dr. Federico G. Cervera directed me to little-known sources and found a place for me to work in the afternoon when the provincial archive was closed. Though not a Spaniard, Jacques Barbier has extensive knowledge of the Archivo de Indias that was a great help in locating materials there.

A number of colleagues read portions of this manuscript critically, and I have benefited from all their comments. They include Suzanne A. Alchon, Mike Baylor, John Chance, Jerry Cooney, Susan Deeds, Gastón Doucet, Donna Guy, Kris Jones, James Lewis, Murdo MacLeod, Lynda Martz, Marcela Mendoza, Roger Nichols, Mario Pastore, Bill Shade, Jean Soderlund, and Eric van Young. John TePaske guided me toward the Río de la Plata when I was his struggling student and read portions of this work. Along the way, he encouraged me and provided an example of how joyous an active professional life can be. Mark Burkholder and Lyman Johnson read and commented extensively on the entire work. Their efforts were generous. If the reader finds errors of fact or interpretation in this account, please blame me, not the previously named scholars.

Finally, I could not have done the research for this book without the financial assistance of a number of institutions. Many offices at Lehigh University, including the Gipson Institute for Eighteenth Century Studies, the Department of History, and the Office of Unsponsored Research, provided funds for travel. The Fulbright Commission sponsored my most fruitful research trip to Argentina. The National Endowment for the Humanities enabled me to visit the University of Arizona to study with Roger Nichols for a summer. The Mellon Foundation awarded me grants for two research summers at the University of Pittsburgh. Janet Walters gave me invaluable assistance at all stages of research and writing.

Finally, I want to thank Barbara, Jamey, and Ted, for their understanding, patience, and love.

The Chaco Mission Frontier

CHAPTER 1

The Rise and Fall of Guaycuruan Power

In 1700 the Guaycuruans of the Gran Chaco scorned missions and the people in them. They thought their hunting and gathering ways and martial cultures made them superior to their neighbors who cultivated the soil. Abipones, Mocobis, Mbayás, Payaguá, and the Toba, the major Guaycuruan groups, dominated the Gran Chaco and its peripheries. These nonsedentary peoples found substance and security on the move. Except for the riverain Payaguá, Guaycuruans were now equestrians. At the beginning of the eighteenth century, a concept of time meaningless to them, they reached the apex of their power.

They hunted, fished, and gleaned in the Chaco and raided and traded with such Hispanic communities as Asunción, Corrientes, Santiago del Estero, and Jujuy. Although their methods of subsistence resembled the "raiding economies" of the peoples of the desert grasslands of the northern and southern frontiers of the Spanish Empire—the Comanche in North America and the Araucanians in South America[1]—their economies were complex.

Their Chaco habitats were savannahs, forests, scrub forests, and marshes intersected by numerous rivers and streams. The eastern and southern Gran Chaco is a low-lying region that slopes gently from east to west. The word *Chaco,* originally Quechua, designates a hunting area. Characterized by forests, scrub forests, marshes, plains, and numerous small, mostly non-navigable rivers and streams, the Chaco is bounded on the west by the Andes and on the east by the Ríos Paraná and Paraguay. It runs from contemporary Santa Fe, Argentina, north over the

Bermejo, beyond the Pilcomayo and even farther north to an area just beyond the present Paraguay-Bolivia border. Spanish expeditions could not long survive in the Chaco. From October to April, swamps abounded, and only Chaco peoples knew their way around them. The rest of the year water was scarce, and invaders lacked knowledge of watering places.

Southern and northern Guaycuruans had infrequent contact. The Guaycuruans of the southern Chaco, Abipones (Acallagaec to themselves), Mocobis (Amocovit), and the Toba (Notokowit and other names), had sought refuge in the Chaco centuries earlier to escape their enemies in the pampas of Argentina, their former home. They brought a pampas-like culture to the Chaco.

In the Chaco Austral, the southern third, between the Río Salado and the Bermejo, Abipones and Mocobis ranged. Concentrated in the southeastern Chaco between the Río Salado and the Río Bermejo north of Santa Fe, now Argentina, Abipones claimed lands bordering the Río Paraná, although some groups had moved north into the contested territory along the Río Paraguay between the Bermejo and the Pilcomayo Rivers. Mocobis exploited the southwestern Chaco between the city of Salta and the Río Bermejo, although some bands were relocating to the lands east of the Abipones. The Toba lived mostly in the western Chaco between the Río Bermejo and the Río Pilcomayo, although some later moved east into lands along the Río Paraguay contested by Mocobi, Abipon, and Toba groups.

North of the Pilcomayo was the Chaco Boreal, where Mbayás made serfs of their Guaná neighbors. Beginning about fifty miles north of Asunción, Mbayá lands were divided by the Río Paraguay. Some inhabited the eastern Chaco above the Río Pilcomayo, while others had left these homelands to move even farther east across the Río Paraguay; there they occupied the palm groves between the Río Jejuy and the Itatín region from which missionary Jesuits and neophyte Guaranis had fled decades earlier. The Payaguá, going about their daily lives mostly in canoes, camped along the Paraná-Paraguay river system from south of Corrientes north to the Pantanal in the Mato Grosso of Brazil.

Other Guaycuruans included the Pilagá, closely related to the Toba,[2] the Payaguá, and smaller groups such as the Aguilotes, who later merged with the stronger Abipones. Non-Guaycuruans in the Chaco included the semisedentary Guanás (Chanés or Naperús), Lules (called Isistines and Toquistines), Vilelas (including Chunupíes and Pasaínes), and the mounted Lenguas (Enimagás), Matacos, Mataguayos, Matarás, and others. Few of these groups menaced Guaycuruans, although other equestrians were troublesome.

The Guaycuruan groups, once inaccurately called "tribes," were connected by a common language, not political organization. Guaycuruan peoples normally felt no political loyalties beyond the band. Language groups did not establish boundaries to the areas in which they lived and hunted; the bands into which they were divided did that, and a crazy-quilt Guaycuruan residence pattern was the result. Thus a Mocobi band might be sandwiched between Abipon groups or hold territory beside a Toba concentration. Toba and Mocobi bands often occupied neighboring regions. Mbayás frequently held lands adjacent to their semisedentary Guaná clients. They defined themselves partly in opposition to the Hispanic societies with whom they had fought and traded since the earliest contacts.

Guaycuruan-Spanish Contact: The Early Years

In the year that their new white enemies called 1542, Guaycuruans in the Gran Chaco learned of an impending attack. Across the Río Paraguay, their Guarani adversaries had acquired European allies five years before, and Guaycuruan intelligence about the over-river people was keen. Alvar Núñez Cabeza de Vaca, *adelantado* of Paraguay, had earlier sent fifty men, including two priests, to pronounce the Requerimiento and ask the Chaco warriors to submit. The Guaycuruans rejected the overture, and their arrows put the emissaries to flight.

The largest linguistic group in the Chaco, Guaycuruans communicated easily with each other, even though several related languages defined their group identities. Guaycuruan languages had similar origins and were "as much alike as Spanish and Portugueze." The tongues differed, however, "not only in dialect, but also in innumerable little words."[3]

In 1542 those in closest contact with the Spaniards were the Mbayás, or Eyiguayegis, "the people of the palm," as they called themselves. One regionally designated band of Mbayás, whose name is now lost, lived in the northernmost Chaco between the Río Verde and the Río Pilcomayo across the Río Paraguay and northeast from the recently founded Asunción (1537). Proud hunters and warriors, they scorned the sedentary, corn-growing Guaranis across the river and often seized Guarani women for service and barter. The beleaguered Guaranis yearned for vengeance but alone were unable to defeat the Chaco groups. Cabeza de Vaca therefore organized a conquest expedition of four hundred Spaniards and ten thousand Guaranis. The battle was brief. The Guaycuruans lost. Some died in combat, others became property of the enemy, and still others scattered. No longer contemptuous of the Guarani, the Chaco hunters faced a Guarani-Spanish alliance now militarily dominant.[4] The horses of the newcomers and the iron pikes and swords that sliced through Guaycuruan weapons of wood and bone gave the Spanish superiority.[5] The people of the palm became determined to acquire them.

In the following decades, the Guaycuruan peoples roamed the Chaco adjacent to the eastern region of modern Paraguay. Although surviving documents are silent about population losses, Guaycuruans certainly suffered from the epidemic diseases introduced by the invaders. Like other native peoples of the Americas, their populations were undoubtedly reduced by some 60 to 90 percent over a century or more. Thus the Guaycuruan population of the Chaco, some 40,000 in the mid-1700s, might have been 250,000 to 500,000 before contact. The 35,000 to 45,000 Guaycuruans of the mid-1700s were descended from the larger bands of the 1500s.[6]

Spanish cities sprang up around the Chaco periphery, including Santiago del Estero (1553), San Miguel de Tucumán (1565),[7] Córdoba and Santa Fe (1573), Salta (1582), Concepción on the Río Bermejo (1585), Corrientes (1588), and Jujuy (1593).[8] As these grew, the invaders and their servants, the now-subjugated sedentary and semisedentary natives, pushed into the adjacent countryside.

In 1563 the cities of the Río de la Plata were divided administratively between the provinces of Paraguay–Río de la Plata in the east and Tucumán to the west. They obeyed Spanish principles of authority; even the tiniest Indian municipality owed allegiance to the king in Spain. This network of obligations extended from Paraguay to the Audiencia of Charcas, in modern Bolivia, to the viceroy in Lima, and to the Council of the Indies and the king in Spain. The Spanish were nevertheless so ineffective in deploying their authority that Guaycuruans maintained superiority in their own lands for another two centuries. In 1617 the eastern province split into Paraguay and Río de la Plata. Seldom could the three Platine provinces cooperate against Guaycuruans.

In the northeastern Chaco, Mbayás raided and traded with residents of the capital city of Asunción and its satellite communities. They coveted the agricultural surpluses, artifacts, and animals of the Paraguayan reductions founded by Franciscans in the late 1500s, such as Altos near Asunción and Ypané and Guarambaré to the north. Such missions invited Mbayá raids.

Southeastern and riverain Guaycuruans, only later known as Abipones, Mocobis, and Payaguá, sought plunder in the Jesuit-Guarani missions founded after 1610 near the Ríos Paraguay and Paraná. These reductions housed traditional enemies with abundant crop foods, horse and cattle herds, and iron tools. In what is now northwest Argentina opposite the southwestern Chaco of the Toba and Mocobi, the growing cities of the province of Tucumán contained lesser but still significant numbers of sedentary Native Americans.[9] The rising centers of Santa Fe[10] and Corrientes became important sources of Guaycuruan revenue, as did Santiago del Estero, San Miguel de Tucumán, Salta, and Jujuy.[11]

Although Guaycuruans and Europeans were often at war, occasional Spanish emissaries visited the Chaco. Guaycuruans heard and sometimes executed the Spanish priests who extolled a distant European power and claimed moral superiority.[12] Seventeenth-century Guaycuruans found Christianity insufficiently compelling to submit to European assertions of superiority, especially after they acquired the horses and iron that heightened their military capability and changed their lives. The Chaco contained no riches—no minerals, fertile lands, or large populations—to attract Spaniards. Half the year was so dry that finding water was a test. During the other half, incessant rains made the region swampy and impenetrable. Protected by their poverty, Abipones seized mounts before 1600. They took a handful of horses from Santa Fe, and with these acquired more. At the time, Spanish herdsmen were few, unarmed, and ineffective. Horses facilitated Guaycuruan raids on Spanish settlers and Hispanized Native Americans in Tucumán, the Río de la Plata, and Paraguay. In the 1600s, "In the space of fifty years, an [*sic*] hundred thousand horses were driven from the estates of the Spaniards, by the Abipones."[13] Northern Guaycuruans (Mbayás) near Asunción, crossed the Río Paraguay for horses and cattle. They hunted the new beasts like large game, but they also traded for animals and artifacts. The pattern was similar in other jurisdictions on the Chaco frontier.

The growing market for livestock and captives, as well as Chaco skins, honey, wax, and salt, provided new opportunities. In a designated barrio of Asunción, for example, Mbayás traded with Paraguayans. Once dependent on Payaguá brokers for European trade goods, inland Guaycuruans now acquired iron knives and hatchets directly from Spanish merchants. They sought raw iron for lance and arrow points and bartered it to Chaco neighbors.[14]

The horse complemented the Guaycuruans' warrior ethos, and they developed a "horse culture" similar to that of the Plains peoples of North

America or the Mapuche of Chile. Among the many influences of European derivation, only the horse rivaled iron in importance. Horses created revolutionary changes. They allowed Guaycuruans for almost a century to maintain military superiority over Spaniards on battlefields of Native American choosing, and they made mounted Guaycuruans superior to other Chaco peoples such as the Vilelas and the Chané (Guaná), who remained pedestrians. Agrarian Guaranis in and out of the Spanish orbit suffered even more. Horses provided Guaycuruans vastly greater mobility, increased their economic alternatives, and made more productive their bellicosity. Horses intensified the conflict between Native Americans and between Guaycuruan and creole society. Guaycuruans could now raid over a vast area. On horseback they exploited the growing cattle herds on the plains adjacent to the Chaco[15] and added beef to their diet.

Unlike the inland Guaycuruans, who after 1600 became equestrians, the Payaguá remained water-borne. Their great war canoes imperiled Spanish shipping on the Río Paraguay over two colonial centuries. As they acquired Spanish goods, they became brokers between Spaniards and other Guaycuruans.

Guaycuruan Culture

Guaycuruans lived by hunting wild game, fishing, and gathering fruits and vegetables. They moved their homes periodically, traveling within a familiar area. Killing large animals such as deer and jaguars brought men prestige and meat and symbolized their life; however, they gained more of their nourishment, as well as clothing and utensils, from such vegetable foods as the *algarroba* and palm tree (see chapter 3). Most Guaycuruans continued aboriginal economic pursuits, but goods and animals of European origin modified their work habits and eventually brought them into eighteenth-century missions.

Because the economic potential of the Chaco did not allow many people to congregate for very long, Guaycuruans traveled in small family groups (see chapter 4). Bands periodically coalesced to trade, to socialize, or for plunder and war; but they soon dispersed again into small groups.[16] Each Guaycuruan group claimed exclusive right to its own hunting and fishing area, and the ideologies of all Guaycuruan groups sanctioned aggression and the violent seizure of the property of others. Guaycuruan religion reinforced their martial ways (see chapter 6). It encouraged combat and glorified the warrior. The Guaycuruans' supernatural beings sanctioned hunting and war.

Hereditary chiefs with limited authority normally led Guaycuruan bands (see chapter 5). Other men, not chiefs, led war parties and hunting expeditions; but none had the power of command. Thus expeditions for plunder and war were highly democratic—and disorganized—affairs. The lack of central authority and small size of bands were Guaycuruan strengths for much of the colonial period. Decentralized societies prevented Spanish forces from apprehending a commanding chief, as they had done in the Mexican and Peruvian conquests.

Without a strong "principle of authority," the Guaycuruan peoples grew stronger throughout the 1600s, and with more food from horses and cattle, their living groups became larger. Despite periodic defeats by Spanish forces that chased Guaycuruan raiders around the Chaco, Guaycuruans seldom suffered lasting harm. Conversely, the stronger authority of Spanish society provided no benefit in the 1600s (see chapter 2);[17] and alternating between war and trade Guaycuruans thought more beneficial than submission. Spanish clerics concluded that nomadic Guaycuruans were unsuited to missions and left the Chaco for a century.

Conflict was central to Guaycuruan culture. Abipones fought other Abipones, as well as the Toba and Mocobis. Members of an Abipon group such as the plains-dwelling Riikahés, for example, might remain on good terms with Mocobi neighbors while carrying on a decades-long conflict with a rival Abipon group such as the Nakaiketergehes, although not even these regional groupings commanded political allegiance. As another example, the Codalodis (Mbayás), who joined the short-lived mission of Santos Magos in the 1610s, their descendants recalled, disappeared as a group after defeat by other Mbayás.[18]

Guaycuruan Offensives and Spanish Reprisals

Guaycuruan attacks on Spanish objectives were rewarding. Additionally, they contributed to indigenous security by retarding the growth of Spanish society north of Buenos Aires. On occasion Guaycuruan wars of attrition destroyed Spanish cities. Mocobis and the Toba, along with Payaguá, for example, besieged Concepción del Bermejo in the late 1500s and forced its abandonment in 1632. At the same time, raids by mounted and riverain Guaycuruans on Paraguay inflicted pain on the exalted and the humble alike. The nomads kidnapped the sister and the niece of Hernando Arias de Saavedra (Hernandarias), several times the Platine governor,[19] and killed the family's Guarani servants. They ransomed the niece but kept the sister. Guaycuruan raids in the seventeenth century almost destroyed Santiago del Estero and in 1660 forced relocation of

Santa Fe to the south. By 1686 Guaycuruans had nearly ruined the city of Esteco, and an earthquake finished the job.[20]

Partly because their relations with Guaycuruans were complex, Hispanic settlers had difficulty defending themselves or even retaliating effectively. In February of 1660, for example, a hundred Mbayás visited Asunción to trade Chaco products, as they did periodically. They negotiated in Guarani, even then a language of commerce and diplomacy, as it likely was before contact. Their business over, the visitors recrossed the Río Paraguay, but they returned almost immediately to take horses from creole owners.[21]

Like the residents of Corrientes, Santa Fe, and the frontier cities of Tucumán, most Paraguayans were dispersed on farms and ranches, and their militias assembled for retaliation slowly, although Guaycuruan raiders normally skirted Hispanic fortifications. Even though the garrisons were small, poorly trained, and undisciplined by European standards, they were sufficiently powerful that Guaycuruans avoided them unless victory was certain or honor demanded it. By avoiding pitched battles with Spanish forces, Guaycuruans showed their respect for Spanish discipline, authority, and command.

A typical raid occurred on October 29, 1674, when Mbayás were dispersing from the Chaco Boreal to northern Paraguay. Because the palms (*mboyacá namogoligi*) on the eastern side of the Río Paraguay were more succulent,[22] they crossed into Paraguayan territory. The Mbayás killed or captured sixty Paraguayans, including a priest. The Mbayás saw him as a threat because they believed that enemy shamans killed rivals by supernatural means. They took two hundred horses and tools, trinkets, and trophies. The raiders alarmed the five forts (*presidios*) then along the Río Paraguay, but the Paraguayan militia could neither intercept the attack nor cut off the retreat. The Mbayás recrossed the river far ahead of the Paraguayan militia. Although Paraguayans eventually mustered a massive force of 1,800 men, it could not leave until December 23. After four days' march the Paraguayans found a handful of encamped raiders, who offered to repatriate captives. The vengeful Paraguayans attacked this small band of Mbayás, killing some and scattering others. In all, Mbayás monitored the movement of the Spanish force for three hundred leagues.

Although Guaycuruans usually suspended hostilities for some months after a Spanish reprisal, Platine provinces could infrequently afford large deterrent efforts. Furthermore, the Spanish *entradas* accomplished little in the short run. Creoles undertook punitive expeditions for revenge or honor. Occasionally, a new governor would mount an inconclusive foray before facing the military realities. Thus in 1664 Paraguayan Governor Felipe Rege Corvalán vainly tried to subdue the Mbayás.[23] A successor, Francisco de Monforte, led six patrols to the Chaco in 1685–86. In 1686 Paraguayans under Monforte spent five months in Mbayá lands, including the winter. Guaycuruans were more vulnerable in winter when they lighted fires for warmth. When Monforte's expedition encountered a band of Mbayás, they killed sixteen men, including three chiefs, and captured seventy women. These captives then became *piezas,* who served in Paraguay, often in the *encomienda originaria,* a lifetime bondage not unlike slavery. The Paraguayans also took 340 Mbayá horses,[24] valuable to both cultures. Occasionally other military expeditions from Paraguay, San Miguel de Tucumán, Corrientes, or Santa Fe encountered Guaycuruans. But because the Chaco societies were decentralized, Spaniards only infrequently encountered large numbers of Guaycuruans—unless the Guaycuruans wished it.

In the southwestern Chaco, hostilities followed much the same pattern. On July 4, 1673, Governor Angel de Peredo of the province of Tucumán led six hundred militia and Indian auxiliaries against Mocobi and Toba raiders. Troops from Jujuy, Salta, and San Miguel de Tucumán patrolled the Río Bermejo for twenty days. Boasting, as would Governor Urizar in the next century, that he had brought civilization to thousands of Indians, the governor returned home, mistakenly claiming victory; few captives were truly Spanish enemies, however. Only fifty were Mocobi or Toba. The non-Guaycuruan captives were to serve in encomienda for two generations (*vidas*). But four years later even these captives had returned to the Chaco. Undaunted by Spanish expeditions, by 1677 the Guaycuruans were again raiding Tucumán province. The demoralized citizens of Jujuy feared their city would disappear.[25]

As the eighteenth century approached, Guaycuruan offensives had five cities of Tucumán reeling. Jujuy and Salta were stable but suffering, but Santiago del Estero, San Miguel de Tucumán, and Esteco were tottering. The Toba and Mocobi had ruined *haciendas* as close as five leagues from the cities. The twenty or thirty soldiers at the fort of Esteco rarely contested Guaycuruan forays, because the raiders took the militia's horses. In the late 1600s Guaycuruans advanced on Tucumán over a hundred-league, mostly wooded front, terrain which made Spanish pursuit difficult.[26]

Spanish officials and clerics unrealistically pondered offensive war.[27] No Platine province could muster a force large enough to make the Guaycuruans surrender. Despite the Spanish principles of unified authority and collective obedience, Tucumán, Paraguay, and the Río de la Plata could not coordinate military efforts over the vast Gran Chaco, and local interests prevailed.

In the late 1600s and early 1700s, Mocobi and Toba attacks on the frontier cities of Tucumán, and Mbayá efforts in Paraguay, forced outmigrations from imperiled regions. All the while, Guaycuruans nurtured commercial relationships with the selected Spanish locales spared from their raids.[28] Able to eat or ride only limited numbers of cows and horses, they sold surpluses to Hispanic purchasers. Around 1700, Guaycuruan bands participated in an exchange network throughout the upper Plata region and western Brazil. Thus, while Guaycuruans inflicted pain on some Spaniards, their activities actually benefited others, especially those to whom they sold stolen horses and cattle.

On the southeastern frontier of the Chaco opposite the cities of Corrientes and Santa Fe, Abipones and Mocobis repeated the strategies of the raiders of Paraguay and Tucumán. After 1665 they attacked Corrientes almost yearly. At the same time they communicated with some urban residents, almost certainly including captive Guaycuruans, who reported the movements of local militias. In 1677 a Guaycuruan servant woman in Asunción warned her Spanish mistress that apparently peaceful Mbayás were poised to assault the city, foiling their plans. Such intelligence traveled both ways and helped Guaycuruans evade Spanish expeditions. In these wars of maneuver, Spaniards moved more slowly than Guaycuruans. Local needs prevented military cooperation among Spanish militia. In 1665 Corrientes refused to aid Tucumán against the Toba and Mocobis, because Corrientes feared nearby Abipones. In 1686 poverty-stricken Santa Fe could not even defend itself against the Abipones then taking livestock and captives.[29]

A Paraguayan massacre of northern Guaycuruans (Mbayás) shows how peaceful and hostile relations alternated. In 1677 Mbayás camped near Asunción for trade, a social occasion celebrated by heavy drinking. They terrified Paraguayans. Three hundred Mbayás accepted a Paraguayan invitation to a party and crossed the Río Paraguay. The host, José de Avalos, addressed them cordially and presented them with gifts. The guests, mostly elite Mbayá males (see chapter 4), entered Paraguayan homes and drank to stupefaction. The Paraguayan militia slaughtered them. Never again, the Mbayás said, would they trust the lying Paraguayans, and never again would they visit Asunción. Although in time they revisited the capital to trade, they called the Paraguayans deceivers ever after.[30]

As horses, cattle, and iron encouraged greater population concentrations, Guaycuruan bands grew larger and increased their military potential. In the early 1700s Guaycuruans of the south-central and southwestern Chaco typically scoured Tucumán in parties of fifty to sixty men, but every other year or so raiding parties swelled to three or four hundred riders. They avoided European-style battles, but as proud warriors obligated regularly to prove themselves, they required some combat. If Spaniards gathered quickly with good leaders and good horses, they might recover livestock from Guaycuruan drovers, who included most male Guaycuruans. Normally, though, Spaniards followed raiders only a short distance—a day's ride or two or three—because they soon exhausted their provisions. As Guaycuruans increased their penetrations, they pushed the frontier back in all three Platine provinces.[31]

In the early 1700s Mocobi and Toba societies were experiencing serious pressures from within. Their successes had produced environmental, economic, and security problems. They responded by intensifying their attacks on Tucumán. Mocobi chief Notiviri frequently led his men to Salta and Jujuy to steal livestock and the merchandise of the cart trains supplying the mines of Potosí. Although these Mocobis had earlier preyed on the caravans between Santiago del Estero and Jujuy, the rich cart and mule trains were increasingly well guarded. Nevertheless, Mocobis acquired booty at virtually every hacienda along the two-hundred-league Tucumán frontier. They avoided combat unless certain of a favorable outcome.

Mounting Guaycuruan successes caused Spanish authorities to retaliate, "to carry the war by fire and blood" to their tormentors, "barbarians of the forests that shelter them."[32] Esteban de Urizar y Arespacochaga, an able, ambitious, and newly appointed governor of Tucumán in 1708 requested funds for an offensive war in the Chaco. Defensive operations, the Spanish claimed, were useless.[33] Precisely at this time, Guaycuruans faced greater difficulty obtaining livestock, owing to increased Spanish protection and a reformed Tucumán militia. Like many of his predecessors, Governor Urizar imagined a military solution to his Indian problem was possible. He planned a strategy of terror to overawe Guaycuruans and prepared to penetrate the Chaco in 1710.[34]

Guaycuruan Brokers and Leaders

Three Guaycuruans played notable roles in resisting Urizar's expedition. The first, a conduit between creoles and Guaycuruans, was a mestizo whom Spaniards called Ignacio the Apostate. Born to a Mocobi captive and a man whom she met while in bondage, he was reared on a Jesuit *estancia.* When Ignacio grew older, his mother sent him to her people. Because his mixed race conferred low status in Guaycuruan as in Spanish society, he was not a desirable husband to Guaycuruan women. Ignacio thus married a Palomo woman who had fled to the Chaco from Tarija. Dressed as a Spaniard, he entered the cities on the Chaco frontier anonymously. He refrained from shaving his hair or plucking his beard or eyebrows in the Guaycuruan manner, which would have given him away. He encountered garrulous people, gathered information, and reported to the leaders of his band. Then he led Mocobis to rich rewards with low risk. He was eventually killed by Urizar's army in 1710.

Distinctive because of his beard, Chief Anegodi was the most respected Mocobi of his time. Like other chiefs, he derived his influence from his powerful oratory, brave deeds, and good decisions: he could persuade but not command followers. Anegodi was assisted by a lesser chief, Coquini, bilingual in Mocobi and Spanish, who later fell into Spanish hands.[35] Such were the leaders who faced Governor Urizar.

As Urizar began the entrada of 1710, Guaycuruans confronted the largest Spanish force they had faced in a generation. With contingents from Jujuy, Santiago del Estero, Salta, and San Miguel de Tucumán, the army of Tucumán province numbered 1,316 soldiers, including Spaniards, Indians, and free *pardos.* They drove 6,260 horses and mules, carried 2,056 *arrobas* of hardtack and 1,704 arrobas of wheat flour, and drove enough cattle to feed the army for months.[36] While most Guaycuruans could evade this ponderous column, some were unable to do so and were forced to negotiate.

Mocobi chiefs, including Talexmati, the brother of Anegodi, met with Urizar. Coquini, now a captive in Tucumán, asked Mocobis to submit. Unusually large numbers of Mocobis assembled in the southern Chaco to discuss the approaching threat; one congregation had three hundred fires, a thousand or more persons. To buy time Mocobi emissaries informed Urizar that they would recognize Spanish authority if the governor would halt. This pause allowed them to lead their bands eastward to safer hunting areas near the Jesuit-Guarani reductions of Paraguay and the city of Santa Fe, where Notiviri allied with local Abipones. Nevertheless, Urizar's pressure intensified rivalries among Guaycuruans. The bristling defenses of Tucumán made the eastern provinces temporarily safer.

As Mocobi and Toba bands retreated northward and as sedentary Chaco peoples came under Spanish control, creoles seized new opportunities. Landowners extended their farms and ranches a hundred leagues into the Chaco, taking valuable lands from Guaycuruans. Seventy new haciendas appeared on the northern frontier of Tucumán. Loss of this territory pushed the Toba and Mocobis of the region into the lands of others, thereby increasing friction among indigenous groups and intensifying the stress in the Chaco.[37]

Not all Guaycuruans migrated from the area, however. Some Toba and a few Mocobis skirmished with Urizar's angry army as it entered the Chaco. When the creoles captured a Mocobi named Jacinto, a fugitive from Tucumán, they executed him summarily. They captured six hundred inoffensive Malbaláes,[38] non-Guaycuruan agrarian residents of the Chaco. Twice as many Lules, also non-Guaycuruans, were captured and agreed to settle in a new reduction called San Esteban de Miraflores.

Relationships among captives demonstrate how communications flowed from Guaycuruans and others in the Chaco to Spanish communities. In one case, two Isistines (a subgroup of Lules), came to Miraflores with their Mocobi wives, who maintained contact with their families. Such arrangements enabled peoples in conflict, Chaco Guaycuruans and creoles of Tucumán, to exchange information.

Threatened by the Urizar expedition, semisedentary Chunupíes and Vilelas, other non-hostile Chaco peoples, also submitted. Urizar's soldiers brought home docile Indians as piezas, virtual slaves, as their ancestors had done in the 1600s, but only a few Guaycuruans became Spanish prisoners. One, Toba Chief Tabagui, they executed. Mocobis lost ten-year-old *criolla* Francisca de Tobar, whom they had seized near Salta a year before. Incorporating her into their society, Mocobis had renamed her Tehegelgo. Soldiers almost shot the girl, because her recently shaved head and tattooed arms gave her the appearance of a Mocobi.

The Merging of Guaycuruan and Spanish Societies

Those captives from the Chaco kept in Spanish centers were usually females or young males, those best suited fof service. When Guaycuruan men encountered a Spanish entrada, they seldom fought, even to defend their families. Mobility was their principal defense. They hid the women and children and attempted to draw Spanish troops away. Sometimes they were successful and sometimes not. Thus Spaniards on the Chaco frontier acquired Guaycuruan servants and slaves, whom they forcibly converted to Christianity. The older the captives were when captured, however, the more likely they were to retain contacts with friends and relatives in the Chaco.

Several records of Guaycuruan servants survive. In 1738 in Salta, for example, a thirty-year-old Toba woman served Doña Juana Ruiz de Villegas, and Teresa, a twenty-five-year-old Mocobi, attended Doña Leonor Alarcón. In the early 1740s, one Juan José was an adult Mocobi slave of Sergeant Major Don Juan de Aguirre; a different Juan was a three-year-old slave of Bernardo Hidalgo. Numerous other Mocobi and Toba servants resided in Salta, and surely in the other cities on the Chaco frontier, in the first half of the eighteenth century.[39]

By the early 1700s the barriers between Native American and Spanish societies on the Chaco frontier were crumbling. On the Chaco side, Guaycuruan bands included renegade whites, called *españoles de mal vivir* by the societies they rejected, as well as mestizos. Among the latter were such men as Ignacio the Apostate (mentioned previously), and Fulgencio Chaparro, a Paraguayan captured as a boy and raised by Mocobis. As an adult he led Mocobi expeditions to Paraguay. When his Mocobis later sought a mission, Chaparro negotiated for them, and Paraguayans seized him to prevent his return to the Chaco.

In another instance Nakaiketergehes Abipones captured young Cristóbal Almaraz from Santiago del Estero. His political and martial abilities earned him a position of leadership in their society. He later spoke for peace with Spaniards. After his band was reduced to a mission, he rejoined the Spanish world; there he prospered practicing folk medicine because it was rumored in creole society that Almaraz possessed Native American healing secrets.

Riikahé Abipon Ychoalay (later José Benavides) moved voluntarily to Santa Fe in the early eighteenth century. There he broke horses for a man named Benavides, whose name he used among Spaniards. Ychoalay-Benavides learned Spanish, became a drover, and worked in Chile and Mendoza. After quarreling with an employer, he returned to the Abipones. He then became a war leader, raiding Córdoba but not Santa Fe, where he maintained his previous connections. Much later he became an important leader in mission society (see chapter 2). Other Guaycuruans in frontier cities became culturally Spanish and rejected Guaycuruan ties.[40]

Dispersal and Concentration: The Early 1700s

The eighteenth-century Guaycuruans belonged to regionally designated social groups comprised of numerous bilateral bands. Over the years the bands dwindled and grew, divided and merged, and acquired new names. War, disease, diplomacy, and economic factors altered the boundaries of their territories. In the early 1700s, the Abipones, or Acallagaec, lived between the Río Salado near Santa Fe in the south and along the tributaries of the Río Paraná. Their hunting lands stretched from the Ríos Blanco and Rubio in the north and to the Río del Rey and the Malabrigo to the south. Although often on the move, pursuing vegetable food, game, and booty, they thought of the territory between the present Argentine cities of Resistencia and Santa Fe as home. They migrated there from lands between the Bermejo and Pilcomayo rivers in the 1600s. Divided into three groups, they identified themselves by their habitat. The Riikahés were plains people from the northwest of Santa Fe; the Nakaiketergehes came from the forests around Santiago del Estero; and the Yaaucanigas, formerly a separate "nation" who became recognized as Abipones after a slaughter thinned their numbers, occupied the northernmost region of the Abipon area, to the west of Corrientes, which they visited to trade.

The Mocobis, the Abipones' neighbors to the west, were the largest Guaycuruan language group in the colonial era. Calling themselves Amocovit, they lived in band-level societies, but their eighteenth-century regional designations are unknown. Their residences and hunting areas stretched from the Río Paraná along the Bermejo west to Salta and Jujuy. Frequently, Mocobi and Abipon bands were distributed randomly among each other. Even more irregular in terms of ethnic demarcation was the mix of Mocobis and Toba.

Frequently allies of the Mocobis, the Toba referred to themselves as the Qom or the Nam Qom or the Natocowit. They were divided into eastern, central, and western groups, and their western lands were generally north of the Río Pilcomayo. In the east, however, the Takshik Toba moved between the juncture of the Ríos Bermejo and Pilcomayo and the Paraná. In the west, the Komlek Toba toured the lands of the upper Río Pilcomayo. The central Toba lived between the mid-Pilcomayo and mid-Bermejo and often fought the Abipones, Vilelas, and Matacos. The eastern Toba and northern Abipones fought for dominance in the lands near the Río Paraguay now near Formosa, Argentina. Smaller groups of Guaycuruan speakers, such as the Aguilotes, migrated southeast and joined the Abipones after the Urizar expedition, as the Pilagá moved closer to the Toba.[41]

In the northeastern Chaco (and by the 1700s spilling into the northeastern section of modern Paraguay) lived the Mbayás. They had in 1750 six regionally designated groups. West of the Río Paraguay were the Cadiguegodis and the Guetiadegodis. Past the east bank of the Río Paraguay were the four other regional groups, including the majority of Mbayás.

The Apacachodegodegis, whose name meant "from the lands of the rhea," founded the first Mbayá mission. To their north were the Lichagotegodis, people "of the land of the red earth." North of them were the Eyibegodegis, or Enacagas, "the people hidden among hills and marshes." The Gotocogegodegi, "the people of the cane field," lived to the east of the others.

Most Mbayás lived near the villages of their clients, the Guanás (Chanés), who were pedestrian, Arawakian agrarians that Mbayás had earlier subjugated. Guanás provided Mbayás with crop foods and wives (for chiefs) in exchange for security and iron tools, a subordinate reciprocity resembling European vassalage. These relationships had been well established since the 1500s, when the Guanás were pushed south to the fringes of the Chaco by aggressive neighbors. Guanás retained their own social structure and language. They lived in villages of a thousand inhabitants and may have been the most numerous group in the Chaco in the 1600s. Lacking direct contact with Spaniards until the eighteenth century, they received European artifacts through Mbayá intermediaries.[42]

Guaycuruan leaders and bands competed for the best territories. Potentially rich lands bordered Spanish centers. Guaycuruans required purchasers for cattle, horses, and mules stolen from Spaniards or other Native Americans. Leaders cultivated good relations with one Spanish locale, their customary market, while plundering others. After returning to Abipon life, for example, Ychoalay remained on good terms with Santa Fe, while he raided in Tucumán and Paraguay.

One major Guaycuruan group, the Payaguá, never joined a mission. In the early colonial era, the riverain Payaguá were divided into two main groups: the Sarigués, who traveled the Río Paraguay north of Asunción, and the Siacuás, whose canoes plied the river to the south. Like other Guaycuruans, the Payaguá were nonsedentary militarists, but they found no use for horses. Paddling large war canoes and smaller family vessels, the Payaguá lived by fishing, gathering vegetation along the river, and raiding their wealthier agrarian neighbors, especially the Guarani. After 1537 they extended their enmity from Guaranis to the Spanish. Armed with arrows, clubs, and spears, the Payaguá made travel on the Río Paraguay hazardous for Spanish merchants, shippers, and Guarani crews for two centuries. Iron hatchets and knives enabled them to build their canoes more efficiently, and iron-tipped weapons made their raids more deadly and profitable. Periodically hostile to Paraguayans and later to Brazilians traveling to the Mato Grosso, Payaguá regularly visited Asunción to trade. They became intermediaries between Spaniards and Guaycuruans in the Chaco, trading iron objects and fiber clothing to interior peoples for skins and honey from the Chaco. Later, Payaguá males bartered fish, wax, and woven mats in Asunción for hatchets, machetes, and knives. They could speak Guarani and were in close touch with the lower classes of Asunción. Guarani men and women of the capital joined visiting Payaguá clandestinely for religious ceremonies and sex. In 1704 Payaguá canoes transported Guaycuruans from the Chaco to assault Guaranis in the encomienda town of Guarambaré. In 1717 Payaguá encampments near Asunción succumbed to an attack ordered by Governor Diego de los Reyes. By 1730, though, some Payaguá felt comfortable enough in Paraguay to camp in Asunción.

In the 1740s, the traditional Payaguá economy was producing less, and southern Payaguá began to settle on the outskirts of Asunción. The northerners, the Tacumbús, still lived in three concentrations above Asunción. In 1753 northern Payaguá Chiefs Aypara and Quati initiated peace negotiations with Paraguay. In a transaction that resembled ransom exchanges on the pampas,[43] the Payaguá agreed to sell Paraguayans their captives and not to molest provincial shipping. Initially most of the men kept their families upriver, but they moved them to the Paraguayan capital in the 1790s.[44]

Payaguá movement to the margins of the Spanish world paralleled the social trajectory of mounted Guaycuruans who chose missions. There were differences, however, because the Payaguá never sought or accepted a mission, as did Abipones, Mocobis, Mbayás, or the Toba. Most who rejected mission life—including the Payaguá and those mounted Guaycuruan bands who never secured their own reduction—nevertheless moved culturally and physically closer to the Hispanic world and grew more dependent on it. Before accepting Spanish institutions, though, Chaco Guaycuruans mounted a series of spectacular military offensives. These attacks were manifestations of Guaycuruan weakness, but they terrified Spaniards and induced them to renew their offer of missions.

The Zenith of Guaycuruan Power

For a decade after the Urizar entrada, Guaycuruans refrained from attacking Tucumán, a repetition of the pattern of the 1600s. Diminuendo and crescendo had always characterized hostilities; Guaycuruans traditionally raided, then rested. As southeastern Mocobis turned toward Santa Fe and Corrientes, east-central bands and Toba contingents looked to Asunción. In the mid-1720s, though, western Mocobis returned in force to plunder the settlements of Tucumán.[45]

Guaycuruans approached Spanish settlements for two reasons. One was profit, including livestock, trade goods, and women and children as captives. As before, slow-moving militias pursued until their mobile adversaries dispersed in the vast expanses of the Chaco, and casualties were usually minimal. A second type of clash was for military and symbolic purposes. Guaycuruans might, as they did in March 1732, kill isolated males in the countryside of Santa Fe. Large Guaycuruan groups sometimes attacked small Spanish patrols. These combats were important. They enabled Guaycuruan men to boast of their valor and enhance their prestige.[46] Seldom, though, did Guaycuruans initiate fights with numerically equal Spanish forces, even though individually the Guaycuruan warrior was on balance superior to his Spanish counterpart in the opinion of both sides.[47] The Guaycuruans' lack of command authority, discipline, and organization meant that they could not win set battles unless their numbers were overwhelming or they had the advantage of surprise. Nowhere was the difference in principles of authority between Hispanic and Guaycuruan societies more dramatically evident than in their military styles.

In Santa Fe, hostilities climaxed in 1732. Desperate Guaycuruans pressed hard. Economic, environmental, and security problems, especially strife with other Guaycuruans, were causing intolerable stress. Guaycuruan raids caused Spaniards to protect livestock in corrals. Although expensive for creoles, the enclosures were effective in restricting Guaycuruan access. Guaycuruan profits from raiding convoys declined, because merchants avoided the upper Plata region. Guaycuruans then paralyzed the Santa Fe economy, and in March and April Abipones killed Native American servants of a Dominican convent. They assaulted Catholic symbols knowingly. Religion, they believed, gave the enemy power over them. They vandalized churches and threatened priests, because a measles epidemic currently afflicted residents of Santa Fe, and clerics went about to attend the sick unguarded and thus vulnerable.[48]

In the central and western Chaco, Guaycuruans mounted even bolder offensives. Because authorities had again allowed the militia to deteriorate, the mounted Chaco peoples roamed more freely through Tucumán province than they had before 1710. Mocobi Chief Cithaalin often led three hundred men against Salta, San Miguel de Tucumán, Córdoba, and Santiago del Estero. Mocobi Chief Nevedagnac frequently brought contingents rivaling Cithaalin's to Tucumán province. Mocobi attacks on Santiago del Estero in 1734 cowed its inhabitants and caused settlers to abandon their homes.[49]

The Guaycuruan bands of the southwestern Chaco, mostly Mocobis with Toba allies, intensified their attacks in 1734. In previous years, they had staged progressively larger offensives. They virtually closed the road through Jujuy to Potosí and carried off some three thousand horses and mules, as well as cattle and sheep.

Their grandest attack began at the end of the European year. The invading force numbered one thousand, including Spanish-speaking renegades[50] and at least one Quechua speaker. As rain silenced Spanish muskets, the raiders penetrated the Salta area in three bodies in early 1735. Fanning out over five leagues, they hit a small Jesuit property, the haciendas of the Reyes, Escalante, and Mercado families, and the homes of the humble. They found a treasure trove of booty, including hundreds of horses. They killed or captured hundreds, executing the dangerous or valueless captives—men, boys, and undesirable women.[51] Executions brought honor to the executioners. Of the surviving captives, a few were put into service and the majority ransomed. The raiders halted a quarter league from Salta, because the city itself was too strongly defended. When they withdrew, about 150 poorly armed Salteños chased the dissolving force. As the pursuers closed on them, fleeing Mocobis killed the prisoners slowing them down, and the majority returned to the Chaco.[52]

After this triumph, Mocobi orators bragged about their intent to destroy Salta during the next raiding season and San Miguel de Tucumán in 1737.[53] But their greatest glories were past. Their raids would decline in intensity in the coming years. Succeeding Guaycuruan expeditions encountered more vigorous opposition. A new governor, Mathías Anglés y Gortari, reorganized defenses and mounted an attack against Guaycuruans. But creole troops found only deserted settlements along the Bermejo. The Spaniards returned to Salta in early January 1736, with little to show for their efforts.[54]

Guaycuruan Decline: Environmental and Other Disasters

The Chaco peoples now faced a more deadly enemy. In the mid-1730s a smallpox epidemic ravaged their societies, as well as Hispanic communities and Guarani missions. In one encampment in May 1736 the militia of Santiago del Estero encountered a tragic scene of devastation. Many Mocobis had gathered there to die. Unable to complete their normal funeral rites, the survivors hastily buried a thousand people. Like Spaniards, who viewed the disease as a gift from God, Guaycuruans believed that such calamities had supernatural origins. Creoles sensed weakness, and they gave no quarter. After a party of Guaycuruans raided near Salta on May 7, 1736, Governor Anglés and sixty-four soldiers pursued them. Following a hard day's ride, they caught fourteen Guaycuruans, slowed by captives and livestock. Two leaders fought bravely until they died of bullet wounds. All fourteen died in the fight. Spaniards recovered women and livestock and displayed the heads of the fallen warriors. The governor had the trophy heads on lances carried through Salta to rally his own people and overawe the Guaycuruans, although such demonstrations seldom had a long-term effect.[55]

Similarly, Mbayá attacks on Paraguay peaked in the 1730s. They typically raided most frequently from October or November to February or March, the rainy season. In multiple raids the Mbayás obtained six thousand head of livestock and the lives and scalps of five hundred Paraguayans.[56] But in Paraguay too, these furious attacks abated by 1740, only partly because of a better provincial defense. A greater blow to Mbayá autonomy was that Hispanic Paraguay was moving north, reducing the mobility of hunting and raiding parties and pressing on food supplies. Furthermore, Mbayás now encountered difficulty marketing their prizes. Governor Moneda's prohibition in the 1740s against Mbayás entering Asunción to trade was effective, although the northern bands still traded with Brazilians.[57]

Mbayás, moveover, increasingly were competing with other Guaycuruans for Paraguayan wealth. In the late 1730s, Abipones and Mocobis, now at peace with Santa Fe and Corrientes, turned toward Paraguay. The eastern Toba too found opportunities in the province, and they fought Abipones for possession of the lands across the Río Paraguay from the Jesuit-Guarani reductions, especially San Ignacio–Guazú, Santiago, Santa Rosa, and Nuestra Señora de Fe.[58]

Stresses in Guaycuruan Society

Around the Chaco frontier, the Guaycuruan bands closest to Spanish settlements—such as the Mocobis of Ariacaiquin and the Riikahés of Ychamenraikin, who asked Santa Fe for an armistice in the 1730s—initiated a process that extended around the Chaco and over the rest of the century. In 1750 Yaaucaniga Abipones agreed to an accord with Corrientes, a compact identical to that between Nakaiketergehes Abipones and Santiago del Estero. In 1759 two Mbayá groups, the Apacachodegodegis and the Lichagotegodis, asked the Paraguayan government for a treaty of peace. In the early 1750s, a contingent of western Toba sought peace with Jujuy.

Customarily, Guaycuruans granted Spaniards peace but expected reciprocity, especially payment in Spanish hats, clothing, and knives.[59]

The Guaycuruans' greatest problems were ecological. By the 1730s an environmental crisis that had been gestating for two hundred years finally had overtaken the Chaco peoples. To understand it, we might contrast it with how rapidly a similar crisis overtook the Great Basin natives in Utah in the 1800s after the Mormons invaded their lands. In the Great Basin ecosystem—from northern Arizona to southern Idaho and between two mountain chains, the Rockies and the Sierras—the Shoshonis, Utes, and Paiutes witnessed the devastation of their environment in little more than a decade.

Like Guaycuruans, the Shoshoni, Paiute, and Ute were hunting and gathering peoples whose entities, or "tribes," were really many smaller, culturally linked groups without political connections. They lived by hunting and collecting wild fruits and vegetables. Because vegetation was sparse, the native peoples moved frequently. Their environment denied them surpluses, but they had little use for surplus goods. Their societies were decentralized and flexible. They chose leaders for specific tasks and brief periods. Their relationship with nature was reciprocal and interactive. In 1847 their population was eighteen thousand.[60]

The Mormons who settled in Utah in 1847 initiated environmental changes that would devastate the natives, because they worked to accumulate wealth. The Mormon Church monitored the spread of seventy-five towns over a vast area. The newcomers valued water and soil for intensive agriculture and grazing, and they had to irrigate. Their crops squeezed out the natives' wild fruits and vegetables. Native Americans needed water; Mormons hoarded it. As intensive cultivation destroyed Native American staples, Mormons also purposely annihilated game. The animals that destroyed Mormon crops had sustained native societies. As Mormons prospered, natives suffered. Numbering eighty thousand by 1869, the Mormon population overwhelmed the numerically inferior and declining Native American populations of the Great Basin. By 1860 the Mormons had won, and the Native Americans had lost.[61]

Guaycuruans too suffered from a crisis with multiple causes. Although environmental degradation of the Chaco was the most serious, military threats were more obvious. The disasters eventually pushed many from the Chaco toward the lands of the Spaniards, and one result was the foundation of missions. For Guaycuruans, conflict among themselves and with Spaniards had become an intolerable burden by the

1730s. Peace with Spaniards reduced threats from their most lethal adversary and provided a comparative advantage over Native American rivals, whom they often hated more. A century of confrontations with creole forces paradoxically had intensified confrontations among Guaycuruans. The iron weapons and horses that increased military effectiveness against provincial targets also killed more Guaycuruan enemies. Guaycuruans also suffered devastating illnesses. Although they had encountered plagues of European origin before and had acquired partial immunities, periodic epidemics were still deadly. In 1732–36 the smallpox and measles that raged through the Guarani-Jesuit missions and Santa Fe spread to the Chaco, staggering the Mocobis. Now most Chaco peoples also found fewer game animals because of overhunting. For decades they had hunted to satisfy the growing provincial and European markets for furs, skins, and hides, as well as for food. Markets in Spanish provinces drew resources from the Chaco. Despite having domesticated animals, Spanish society still required game. Mbayás used deer for clothing and bedding and still preferred venison to beef. But Spaniards paid for furs and skins in knives and needles, which Guaycuruans prized above their own rules against hunting to excess. They intensified their search for skins, and game declined.[62]

Vegetation in the Chaco, a source of food, clothing, needles, and netting, was now less abundant. After harvesting wild plant foods with iron tools for two centuries, Guaycuruans abruptly felt the decline of life-sustaining palm groves. Because Spaniards used algarroba for buildings and furniture, Guaycuruans surely found less of it, the most important source of sustenance for the southern societies. Grazing animals further damaged the Chaco environment. As if ecological debasement were not enough, Guaycuruans had increasing difficulty obtaining cattle and horses. Ranchers in the upper Plata after 1720 began to acquire ownership rights to formerly feral cattle, and they hired men to protect them. Fewer animals now roamed. At the same time Guaycuruans also found themselves confined by Spanish encroachment. They needed great spaces through which to migrate, land that was no longer available as land-hungry Spaniards pushed back the Chaco frontier.[63]

These calamities brought economic crises, increased security problems, a breakdown of Guaycuruan ideology (see chapter 6), and a loss of self-confidence. Guaycuruans interpreted these misfortunes as signaling that their traditional deities had lost power, so they decided to investigate the spiritual forces of Europeans. Abipones and Mocobis made peace with Santa Fe in 1734 and requested missions. Over the next half century most Guaycuruans asked for missions, although probably only about half lived in one for any length of time.

As the Chaco missions grew, other Guaycuruans trickled into the Spanish world. The Payaguá, who moved to Asunción in the mid-1700s, were the most visible, but there were others. Abipones settled at several sites on the Río Paraguay north of the Bermejo. After 1773 non-mission Mbayás lodged outside Concepción in northern Paraguay and in the Brazilian Mato Grosso. Some Guaycuruans, especially the western Toba and the Pilagá, the most remote, remained in the Chaco, living as traditionally as they could; but they too often visited missions to trade and raid. They mounted attacks on Spanish localities less frequently. Peace with one city, even after settling in a mission, however, did not represent to Guaycuruans a general alliance and subservience to Spanish society, as it did to Spaniards. Guaycuruans in missions retained their mobility and the option to reject mission life. Thus, the Guaycuruan missions of the Gran Chaco provide an important perspective on the history of Catholic missions in the Americas, because Guaycuruans learned new ways while remaining culturally Guaycuruan.

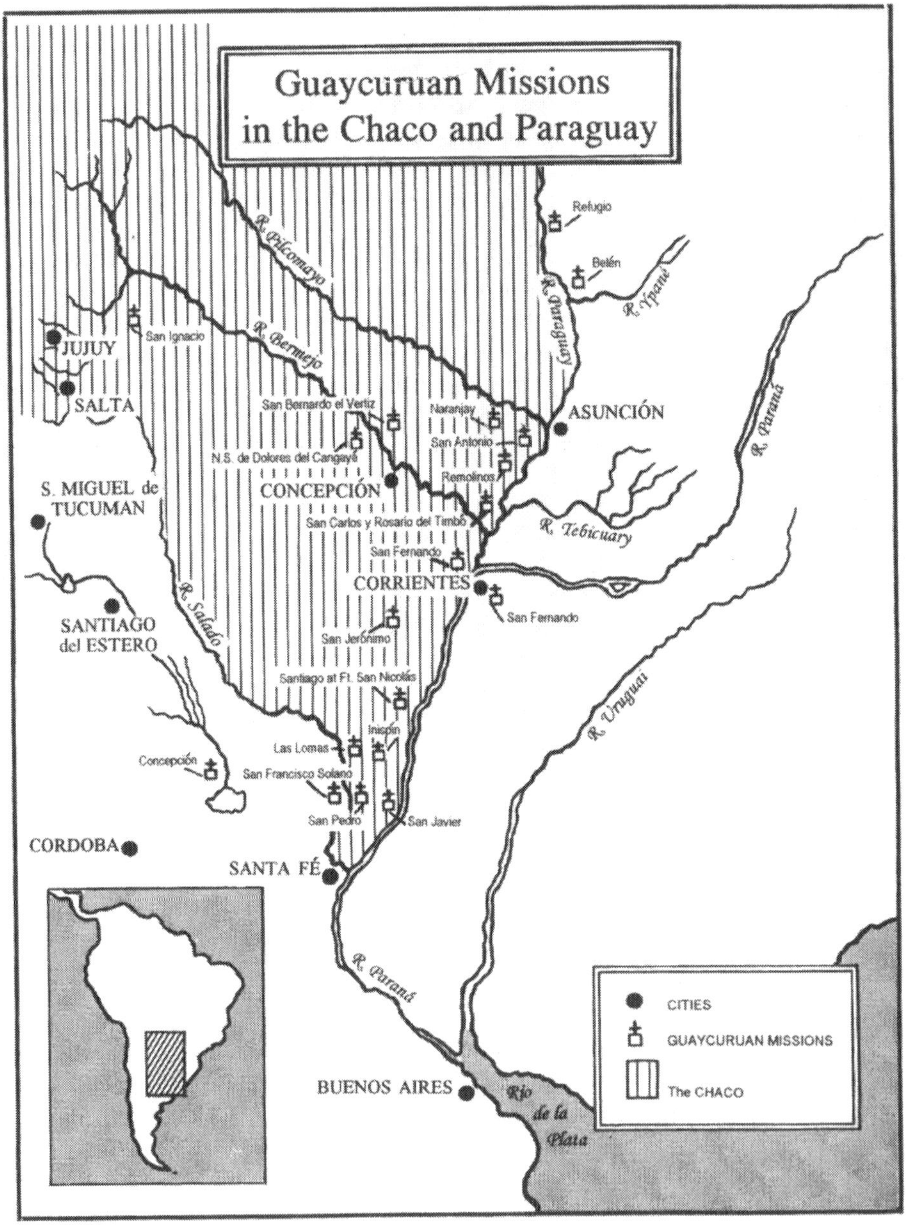

Guaycuruan missions in the Chaco and Paraguay.
(Map by Jane Gaughran)

CHAPTER 2

The Growth of Guaycuruan Missions

Guaycuruan society in the mid-1700s was beset by severe economic, environmental, and security problems. The survival strategy of most Guaycuruans was to adapt to these pressures by moving to Catholic missions, although many were unsuccessful in this quest. In this chapter I will investigate the growth of Guaycuruan missions in the Gran Chaco and northern Paraguay. I will examine how mounted Guaycuruans, who tried and rejected missions in the 1600s, embraced them after 1743. I will consider mission foundation and growth, obstacles to mission survival, and successes and failures.

Early Experiences with Missions

Guaycuruans first heard of missions after their Guarani adversaries gathered under Franciscans at Altos in Paraguay in 1580.[1] Guaycuruans maintained keen intelligence about Guarani affairs, and spies and scouts unquestionably brought news of mission life to the Chaco.

Guaycuruans next learned of missions directly from missionaries. In the seventeenth century, southern Guaycuruans heard and rejected claims about the superiority of the Christian God and the beneficence of Spanish rule from Fathers Alonso de Bárzana, Pedro de Añasco, and other missionary preachers in the Chaco.[2]

A few seventeenth-century Guaycuruans, though, were curious enough to experiment with missions. The Codalodis, a band of Mbayás, sampled mission life from 1609 to 1626. In exchange for material rewards, Chief Guayicota and his people welcomed Jesuit Fathers Vicente Grifi and Roque González de Santa Cruz to Guazutinguá west of Asunción. The priests appointed the chief a cacique, and renamed him Don Martín and his wife Doña Francisca. The Codalodis built a chapel under Jesuit direction. The Europeans planted crops. Uncomfortable with agricultural life, the Mbayás, according to the priests, ate the maize and wheat prematurely. They avoided mass, although some permitted priests to baptize their children. During an epidemic, a spirit warned Mbayás to fear Christianity and gave the missionaries an opportunity to elaborate their doctrines.[3] Like the Jesuits, the Guaycuruans wanted the sick baptized first, but the Guaycuruans expected the ceremony to cure, not understanding the Jesuits' preaching about eternal salvation. The mobile Guaycuruans' lifestyle frequently pulled them from the settlement to hunt animals and ripening plant foods, causing the mission to deteriorate. After the first mission failed, Jesuits and Mbayás established another, Santos Reyes Magos, at Yasocá.

Because missions made little sense to Guaycuruans in the 1600s, indigenous residents of the reduction of Santos Reyes Magos left for good in 1626.[4] In the early seventeenth century, Guaycuruans had recently acquired horses and iron weapons and tools, and were developing a "horse culture."[5] They began a century of political expansion and economic growth. They reaped increased benefits from violence on horseback, including iron knives and hatchets, and also the Native American and creole[6] women who maintained their numbers. Most prospered. Missions, however, remained embedded in the Guaycuruan collective memory.

In the southern and western Chaco, Guaycuruan experiences with missions in the 1600s resembled that of the Mbayás. The ancestors of the Abipones, Mocobis, and Toba who sought missions in the 1740s first observed the missions on the periphery of their territories. When the seventeenth-century San Javier de Mocobis was founded near the city of Talavera de Madrid (called Esteco), it predictably failed.

A group of Abipones led by Chief Caliguila also experimented briefly with a mission in the 1600s.[7] In 1638 Tobas and Mocobis asked Father Gaspar Osorio for a mission, but they must have reconsidered, because they took the priest's head in 1639. In 1641 a group of Abipones welcomed Father Juan Pastor to their seasonal settlement east of Santiago del Estero. They accepted "scissars, [*sic*] hooks, needles, and glass beads," but their desire for mission life was transitory. Abipones for the next century "over-ran the whole province with hostile, and generally victorious arms."[8] Fortunate in war, they lacked incentives to join a mission.

Changing Attitudes toward Missions

By the early 1700s Spanish artifacts had become economic requirements, and Spanish clothing and jewelry were social necessities. Raids brought horses, but excessive bartering of horses to Spaniards diminished Guaycuruan wealth and power. By the 1730s Guaycuruans found cattle, now an important source of protein and a trade item, increasingly protected by Platine cowboys. Intertribal strife grew intolerable. Smallpox and measles spread through the upper Plata region from 1732 to the 1740s. Food shortages followed epidemics, and ecological damage to plant foods from iron tools and grazing animals intensified the crisis. Spanish violence and intra-Guaycuruan conflicts also destabilized many groups.[9]

After the 1730s Guaycuruan eagerness for combat with Spaniards declined, not through a major cultural change but rather a recognition of altered power relationships. No longer were Guaycuruans uniformly hostile to Spaniards. A mission, Mocobis decided, would ensure their now-precarious food supply and safety. Mission Guaycuruans would receive a steady supply of now-necessary European artifacts. They could locate food with less effort and would be better prepared to confront Native American enemies. It also would provide them a new vision of the world and reconciliation with Spaniards. Because the two cultures often misunderstood each other, Guaycuruans sought missionary priests to act as intermediaries with the Spanish world.[10]

Mission Foundations and Mission Demography

The policies of Chaco missionaries resembled those on other Spanish American frontiers. Jesuits in the Chaco, like their brethren in Moxos, now Bolivia, aimed "to transform those ignorant of laws and government into communities that reflected European conceptions of orderly society;" from the missionaries' perspective this meant "the transformation of Indians from gentiles into neophytes."[11]

In 1734 the Abipon and Mocobi bands closest to Santa Fe made peace with that municipality.[12] By 1741 Mocobi Chief Ariacaiquin had requested a mission, forthcoming in 1743. In the intervening months, Mocobis visited the Jesuit *colegio,* where they received presents and advice.[13] This mission became San Javier, the first permanent Guaycuruan mission. (This mission is discussed in more depth later in the chapter.) The first founding of San Javier in June 1743 was on the site of the original city of Santa Fe, which Mocobis had forced Spaniards to abandon eighty years earlier.[14] After several moves, it was finally located about forty leagues north of Santa Fe. Mocobi Chief Aletin, whose band had joined Ariacaiquin's, and Jesuit missionaries Jerónimo Núñez and Francisco Burgés chose a site with woodlands, pasturage, water, and fish in the streams, all essential to survival. The mission's dimensions, according to Spaniards, were two leagues from north to south along the Río Paraná and four leagues from east to west, although Mocobis had a more expansive notion of their homeland. Fifty Mocobi families, 246 persons, established the reduction. They took possession of cattle and oxen for plowing. Guaycuruans were exempt from Spanish labor demands, from personal service, and from normal taxes, as were most other Platine Jesuit reductions.[15] Across the Río Paraná, mission Guaranis paid a silver peso a year in tribute for each adult male under fifty,[16] but to the end of the colonial era, the Guaycuruan reductions received more in subsidies than they paid in taxes.

In 1748 the Riikahés Abipones settled the mission of San Jerónimo del Rey, thirty-eight leagues north of the Mocobi mission;[17] early priests included José Cardiel, a veteran of San Javier, and Francisco Navalón. Abipones likewise located their reduction in their own lands, surrounded by plains, woods, game, water, and good soil for crops.[18]

Elsewhere in the southern Chaco, similar foundations were laid. In 1748–49 the Nakaiketergehes Abipones helped establish the Concepción mission in Santiago del Estero, and in 1750 the Yaaucaniga Abipones moved to San Fernando across the Río Paraná from Corrientes, now the city of Resistencia. In 1756 a band of Toba and Jesuits created San Ignacio de Ledesma in the southwestern Chaco, a day's ride from Jujuy.

In northern Paraguay, the Apacachodegodegis, an Mbayá band, selected in 1760 a site for mission Belén on the Río Ypané just east of the modern Paraguayan city of Concepción. Abipon refugees from other missions in 1763 selected Rosario del Timbó, seventy leagues south of Asunción on the Chaco bank of the Río Paraguay, on lands that eastern Toba also claimed. In 1765 Mocobi relatives of San Javier people formed San Pedro, southwest of San Javier on the Río Ispín, or Inispín Chico, the last mission Guaycuruans founded before the Jesuit expulsion.

Jesuit priests staffed these missions for several reasons. First, they aggressively sought the appointment, whereas the other orders were passive. Second, Jesuit resources could finance the new settlements.[19] Prosperous Jesuit businesses in the Plata region and the surpluses of the Guarani missions provided subsidies to supplement grants from the crown, viceroys, municipal governments, and local philanthropists.

The most pronounced demographic result of Catholic missions in

Latin America was normally population decline.[20] According to one scholar, mission populations in northwestern New Spain were "not viable as a consequence of chronically high rates of mortality," and there was "no long-term recovery from periodic epidemics."[21] Even the famous Guarani missions of Paraguay, which held their own from 1702 to 1767, declined after 1768.[22] But the demographic record might be more complex than gloomy. In Sonora, for example, "alternative interpretations of the population history" include "the partial destruction of the community as a fixed entity and its reconstitution in other forms."[23] Chaco missions declined more often from desertions than disease.

As in other areas, Guaycuruan mission populations were unstable (see appendixes). Missions usually started with small populations, rose to a peak in a few years, and then fluctuated thereafter. The peak was probably reached in the early 1780s, when five to six thousand Guaycuruans lived in missions, or 20 to 30 percent more than in the last years before the Jesuit expulsion. These population shifts were less the result of the lethal epidemics and chronic diseases found in missions in areas of new European occupation than of Guaycuruan habits of mobility. The populations were constantly changing as mounted Guaycuruans arrived and left. Occasionally men left alone; more often they departed in nuclear or extended family groups. Large congregations dwindled for several other reasons as well. Lack of economic support from the Spanish world was one reason, and ethnic rivalries and warfare played a part as well.

Most missions outside the jurisdiction of Santa Fe, where they were larger, had core populations of between 250 and 600. Moreover, whatever the size of a mission at any time, a larger number than indicated by census records normally formed the mission society. These were vastly greater permanent concentrations of people than in previous Guaycuruan experience. In the Jesuit years, San Fernando de Abipones averaged 359 persons, while more than a thousand Mocobis lived in San Javier. San Jerónimo normally had about 650 Abipon residents. In 1767 the Guaycuruan mission population was around 3,860. Concepción housed 400 Abipones, San Jerónimo from 700 to 800, San Fernando about 400, and Rosario del Timbó about 350. At the time San Javier had 1,000 Mocobis, while 150 of their kin lived in newly founded San Pedro. Approximately 600 Toba lived in San Ignacio, and 260 Mbayás lived in Belén, a temporarily low figure for a mission whose population was in the high hundreds just before the Jesuit exile.[24]

The population of Belén declined after the high point of 1,300 in the early 1760s because the Lichagotegodis and Apacachodegodegis, rival bands, clashed. The Lichagotegodis requested their own mission, and they received Refugio.[25] It was founded in 1769 near Ytapucú under Franciscan Friar Francisco Méndez, but disappeared in 1775 when he died.[26]

San Jerónimo de Abipones illustrates population fluctuation. It rose from 800 in 1767 to 1,254 in 1777 and fell to 681 (or 598) in 1785 and then to 482 in 1793. San Javier, the oldest and most stable of the Guaycuruan missions had 1,028 residents in 1785 but declined to 674 later that year. By 1793, however, it had recovered, because 1,308 Mocobis lived there. The original 150 Mocobis of San Pedro became 400 in 1776 and then 900, but the mission oscillated between 400 and 643 residents from 1767 to the end of the colonial era. In San Fernando de Abipones during the Jesuit years, the population reached a high of 679 and a low of 151, averaging 359. San Ignacio housed 365 Toba in 1757, 332 in 1771, and 334 in 1778,[27] a remarkably steady figure for a mission so exposed to Chaco influences and exploited by the post-Jesuit officials of Tucumán.

The largest mission foundations of the post-Jesuit era were San Bernardo de Tobas, with 1,070 in 1781 and Santiago de Cangayé de Mocobis, with 905 in that year.[28] Both disappeared in the 1790s because of lack of government support and remoteness from Spanish economic and military institutions. Another post-Jesuit establishment, Remolinos, for Mocobis south of Asunción, had 500 to 600 Mocobis in 1779, a year after its foundation.

Characteristics of a Successful Mission

The first Guaycuruan mission, San Javier de Mocobis, was a model for others. Its founding began when Mocobi Chief Ariacaiquin (through captive interpreters) asked civil authorities, not Jesuits, for a mission.[29] The chief promised to become a Christian and behave as Europeans wished. Although he died soon after, his brother, Cithaalin, led his people to mission life. Chief Aletin's people soon followed. San Javier de Mocobis formally commenced on June 27, 1743, at Pueblo Viejo.

A mission needed a sound economic base. Therefore, Cithaalin contacted Jesuits in Santa Fe, whose colegio owned an estancia with 23,000 cattle and could help the Mocobis financially.[30] Although initial subsidies for San Javier from secular authorities and private donors were small, Mocobis received enough for a start. Beef was essential, because Guaycuruans were meat eaters. Usually, five families shared a cow a week.[31] The mission's initial endowment was 187 head of cattle, 451 sheep, 137 varas of locally made clothing, 3 arrobas of *yerba*, and boards for doors of the church and the priests' homes.[32] Support from Santa Fe continued, as its city fathers, in effect, paid for peace. San Javier received 40,000 pesos from that city from 1743 to 1760, and San Jerónimo de Abipones received 27,000 pesos from the same source between 1748 and 1760.[33] Jesuit colegios and the Guarani missions also provided cattle. From 1743 to 1767, each Guarani mission contributed 100 pesos a year to Guaycuruan reductions.[34] Others occasionally contributed as well. For Concepción de Abipones, the viceroy of Peru in 1750 allocated four thousand pesos, an exceptional grant.[35]

Guaycuruan missions required continuing support. A consignment of two thousand sheep in early 1752, which Santa Fe authorities allotted from the *diezmo* of livestock, kept San Jerónimo afloat.[36] Authorities preferred subsidizing missions to the military expenses of the past. Officials hoped that livestock, agriculture, and workmanship would enable the mission eventually to support itself,[37] but nomadic Guaycuruans needed more encouragement than did peoples whose pre-mission cultures had been sedentary or semisedentary. The Guaranis who lived across the Río Paraguay–Río Paraná system from the Guaycuruans or the Arawak-speaking peoples of Moxos in upper Peru were better prepared for missions than the Abipones or the Toba. From the 1740s onward, however, the desire of Chaco peoples for missions was greater than Spaniards' willingness to pay for them.[38]

Physically, a mission resembled a European village with Guaycuruan modifications. At the center was the mission town. San Javier was typical. Woods, pastures, and water surrounded the town. With Jesuit advisers and Guarani assistants, Mocobis built small adobe houses with peaked, thatched roofs. They were arranged in the Guaycuruan fashion in a semicircle around an open, grassy area. Of varying sizes, the homes were square, rectangular, or L-shaped. Commoners' homes clustered around the houses of the five to ten caciques in residence there. Small wooden stockades surrounded a few individual homes, or now and then a pair, but most family dwellings were not enclosed. After a few years, San Javier's ranch possessed thousands of cattle, horses, and sheep—in the good times. In addition, caciques owned ranches beyond the town. A few corrals dotted the outskirts of the settlement, but most animals grazed in the open. Abutting the indigenous semicircle, a solid wall protected the mission church, priests' quarters, warehouses, sheds, and an enclosure for the stretching and drying of hides. Vegetable gardens, fields, and an orchard adjoined the Spanish section.[39]

A Precarious Foundation

The Mbayás' experience provides a useful contrast to that of the Mocobis. The Mbayás closest to Spaniards had more frequent contacts with Spanish culture and were the earliest to request missions. In 1759, four hundred Mbayás came to Asunción to request a mission, and at one time or another all Mbayá groups, seven thousand to eight thousand people, requested Spanish missions.[40] Asunción officials rejoiced, expecting these reductions to buffer Paraguay against Indian attack and Portuguese expansion along the Spanish-Portuguese frontier, a zone of frequent hostilities.[41] Their strategy was only partially successful, however; groups more remote from Paraguay later migrated toward Portuguese centers.

Civil authorities approved an Mbayá mission in 1760, and construction of Nuestra Señora de Belén began the next year. Anti-Jesuit Paraguayans unsuccessfully advised Mbayás to spurn the Jesuits.[42] Possibly because of anti-Jesuit sentiment, few citizens of Asunción helped, and the initial request for donations raised only a hundred pesos, less than 1 percent of the cost of a new reduction. Although Paraguayans wanted the reduction to pacify the northern frontier, they assumed that the Jesuits would underwrite the cost and had no desire to do so themselves.[43] Belén did pacify the frontier,[44] but only because the Jesuit colegio of Asunción assumed the financial burden.

On August 20, 1760, Mbayás, Jesuits, four Guaranis, and fourteen Paraguayan militia men arrived at the northern bank of the Río Ypané a few leagues east of its confluence with the Río Paraguay.[45] Jesuits opposed Mbayás' contacts with civil society, except for those contacts with the minority of Paraguayans who supported them.[46]

Mbayás and Jesuits surmounted the language barrier. Mbayás first communicated with priests through captives, who spoke Mbayá, Guarani, Spanish, and Portuguese. Initially missionaries learned the Mbayá tongue from women, but the men, who spoke a different dialect, ridiculed them. Soon the priests learned to speak like Mbayá males.[47]

Construction projects were huts for Mbayás, a house for the missionaries, and a warehouse to protect provisions from the elements and from Mbayás. Paraguayan philanthropists provided sheep. Hoping to entice Guaycuruans toward sedentary agriculture, Jesuits and Guaranis initially sowed maize, watermelons, sugar, and manioc. Jesuits controlled the maize and manioc, as they did tobacco. Mbayás craved sugar, and priests used sweets to reward compliance. Additionally, Mbayás demanded bread, beef, and shoes.[48] Guaycuruans had long obtained Spanish foods and clothing in limited quantities but now gained regular access to these commodities.

The first Mbayás at Belén were Apacachodegodegis of Chief Epaquini, who boasted that Guayicota-Martín, founder of the short-lived Santos Reyes Magos mission of the seventeenth century, was his great-grandfather. The Lichagotegodis also lived at Belén for two years. Both left according to the cycles of the palm, the algarroba, the hunt, or for war and commerce. Like other Guaycuruan leaders, Epaquini could not command followers, but he promoted the mission experiment, as did his wife, renamed Margarita.[49]

Typical of the early instability of the Guaycuruan reductions, Belén was nearly deserted at one point. When the Mbayás decided to go to Asunción, most likely to trade, they packed up and rode south, leaving in Belén only a few people, mostly aged and infirm but also the healthy adults who declined to follow Epaquini, now Cacique Jaime. Missionaries attributed this mobility to a supposedly childlike Indian nature, calling it "fickleness" and failing to recognize the faithfulness to tradition that it actually represented.[50] Customarily, Jesuits awaited the Indians' return, were confident that they would return, and had the resources to support the dependent Indians who remained behind. They distributed food, clothing, and tools as incentives to Indians who returned.[51]

In the first year or two, conditions in Belén were trying. Food shortages occurred. Paraguayans, now less fearful of Mbayás, continued donating little. Some even obstructed the enterprise.[52] Missionaries and their Mbayá neophytes had to draw on Jesuit resources and acumen to resist land-hungry Paraguayan ranchers and yerba traders.

By 1762 many subsistence problems were on the road to solution. Sheep, grain, and cotton came occasionally from private citizens.[53] Cattle came from the Guarani missions in nearby Taruma, and the cattle ranch essential for sustenance was founded. When Mbayás left the mission, they often went hungry,[54] despite periodic abundance in their lands, and returned for food. Well-fed Mbayás left the mission less often,[55] but war periodically drew them away.

The Guaycuruans' martial values retarded the development of a mission culture. Moreover, Guaycuruan contact with Spanish and Portuguese secular societies provided few models of pacific behavior. The frontier was violent. Guaycuruan men's desire for combat, which had provided security, sustenance, women, and prestige for centuries, could not be preached away. Economic opportunities beyond the mission caused Mbayás to look for captives to use as servants and to sell.[56] Over time, however, male prestige from hunting, war, and raiding declined.[57] Belén Mbayás learned more of the Hispanic world from priests and Hispanized Guaranis, and missionization accelerated the changes already underway in Mbayá life.

Since Mbayás had kept livestock for a century,[58] animal management required few lifestyle changes and was adopted fairly readily. In contrast, Guaycuruans had scorned sedentary "corn growers" such as Guaranis for centuries, and the transition to agriculture was more difficult, especially for the men. Accustomed to harvesting wild foods when hungry, Mbayás ate newly planted crops before they ripened. Because agriculture had always been women's work, for Mbayá women the switch to sedentary agriculture was not as great a departure (see chapter 3). Men resisted working in the fields, however. In time Mbayá men began working periodically in the fields, but many preferred working for wages as cowhands, guards, or artisans.

Young women appreciated the added security of the Christian agricultural revolution, but older women, young men, and shamans resisted the loss of influence and status (see chapter 4).[59] One of those who resisted was Epilig Iyegi (renamed Lorenzo by the Jesuits), Cacique Jaime's son and heir. Lorenzo's mother was a Payaguá from Asunción, where the boy lived until he was ten. His childhood in Asunción, fluency in Guarani, and prior relationships with Paraguayans connected him to the Spanish world independent of Jesuit mediators. He often visited the capital on business.[60] Young Guaycuruans such as Lorenzo and Antonio, his cousin and fellow alumnus of a European cultural education, voiced the discontent of young Mbayás. They challenged the priests who were their rivals for leadership and reduced their status as warriors. In the mid-1760s, for example, Antonio plotted the execution of Father Sánchez. Only the intervention of Lichagotegodi warriors saved the priest. Disobeying Jesuit directives, Lorenzo led a raid on the Guarani Jesuit mission of San Estanislao.[61]

The Spanish-Portuguese imperial rivalry in the upper Plata also hindered the missionary enterprise. In 1762 word of hostilities between Spain and Portugal reached Belén, and Mbayás prepared for attacks from the north.[62] Mbayás felt vulnerable at Belén. They lacked their old protective mobility, and they remembered atrocities committed by subjects of both European empires.[63]

Secular society was another force that pulled Mbayás from Belén.

They joined Spaniards in contraband activities. Contact with Paraguayans weakened the priests' influence. Innocent encounters brought unexpected results. One Mbayá woman, for example, returned from Paraguay and insisted that she needed no baptism. Recently a guest of a Paraguayan woman, the Guaycuruan was received in such a way that she believed she was already baptized. The priests' efforts to convince authorities to prohibit Indian travel were seldom successful.[64] The land was vast, Spanish forces distant. Unlike missions in northern Mexico, few Spanish presidios adjoined Guaycuruan missions in the early decades. Thus, mounted people were able to evade Spanish coercion.

Guaycuruans, even in missions, frightened creoles. In 1764, for example, a confederation of Abipones, Toba, and Lenguas from the southern Chaco threatened central Paraguay. Belén Mbayás came to Asunción to aid Paraguayans against mutual rivals. The governor panicked. He tried to starve the Mbayá volunteers back home and sent smallpox victims to their encampment. The governor's strategy worked. Hunger forced the Mbayás to return to the north, and smallpox infected them en route. They brought the pestilence to Belén, where two hundred people died. That the epidemic was not more severe was due to prior Guaycuruan contact with the disease. By the 1760s diseases of Old World origin were no longer wholesale killers of Native Americans. Epaquini-Jaime and many other Mbayás had survived smallpox infections and were thus immunized. Yet smallpox was still fearsome, and when the disease struck in 1764, terrified Mbayás fled Belén.[65]

Ironically, when hunger visited Belén in 1764, Hispanized Guaranis suffered most. Mbayás continued to make flour from palms and sold it to Guaranis for clothing. By this time as well, adult Mbayás of both sexes worked family fields,[66] although like other mission Guaycuruans, they retained their nomadic habits into the mid-1760s. Most families appreciated the mission's security but tired of its regimentation and frequently left for periods of time. Children were the first to welcome the new ways. By 1765, when the Belenistas traveled, their sons and daughters begged to return to the mission.[67]

Nevertheless, after seven years of Jesuit tutelage at Belén, the fusion of the Mbayá bands with the Guarani-speaking subculture of the Upper Plata region was underway. A few Mbayás now communicated in European languages acquired through commerce and from captives. Several examples of acculturation were notable. As one example, Lorenzo served for a time as foreman of a cattle ranch in distant Santa Cruz,[68] now Bolivia. As another, one band far from Asunción in 1767 had six women from Asunción among the captives. Finally, a Brazilian man and a woman of the Cuyabá elite served Chief Caminigo of the Eyibegodegis.[69]

Charles III's order to expel Jesuits from Spanish dominions, carried out in Belén in August 1767, ended the Society's tutelage of Mbayás. Mbayás watched Paraguayans swarm into their lands after Lorenzo helped found Villa Real de Concepción near Belén in 1773.[70] From the Mato Grosso, Brazilians pushed south, catching Mbayás in a pincers. Southern Mbayás formed alliances with Paraguayan *yerberos* against unsubdued Guaranis who harassed the yerba trade. Mbayás suffered further as their Guaná clients sought Paraguayan employers to shield them from Mbayá domination. Non-mission and former mission Mbayás camped at Villa Real and made peace in return for salt, meat, blankets, and tools.[71]

Refugio, founded for exiles from Belén after the Jesuit departure, died and no other Mbayás received missions, but Belén limped along until the end of the colonial period. It received less material support than Guaycuruan missions closer to Spanish centers, and in 1789 its people were naked, without food, and in debt.[72] With the exception of Rosario y San Carlos de Timbó for Abipones, no other mission founded in the Jesuit era fared worse. Nevertheless, Belén survived. It remains today a town in northern Paraguay, although its Mbayás long ago assimilated into the Guarani-speaking population of the region.

Post-Jesuit Developments

The Jesuits' departure did not lessen Chaco peoples' continued desire for missions. Non-Guaycuruans and the Toba of the Tucumán frontier requested new settlements, but Spanish financial limitations often frustrated their quests.[73] By 1778 Franciscans officiated in the Mocobi missions of San Javier and San Pedro, and in Concepción de Abipones, San Fernando de Abipones, San Ignacio de Tobas, and San Francisco Solano de Remolinos de Mocobis in Paraguay. Later Franciscans also took over San Jerónimo from Mercedarians. Sometimes the missions had two priests, sometimes one, and toward the end of the colonial period, some at times had no priest at all.[74]

All these missions survived until the end of the colonial era, although San Fernando disappeared for a time after the Jesuits' departure. Its Abipones temporarily moved to San Jerónimo but returned in the 1770s and refounded their mission as San Fernando de Garzas on the east bank of the Río Paraná.

Post-Jesuit transitions were stormy for some missions and less difficult for others, particularly the well-established ones. From 1767 to 1773, four priests served in San Fernando de Abipones, a turnover that brought uncertainty and unrest. Finally Friar Francisco Rodríguez arrived and stayed for twenty-three difficult years, while the mission continued to develop.[75] In contrast, San Jerónimo de Abipones and Concepción both generally prospered.[76] In 1773, for example, San Jerónimo de Abipones kept thirty thousand head of cattle.[77] Such firmly established missions even endured without regularly appointed priests, as Abipones in San Jerónimo did from 1787 to 1795.[78]

Lacking Jesuit financial support after 1768, mission Guaycuruans became more dependent on emergency subventions from local governments. In early 1769, for example, a fire destroyed part of San Jerónimo de Abipones, and Cacique José Benavides begged Santa Fe for help. The Abipones could cut the wood and prepare the other materials for reconstruction but needed money to hire a builder and *peones.* (Peones' wages were a normal expense. They performed such tasks as cart making and, in the early years, agricultural jobs.) Fortunately, the governor underwrote slaves, masons, carpenters, peones, and carts for rebuilding.[79]

Some missions did better economically than others. In 1769 Concepción de Abipones was affluent. Some 229 Abipones worshiped in Concepción in a nice church, though in need of new roof tiles. Long and narrow, it was forty-two varas long by eight varas wide and it stood seven varas high. The mission also had a well-equipped smithy, seven corrals, one oven for lime and another for bricks, brick-making tools in good repair, and jail equipment, including a stock and chains. The mission owned about 4,000 mares and colts, 600 horses,[80] 400 mules, 17 oxen, and 1,500 head of cattle.[81]

In contrast, the Toba of San Ignacio encountered trouble. A few years after the expulsion, the mission still held 2,232 cattle but only 70 oxen, 28 mares, and 14 tame mules. The foreman received no salary, and no one checked his books, a license to steal. Improvident Toba and greedy outsiders consumed the animal resources of the mission. Tucumán governors used Toba lands for winter pasture for thousands of mules. In 1771 the 332 Toba of San Ignacio finally received a subvention of tools, seeds, cattle, and 300 pesos,[82] and the mission survived. In 1776 a visitor found a new three-room adobe building with stone foundations, wooden doors with lattice work, working locks, and wooden floors, altogether worth 291 pesos. Additionally, the mission still possessed ornaments, sacred vessels, books, and such tools as saws, hoes, adzes, chisels, shovels, sickles, kettles, cauldrons, cook pots, yokes, scales, branding irons, storage boxes, adobe molds, and nails. In the garden eight mature orange trees grew beside a grape arbor and apple and other fruit trees. But the livestock, on which everything else depended, was almost gone by 1776. Only fifty oxen, thirty cows, and five worthless mission horses remained for the 342 mission Toba.[83]

By 1778 the church, like all adobe structures demanding constant repair, was in ruins. The Toba mostly lived beyond the town itself. Nevertheless, some 383 persons were near enough to gather at the pueblo when the governor of Tucumán sponsored the first mass in three years. Because their priest had deserted them, no children had been baptized. The governor brought the Toba two thousand cattle and promised two thousand more. Some authorities judged five hundred pesos annually enough to subsidize a Guaycuruan mission, but this was inadequate.[84] Such calculations ignored emergencies—fire, war, plague—which came in bunches.

Like that of the Guales in Florida,[85] the behavior of Guaycuruans tried the patience of Spanish officials, even those raised on the Chaco frontier. In Spanish eyes, the Mocobis of San Pedro, a recent foundation, lacked subordination. The Mocobis agreed; they were proud of their independence. In 1768 they gave little indication of adjusting to mission life, because their adaptation was slow. When fugitives took cattle, they exposed the mission to ruin. Prior to their expulsion, Jesuits had had the resources and credit to renew a depleted mission herd, but by 1769 San Pedro de Mocobis was heavily in debt.[86] It was not alone; the three Santa Fe missions were 17,000 pesos in debt in 1768.[87]

Relations with the Spanish World

By the post-Jesuit era, Guaycuruans had entered the legal Spanish economy. They raised and sold livestock and crops and sold their labor services in the local market.[88] At the same time, unlawful economic activities, especially rustling and smuggling, were crucial to missions. For example, in the 1790s Correntinos dismissed San Fernando de Garzas as "a nest of highwaymen," revealing that Abipones continued participating in the underground economy even as they were raising crops and cattle.[89] Most missions participated in the larger imperial economy at both controlled and free levels, selling products legally in nearby towns and illegally trading with smugglers and receivers of stolen property.

Open Chaco spaces invited contraband. Brazilian traders visited countrymen in Santa Fe, then rode to the Río Bermejo region on business. Mission and non-mission Guaycuruans of the central Chaco were good partners. They guided trains of untaxed yerba and tobacco from Paraguay and the Guarani missions through the Chaco to Upper Peru and escorted the silver returning east. In 1775 Abipones in San Jerónimo were caught unloading untaxed goods from Paraguay, tobacco and honey destined for markets in Tucumán. In the missions, merchants from Paraguay, Corrientes, and Santa Fe and their Guaycuruan partners avoided taxes.

Another enterprise favored by most missions was cattle rustling. In 1779 the Abipones of San Jerónimo, then at war with San Pedro Mocobis and their non-mission Mocobi allies, survived on stolen livestock. As in the past, they shipped horses and hides to Corrientes and Santiago del Estero. Hispanic purchasers did not question ownership. Luis Pavón, a Portuguese merchant, bought hides from Abipones at San Jerónimo, and merchants from Santiago del Estero traded ponchos for stolen horses and mules.[90]

As mission Guaycuruans struggled to maintain their new homes, their friends and rivals sought reductions of their own. For two decades after 1767, Guaycuruans from the Chaco interior repeatedly petitioned the government for missions, but their desire exceeded the Spanish ability to underwrite such ventures. Northeastern Mocobis asked Paraguay in 1776 for a mission and founded Remolinos in 1778, forty leagues south of Asunción. Neighboring Paraguayans were to serve as examples, employers, and trading partners. In 1779 Remolinos de Mocobis had five hundred to six hundred people. Although presidios came relatively late to upper Plata missions, across the river from Remolinos such a fort now stood; this situation became increasingly typical in the late eighteenth century, as reductions and forts were paired along the Chaco frontier. The development of the Chaco differed from that of northern New Spain and California, where the presidio, present from the beginning, "eclipsed missions to become the dominant institution on Spain's North American frontiers."[91]

Remolinos Mocobis received from Paraguayan officials enough cattle, tobacco, and salt to survive. Owning five thousand cattle in 1782, they nevertheless frequently took livestock from the royal estancia, and a fifty-man garrison was ordered to restrain them. Mocobi men angered creoles in other ways, especially when drunk, but Mocobi women's industriousness pleased Paraguayans. Remolinos Mocobis seldom attracted attention, except for periodic reports of missing Paraguayan livestock. In 1807 and 1812, the mission received government subsidies, but its men now worked their own fields. They grew corn, cotton, manioc, sweet potatoes, and watermelons. The population was somewhat reduced from the 500 to 600 founders, although its exact size is unknown. The mission was home to 166 women and children, and 93 of the women were formally married to their husbands around 1810. Remolinos survived many hardships but finally succumbed to the anticlerical hostility of Dr. Francia, the Supreme Dictator of Paraguay. By 1821 it was abandoned.[92] Some Mocobis eventually followed their cacique across the Río Paraguay to live in creole Paraguay.

Imperial expansion in the late Bourbon era led to a few more Guaycuruan missions. In the late 1700s the Guaycuruan desire for missions coincided with Spanish aspirations for a commercial route across the southern Chaco,[93] dominated by Mocobis and Toba. Tucumán officials helped found two more Guaycuruan missions. On July 24, 1774, the celebrated Mocobi Chief Paikin signed a treaty of peace with Governor Gerónimo Matorras and accepted Spanish promises of missions for his people and his Toba allies.[94] In 1780 another expedition from Tucumán established Nuestra Señora de los Dolores y Santiago at Cangayé for Mocobis and San Bernardo el Vértiz for the Toba on the Río Bermejo.[95]

Despite crown support for the new Chaco missions,[96] the reductions of Cangayé and San Bernardo were doomed. Large by Guaycuruan standards, they were still tiny compared to Guarani reductions.[97] The San Bernardo mission began in late 1780 with 1,070 persons, and Cangayé had 905 Mocobis. Neither prospered, because both were too distant from Spanish subsidies, markets, and protection. The priests of the two missions were often in Corrientes, some eighty leagues to the east. Absentee priests were not uncommon in other Guaycuruan missions in these years, but departures proved fatal to new enterprises. Residents of the Río Bermejo missions resumed old ways, raiding Spanish ranches of Corrientes and Santa Fe and the missions along the Río Paraná and Río Paraguay.[98] Soon the missions disappeared. While one group hived off to settle along the east bank of the Río Paraguay between the Bermejo and the Pilcomayo, others remained in the vicinity of the former missions.

The last Guaycuruan mission founded in the colonial period was Jesús Nazareno de Ispín (or Inispín) for Mocobis. In 1795, 511 Mocobis settled there, and 119 more arrived in 1796, leaving about 3,000 non-mission Guaycuruans along the Chaco frontier of Santa Fe and more in the interior. In 1809, on the eve of the independence struggles that doomed the colonial missions, Mocobis of Ispín, besieged by Chaco Toba, asked to move their mission closer to Santa Fe for protection,[99] showing their attraction to mission life and their unwillingness to return to their old ways.

Internal and External Conflicts

Violence plagued all Guaycuruan missions, because missionaries could persuade but—lacking nearby military force—could not command Guaycuruans. Ancient enmities pushed the residents of various missions against each other. Mission residents also harried distant creoles, who themselves contributed to the culture of violence. Two conflicts of the post-Jesuit years are instructive: the Abipon-Mocobi war of the missions of Santa Fe and the involvement of the San Ignacio Toba in the uprising of Indians and castes in Jujuy in the fateful Andean year of 1781.

Several developments of 1775–76 sparked an Abipon-Mocobi war, which persisted into the 1780s. The feud between Cacique Ychoalay–José Benavides of San Jerónimo and non-mission Mocobi Chief Paikin set the stage. Another cause was the pro-Mocobi policy of Santa Fe's *teniente*, Melchor de Echagüe y Andia, and his subordinate, José Tarragona, mission administrator.[100] Echagüe discontinued the even-handed policies of his predecessors and openly favored Mocobis, permitting them to harass mission Abipones without retaliation. Abipones also claimed that Tarragona, who controlled legal trade, discriminated against them. Through his Mocobi godson, Tarragona was related to mission Mocobis, giving him financial incentive to favor Mocobi traders. The non-mission Mocobis from the Río Bermejo who visited the Santa Fe missions to trade eventually ruptured the amity between the Abipones of San Jerónimo and the Mocobis of San Javier. Paikin's band was especially persistent. They visited friends and relatives in San Pedro, who were also tied by kinship to the Mocobis of San Javier, and they raided San Jerónimo for livestock, captives, and scalps.

In 1775 Chaco visitors brought the population of San Pedro, only a decade old, from five hundred Mocobis to nine hundred. All venerated war in the Guaycuruan manner, and the newcomers loathed Cacique José Benavides of San Jerónimo and his people. San Pedro men allied with Chief Paikin, who in 1774 asked for a mission specifically in order to defeat Benavides.[101]

Abipones killed Paikin in 1775 as his people besieged San Jerónimo, expanding the conflict.[102] Paikin's death aroused San Pedro, whose cacique, José Pablo, called on his connections in Santa Fe. He brought with him Paikin's nephew and his wife, Doña María Micaela de la Riva Herrera, whose name revealed her kinship ties to a previous teniente. Mocobis of San Javier joined them.[103] Cacique-Corregidor Benavides of San Jerónimo sought countervailing help from Governor Pinedo of Paraguay. Pinedo offered to intervene in the Guaycuruan dispute because Mocobi raids on Paraguay gave him and Benavides common enemies. As Corrientes and Asunción sided with the Abipones of San Jerónimo, worried Santafecinos forged stronger ties to mission and non-mission Mocobis.

In August 1775 Governor Pinedo and Benavides agreed to a joint expedition to chastise their mutual Mocobi adversaries. Three hundred Abipones hoped to join a like number of Paraguayans to punish the Chaco Mocobis. The force was intended to have complementary skills: the weapons, organization, and discipline of the Paraguayans[104] with the Abipones' combat abilities and knowledge of the terrain. However, Pinedo found that Echagüe, who as teniente of Santa Fe was Benavides' nominal superior,[105] strongly opposed the expedition, so he canceled it.

In 1775 and 1776 conflict between San Jerónimo Abipones and the Mocobis of San Pedro intensified, and the war ensnared San Javier. Men from both Mocobi missions joined Chaco Mocobis and their Toba confederates against Abipones.

Eventually, San Jerónimo Abipones retaliated against San Javier. After they stole brood mares from the estancia of Cacique-Corregidor Domingo Nevedagnac, authorities in Santa Fe supported Mocobis. Corregidor José Benavides denounced Echagüe's refusal to protect his mission, while the teniente responded that the discord between Mocobi and Abipon missions was long-standing, an assertion that was only partly true. The real source of the hostility was the feud between Paikin's band and their San Pedro allies against the Abipones of San Jerónimo, a feud clearly exacerbated by Echagüe's own behavior.

Antagonisms became further inflamed, despite mediation by Echagüe and the missionary priest of San Javier, Father Julián de Obelar. Spaniards joined Chief Daanotin (leader of the Mocobis who would settle Remolinos in Paraguay in 1778), Cacique Nevedagnac of San Javier, and two caciques of San Pedro to parley.[106] The widening conflict entangled the Abipones of San Fernando.

The Guaycuruan missions of Santa Fe fought from 1776 to 1782. Because San Pedro Mocobis had relatives in the mid-Bermejo region, raids brought reprisals against the mission. With four hundred warriors, the Abipon force menaced Santa Fe, whose militia was not much larger. The Abipones did not seek to attack the Spaniards, but Santafecinos feared that Indian warfare might engulf them. Meanwhile the viceroy in Buenos

Aires understood that the missions protected Spanish settlements and counseled the teniente to exercise restraint. In 1779 when 300 Abipon warriors of San Jerónimo confronted a 430-man militia unit from Santa Fe, the Abipones feared Spaniards less than their Mocobi auxiliaries. The Abipones of San Fernando came to San Jerónimo for safety, but it was dangerous for individuals to leave San Jerónimo or even to till the mission fields. Livestock scattered, the fields lay fallow, and Abipones resorted to raiding and selling the booty in Corrientes and Santiago del Estero.[107]

In 1780, as the conflict heightened, José Tarragona, the anti-Abipon administrator of Santa Fe's missions, advised that conditions in the Mocobi pueblos were deplorable. Viewing the conflict in light of his anti-Abipon prejudices, Tarragona reported that the Mocobis were destitute because they were friends of Spaniards. His ties to Mocobis gave him a financial stake in the dispute, and he demanded punishment of the Abipones.[108]

In 1781 Abipon Cacique Miguel Jerónimo Benavides, son of the late José Benavides and now *corregidor* of San Jerónimo, traveled to Montevideo to complain to the viceroy. Don Miguel Jerónimo claimed that Tarragona was a business partner of San Pedro and San Javier. He wanted the connection broken and less bureaucratic interference.

A peace of exhaustion ended the war, just as wars had ended in indigenous society. In 1782–83 all parties wanted peace, and the missions concluded an armistice. Teniente Echagüe took priests, the political and military leaders of the Mocobi towns, and Chaco chiefs to San Jerónimo, distributing cattle to needy Indians. Strife among the Guaycuruan missions of Santa Fe declined,[109] partly because, between 1778 and 1782, many of the most belligerent Mocobis and Tobas had themselves settled into missions at Remolinos, Cangayé, San Bernardo, and San Antonio.

Another violent episode involving mission Guaycuruans occurred in 1780–81, when almost half the Toba of San Ignacio took advantage of the great Andean uprisings. In September and October 1781, news of Indian rebellions in upper Peru reached Jujuy. The revolts emboldened men on the margins of local society such as José Quiroga, a mestizo soldier who led the Toba insurrection. He had served as interpreter for the Toba of San Ignacio, and he proselytized among them and the Hispanized lower classes of the region, including Indians, mulattoes, and castes. Quiroga preached that the Jujuy elite was iniquitous and promised his followers riches and elite women.[110]

The Toba response to the Andean rebellions had little in common with that of such rebels as the Indian governor in the Andean village of Rinconada, Manuel Callagara, who saw the Cataris and "Tupamaro" as legitimate political leaders. Although Quiroga professed allegiance to "the Inca king," the Toba were as wary of Andean peoples as of Spaniards, and the logic of this advocacy escaped them. Motivated more by the promise of wealth in Jujuy, hostility toward Europeans, and the dream of a return to the days when warriors seized goods and captives from Spaniards, about seventy mission Toba, led by Cacique Santiago and Cacique José, joined Quiroga. Like their forefathers, the Toba dissidents wished to despoil Jujuy.[111]

In 1781 the mission divided politically, reflecting preexisting political divisions. Many Toba rejected Quiroga's blandishments, and when the rebels left, a larger number remained in San Ignacio with Cacique Tesodi. Most Toba of San Ignacio, whose population in these years fluctuated between 250 and 600, were not actively involved in the uprising.

Accompanied by renegade militiamen on March 28, 1781, the rebels attacked. At Fort Ledesma they killed the commanding officer and joined other rebels on the outskirts of Jujuy. When challenged by five hundred Spanish soldiers, Caciques Santiago and José and one hundred Toba followers retired to the Chaco. The Toba and Mocobis of the new missions of San Bernardo and Cangayé refused to help them. On May 29 the fugitives surrendered; Jujuy officials executed the leaders and returned almost a hundred followers to the mission.

The situation at San Ignacio did not change much after 1781. The Toba retained their identity and martial attributes. They came and went, angering Spanish officials and priests, and regularly reported to nonmission Toba on the deployment of Jujuy soldiers; their priest regarded them as hostile to Hispanic society. In 1807 and 1809, the mission Toba protested their inadequate subsidies on the one hand, showing their acceptance of the colonial regime, and the degree of Spanish interference in their lives on the other.

In 1809 they participated in the royal campaign of smallpox vaccination, a further demonstration that they received and benefited from Spanish gifts, even while resisting Spanish authority. They were pleased, they said, that inoculation freed them from the disease.[112]

Provincial Neglect and Imperial Rivalry

In Paraguay Mbayás continued to reside at Belén after the Jesuits left, but many saw the mission merely as a convenient social and commercial center. Often mission residents dealt with Paraguayans directly, bypassing missionary mediators. Franciscans labored in Belén and in Guaná and Guarani missions, but they lacked the capital of the Jesuits. Franciscans were too poor even to celebrate mass very often.[113] Paraguayan authorities gave little support to missions in the north, even while they helped Remolinos and San Antonio to the south of Asunción.[114]

As the colonial era closed, Mbayás drew closer to the encroaching European worlds. By 1775 Paraguayan farms and ranches in the Concepción area were scattered among bands of Mbayás and Guanás. The Indians visited Paraguayan farmers, ranchers, and troops. Some Mbayás collaborated with Spaniards, while others pilfered livestock. Still others cooperated with Portuguese. The Mbayás who had joined Belén and Refugio, and their descendants, were the most Hispanized. Even though they respected Presbyter Domínguez of Belén, who himself "went native" ("se hizo Mbayá"),[115] they still remained Guaycuruans. They extorted food from farmers and took grain and animals by force, knowing that the scattered settlers had difficulty retaliating. The number of Hispanized Mbayás was growing, showing that Guaycuruans without missions were also assimilating into the Spanish world. In season a thousand Mbayás camped at Concepción, receiving subsidies—tobacco and salt for commoners and knives, needles, and mirrors for leaders. Mbayá men scouted for Paraguayans and reported on Portuguese activities.[116] Mission Mbayás traveled as before, although they loved Belén and considered it home.[117]

Less Hispanized Mbayás lived on the Chaco bank of the Río Paraguay near present-day Puerto Stanley. They traveled by canoe to Concepción but refused to pass south of the settlement.[118] The descendants of southern Mbayás who had requested missions in the 1760s cooperated with Paraguayans in various ways in the 1780s and 1790s, often receiving direct subsidies; meanwhile the northerners slipped into the Brazilian orbit.

Belén eventually became a center of Guarani speakers. Some increasingly sedentary Mbayás lived there. They no longer dominated Guaná clients, because some neighboring Guanás obtained government protection from Mbayá exploitation while others left for central Paraguay. Still other Guanás became bellicose, more like the old Mbayás.[119]

By the late colonial era, little had changed. Belén and the Guaná missions in northern Paraguay continued to lack support. Priests were ignorant of Indian languages. They failed to minister to the spiritual needs of their flocks. Mission residents often went unclothed and hungry. Many non-mission Mbayás lived among Paraguayans, especially in the spring when wild plant foods were scarce and also during harvests.[120]

Late Colonial Developments

Because of the inability of Spanish authorities to create as many reductions as Guaycuruans wanted, a considerable number remained outside missions. Even after the founding of Remolinos, San Fernando, and Cangayé in 1778–81, non-mission and central Chaco–mission Mocobis raided San Jerónimo de Abipones in Santa Fe and the Spanish outpost at Curupaity between Corrientes and Asunción, where other Guaycuruans were settling. Even San Javier, the oldest Mocobi mission, suffered from raids by hostile Mocobis. Some nonsedentary Mocobis settled in the mission of Ispín (or Inispín) in 1794–95, the last Guaycuruan mission of the colonial period. Others lodged near the Río Paraguay. Groups of Toba and Mocobis from the now-abandoned missions of San Bernardo and Cangayé migrated to the Chaco frontier of Santa Fe, while more traditional groups remained near the mission sites.[121]

Around 1800 Guaycuruans drifted to the outskirts of the Spanish world, as a few had done before the coming of missions in 1743. A common destination was Curupaity, a settlement of Guaycuruans, Spanish renegades, and other displaced persons (including mission Mocobis and their priest from the central Bermejo) on the Río Paraguay north of Corrientes.[122] Most survived in the Spanish underworld. They helped themselves to the livestock and other goods of the *vecinos* of Ñeembucú, and sold their booty to Spanish protectors.[123] Groups refrained from raiding the area where they marketed their produce, reestablishing the seventeenth-century pattern of forming alliances with some cities while preying on others.

Non-mission Guaycuruans on the margins of Spanish society included the Payaguá, or Evueví, the nonsedentary river Guaycuruans. Spaniards never provided a mission for the Payaguá, and a spectacular baptism of 153 Payaguá children in Asunción in 1793 had no lasting effect. Long dependent on iron tools—knives, hatchets, and fishhooks—the Payaguá eventually damaged their environment, and suffered from its degradation, just as the mounted Guaycuruans had done. Extensive cutting of trees for canoes eventually destroyed their way of life. As their society deteriorated, the Payaguá began accommodating themselves to Hispanic culture.[124]

Payaguá trickled into Paraguay after 1730 in families and small bands while, like northern Mbayás, northern Payaguá began clustering around Portuguese settlements. In Asunción they sold wild rice, wax, and the spoils of their raids on river commerce, and were the city's exclusive providers of fish. They also turned their experience as river dwellers to economic advantage. "Evueví canoe men worked for the state as guides, paddlers, and couriers on the Paraguay River. Following the independence of Paraguay . . . the Evueví served as the country's river police." Their canoe patrols warned of rustling by mounted Guaycuruans.[125]

Many Guaycuruans never obtained reductions. For example, most western Toba inhabited lands remote from Spanish settlements and remained in Native American–controlled sections of the Chaco until the late 1800s. The few Toba who chose missions moved to such non-Guaycuruan institutions as Macapillo in Tucumán. Other Guaycuruans tried and rejected mission life, or found the irregularity of subventions distressing and departed. Nevertheless, a substantial percentage of Guaycuruans in the 1700s spent at least some time in missions, where they adapted to a changing environment. They experienced significant economic, social, political, and religious change, as the next four chapters will show. They also retained large, indissoluble pieces of Guaycuruan culture.

Summary

Having observed Native American neighbors assemble in reductions, bands of Guaycuruans tried and rejected mission life in the 1600s. As economic, environmental, and security problems mounted between 1710 and 1740, their descendants sought missions for survival. There they acquired benefits once obtained by violent acquisition and independent trade: Spanish artifacts, food, and security.

New Guaycuruan reductions were unstable; equestrian inhabitants came and went, because old habits survived. Mission populations fluctuated. Critical factors included subsidies or absence thereof, group and individual economic opportunities in the Spanish world, and security. For two or three generations subsidies sustained all Guaycuruan foundations.

Subventions before 1767 came mainly from Jesuit sources. After the Jesuit exile, the imperial and local governments were unable to match Jesuit aid, and Guaycuruan reductions faced a precarious financial situation, with some faring significantly better than others. The best established—including San Javier de Mocobis, San Jerónimo de Abipones, and San Ignacio de Tobas—became stable communities. Despite somewhat erratic and inadequate support, the government managed to keep most existing missions afloat and even founded new ones. As a result, the mission population grew substantially in the fifteen years following the Jesuits' exile, but scarcities led to renewed violence.

By 1800 mission and non-mission Guaycuruans had divergent survival strategies. The former were becoming artisans and agriculturalists. The latter survived by hunting and gathering. They reduced their violent acquisitions, exchanging outright warfare for cattle rustling. Other non-mission Guaycuruans filtered into the Spanish world, losing their indigenous identity after a generation or so.

CHAPTER 3

Economy

During the eighteenth century, many Guaycuruans transformed their livelihoods. Leaving a semi-nomadic existence in the Gran Chaco, where their indigenous production,[1] characterized by "immediate-return economies,"[2] included raiding, gleaning, hunting, and fishing, they took up residence in missions. There they continued indigenous but no longer aboriginal activities and added pursuits typical of European society. In fact, the quest for economic security was a primary reason why Guaycuruans chose missions over other alternatives. In this chapter I will discuss the postcontact work habits of women and men in the Chaco from about 1600 to 1740, how these changed in missions, and mission economies from the 1740s to 1810 and beyond.

Women's Work Prior to Missions

Guaycuruans practiced gender complementarity in their work habits, but this did not lead to the idyllic gender relations that Irene Silverblatt claims characterized pre-Inca Andean societies.[3] In the prehistoric period a large portion of a Guaycuruan band's sustenance came from the labor of women, who worked tirelessly. Thus, scholars who emphasize the abundant leisure time of hunting peoples denigrate the activities of women. Guaycuruan women's work began when a settlement was chosen. The women set up camps and dwellings and then killed poisonous snakes. Major female obligations revolved around finding food, preparing it for meals, and storing it, including drying meat. Females also found and fetched precious and frequently scarce water and made pots and vases. They sought honey and prepared it for fermentation into a

A Mocobi chief with his wife and son. [From Florian Paucke, *Hacia allá y para acá (una estada entre los indios Mocobíes, 1749–1767)*, vol. 2, fol. p. 154]

potent intoxicant, drunk almost exclusively by men in a rigidly controlled ritual.[4]

When Mocobis were on the move, as all Guaycuruans frequently were, they might travel up to two hundred leagues for food. On these journeys women cared for their children, their own horses, and often extra mounts. They packed on their animals household goods, including pots, vases, mortars, nets, scissors, needles, looms, bedding, and the spare weapons of men. When the band was encamped or, as it more frequently was, dispersed in extended family units, women gathered firewood and also hunted for small game. Occasionally they even accompanied men on expeditions for large animals.[5]

Abipon women had similar responsibilities. As bands roamed to find food, women brought along on their horses not only children but also "all the domestic furniture, all the pots, gourds, jugs, shells, balls of woolen and linen thread, weaving instruments . . . contained in boar-skin bags, suspended here and there from the saddle."[6] Manufacturing these household goods and obtaining the raw materials from which to fabricate them also fell to females.

Guaycuruan women practiced creative strategies for food gathering. A common food source, even after settlement in missions, was the locust. Mocobi women and children surrounded a swarm of locusts, much as men did jaguars. Waving blankets and skins, they drove the insects toward a pile of straw, steadily closing the circle, then set the straw afire to cook the insects. They also stewed locusts and locust eggs and served them in gourd dishes using spoons of leather, shell, and horn. Abipones, too, roasted locusts but ate only the female ones.

In all Guaycuruan societies, women harvested and prepared the principal vegetable food. For the Guaycuruans of the southern Chaco—the Toba, Abipones, and Mocobis—this was the algarroba, and for the Mbayás in the north it was the palm. The palm was not only their main source of sustenance but was also integral to their identity. Mbayás called themselves Eyiguayegis, "the people of the palm" (Eyiguá being the name of one type of palm). Mbayá women and their (usually female) servants and slaves imaginatively exploited the many varieties of palms. They gathered hearts of palm and dates, which were eaten raw. Coconut palms were a source of flour, ground from coconut meat, as well as oil and thread.

Although palms were less important to the southern Guaycuruan groups, women of these groups also harvested palms for "meat, drink, medicine, habitation, clothes, arms . . . ."[7] The Guaycuruans first obtained knives and hatchets in the 1500s, and by the 1700s they had devastated the palm groves. The loss of this vital resource was one of a series of ecological changes that depressed their economies and led them to ask for missions.[8]

For southern Guaycuruans, the primary source of food and drink was the algarroba, or carob bean. Women gathered and prepared two varieties of algarroba, white and black. Black algarroba fruit was sweet. Mocobi women picked it and dried, mashed, and strained it through a colander to make flour. After the addition of water, the resulting dough was molded to the proper size and dried in the sun. It became as sweet as sugar and had a similar consistency. Other food resources were wild roots and tubers, which women collected with a digging stick, a single piece of wood with two broad, flat ends and a narrow rounded middle resembling a modern sport-kayak paddle.[9]

From the fruit of the algarroba and from honey, women also brewed intoxicants, although only elderly women were permitted to drink. Drinking rituals were major social events for men, and beforehand women hid the weapons for their own and their children's protection,[10] as well as that of men.

Guaycuruan men did in fact collect food occasionally. Mocobi men, for example, at times foraged for honey.[11] They were also often away from their homes and families on raids for weeks and at those times necessarily gathered vegetable foods. Still, gathering was defined as women's work. For Guaycuruan women, as for those of other Chaco peoples, the collecting of vegetable foods was not only a subsistence activity but was also an act with religious significance, as hunting was for males. The sun, for example, in its human form was a female. She was the first harvester of the algarroba, and Guaycuruan women followed her example.

A few women—and only women—of some Guaycuruan groups even practiced limited cultivation. All Guaycuruans believed strongly that planting and harvesting were female pursuits inappropriate for males, a conviction that helps explain the initial male resistance to agricultural labor in missions. Comprehending the gendered apportionment of work and the feminine connotation of harvesting also shows what a culturally revolutionary[12] choice Guaycuruans made when men took up plows, spades, and hoes to work in mission fields.[13]

Vegetable foods likely made up a majority of the average Guaycuruan's caloric intake per day, but meat was more important symbolically. Men and women believed that meat was essential to their material and religious lives. Before joining missions women generally cooked meat by roasting or boiling it without salt. Sources of meat included rabbits, nutrias, snakes, crocodiles, wild cats, rhea eggs, and after about 1600 cattle and horses.[14] A further task of food preparation was the drying of meat for preservation. Before contact with Europeans, women cut raw meat into strips with knives of hard-to-obtain stone or bone, an arduous and time-consuming job. The strips of meat then were hung to dry from thin poles placed horizontally between the forks of trees. The preparation process became much more efficient after the introduction of European knives in the sixteenth century. Women valued these tools highly, even though iron implements wore out quickly in the Chaco, where it rained daily for half the year.

Guaycuruan women were artisans as well as foragers, harvesters, and cooks. They fashioned household utensils, clothing, houses, and pottery. Net bags to hold possessions were one of their most characteristic manufactures, because most groups lacked baskets. Unlike most non-Guaycuruan Chaco groups, who fashioned nets from fibers of the *caraguatá,* the women of the southern and western Guaycuruan bands made their netted luggage from leather.

Clothing was usually fashioned of nutria, jaguar, or deer leather. After men with dogs caught a game animal, women were responsible for skinning it and tanning the hide. The skins of deer and jaguars had to be scrubbed until they were flexible and soft. Nutria hides had to be skinned from the carcass, dried, softened by hand, and sewed together. Iron needles, when available, made sewing more efficient, but the women typically had to use needles fashioned from thorns. Skirts might contain twenty nutria skins, although deerskin skirts were also common. Blankets, usually consisting of eighteen to twenty nutria skins, were decorated by painting each skin with a red design before sewing it to the others.[15]

After the introduction of sheep in the seventeenth century, Mbayá women sheared the sheep, spun wool, dyed it, and wove it into blankets and clothing on back-strap looms of wood and reeds. Woolen blankets were woven not only for domestic use but also for barter to other Native Americans and Spaniards.[16]

Without a potter's wheel or oven, Abipon and Mocobi women made clay pots for cooking and eating. Mocobi women made pots, dishes, cups, and water jugs by modeling the wet clay to the desired shape and thrusting it into the center of an open fire. With a long stick they turned the objects until they were baked all over.[17]

Most Guaycuruan peoples constructed similar types of dwellings, and all groups entrusted this responsibility to women. Mbayá and Abipon women cut rushes, wove them into mats, and secured them to poles stuck into the ground. Although these homes gave imperfect protection from the sun, wind, and rain, they could be easily erected and disassembled, accommodating the mobility of nonsedentary people who moved from one area to another every two weeks or so. To prevent their homes being flooded, the women dug channels to divert rainwater.[18]

Men's Work Prior to Missions

In all Guaycuruan groups, men's work, particularly hunting, carried high social and religious status. Guaycuruans saw themselves as living within three interlocking worlds: the sub-world, the earth, and the super-world. The super-world of the Toba—and surely that of other Guaycuruans—was an ideal hunting ground.[19] This hierarchy of the universe, with perfect hunting areas at the apex, clearly reveals the paramount importance of this activity.

Hunting techniques of Guaycuruans varied less from group to group than from animal to animal. For safety and success, men usually hunted collectively, and rigid rules governed the division of the slain animal. For example, the Mocobi typically hunted in parties of three or four hunters, and the hunter who killed an animal took the hide and the choicest cut of meat, the next on the scene took second best, and so on. Groups seldom debated how to distribute surpluses, for there were few surpluses.

All initiated hunters learned the fables of animal behavior. These lessons taught a man to master his quarry, the traits he could gain from conquering an animal, and the rules to follow to placate the spirit owners of animals. For example, the fortunate hunter who felled a rhea got the speed of the slain bird. As the leaders of society, successful hunters also earned characteristics of animals that they consumed. Thus, men avoided eating those animals whose character revealed cowardice and submission, including sheep, chickens, and pigs—animals with which they came into daily contact in the mission period. They scorned similarly undesirable personality traits of smaller wild animals.

While men preferred to hunt large game such as deer, jaguars, wild boars, and rheas, they also sought anteaters, nutrias, rabbits, geese, ducks, land tortoises, coatimundis, and tapirs. When they could, they supplemented the fruits of the hunt with fish.[20] The most prestigious prey was the most dangerous, especially large game and, of course, other people. Like other Guaycuruans, Mocobis hunted jaguars as religiously venerated adversaries and objects of value for their meat and skins. A hunter who ate jaguar meat shared the beast's bravery and strength. Wearing a tunic of jaguar's hide proclaimed a hunter's skill.[21]

Hunters took animals of the forest, field, and stream not only for food but also for clothing and the raw materials of artifacts to be processed and fashioned by women. One kind of wild boar, for example, yielded a skin for women's traveling dresses and bristles for combs. Rheas provided not only meat, but feathers for adornment, skin for clothing, bones for weapons and other artifacts, and eggs. Fish jawbones and spines became scraping tools; other fish bones served as tweezers to pluck hair from the scalp, body, and beards. Deer horns were used for tobacco carriers; later cattle horns served this need. Bones of large animals became deadly arrow points that festered in flesh.[22]

One of the best-recorded aspects of Guaycuruan material culture is weapons technology. The weapons of the Guaycuruan hunter were simultaneously simple and complex. They included only spears and harpoons, bows and arrows, maces, boleadoras, and lassos. Within these categories, though, there was surprising variety. Both shock and projectile weapons became more formidable after the acquisition of iron. Guaycuruans affixed metal points, edges, and slides to their arms, but most weapons remained of the wood and bone variety; iron was hard to come by and supplies uncertain, while wood and bone were plentiful. Even stone weapons and tools were dear in the stoneless Chaco. Through extensive precolonial trade networks Guaycuruans imported stones suitable for weapons to the Chaco. Mbayás killed large game with a wooden club, which was difficult and dangerous, but left a whole skin for use or sale. For the multiple needs of hunting and war, Mocobis in the 1700s employed at least five different kinds of spears and used them as javelins or lances. Some were quite long, taller than the man who wielded it. Only one type carried an iron point. The simplest was a long piece of dried hardwood sharpened at both ends and probably hardened in fire. The throwing spear, accurate up to twenty paces, had flitches on one side below the point and was useful against such water animals as carpinchos and crocodiles. A fourth spear had a diamond-shaped point of flattened wood. A fifth, used in war, carried a point made from a deer's horn, which broke off and festered in human flesh. Hunters and warriors also made arrows of six varieties for different quarries. They constructed two kinds of bows, the shorter for horsemen and the long bow to be used on foot. Men communicated with each other in battle and while hunting by blowing horns and whistles of wood and reeds. Lassos, about eleven *varas* long, were of crude leather with, after contact, an iron fastener or slide at one end. Boleadoras, thrown around the feet of large game, and later cattle, could bring down an animal from thirty paces.[23]

Economic practice and religion connected hunting with war, both honored methods of economic acquisition. Warlike Guaycuruans were proud of their martial abilities, and sought power more than possessions. Belief systems encouraged aggression, giving religious sanction to combative urges, which initially strengthened—and later destroyed—their economies. In the eighteenth century, the Mbayás venerated a spirit called Karakará, their original benefactor. Karakará had not given them a homeland, but rather weapons, the right to conquer others, and the bravery and martial skill to do so, in order that they could subsist by combat.[24] Similarly, Abipones believed that their mythical grandfather, Keebet, gave them bravery, which together with their right of violence against neighbors, assured their survival.[25]

The "spiritual component" of hunting was central to the beliefs of a number of Native American groups, including both Guaycuruans and northeastern Algonquians, and had the effect of protecting animals from overhunting. In northeastern North America, the "Indian-land relationship was suffused with religious considerations which profoundly influenced the economic (subsistence) activities and belief of these people,"[26] and this religious connection among supernatural beings, hunting and hunters, and animals mirrors the Guaycuruan experience. Like the Algonquians, Guaycuruans saw a spiritual relationship between humans and animals. They depended on nature's resources for subsistence and venerated nature. They had few possessions and felt little desire for surpluses; nor did they seek to possess as property such natural things as wild animals. They conceived of inhabitants of the unseen world as the true owners, as well as protectors, of animals; therefore, these spirits had to be propitiated by shamanic activity and strict taboos. Guaycuruans believed that, like humans, animals had souls, which might in fact be those of their deceased relatives. Thus, Guaycuruan hunters usually killed only enough animals for their bands to consume, or occasionally a few more to trade for maize, kidnapped relatives, or rocks and stones hard enough to hold a cutting edge for weapons.[27] In the precontact era, only fools irritated spirit guardians of animals by unrestrained slaughter.[28]

In summary, the Guaycuruan moral code was quite divergent from that of Europeans: it sanctioned the killing of humans but circumscribed the hunting of animals. For pre-mission Guaycuruan males, violent economic acquisition was a culturally appropriate way of satisfying wants.

War was a major economic activity. The jobs of adult Mocobi males were first to hunt animals and then to raid other humans for their women and material possessions.

European Influences on the Guaycuruan Economy

The growth of Spanish society from about 1550 to 1700—centered around Asunción, Corrientes, and Santa Fe in the east, and in the west spreading out from Salta, Jujuy, and Santiago del Estero—changed the Guaycuruan economy, especially during the seventeenth century. Trade and war with Spaniards became intensive. The Guaycuruan economy evolved from subsistence-based to barter-based. Beef supplemented game, fish, and wild plants in the Guaycuruan diet, and many bands raised sheep to provide wool and food for women and children. Men continued to disdain mutton because they believed it conveyed to the consumer the submissive personality traits of the animal. Animals of European origin, however, became staples for food and commerce with Spaniards. The Native Americans traded Spanish, Guarani, and other captives; horses; honey; wax; skins of large game animals; and brightly colored feathers for a diverse array of items. These ranged from friends and relatives taken by Spaniards to knives, hatchets, needles, hooks, iron for projectile points, beads, and clothing.[29] Horses and iron weapons ultimately revolutionized Guaycuruan material life. In the 1600s Guaycuruans shaped their aboriginal beliefs and practices to the new ways, as bands increased in wealth, numbers, and power. By the early 1700s, however, these transformations were undermining their economies and religions.

HUNTING

European influences changed both Guaycuruan hunting techniques and the activity's religious significance. The hunt became more efficient after about 1600, when mounted Guaycuruans began using iron lance points. After 1600 Abipones, Mocobis, and Mbayás increasingly hunted on horseback. The Toba employed horses but preferred to hunt on foot with dogs, used by most Chaqueños, pedestrians and equestrians alike, in the colonial era. Hunting jaguars now not only brought strength and prestige to the hunter; bartering pelts to Spanish buyers brought another kind of good fortune. Thus, hunters took care not to damage a hide. Hunting in small parties on horseback and foot, most lassoed or trapped the animals instead of dispatching them more safely with an arrow; some men speared the great cats in the belly to protect the most beautiful part of the pelt.

Until whites created a commercial market for hides, many Native American peoples throughout the Americas abided by their religions' insistence that hunters be moderate. A major alteration of aboriginal beliefs occurred when Native Americans began to disregard the sanctity of animals. In the Chaco, as in the woodlands of North America, the developing European market for skins and pelts encouraged overhunting, producing a deteriorating economic base and ultimately an erosion of traditional life. For the Guaycuruans this process began in the 1500s, when they learned to want the European artifacts that made life easier. They ignored the religiously sanctioned guidelines about moderation and began hunting commercially, setting in motion forces that eventually pressured them to choose missions.

Guaycuruans justified their departure from traditional practices by concluding that the domestic animals of Spaniards chased away the spirits who protected and owned game animals. The supernatural protectors fled to distant forests and far mountains. With the equilibrium between mankind and animals broken, Chaqueños' commercial harvesting of deer, nutrias, and other game depleted the animal population of the Chaco and northern Paraguay, endangering the survival of all people there.

LIVESTOCK

The arrival of domestic animals on the Chaco periphery in the sixteenth century forever altered the Guaycuruan way of life, but the changes began slowly. Guaycuruan males, in fact, for decades conducted hunts for wild horses and feral cattle as if they were game animals, in the manner of Hispanic cowboys of the region. Guaycuruans increasingly came to depend on Spanish horses and cattle, relatively easy to acquire in the 1600s, when most ran wild. No legends about livestock existed; they lacked souls and had no vital force related to fighting ability. Men forged no spiritual community with cows, as they had with game animals.[30]

After a time, the Guaycuruans began taming and breeding their mounts but through the 1600s continued to hunt wild cattle. In the eighteenth century, they raided the growing number of Spanish ranches of the Plata region for livestock. As they later would in missions, teams of men working from horseback and on foot caught cattle with ropes. A rider lassoed the horns of the cow while the dismounted hunter threw a rope around her feet to bring her to the ground, a Hispanic technique observable in contemporary Mexican rodeos.[31]

ARTIFACTS

Guaycuruans adapted several artifacts from Spanish models to suit their needs. Crude equipment, not lack of skill, limited their production. The talented artisans who made the tools of hunting and war with wood, stone, and bone performed wondrous feats with simple equipment. They fashioned devices to harness the new potential of domestic animals, including hobbles for the front legs of horses. These were simple cord fetters to keep the animals from straying. Mocobis made spurs from forked tree branches, resembling in shape the cavalry spur of the U.S. Army in the early twentieth century. Most Abipones, in contrast, rejected spurs.[32]

Another technology that Guaycuruan men in the Chaco developed was the gear that prepared a horse for hunting and war. To guide their horses, Mocobis and Abipones fashioned simple bridles, imitations of Spanish tack. Leather straps slipped over the horse's head and held a bit made of wood, bone, or occasionally of metal and resembling the wicked Spanish curb bit; this bit was joined to cowhide reins. Mocobis made bridle bits somewhat differently. Their bits were fashioned from horn cut to a precise form and fitted to the reins by lateral horns. Guaycuruans made bridles so artfully that Spaniards paid a handsome sum, two *pesos duros*, for them. Abipon and Mocobi saddles consisted of leather coverings mounted on wooden or reed frames. They usually lacked stirrups. After moving to missions, Mocobis began suspending from either side of their saddle a leather thong ending in a horizontal piece of wood extending slightly beyond the width of a human foot, a simple stirrup that the hunter gripped with his toes. These stirrups and saddles improved hunting. Without stirrups, a lancer could be thrown from his horse on impact with his quarry, and a roper without a saddle could be dragged to the ground by a cow or jaguar.[33]

RAIDING AND TRADING

After the arrival of Europeans, the Guaycuruan hunter-warrior began to accumulate material goods. He developed a sense of hereditary, private property. He could trade with and raid his Hispanic neighbors for animals and for the iron weapons and tools that made his work more productive. From Spanish settlements he took captives to share the menial work and bolster the population of the band. Thus, the economic importance of war increased through the seventeenth century. Jesuit Father Dobrizhoffer reported, "Their whole souls are bent on arms"—a statement he knew to be an exaggeration but which conveyed the cultural importance of martial aspirations to Guaycuruans.[34] They were also, however, pragmatic people who often bartered for things instead of fighting for them. Nevertheless, the pragmatism that made them traders has only a small place in the archival record, because it was of little interest to Europeans.

Guaycuruans obtained much that improved their standard of living from the Spanish settlements on the Chaco periphery by violence. Abipon attacks on economic targets of Santa Fe in 1730 were raids for profit. On June 30, at Colastiné on the east bank of the Paraná, they overwhelmed twenty-one carts and a wagon bringing goods through Santa Fe to Córdoba. They scattered the thirty-three escorts and seized the wagon stock and a load of *aguardiente*. They searched for booty around Santa Fe and caught three hundred cattle and horses, although Santafecino counterattacks recovered all but fifty. The Guaycuruans' objective was economic gain not warfare, and they refused to fight. Faster than the heavily laden opposition, they plunged their unburdened mounts into the Paraná to escape. Guaycuruans staged another lucrative raid on Santa Fe in October, as they captured a herd of four hundred horses and two hundred mules, guarded only by the animals' Spanish owner and seven peones, four of whom they killed. The raiders then took the animals to ride and sell. They easily eluded the pursuers from Santa Fe.[35]

Although they appropriated thousands of head of cattle from the Spanish settlements, Guaycuruans did not become true cattle herders until they moved to missions. Rejecting husbandry, they exploited cattle as traditional hunters and consumed or traded the animals as they got them, it seemed to European observers, with little regard for future needs. Yet they often sold the proceeds of a raid on Santa Fe in Corrientes or Asunción and thus were in transition from an aboriginal economy to an early form of commercial capitalism.[36]

DEVELOPMENT OF A MARKET ECONOMY

Economic opportunities resulting from external markets brought great changes to the Gran Chaco. Guaycuruan leaders established personal relationships with creole purchasers and now could sell merchandise destined for local, regional, and international markets. Political leaders received no greater reward than others from sales to Europeans. Achievement determined who got what, according to the rules of the hunt.

The mining community of Potosí was a major regional market for Guaycuruan goods. Guaycuruan products ultimately reached upper Peru, after transactions in such localities as Corrientes and other Platine centers. A second external market, "more expansive in nature," was "the European trading community," whose links to Guaycuruans ran through Buenos Aires and then by "mules, oxcarts, [and] riverboats" to cities on the Chaco frontier.[37] Cowhides and more precious wild animal skins went from the Chaco through regional trading centers to Buenos Aires and to Europe. In 1708 in Corrientes, for example, a deerskin brought two pesos, while that of an elk fetched six pesos. A horse broken to ride—and Guaycuruans were expert horsemen—also brought six pesos.[38] Because of the illegality of many transactions with the Hispanic world, Guaycuruans were typically unable to obtain the same prices for their products as creoles received, but their labors brought them greater rewards than subsistence activities.

The coming of market relationships to the Gran Chaco and their transformation of Native American economies resembled the experience of the natives of the southern Piedmont region of North America at about the same time. In the seventeenth century several societies from South Carolina to Virginia entered a three-stage process. First alien microbes brought mass death. Then European technology drew Indians into the world market. Finally, as settlers acquired Indian lands, peoples such as the Saponis, Occaneeches, and Tutelos merged into the Catawba nation.[39] Their economic transition began in earnest after 1650, because they "were glad to barter for the more efficient tools, more lethal weapons, and more durable clothing that colonists offered," acquisitions which had "revolutionary consequences." Like Guaycuruan and non-Indian residents of the Plata and Piedmont regions, Catawbas produced "raw materials for foreign markets and found themselves caught up in an economic network." Piedmont peoples exchanged slaves and deerskins for European tools, weapons, and clothes, but because they never acquired the technology of manufacture, they continued to depend on colonial suppliers.[40]

Initially, the Native Americans controlled trade. They bought useful goods and rejected undesirable ones. They lost this advantage, however, in the Yamasee War, when English colonists recognized Indian dependency. After Catawbas invaded South Carolina in 1715, colonial merchants halted trade. At this point the Catawbas realized their need for a partnership with the English. When the wells of slaves and deerskins went dry, they related to English colonists in new ways, serving, for example, as guards on the frontier, as did Guaycuruans in missions. "In the space of a century, the [Catawbas] had become embedded in an alien economy."[41] For the Guaycuruans of the Gran Chaco, the process was much the same, although in the Chaco the changes took place over more than two centuries instead of one, owing largely to the fewer Spanish than English intruders in relation to a larger territorial expanse.

The Transition to Missions

In the 1730s Guaycuruans began their movement toward missions. Many forces pushed and pulled them toward missions, but economic factors were paramount. Now dependent on cattle, Guaycuruans found them harder to acquire because Spaniards established ranches with corrals and cowboys to safeguard livestock. The ecological damage to their habitat from their own iron tools, the grazing habits of domestic animals, and Spanish exploitation of the forest resources of the Chaco intensified the struggle for subsistence. The declining game supply, reduced by the market for Chaco animals, increased the difficulty in finding food. Some bands sought peace with the Spanish world—beginning with Santa Fe in 1734. In the next decade, they began to settle into reductions staffed by Jesuit missionaries. By the end of the century, Guaycuruans and priests had founded fifteen or sixteen more missions in Santa Fe, Corrientes, Tucumán, and Paraguay (see Appendix A).[42]

Material acquisitions had already wrought momentous changes in Guaycuruan life. Old economic practices could no longer feed and clothe men and women, boys and girls, as they had in the past. Culturally innovative Guaycuruans began the search for new ways to explain and control the world. In missions they found men who could supply those explanations and techniques.

To make economic sense of the Guaycuruan leap from their indigenous world to the mission environment, one should compare their aboriginal pursuits to mission life: the journey was shorter than one might suppose. Guaycuruans in missions exchanged a nonsedentary lifestyle for a sedentary existence based on livestock, agriculture, and artisan's crafts, but they also retained most old methods—hunting, gathering, and fishing—to complement the new occupations, partly because the missions to which they moved were seldom prosperous. In the mission of San Jerónimo de Abipones in 1788, for example, forty years after the reduction's commencement, a time when the Indian leaders were all second-generation mission residents, hunting was still necessary to sustain life, although agriculture was now also essential to their well being.[43] In part, gradual changes reflected a cultural continuity, as men could depart the missions when they wished. Hundreds of people failed to adjust to life in missions. They left individually, in families, and in larger groups. Some resumed an indigenous existence after withdrawing. Others moved to the peripheries of the Spanish world without the benefits or the discipline of missions, as did the Payaguá in Asunción, the Mbayás at Concepción, and Abipones and Tobas at Curupaity.

Women's Work in Missions

Women more than men found continuity in their daily tasks during the transition to mission life. Many women's chores in missions were identical to those in the Chaco. Women still gathered algarroba and palm fruits, wove, potted, and prepared and cooked food. Like men, they experienced momentous changes in subsistence activities after contact with Europeans, but the greatest economic changes came in the 1600s, before the mission experience. During this time, horses, cattle, and iron artifacts increased Guaycuruans' productivity and enabled women to work more efficiently.

Once in missions, women needed to alter aboriginal skills only slightly. Most tasks of food preparation, food gathering, and household chores were unaltered. It is true that women added a few new touches to their household economy, including the use of salt in cooking. A number of tasks, though—including sewing, weaving, and cooking—were not so much revolutionized as rendered more efficient in missions by the increased availability of artifacts (such as iron needles, knives, scissors, and pots) that they had used for decades but in limited quantities. Although in San Javier women also tended cattle and some even claimed them as personal property, most mission women worked at traditionally female occupations.[44]

Yet changes in feminine economic patterns did occur. One departure was the introduction of a small, open-air factory for textiles in some missions. In San Javier a Mocobi widow from the cacique class instructed girls in the manual arts, enforced discipline, and inflicted punishment. Soon, fifty adolescent girls diligently spun and dyed wool. Within six months Mocobi women were turning out brightly colored rugs and blankets under the tutelage of another woman returned to her people from Spanish captivity. The first stimulus to increased production was local; mission Guaycuruans rejected leather vestments and donned locally made, multicolored fiber garments.[45] Soon, however, women began producing blankets for a wider market. In a notable transaction three hundred blankets were sold by Jesuit intermediaries in Asunción, where goods were scarcer and prices higher than downriver. Most blankets brought twelve *pesos fuertes*, although the best sold for twenty-five pesos.

In commodity exchanges, the normal mode of exchange in rural Spanish and Indian areas of the Plata region, a blanket brought twelve to sixteen sheep. In another sale in Asunción, seventy-three blankets brought forty-eight *quintals* of yerba, fifteen of tobacco, and some sugar. In 1762, seventy-two ponchos, "well woven and of beautiful colors" brought fifty pesos each in Paraguay. Women urged their husbands to cooperate in the new venture, and the men procured the sheep to keep the new business going. In San Fernando de Abipones, clothing manufacture was sufficiently developed that one regular purchase for the mission was indigo, a dye for textiles.[46]

In the Belén mission, Mbayá women also tended family-owned flocks of sheep and spun and wove wool. They dyed and embroidered woolen blankets for sale in Asunción. They quickly acquired Spanish techniques of needlework and design from Paraguayan women and created fine vestments for clerics. In Abipon missions the women, noted by priests for "their assiduity and almost avidity in labour," sheared sheep and expertly spun, dyed, and wove wool into blankets so pleasing to the eye "that you would take it for a Turkey carpet, worthy of a nobleman's house in Europe."[47] Of the twenty-three women in the tiny Abipon mission of Santiago in 1793, there were sixteen weavers, six spinners, and one pot maker.[48]

Most females in Guaycuruan missions, like the Mbayás of Belén, labored in the fields.[49] Because they had not practiced cultivation before they joined missions, this activity appeared revolutionary to the missionaries. Yet there was continuity with the chores of aboriginal days, when women harvested ripening fruits and vegetables.

Men's Work in Missions

In missions, to the surprise of many Europeans, Guaycuruan men became blacksmiths, carpenters, and builders. Their skill at artisans' practices of Spanish origin the priests found striking, yet the change was less than it appeared. Postcontact Chaco male artisans of the period from 1600 to 1740 had fashioned weapons, bridles, and saddles with tools made from shell, fish spines, wood, and bone. In missions they learned such skills as smithing, house construction, woodworking, and carpentry using iron and steel tools. The evolution was not a major one, either culturally or occupationally. Moreover, it required little ideological modification, because no taboos labeled these pursuits as feminine or inferior. On the other hand, with a reliable supply of sharp, durable tools, the productivity of artisans expanded dramatically in the new settings, in the same way that Guaranis could clear larger fields with iron than with stone axes. Similarly, exchanging the hunting of cattle for the herding of them involved little change of either work habits or ideology, since men and women previously had hunted, skinned, and cooked cattle and had long raised and ridden horses.

As Guaycuruans moved to missions, though, the work habits of men changed more than those of women. Evidence from several missions corroborates that males eager to learn from the Hispanic world generally chose artisan's skills before those of the agriculturalist. Other transitional occupations in the missions of the eastern Chaco were logging and woodworking. Although wood was scarce in the southern Plata region, especially around Buenos Aires, softwoods were plentiful around Santa Fe and Corrientes. As one traveled north the quality of wood improved steadily. Even the soft but abundant algarroba yielded furniture for Spanish homes and offices and carts for transport. Guaycuruans in the Chaco had felled trees before joining missions, and European axes provided by missionaries merely facilitated the work. In San Javier twenty-five Mocobis served an apprenticeship under the direction of a Hispanized Indian who was a master cart maker. They later constructed independently the ubiquitous two-wheeled carts that transported goods throughout the Plata region. By 1767 they had made thirty-six of the vehicles. Some carried the reduction's hides and surplus crops to market. Others surely were sold to help pay the expenses of the heavily subsidized and indebted mission. Mocobis also constructed wooden rafts that carried their goods to market. A few men became wood carvers. Four who plied this trade made altars, and their pieces adorned the Jesuit church in Santa Fe. Another four became turners. Eight Mocobi carpenters made windows and doors. Their first efforts provided daylight for the mission church and the priest's house. Some males apprenticed at a smithy in Santa Fe. Returning to the mission with their hammers, anvil, forge, and files, they were able to make a hoe from a slab of iron. Their new skills were marketable almost anywhere in the Americas in the eighteenth century, and if they wished to sever ties to their people, they could support themselves in the Hispanic world. In San Javier, Mocobis also made bricks and tiles for themselves and others.[50] This facilitated the transition from indigenous to European housing styles.

In San Jerónimo de Abipones, Spaniards from Santa Fe built three small huts and departed. Guaycuruan artisans did the rest, constructing institutional buildings and residences, as well as their own houses. Under the direction of war leader Ychoalay, Abipon men used the many Spanish axes, part of the capital grants of the new mission and a tool with which they were familiar. They felled thousands of trees, dragged them to the center of the reduction, and cut them to their needs. They first built a chapel, homes for the priests and shepherds, and then corrals. Next they raised a stockade to protect against enemy attack, and finally they assembled one-room homes of wood and adobe bricks, like those of the rural Hispanic lower class, to replace huts of reed matting.

Mocobis in San Javier also built large buildings. After initial instruction they were on their own. Working with little supervision from lay or clerical Spaniards, they stuck paired wooden posts into the ground to create a form in the outline of the future edifice, usually a square or rectangle. Between the forms they placed sifted earth, piling up loads of mud and tamping them down. When the walls reached the desired height, the workmen removed the posts and roofed the structure.[51]

Mbayás were proficient at the working of metal and were the only Guaycuruans to practice metalworking in the indigenous period. Before contact they had obtained silver for adornment from Andean peoples through aboriginal trade networks. After the 1540s, they sought iron for economic and military uses but continued to acquire silver and bronze to symbolize good fortune. Other Guaycuruan peoples had not practiced metalworking, but had traded for metal ornaments and objects of ceremonial value with other Native Americans before contact; they continued these exchanges from 1550 to 1740, although Hispanized communities became the major source of such goods.[52] As Guaycuruans moved to missions, around 1740 to 1780, requests for jewelry declined but did not disappear. Items for personal display were now primarily silk thread and ribbons and only occasionally rings and semiprecious stones.[53]

Eurocentric interpretations of these transactions credit missionaries with putting a stop to such senseless activities as spending hard-earned goods for "worthless trinkets" like rings and stones. Fortunately more persuasive explanations of Native American mercantile behavior are available. One North American experience sheds light on the behavior of Guaycuruans. In the northeastern woodlands of the United States and Canada in the early colonial period, Native Americans valued bright objects of glass and metal, scorned by Europeans as of slight value. They were initially great prizes for Indians, not because they were new and different, but precisely because they were familiar, resembling objects of ceremonial value in aboriginal society. Many peoples found that European jewelry could replace scarce traditional objects and incorporated these nonutilitarian trade goods into their ceremonies. When the Indians' ideological world was shattered, as was the Guaycuruans' in the mid-eighteenth century, the "magical crystals became cheap glass beads."[54] Like aboriginal Canadians, Guaycuruans sought scarce necklaces, rings, and beads for the prestige that they conferred.[55] When these items become plentiful, they conferred little prestige. Thus the missionaries' efforts to convince Indians that such purchases were worthless reinforced an indigenous reappraisal of items of value.

By 1700 Guaycuruan males had acquired metalworking skills. They were making arrow and lance points from raw iron. Mbayá artisans employed scarce, precious rocks as anvils and hammers, set fires in the earth as forges, and used hardwood tongs.[56] In Belén the men found the step to becoming blacksmiths and farriers a short one; familiar tasks were also made easier by the blacksmith's tools of the mission's smithy, a shop found in many Guaycuruan reductions, as surviving inventories attest.

Mocobi boys in San Javier became musicians. Under Father Paucke's tutelage, twenty boys formed an orchestra of two double basses, two harps, eight violins, a cello, a *trompa marina,* and voices. They served as apprentices from 1750 to 1753, performing at masses in the mission and at vespers in the Jesuit colegio in Santa Fe. In 1755 they traveled to Buenos Aires. They played and sang for lay audiences there and for the bishop, who paid them a handsome fee. They returned to the mission with ten thousand needles, eighteen dozen knives, twelve dozen metal bells, and fifty pesos duros. They earned for themselves European-style clothing, new saddles, and cash.[57]

Most Guaycuruan men who chose to live in missions adhered to their traditional work as much as possible. Warfare was a calling easily transported to the new environment. All men performed military service defending the mission, but some also soldiered for Spaniards. The effectiveness of their warfare improved because they now had easy access to iron lance points and sabers, more deadly than wood, bone, and stone. Thirty Mocobis a month served the teniente of Santa Fe as auxiliaries. On one occasion the mission auxiliaries received five hundred head of cattle for their services. They generally fought Guaycuruans who were enemies of both the bands of San Javier and of creole settlers. When these Mocobis rode on punitive expeditions with local authorities, they received five hundred cattle and four hundred pesos per entrada. In 1758 seventy-one Mocobis from San Javier, led by Caciques Xavier Aletin and Francisco Cithaalin, fought beside Santafecinos against raiders from the Chaco. Individual warriors received payment in the form of booty taken from the vanquished, an ancient tradition. In 1764 fifty-five Mocobis fought under Sargento Mayor Bernardo Garmendia against rival Guaycuruans in exchange for the lances and saddles of the fallen.[58]

Caring for mission animals similarly provided continuity with the past. The twenty adult males in the small (fifty-eight-person) Abipon mission of Santiago at the frontier fort of San Nicolás were described by Spaniards "hard-working" men; five worked as horse breakers or "bronco busters," and nine were teamsters who drove oxen for cart trains. Only five worked as laborers, probably in odd jobs around the fort and in agricultural tasks.[59]

Men in reductions also worked the cattle on the community and caciques' estancias. Guaycuruans brought from the Chaco proficiency in the often romanticized but actually dangerous and arduous management of cattle: excellent horsemanship, the ability and bravery necessary to rope the unruly animals, and the strength and skill to skin the hide from the animal's carcass. In all missions, males herded, roped, branded, and slaughtered cattle and stripped the hides. Guaycuruans exploited livestock in a fashion common to the Hispanic cattlemen of the region. Workers drove cattle to a destination, riding behind the animals, shouting and waving the lassos and boleadoras used to bring them to the ground for branding or slaughter. Of these tasks the only important new aptitude developed in missions was the branding of stock. The mission estancia in San Javier used eighteen branding irons (made by Mocobi smiths), which burned the mission's brand, an X superimposed on an S, onto livestock.[60] Evidently branding did not put a stop to Guaycuruans' propensity for raiding, as Spaniards reported that the Mocobis illegally appropriated animals from other missions.

The growth of ranching as an economic activity is clear from mission censuses. At the end of the Jesuit period in San Javier, the mission livestock on the two common estancias of the mission numbered 24,000 head of cattle, which forty men herded more or less full time. The mission also possessed 3,000 horses, 1,300 brood mares, 400 mules, 180 burros, and 1,700 sheep. The mission cattle not only provided food for the residents, but were also valued for their hides, which Mocobis shipped to Santa Fe and Corrientes to buy things that they did not produce themselves. It is probable that they had ongoing relations with specific merchants and their patrons in the local government, as exemplified by the Mocobi relationship with Teniente Echagüe and his man Tarragona (see chapter 2). Similarly, San Jerónimo Abipones dealt clandestinely with merchants from Santiago del Estero and Asunción.

In addition to the common property of the various missions, Guaycuruan leaders owned private property, a departure from distribution practices expected of chiefs prior to missions (see chapter 5). In San Jerónimo de Abipones and in San Javier, Abipon and Mocobi leaders owned private estancias and farms. In San Javier Caciques José Nedlaniguin, Quevagij, Domingo Nevedagnac, Nevedagnac's brother Juan Canotdin, and Passodin all owned improved properties, equipped with corrals and stockades.In San Jerónimo both Ychoalay–José Benavides and Laberequin had large estancias. Ychoalay profited from the sale of crops as well as cattle, while Laberequin owned more than ten thousand head of cattle in 1759, an impressive number when one considers that in 1767 the mission's common herd numbered only sixteen thousand head. Ychoalay's son, Miguel Jerónimo Benavides, continued his father's ranching tradition; his personal herds were sufficiently large that in 1781 he protested the recent loss to rustlers of more than three thousand head of livestock.[61]

By the late 1770s Guaycuruan males were also working for Spanish ranchers at seasonal jobs, as non-Indian Argentine cowhands often did. Slatta claims that "most gauchos worked as ranch hands only a few weeks or months a year." For day wages, "these migratory . . . hands circulated to many different ranches and worked as needed a few days at each."[62] In 1781 more than two hundred Abipones worked as cowhands for Don Francisco Candioti for two *reales* per hide.[63]

Most Guaycuruan males, who for centuries had viewed cultivation as demeaning, initially resisted labor in the fields and other agricultural tasks. In the pre-mission era, cultivation was appropriate only for women or such ethnic inferiors as Guanás or Guaranis, whose very devotion to agriculture revealed their inferiority. Some men nevertheless made this "revolutionary"[64] leap to agricultural duties, a wrenching change. Within a year or two of the establishment of Belén, many male Mbayás had adjusted to working at least periodically in the fields. Still, in the early years, the men of Belén and other missions worked at stoop labor only sporadically. Men and even women left the mission fields when the palm or the algarroba ripened. They generally also resisted toiling on the mission's common properties, preferring to work on private holdings. Reports from San Javier de Mocobis, however, make it clear that men there eventually cultivated wheat and corn with teams of oxen and wooden plows. They improved their plots with rakes of tree branches. Inside wooden palisades, they threshed and winnowed grain and stored it in cowhide containers. They also stored produce in sacks and bins made locally, probably by Mocobi women. By 1766 Abipones of San Fernando, known among Spaniards and among other Abipones as a difficult group, were laboring in the fields with less reluctance than earlier. By 1785 they cultivated wheat, sweet potatoes, manioc, watermelons, and other fruits and vegetables.[65] In San Jerónimo de Abipones, innovator and priestly favorite Ychoalay was an adept cultivator of wheat for personal profit. With money from the sale of grain, he bought Spanish-style clothing, and other Abipones soon followed his example.[66]

Mission Economies

Some Guaycuruan missions—San Javier, San Jerónimo, San Fernando, Belén, San Ignacio, and others—survived until the end of the colonial period.[67] Others—such as Timbó for Abipones, Cangayé for Mocobis, and San Bernardo for Tobas—disappeared after a few years. An institution usually endured or disintegrated for economic reasons. In most transitory foundations, the mission deteriorated when the subsidy ran out. In addition, such missions as Cangayé or Timbó were too distant from Spanish centers to permit easy trading with creoles. It made little difference to the viability of a reduction whether its economy was based on legal trading such as marketing hides or illegal activities such as selling rustled horses. One way or another, however, Guaycuruan missions had to connect their activities to the larger economy.

Missions founded from 1743 to 1767 with Jesuit support were more likely to survive than those founded after 1767, largely because of the greater material help Jesuits provided their missions. Nevertheless, some later foundations were successful, including Remolinos and Ispín for Mocobis and San Antonio for the Toba.[68] All missions began with a subsidy of cattle and often horses, asses, sheep, tools, and clothing. Many missions also needed money to pay Hispanized peones, who served as examples and tutors of the new ways and were essential in the early years of a mission.[69] Between 1743 and 1760, for example, the city of Santa Fe subsidized San Javier de Mocobis to the tune of 40,000 pesos, and San Jerónimo de Abipones from 1748 to 1760 with 27,000 pesos.[70] Governments at several levels provided cattle to hungry neophytes who threatened to leave missions,[71] because Guaycuruan missions never produced great surpluses.

The more successful reductions, however, usually could get by in good years without renewed subventions—as did San Javier de Mocobis in Santa Fe, Concepción de Abipones outside Santiago del Estero, or San Ignacio de Tobas near Jujuy. Absent extensive hostilities or natural disasters, in fact, their economies were strong. In 1769, for example, San Javier produced goods and services valued at sixteen thousand to seventeen thousand pesos a year.[72] Between 1777 and 1785, the beginning of an economic downturn, Abipones of San Fernando provided for themselves so abundantly from their farms and animals that their surpluses fed the creole poor of their *partido*.[73] In periods of prosperity and self-sufficiency, the Guaycuruans in missions sold cattle products, hides, tallow, blankets, crops, lumber, and carts. They hired themselves out as escorts, guides, and scouts. Situated beyond the scrutiny of overseers, missions were prime locations for officially prohibited transactions, and most missions participated to some extent in the underground economy of the region. For example, San Jerónimo de Abipones was a depot for the illegal transshipment of Paraguayan tobacco to Tucumán. Priests were seldom in a position to report law breakers.

Many missions found themselves economically imperiled at some point during the eighteenth century, however. War, drought, epidemic disease, or venality of officials brought periodic catastrophes. In the 1770s, for example, the avarice of Administrator of Missions of José Taragona of Santa Fe and Governor Gerónimo Matorras of Tucumán, who siphoned off mission surpluses for their private purposes, reduced the people of San Jerónimo de Abipones and San Ignacio de Tobas to begging. Thus, periodic subsidies remained essential for decades.[74]

The potential earning power of most missions was limited, partly because many people in transition from nonsedentary to sedentary modes were still gaining the skills valued by Hispanic societies.[75] One cultural survival detrimental to mission welfare was the custom of immediately consuming all one could eat, a practice common among hunting peoples.[76] The greatest obstacle to a mission's economic growth, though, was the survival into the mission period of the honored callings of raiding and war. Raiders from the Chaco and Guaycuruans in other missions helped themselves to rivals' livestock. The practice of beggaring neighboring missions began in the Jesuit era and became more frequent after 1767.[77] Clerical mediators in the last third of the century were even less able to adjudicate disputes and vendettas among competing groups than their predecessors had been. By the 1780s there were more missions, more people living in them, and proportionally fewer resources available to pacify potential enemies. In addition, the expulsion of the Jesuits reduced the number of available clerical mediators.

War also periodically threatened prosperity. In the 1770s and 1780s, for example, the Abipon missions of San Jerónimo and San Fernando fought with the Mocobi reductions of San Javier and San Pedro (see chapter 2). In the late 1770s, San Javier lost twelve thousand cattle to Abipon raiders. Even as this conflict ran its course, however, men and women in the warring missions maintained the course that they had elected when they chose reductions. In San Javier and San Jerónimo, farming continued between hostilities, and the cattle trade persisted, albeit at a reduced level. In 1778, as the mission's forces faced combat every few months, the carts of San Jerónimo still traveled to Santa Fe with livestock products and crop surpluses. In the early 1780s, however, San Jerónimo Abipones succumbed to raiding pressure when the oxen they needed to plow their fields were stolen, and they reverted to aboriginal pursuits, intensifying their hunting, fishing, and gathering. San Fernando Abipones were driven from their mission in the 1770s, when they relocated to the east bank of the Rio Paraná for protection, but the mission survived until independence. At the end of the eighteenth century, in fact, Abipones there worked their fields diligently and constructed houses in the Spanish fashion.[78]

Guaycuruan Economic Strategies in a Colonial Context

By the second mission generation, Native American leaders were confident enough in the skills of their people to resist paternalistic Spanish economic controls. Corregidor Don Miguel Jerónimo Benavides, son of Ychoalay, spoke for his mission. He begged the viceroy to allow San Jerónimo residents to negotiate freely with Spanish merchants. Benavides said, "we feel ourselves capable of trading and trafficking by ourselves; and our goods are acquired by our own industry and continual labor and not by the aid and counsel of the Administrator and Protector; and our goods and persons being free, it is also certain that we in our liberty are not in an inferior condition to the Spaniards."[79] He requested that Abipones be able to choose the merchants with whom they traded. Competition would benefit Abipones, he argued, because they could distinguish between honest traders and crooks. His people did business with those Spanish traders whom they trusted. In 1780 they sold their produce to Don Manuel Rubio, a vecino of Buenos Aires, angering the teniente of Santa Fe.[80]

In the early nineteenth century, Guaycuruans' economic activities increasingly resembled those of the Hispanic world, although their economies and cultures were still distinctly Native American. From San Javier, San Pedro, and San Jerónimo, Guaycuruan traders brought mission goods to market in Santa Fe, including clay pottery, halters for horses, lassos, agricultural produce, and tanned deerskins. Even warfare was taking on a European form, as Abipones and Mocobis in the nineteenth century served in the Spanish military. In 1803, for example, Abipon soldiers from San Jerónimo formed a militia company under an Abipon captain. In Santa Fe in the 1820s and 1830s, former mission residents constituted the cavalry units Lanceros del Sauce (Abipones), Lanceros de San Pedro (Mocobis), and Lanceros de San Javier (Mocobis). They made a living combating the enemies of Santa Fe *caudillo* Estanislao López.[81]

In both the eastern and western Chaco, Guaycuruans in the early 1800s were electing to work outside missions, and new occupations put them in more intimate and regular contact with Spaniards. Some men began losing their Guaycuruan cultural identity as they left the missions to work on estancias in Santa Fe and Entre Ríos beside non-Indian gauchos. In 1803 San Jerónimo Abipones were dispersing among Spanish estancias. In 1808 the Toba of San Ignacio seasonally cut sugarcane on three Spanish haciendas in the province of Salta del Tucumán, although the missionary still tried to regulate their service. Also in 1808, several adolescent Toba orphans and young adult males from San Ignacio apprenticed themselves to artisans in Salta: a smith, a mason, and a master tailor. All agreed to work for five years without pay while learning their crafts.[82] Some of the Mocobis of Remolinos, on the bank of the Río Paraguay south of Asunción, were migrating to the valleys of eastern Paraguay, but most labored as their priest wished; in 1809 they cultivated maize, cotton, manioc, sweet potatoes, pumpkins, and watermelons.[83] These peaceful activities of Guaycuruans, however, had a violent counterpoint, as Remolinos Mocobis exploited not only their own livestock but also those with Spanish brands. In 1808 the Remolinos Mocobi best known to Spanish ranchers across the river was a rustler, one of two killed by a patrol of non-mission Payaguás employed by Spaniards.[84]

By the early 1800s, second- and third-generation mission Guaycuruans had accepted Hispanic work habits within and beyond the mission world. Creole landowners, their former enemies, had been encroaching toward the missions' lands since the 1780s.[85] In the last decades of the eighteenth century, for example, Don Lorenzo Revuelta, a vecino of Jujuy and commander of Fort Ledesma, used his position to acquire a ranch near the mission.[86]

After the collapse of the mission system in the 1830s, Guaycuruans continued to move economically toward the Hispanic world. Beset by security problems in the post-independence Río de la Plata, Mocobis formerly of San Javier, for example, accepted the invitation of Santa Fe caudillo Estanislao López to move their village nearer the city, where they worked as peones on farms in the area of Rincón.[87]

As documented in this chapter, Guaycuruans in and out of missions chose to reorder how they earned their livelihoods between 1650 and 1810. Their habits of labor changed significantly. Those men and women who requested missions experienced alterations in their material lives and those of their offspring. Some elected and others were coerced into agriculture on mission properties, labor as artisans, work as weavers and blanket makers, and day labor on neighboring estates. In missions they adopted a host of new technologies that intensified the changes in their material lives which had begun in the 1500s. Yet the most revolutionary changes in their subsistence activities—the utilization of horses, cattle, and iron artifacts—occurred before the people came to reductions and, in fact, were part of the reason for their moving to missions. But the alterations in the Chaco from 1550 to 1740 were invested with indigenous significance; Guaycuruans largely controlled their own economies. Their destinies now depended on their Spanish neighbors, and none could pretend otherwise. Still, they felt, the choice to join missions had been theirs.

CHAPTER 4

Society

This chapter will explore Guaycuruan society in the pre-mission era and the continuities and changes occurring in missions. Although from 1600 to 1750 Guaycuruans lived simpler lives than their Hispanized neighbors and enemies, the Chaco bands were not egalitarian. The social inequalities in Guaycuruan society were indigenous; no evidence shows that direct European influences significantly contributed to the hierarchical social structure. Abipones, Mbayás, and Mocobis recognized sharp class distinctions. Each group had an elite, a class of common people, and a lower order of servants and slaves. The Toba marked their divisions less clearly but still recognized a social hierarchy—leaders, followers, and captives. Guaycuruans made class distinctions based on behavior and appearance, not wealth. As in contemporary Europe, Guaycuruans thought that behavior should be commensurate with lineage. High-status people were expected to be valorous, and vile behavior was assumed to come from vile birth.[1] An insult in Abipon was "Acami Lánaraik," "You are lower-class" (and therefore ignoble).

Social Distinctions

Guaycuruan upper classes included respected men, especially political leaders and the most successful of warriors, and their wives and daughters (see chapter 5 for a discussion of chiefs and others). In Abipon bands the *hĕcheri*, or *nelerĕycatè*, were the most honored class. Most gained honor and status by martial deeds and survived a rigorous initiation. To demonstrate their superiority they used a distinctive dialect, transposing or adding syllables to words used by common Abipones. Names of

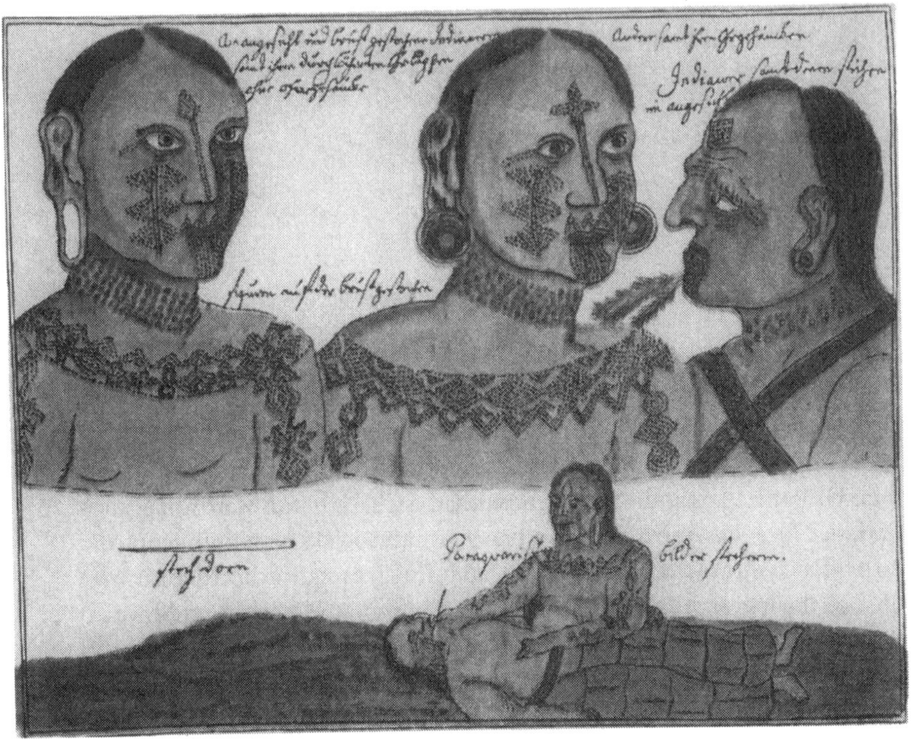

Tattooed Mocobi women and men and a practitioner at work.
[From Florian Paucke, *Hacia allá y para acá (una estada entre los indios Mocobíes, 1749–1767)*, vol. 2, fol. p. 140]

upper-class men and women ended in *-in* and *-en* respectively. One also added the same syllables to nouns and verbs when conversing with noble Abipones. One asked an Abipon commoner, "Have you arrived?" by saying "*Là nauichi?*" The same question addressed to an Abipon noble would be "*Là náuirin?*" Mocobi social structure and language mirrored the Abipones'. Mocobis used four dialects: one for the "military nobility" and the bravest of men, another for male commoners, a third for married women, and a fourth for unmarried women.[2]

Noble Mocobis avoided marriage with common folk and rejected sex with captives, priding themselves on pure Mocobi descent, which distinguished them from commoners. Mocobi men and women who had the choice avoided marriage with non-Mocobis. They married people from other, and presumably distant, bands, because their consanguinity test for incest was more rigorous than the Catholic one. Captives, including Spaniards and Guaranis, and Mocobis returned from the Spanish world formed a low-status group. In the half-century before they joined missions, some Mocobis with poor hunting and fighting skills could do no better than a Spanish woman as a mate. Women belonged to the social class of their defining male relative, usually their husband or father.

Most Guaycuruan bands did harbor outsiders. Some captives were taken by force and were treated as slaves, while other outsiders came by choice, accepting the hospitality of the band. The Toba and Mocobis commonly traveled together. It was not unusual either for a Toba shaman to reside with Abipones or for a non-Guaycuruan Malbalá to travel with Mocobis. Even renegade Spanish males occasionally sought refuge with Guaycuruans, as did blacks and Hispanized Indians. The Toba band of the shaman-chief Keebetavalkin raised a boy taken from Paraguay; he retained a Toba identity after a Spanish-Abipon force massacred his adopted people. When told that he was now free, the youth replied that he was a defeated Toba, not a liberated Paraguayan. The Riikahé Abipones for years sheltered a black warrior-hunter. Originally a captive, he became an Abipon, scouting for them and later even leading attacks on Spanish centers. His bravery won him the devotion of ethnic Abipones. Other captives such as Fulgencio Chaparro from Asunción and Cristóbal Almaraz from Santiago del Estero became important Mocobi and Abipon war leaders (see "The Coming of Missions" later in this chapter). Later they served as negotiators between the Guaycuruan and Spanish worlds.[3]

At the bottom of Guaycuruan societies, captives normally were slaves. Because many had no place to go, captives seldom fled. Among the Abipones and Mbayás captives made up an important work force and a major demographic element. In contrast, Mocobis valued captives principally for their ransom price, and relatively few remained with their captors long term.

Abipones treated with their captives with consideration and many were eventually able to better their situation. Captive females did not fear sexual attacks from Abipon men, probably because men scorned the socially degraded women, liaisons with whom would jeopardize their status. Abipon sexual partners were available for men who wished them. Abipon masters treated their slaves paternally, phrasing their orders as requests. Captives still understood the implied threat of violence behind the entreaties and obeyed promptly. Captive males often accompanied their masters to the hunt and to war. After proving themselves in combat they might take as wives Hispanized women or Native American captives. Among Abipones and Mocobis, captive males of talent had opportunities for social advancement based on ability. Males taken captive while very young could thrive in Guaycuruan settings if they were skilled hunters, warriors, scouts, or interpreters. In particular, males captured as youths from Spanish locales were assets in Guaycuruan wars against their birthplaces, and they could rise to positions of influence through valorous deeds.

All Guaycuruan societies were ethnocentric and proud of their bravery, but Mbayás were the most outspoken in this regard. They integrated male children of captives into society to reinforce their declining population but considered them not warlike and without honor. Children of female captives and Mbayá fathers were considered Mbayá, although their mothers remained slaves.[4] Captives of Mbayás gathered firewood and carried water, dishonorable chores. Because Mbayás kept a relatively large number of captives, their commoners worked at menial chores less often than commoners of other groups such as the Mocobis, who took captives more for revenue than servitude.[5] By the 1700s a significant portion of Mbayá society was made up of captives in two servile categories. Guanás served Mbayás voluntarily, while captives were true slaves who could be bought and sold. At Chief Caminigo's village in the 1760s, captives included six female Paraguayans from Asunción. One worked as an interpreter and hated captivity. Other long-time captives included a Portuguese woman from Cuyabá whose two black slaves accompanied her. Neither voluntary nor coerced servants were socially mobile in Mbayá society, unlike the situation among other Guaycuruan peoples. Although Guaná servants assisted masters in battle, no heroic deed could win them a higher status. Mbayá bands could not string out class logic indefinitely, however, and eventually descendants of captives joined the mainstream. Mbayá Chief Golanigi even married a woman descended from a captured member of the prominent Montiel family of Asunción.

Personal Appearance

Guaycuruans valued physical attractiveness, and men and women enhanced their looks in several ways. Like many Indian groups of North America, Guaycuruans found meaning in hairstyles. Mbayás were easily distinguished from other groups because they shaved their eyebrows, eyelashes, and other body hair, which they thought ugly. Abipones, Mocobis, and the Toba plucked their hair about two inches back from their forehead, and from a distance it was difficult to distinguish them because they all plucked their hair from forehead to crown. For Abipones, this *nalemra,* the bald place, was a religious mark. Cutting youngsters' hair was entrusted to shamans, male and female. Women also shaved the hair at the base of their skull. Mourning Abipon widows and widowers shaved their heads completely, as did all men after the death of a chief.[6]

Guaycuruans also tattooed themselves. For both sexes, scarification was a mark of beauty. Girls and boys were tattooed and scarified in adolescence as they came of age. Abipones rubbed fresh ashes into geometrically arranged thorn pricks to form designs indicating the wearer's social status. The more tattoos, the higher one's station. Mocobi men generally tattooed three parallel lines above the nose and two under the eyes.

Mbayás valued silver earrings as highly as did ladies of Asunción or Santa Fe; they also prized necklaces, bracelets, and rings, especially if silver. Mbayá men dressed for festive occasions by wearing glass beads, feather bracelets, and tin belts. In the lower lip all Guaycuruan groups wore a bone plug, which Abipones rejected at about the time that some began to choose missions.[7]

Guaycuruan clothing was more functional than decorative. Mbayás and Mocobis dressed according to the weather. In the hot months, men often wore only black and red paint; in cooler months, they wore blankets made from skins of big cats, deer, and other animals with desirable personality traits. Unlike males, even infant Guaycuruan females were clothed. Women of the southeastern groups wore leather skirts fastened at the waist and shawls knotted at the neck covering their shoulders and breasts. Occasionally, they wore clothes of vegetable fibers. Mbayá women wore a short blanket in their homes and a longer one for out-of-doors. On special occasions Mbayá women wore dresses covered with shells, and upper-class females displayed more shells than plebeian women.

Some changes in Guaycuruan clothing occurred between the time of contact and the coming of missions. After the acquisition of sheep in the seventeenth century, Guaycuruans began weaving garments of wool. Women, however, continued to wear skins long after men chose textiles for clothing. By the 1600s both men and women in Mocobi bands wore Spanish hats as finery.[8]

Social Rituals

Guaycuruan women passed most days working and conversing about the weather, survival, and their children and husbands. These usually amicable exchanges at times became hostile, when quarrelling women engaged in essentially unarmed combat. These contests followed a pattern. An Abipon woman of the noble class might scold another for her objectionable behavior, shouting insults at her for an hour or more; women of other Guaycuruan groups probably behaved similarly. Common insults were to call a woman ignoble, low-born, or dead. Disputes sometimes escalated from words to physical violence, called *roélakitápegeta.*[9] The women attacked each other with fingernails and teeth, not with fists as men did. Each tried to rip the earrings from the other's lobes, pulled her opponent's hair, and scratched her face. One woman might take a knife to the another, not to kill but rather to mark her. Though these conflicts were bloody, they were never lethal. Nor did they have the potential for escalation to full-scale armed conflict, as did male disputes. Custom forbade men, even husbands of losing contestants, from interfering in women's fights, although they participated as spectators.[10]

Sober men did not quarrel; instead they were exquisitely courteous to each other. Males saved their disputes until drunk. Then aggrieved men of the warrior class initiated combat during ritual celebrations. At times a man might harbor a grudge for months, until an alcoholic festival gave him the opportunity for revenge. As men traded insults over their liquor fistfights frequently erupted, but these caused only bruises or lacerations. If a man found a weapon, he might kill his opponent and would not be stopped from doing so by the other celebrants.

Some of these alcoholic festivals had religious significance, while others were purely social; social celebrations might be held to commemorate a harvest or the birth of a chief's son, or simply because the honey or algarroba to make the beverage was available. Often one man acted as host. Abipones and Mocobis mostly restricted the right to drink to married males, although bachelor sons of chiefs could participate.[11]

Mbayás' ceremonies have been described in the documentary record. They placed a liquid made from honey or algarroba in the sun for three or four days to ferment and beat a drum to mark the fermentation process. Guests fasted before the festival, increasing the intoxicating effect of the brew. At sunset the celebrants began drinking for a solid twenty-four hours, heedless of their own and others' vomiting. Musicians played a squash or cow-horn bugle and beat drums. A boy might sing the praises of the celebrants, who seated themselves in a circle, talking, smoking, and drinking from the cups that women brought them. Each participant extolled his own and others' virtues, boasting of enemies or animals bravely killed. Insults followed boasts. A man frequently disputed how many Spaniards a braggart had killed, calling them few, feminine, and feeble. Frequently the insults ended in physical fights.

Abipones celebrated anniversaries of great military victories with similar bouts of drinking. The men collected honey and sent a crier, perhaps a lesser shaman, through the village announcing the event. Carrying a spear with a bell on the tip, he visited the home of each married man. There, the woman greeted him, took his spear, and seated him by her husband, whom the visitor invited to the festivities. While awaiting fermentation, men built a hall of reeds festooned with enemy scalps. When the celebration began, men would chant two at a time of their deeds to the accompaniment of rattles and drums. The storytelling was competitive, with the best singers receiving the most attention.[12]

Wives and children escorted the drunken and battered men home the next nightfall at the conclusion of the celebration. Family violence, especially the abuse of women and children, was always a threat at such times, and some women hid their children and their husbands' weapons during these debaucheries.[13] The next day remorseful husbands ventured outside apologetic and in pain.

Naming was an important ritual for Guaycuruans. A Guaycuruan's true name delineated presumed character traits, and Mocobi infants often were given the names of animals. This name was so important that Abipones neglected to name some women, as a sign of their lowly status. People were never permitted to speak their own true names nor that of someone who had just died. Even husbands and wives were not to tell each other their true names. Because a person's true name was too important to be spoken, people were addressed by nicknames, which changed frequently. For example, a man's public name might be changed during a drinking bout. At Mocobi drinking parties, one man might even purchase a name from another. Men were given new public names to mark the stages in their life. Mocobi Chief Cithaalin was known at various times as Vadanoquin, Peliguedoin, Ripliligoin, and Ylimodin.[14]

Guaycuruan etiquette was demanding. Away from drinking bouts, Abipon men were reported to control themselves rigidly. All Guaycuruan peoples addressed each other in ceremonious language, and Mbayás particularly valued good manners. Gatherings were orderly. Within a band, theft was virtually unknown. An important ritual was the welcoming of a visiting chief. When whole bands visited each other, they engaged in mock combats and played sports.[15]

Important milestones were occasions for recreation. One important ritual recognized the birth of a son of a chief. Abipon bands celebrated the event for several days. Everyone played a role. Girls circled the infant's home shaking palm fronds, insuring that he would be a great fighter and leader. A formidable woman dressed in rhea feathers brandished a rawhide whip. She roused the men of the village, as girls beat the laughing males with their palm fronds. After eight days of games that polished survival skills—including footraces, horseraces, and war games—the festival ended with a drunken celebration for the men. Another celebration occurred at the full moon, when Mbayás sang until the rise of the morning star, their "master." In the Mbayá festival of branches, a young woman, her face blackened with charcoal, sat dressed in tree branches and surrounded by women and girls who protected her from naked boys who tried to remove the leaves. When the leaves were gone, the girl ran to the river and washed her face.[16] Such simple rituals reflected the stark realities of life in the Chaco.

Family Practices

Permissible sexual activity varied among the various Guaycuruan groups. Unmarried Abipon women, for example, were normally chaste, while Mbayás allowed single women more freedom, as long as they terminated pregnancies. An unmarried Toba woman could have sex and abort a pregnancy or two without a fuss. Promiscuity, however, brought censure and damaged her marriage opportunities. Sexual fidelity in marriage was expected among all Guaycuruan peoples. Although Mbayás were more casual about this than other Guaycuruans, they nevertheless ridiculed men whose wives were unfaithful. Cuckolded husbands sought revenge by repudiating an unfaithful wife or thrashing a rival while drinking.[17]

During pregnancy, both the husband and wife observed dietary and other taboos. Pregnant women abstained from fish, certain meats, and the feet of animals, whose consumption they thought would produce children with twisted legs. Because it was believed that misbehaving males could damage a fetus, Guaycuruan fathers shared the responsibilities of pregnancy and childbirth. Wayward Toba and Abipon fathers, for example, could cause ugly, deformed, or antisocial children. Connected by a magical bond to their embryonic children, Toba men joined their wives in rejecting certain foods and activities. Abipon fathers mimicked the pains of birth and postpartum depression. When a baby died the father was often blamed for deviant behavior during pregnancy.[18]

Guaycuruan childbirth was a simple ritual. Families met with shamans, who officiated at parturition. Mbayá babies were wrapped in blankets to meet their fathers. New fathers painted themselves with black and red designs and plucked offensive facial and body hair. In Mbayá villages only the birth of a chief's son was celebrated outside the immediate family.[19] In Mbayá bands, another nursing infant was paired with the heir to political leadership. This child became an honorary member of the nobility but lacked the right of the blood elite to bequeath noble status to his descendants.[20]

Women could not feed and nurture large numbers of children while on the move. For generations women had regulated family size through infanticide and abortion, as most Mbayás continued to do throughout the eighteenth century. Some women avoided childbirth for fear their husbands would desert them during pregnancy. Women delivered unwanted newborns to shamans, who buried them alive or left them in the woods for the animals. In some groups specially designated women twisted the necks of condemned infants. Married Mbayá and western Toba women practiced abortion by pounding on a woman's stomach in the fifth month of pregnancy.

The surpluses of the horse revolution in the 1600s lessened the environmental pressures that had caused Guaycuruans' rigid limiting of family size. Mocobi mothers were evidently the first of the Guaycuruan peoples to give up routine abortion and infanticide. Population growth followed and partly accounted for the Mocobis' being the most numerous Guaycuruan group by the 1700s. Many Mocobis had several children. Mocobi mothers carried as many as four children on horseback. On the eve of the movement to missions, other Guaycuruans as well were choosing larger families, as the ruthless limitation of family size was disappearing in all but the Mbayá culture. Abipon Chief Oahari and his wife had four sons and at least one daughter before they came to Timbó. Toba Chief Ovagaiqui and his wife raised four young children at one time, three girls and a boy. Mbayás, however, generally obeyed the old rule of having only one child at a time, their descendants in the 1940s recalled.[21] Guaycuruan family planning changed in the early 1700s, even before missions. By the 1740s Mocobi women seldom resorted to infanticide, except when they bore twins or deformed children, when their husbands abandoned them, or when they lacked milk.[22]

Childhood

Guaycuruan children enjoyed a loving childhood with little overt criticism of their behavior. Mocobi children slept with their mothers and sat on their laps as they worked. Mbayá parents so respected their children's wishes that a child's whim could move an Mbayá father to sell a horse. Guaycuruan parents refused to spank or reprimand sassy or disobedient boys because an aggressive boy would likely grow into an aggressive warrior.[23] The son of Abipon Chief Alaykin, for example, threw hard objects at his mother, and Alaykin approved. Such combative behavior in girls, of course, was of less social utility, and girls were taught to be more subordinate than boys. Nevertheless, children were devoted to their parents. When Mocobi mothers or fathers were ill, children ate only fruits and vegetables, because they believed eating meat might cause their mother to die.[24]

Informal but effective, education for young girls and boys was the responsibility of mothers. Although parents normally taught by example, Mocobis revealed what they expected of a son by placing a tiny bow and arrows in his crib. When boys were a year old, mothers guided their hands around the weapons. They encouraged their daughters to carry water jugs about. Fathers taught adolescent boys horsemanship, hunting, and war. Girls learned by assisting their mothers in finding, harvesting, preparing, and cooking foods. They followed them to the woods and rivers with linen nets and water jugs. In this practical educational system, girls learned to sew, fashion utensils, and build houses. Young children generally obeyed when asked to do chores. Abipon boys and girls were happy and playful, but they bathed and played separately. Sexual segregation was the norm in Guaycuruan societies.

Adolescence

Between thirteen and sixteen, Guaycuruan youths began thinking of themselves as adults, and they endured rituals to formalize their new status. Having worn black paint as youths, Mbayá boys now painted themselves red, wore their hair in nets, and prepared to enter the order of soldiers. They passed the tests for hunters and warriors and suffered scarification of their faces and upper torsos and partial mutilation of their penises without showing pain. Finally, a boy dressed in his finest regalia, feathers, beads, and metal ornaments and endured the last ordeal. All day, a drummer beat out a rhythm until, at sunset, a shaman made puncture wounds on the boy's body. If he were truly a man, he endured the pain and impassively watched blood ooze. Finally all eligible males convened in a solemn drinking festival, signifying that the new soldier could now paint himself for war.[25]

When Mocobi boys were twelve, their mothers and grandmothers gave them their first tattoos, an ordeal that most bore stoically, as they were expected to act like men. Fathers had sons bathe uncomplainingly in the coldest water to be found. At this time, men shaved boys' heads from forehead to crown, like all Guaycuruans, giving them an appearance that caused early Spanish colonists to call them *frentones*, "the people of the forehead."[26] At fifteen or sixteen, young men became responsible for a share of their families' subsistence and security. They now gave orders to elders, and parents obeyed.

At the time of their first menstruation around twelve or thirteen, Toba girls also underwent an initiation into womanhood. It was believed the spirit who dominated the rivers recognized their womanhood and would violate them sexually. At this time, therefore, they were forbidden to approach waters in order to prevent flooding. They were secluded, their heads shaved, and their diet restricted for two months, principally through abstention from meat. Finally, the father gathered honey, brewed mead, and drank and danced into the night, proclaiming that his daughter was now a woman and worthy of respect. At the earliest opportunity, a man offered his daughter the head of an enemy to mark her passage. On becoming women, Guaycuruan girls were tattooed for beauty. For Abipon girls this was a four- or five-day ordeal, as women punctured their faces, arms, and breasts with fish-bone needles to form geometric designs. These wounds were injected with ashes and blood, leaving permanent marks. The more elevated her social position and the greater her beauty, the more tattoos a girl was given. If she flinched from pain, women ridiculed her.[27]

Marriage and Divorce

After the horse revolution of the 1600s, Guaycuruans evolved new marriage customs. Mbayás captured females to ensure demographic expansion. Because of infertility, abortion, and infanticide the bands normally had trouble maintaining their population. The necessity of perpetuating the culture overcame ethnocentric ideology. Mbayá leaders themselves sought endogamous marriages, or at least ones with Guaná wives, but they allowed commoners to marry servants and slaves. By the 1770s even such honored leaders as Chief Epaquini had strayed from the ideal. His son and heir to band leadership, Epilig, was born to a Payaguá woman of Asunción. This child's claim to authority was acknowledged by others in the band.[28]

As they approached thirty, Guaycuruan men sought wives ten years younger, whose extended families[29] they would join. Courting customs varied. A Toba suitor had to convince the mother of his intended bride that he was a skillful hunter. An Abipon seeking marriage had to negotiate a price with the parents of his intended bride, usually paid in horses or cattle. The profit potential made girl babies more valuable than little boys. Mocobi parents received jaguar skins, horses or cows, or valuable bead necklaces from prospective sons-in-law. When a girl was eligible for marriage, they cut her hair in a special way.

Mocobi parents often arranged marriages of young children. Mocobi girls prepared for marriage for two years, isolated from young males. As they matured, betrothed boys and girls heard from relatives and friends about the benefits of the arranged marriage. A prospective bride valued a future husband's ability to hunt and to fight, but her main concern was that he not be cross or abusive. If a girl were reluctant, her principal recourse was flight, but she usually had no place to go. Sometimes the girl's feelings would influence her parents to cancel the match, particularly if the prospective husband was potentially abusive.[30] Irascible men were often forced into prolonged celibacy.

Guaycuruan weddings were simple. Mocobi parents stayed at home and awaited the groom or visited his home with their daughter. The groom's parents dragged an unwilling bride to the home of her future husband and threw her inside, where he ignored his wife's anguish. Other women of the band consoled her. Until the birth of a child, the woman owed allegiance to both her husband and her parents. Many new brides returned to their parents for as long as two months while their men were hunting or raiding. On the husband's return, the woman might remain with her parents if she still detested him.

Mbayás had no special marriage ceremony. Between the ages of twenty-five and thirty, a suitor in theory secured the permission of the bride's parents and took the woman to his hut. The groom celebrated the end of his bachelorhood with a drinking party.[31]

Abipones had a more elaborate marriage ritual, which began when the groom paid his in-laws the bride price. Holding a canopy over her head, girls escorted the bride to meet the groom and back to her parents' home. She made several trips to transport her cookware and loom to her new abode. That night, though, the couple stayed with her parents, and during a trial period of several months, the groom had to prove his worth. For the Toba and Mocobis, the period of matrilocal residence might be permanent or temporary, although most Toba pairs eventually went to live with the husband's people. When a man joined a woman from a different band, he lived near his in-laws, avoiding them as much as possible. To this unit husbands brought their own property, usually including captives, horses, and cattle.[32]

Among Guaycuruans, the desire for marriage was not confined to the young. Widowed and divorced women were not always sentenced to living alone, to single motherhood, or to the resources of their own families, although a majority were. Some older widowers and divorced men preferred their wives to be older as well, although the martial nature of the society meant that there were more mature single women than men. Older women exercised more control over whom they married than first brides. They might pair off with captives or other less desirable persons, but Guaycuruan ethnocentrism defined this as a last resort.[33]

Husbands were to be moderate and not beat their wives in the course of daily life, although some women were abused. Although a man did not usually show affection for his spouse, a battered wife might feign death to discover whether her husband in fact cared for her. Family violence commonly followed drinking bouts, when husbands were abusive. Drunken husbands held the power of life and death over their wives and children.[34]

A majority of couples remained together for a lifetime, but divorce was relatively common among Guaycuruans. To some extent divorce was limited by class. Mbayá commoners could divorce several times, but Mbayá leaders were more restrained. Usually it was the man who broke the bond; women also had the right to initiate divorces but normally did not, although occasionally a wife left her husband for a lover. Husband and wife retained separate property, and divorced men and women had the right to reclaim what was theirs. Some men reclaimed the property that they brought to the union while returning the woman to her parents, but others did not bother, because most property was perishable. The families of divorced Abipon women kept the bridal gifts.[35]

Women feared abandonment more than beatings. The loss of a husband, the provider of horses, cattle, skins, and iron trade goods, meant shame and impoverishment. Wives knew that most husbands valued obedience above physical beauty and that men would choose an obliging, homely woman over a beautiful, sharp-tongued one. Independent-minded, faithless, lazy, complaining, or thieving women had trouble keeping a husband.[36] Divorce was so threatening that women even practiced abortion or infanticide to avoid being abandoned. The birth of a child might strengthen or destroy a marriage. Lack of sex during pregnancy and the long lactation period after birth caused some fathers to reject one wife and seek another.[37]

Monogamy was the norm in Guaycuruan society, but all people knew men who had plural marriages, especially chiefs. Privileged Mocobis, chiefs' sons or superior warriors, might take a second wife. Abipones with second wives commonly maintained only one in their own residence, because of the mutual hostility of the two wives. When wives met, they often fought over who would govern domestic life and whom the husband would favor. Wives of the same husband might attack each other with fish bones, attempting to wound and thus make ugly their rival. Abipones called a contest between wives a *nejetenta,* distinguishing it from an ordinary scuffle between unrelated women, which was a roélakitápegeta.[38]

Abipon men more frequently divorced an original wife than took a second, because supporting two families at once was difficult. Thus serial monogamy was more common than plural marriage. When a man remarried, he typically chose a younger, usually more productive worker and no longer provided for the first wife, who was left on her own or returned to her family with her children. Fathers did not normally support their children by former wives, but older male offspring remained with fathers. Losing prestige, some abandoned women took mates from the servile class.[39]

Marital infidelity was rare but not unknown among Guaycuruans. Jealous Mbayá husbands often accompanied their wives, because they did not trust them alone. When a Mocobi woman bore a child from an adulterous relationship, she could save her marriage by confessing. A suspicious husband might kill a wife who refused to confess. If she put the unwanted child to death, her husband usually spared her life.[40] In such matters personal power was decisive. Wives of unfaithful husbands had few rights.

Gender, Aging, and Death

The social aspects of aging worked differently for men and women. Skills of hunting and war deteriorated as men reached their late thirties. As their powers declined, so did the respect that they commanded. As Guaycuruan women grew older, however, their status increased. Aged women enjoyed privileges withheld from younger females. They also remained vital to the society. Older Abipon women, for example, carried cooking and drinking water from the nearby river or stream,[41] a task essential to group survival, although not conveying high social status. Older Mocobi women with religious duties could drink to excess, a badge of honor. Their dances magically kept attackers away. Their Mbayá counterparts danced in celebration when a man brought home an enemy head.[42]

Death was omnipresent. Guaycuruans feared death and tried to avoid the wrath of the spirits who caused it. After someone's death, people changed their public names to make it difficult for the departed soul to injure the living. When Abipon Chief Revachigi's wife died, he changed his name to Oahari. When an important person or family head died, survivors might even change the name of the object from which the deceased person's name was derived. When a Mocobi chief named Ana, meaning "needle," died, Mocobis changed the word for needle. Similarly, when Mocobis died bearing the names of animals, survivors created new names for the animals. Guaycuruans refused to live in houses where a person died; usually they destroyed them. Once Death had discovered a place, he could come again.[43]

The fear of death did not prevent some Guaycuruans from killing terminally ill parents, however. When older Mocobis fell ill, for example with smallpox, and appeared to be dying, children might dispatch them to the next life with a club.[44]

Guaycuruan religious belief controlled death rituals. Mbayá women painted male cadavers red to symbolize the soul's departure. Guaycuruans placed bodies in shallow graves so that the departed soul could escape. Beside the grave were provisions for the afterlife, a man's weapons or a woman's jewelry and cooking utensils, and food and water for the journey. When a child died, parents brought food daily to the grave for weeks, and then periodically after that. Guaycuruans at one time slew the horse of a dying chief or major warrior, so he could ride through the afterworld, but this custom was much neglected by the mid-1700s.

Funerals began before death. Women painted the dying person and adorned him with jewelry. People left the house of a dying Abipon as a precentress beat a drum by his head. Married women mourned outside. Family survivors cut their hair in mourning. All Mbayás in a band cried for an hour at dawn in the days following a death. After a husband died, a Mocobi widow cursed her mate's desertion, shaved her head, and veiled herself. Elderly female mourners, who expected payment for their services, chanted for three or four nights. Surviving Mocobi children comforted a surviving mother but not a father. A widower surrendered his children to his wife's kin and disavowed further responsibility for them. Mocobi and Abipon widowers shaved their heads on the death of a spouse. Men solemnized an important death by drinking themselves senseless.[45]

Status of Women

Guaycuruan societies were bounded by martial values. Although women had subordinate status, they were respected, and many structures were parallel. The economic contribution of women increased after the horse revolution, and Mocobi and Mbayá women owned cattle and sheep. In general, though, women's status changed slowly until the mission era.

The status of Guaycuruan women resembled that of the Ojibway of Michigan, Wisconsin, and Minnesota in the eighteenth and nineteenth centuries. The Ojibway lived by hunting, fishing, harvesting wild plant foods, and cultivating corn. In winter they dispersed into smaller units to exploit large game and precious animal skins. At first glance Ojibway women appeared to be menials, because they constructed the dwellings, cultivated corn, and were seemingly exploited. Nevertheless, they had autonomy in the female sphere and owned what they produced. Like Guaycuruans and many other peoples, the Ojibway judged some tasks more appropriate for women and other tasks, usually the more prestigious ones, appropriate for men. But women and men might work together. Thus, although a task might in theory be considered masculine or feminine, in reality males and females worked interdependently.[46] These activities included hunting, in which women butchered and dressed meat, finished hides, and made leather clothing.

Guaycuruans refused to allow socially designated sex roles to prevent a person from doing something necessary for survival. Although Mbayás labeled the task of catching and hobbling horses as men's work, women routinely performed these tasks during their men's long absences. Despite the constant threat of attack, Abipon women would ride off to harvest "fruits, roots, colours . . . and remain four or eight days in the country, without having any male to accompany them."[47] In these gathering parties, women thought themselves safer than males who went out to hunt.

Guaycuruan women officially could not control the actions of a band and had no independent political voice. Nevertheless, they made their opinions known. At meetings held to decide matters of policy, only Mbayá men could speak to issues of importance. Nevertheless, as men decided policy, women stood behind them. The women talked only to each other, but the men overheard and understood their remarks, though spoken in the dialect of women.[48] Female consensus that a proposal was foolish would inevitably fall on male ears. The admiration and approval of women was as necessary for Mbayás as for any other men. They took notice of disparaging remarks, although they did not acknowledge them openly.[49]

Even war, the most prestigious Guaycuruan activity, was not exclusively a male activity; Guaycuruan women were central to war making. As captives and servants, women were the objects of much conflict. In addition, women's esteem for able hunters and warriors and scorn for incompetent ones were important. The better a warrior, the better his chance for a desirable wife. Furthermore, women performed such war rituals as the dances and chants before battle. After combat, women expressed the collective grief. Guaycuruan women got from war clothing, utensils, jewelry, and captives who relieved their work burdens. War also, however, robbed them of the very favors it brought.

The Coming of Missions

In the 1740s and 1750s, as Guaycuruan families and bands chose Catholic missions, many social customs changed. With the exception of the captives, however, many of whom returned to their places of origin, social relationships among Mocobis, Abipones, the Toba, and Mbayás in missions changed more slowly than did their religious beliefs, economic practices, and political structures. The Mocobi elite, for example, continued to marry among themselves, and missionaries had no objections. European societies recognized even sharper social gradations than Guaycuruans, and the Native Americans of the Chaco missions encountered little sustained effort from missionaries to level their class structure. In fact, at times the opposite was true. Lesser chiefs in missions who had no governing role nevertheless received European confirmation of their elite status. Their social prestige was enhanced by the title "Don." Militia leaders in missions acquired the social prestige that both Guaycuruans and Europeans conferred on warriors.[50]

NEW OPPORTUNITIES

In missions, non-noble but socially mobile men became caciques and cabildo officials, competing with the old elite. When members of the chiefly class earned special privileges in missions, the common classes seldom objected. When an upstart received undue preference from priests, however, the relationship caused problems. One Mocobi parvenu was Bartolomé Citai, servant of the missionary Father Canelas of San Javier. Although Citai was literate in Spanish, he was unable to marry into the leadership class. Yet his services to the priest earned him a tidy estate with cows, horses, sheep, and a Spanish-style home. When Sebastián Cithaalin, son of the cacique, married Estefanía, daughter of Cacique Domingo Nevedagnac, both from the old elite, the bride's father made a special effort to ensure that the couple lived in a house that outshone Citai's; envy then prompted Citai's desertion.[51]

Among the earliest residents of Guaycuruan missions were Guaranis, one-time enemies. Some came as captives of the Guaycuruan founders. Others arrived with the Jesuits to teach sedentary living. They were not always welcomed; the Guaranis of Belén, for example, suffered discrimination from Mbayás. As Guaranis settled around the mission in the 1770s and 1780s, however, it eventually became more Guarani than Mbayá. Tiny minorities in other Abipon, Mbayá, and Mocobi mission societies, those Guaranis who remained after 1767 prospered and suffered with the Guaycuruans. In the spring of 1781, for example, Abipon raiders from San Jerónimo killed a Guarani shepherd of San Javier. So integral was he to the mission that the irate Mocobis sought revenge.[52]

OUTSIDERS IN MISSIONS

Outsiders in missions were of several categories. The most important were those Native American captives whose masters would not permit them to return to their places of origin. The priests—Jesuits and their usually Franciscan successors—attempted to argue for their release, but if persuasion was ineffective, the missionaries usually had no readily available force to summon. Moreover, captive women who had children typically did not wish to abandon their offspring and chose instead to accept their circumstances. Many captives in missions were hostile to priests,[53] who since the Jesuit years had lacked non-Guaycuruan force to enforce their edicts. Similarly, Spanish captives in Mocobi bands were at times more antagonistic to Hispanic institutions than were ethnic Mocobis.[54] Renegades from Hispanic settings—errant husbands with Native American wives, outlaws, and former slaves—also found their way voluntarily to Guaycuruan bands and moved to missions with them. So did renegades from other Native American cultures—shamans in disrepute and losers in factional strife and feuds. Other outsiders included spouses of members of a band.

As Guaycuruans came to missions from the 1740s to the 1790s, secular and clerical authorities pressed them to repatriate their captives, especially those from Guarani missions and Spanish cities, and this was often a condition of Spanish largess. Mocobis of San Javier in the early years, for example, returned seventy-three Guarani children to the missions from which they came. Groups responded to the Spanish pressure to relinquish captives in different ways. For Mocobis, the change was not abrupt, because captives typically had been ransomed rather than retained as slaves. For the Mbayás in Belén, the adjustment was wrenching. Before the 1760s an upper-class Mbayá woman might command as many as four captive servants. In a mission, however, her superior position came under attack, especially if having servants encouraged her to be uppity with priests.[55] Guaycuruans had leverage, however, because they retained a military potential in missions. Thus, some defiantly retained captives, especially those from other Chaco groups, and had the power of life and death over them. When a Toba from San Ignacio killed a Spaniard of Tucumán, the governor demanded justice and threatened reprisal unless the Toba delivered up the guilty party. The Toba response was to kill a captive and bring her head to the governor, maintaining that she was the culprit.[56] Juan Bueno, an Abipon of San Fernando helpful to missionaries, retained his Afro-Argentine slave woman. Mbayás of Belén in the 1760s raided Guarani missions for captives. When Abipones of Timbó defeated Tobas, they took prisoners as property, sold a few, and kept the rest for themselves.[57] In fact, taking captives was one cause of the inter-mission wars of Santa Fe in the 1770s and 1780s.

Even after more than four decades of mission life, captives remained part of Guaycuruan society, some having achieved positions of authority and responsibility. In the Santa Fe missions in 1785, captives served as interpreters for the post-Jesuit, monolingual missionaries, as the Maya schoolmasters of Yucatan had done in the 1500s.[58] Over time, however, captives, some of whom chose to remain with their captors, played a reduced role in many missions. In 1785, after forty years of mission life, captives comprised 7 percent of the population of San Jerónimo.

In missions as before, Guaycuruans professed cultural exclusivity as an ideal. Many Spanish officials misunderstood Guaycuruan ethnocentrism, thinking it more restrictive than it was in fact. In practice most Guaycuruans continued the hospitality of earlier years, as they accepted outsiders of Spanish and Native American origin. Outsiders, friends, and relatives of Guaycuruans—at times numbering several hundred—often spent a few weeks or months visiting a mission. They came to trade for food and luxuries such as tobacco, sugar, and *yerba maté*. From the 1740s to the end of the century, Mocobis from the Chaco and their Toba allies often stayed at San Javier de Mocobis.[59] Many Toba also stayed at the non-Guaycuruan Chaco missions of Tucumán, especially Macapillo and Miraflores, for Pasaínes and Lules. At the Mocobi mission of Remolinos in the late 1770s, at least two Abipon families were in residence.[60]

The universality of Catholic goals and familiarity with language and culture enabled missionaries to encourage traditional ways that benefited the European religion, and they accepted this tradition of hospitality. Thus, mission Guaycuruans made a place for volunteers who came among them.[61] Ultimately some guests yearned for what their friends enjoyed and secured missions for themselves.

The priests were less enthusiastic about some of other useful outsiders whom Guaycuruans welcomed into their missions. One such person was José Ramón Quiroga, a man from a respected family of Santa Fe. Originally married to a Paraguayan woman, Quiroga deserted her, took an Abipon wife, and joined the San Jerónimo de Abipones mission in the 1770s. There he was a war leader, political adviser, and interpreter. Not ethnically an Abipon, Quiroga lived as a respected member of the group.[62] When Spanish officials tried to force him to return to his first family, Abipones protected him.

Other Spanish "renegades"[63] who lived with Guaycuruans included Cristóbal Almaraz and Fulgencio Chaparro. The bicultural Almaraz was born in Santiago del Estero and captured by Nakaiketergehes Abipones while a boy. Raised as an Abipon, he became an intrepid anti-Spanish warrior, accepted and honored among Abipones. He married two Abipon women. One wife was of the elite class and bore him several children. When she was captured by Spanish forces from Santiago del Estero, Almaraz spoke out strongly in favor of joining a mission. Later he helped Abipones negotiate for the reduction, Concepción de Abipones, to which they ultimately moved. Eventually Almaraz returned to Santiago, where he became a folk healer, because Spaniards were impressed with his knowledge of native remedies.[64]

Chaparro was a Paraguayan whom Mocobi raiders seized as a boy. Reared by his captors, he rejected Christianity and lived by Mocobi rules. As an adult he scouted for Mocobi raids on Paraguay. As the Mocobis considered missions, he negotiated between his band and Paraguayan authorities, who seized him as an apostate. They refused to release Chaparro because he would have deserted Paraguay for Mocobi life.[65]

Guaycuruans returned from the white world were often disgruntled outsiders in missions. Some had escaped Spanish captivity.[66] Others had worked voluntarily for Spaniards before missions were founded. Things Hispanic often disgusted returnees. Especially troublesome was the second Abipon wife of Cristóbal Almaraz. She had experienced Christianity in Santiago del Estero and argued that it was no improvement. Its adherents did not become better persons. With Almaraz, she moved to Concepción de Abipones. There she opposed priests and denounced Christianity. After she agreed to remarry Almaraz in the mission church, he spurned her, alleging that she was impious. But his real motivation for the break was his desire for a younger Spanish woman. When the bishop of Tucumán permitted Almaraz to dissolve his marriage to this sharp-tongued mother of his children, on the grounds that she was too closely related to an earlier wife, Almaraz was free to pursue his new choice.[67]

NEW NAMES, DRESS CODES, AND CONFLICT RESOLUTION

Guaycuruans viewed mission life from the vantage point of their own experience. In practice, they adapted priests' teachings to their own ways. They took Spanish names easily, because they had long had a tradition of taking new names. Priests could not, however, make a Guaycuruan forget the true name that formed his or her character, never spoken aloud. Guaycuruans used Christian names first as a convenience. They merely continued the traditional practice of nicknames, now Spanish names, as the public form of address. This involved no break with the past, and the new names pleased priests and civil officials, who discouraged public use of non-Christian names. Thus women and men took or were given Spanish names with or without baptism. Spanish names revealed more significant relationships as well. Doña María Micaela de la Riva Herrera, who married a cacique of San Pedro de Mocobis in the 1770s, was connected by ritual kinship to the important Riva Herrera family of Santa Fe.[68]

Dress measured Guaycuruans' adaptation to missions. Clothing was symbolic, stylistic, and utilitarian. In San Jerónimo, Ychoalay resisted dressing like a Spaniard for many years. He knew that he and his family could provide traditional clothing for themselves, though that of Spaniards was more comfortable. He saw adopting Spanish clothing as another level of dependence on Europeans. As he acquired more of the political power bestowed by Europeans, though, Ychoalay first became a Christian and then began dressing like a Spaniard.[69] In time, most Guaycuruans in the prosperous missions dressed like their one-time enemies. After a few years in a mission, a party of mounted Abipones from San Jerónimo from a distance resembled Spaniards.

Priests provided European clothing to those Guaycuruans whose behavior pleased them. Caciques and favorites of priests wore flannels and Spanish headgear, while the priests' antagonists wore head coverings made from animal skins. Women liked Spanish dresses, although they did not always wear them. Even in missions, Mocobi women might be naked to the waist in hot weather. They wrapped themselves from waist to ankles away from home, and at the urging of priests, they covered their breasts in church.[70]

Young women and men opposed the painful processes of tattooing and scarification. They gladly gave up the painful process of tattooing after missionaries disparaged it. In the face of priestly criticism, parents decided that these marks no longer symbolized social status, ethnicity, and beauty.[71]

Under pressure, women altered their standard method of conflict because these disputes made the priests anxious. Guaycuruan men traditionally had been unwilling to intervene in women's affairs. Although Abipon men still refrained from involving themselves directly in women's quarrels, husbands now sometimes solicited a missionary's help in ending disputes. In like manner, when the Mocobi women of San Javier went at each other with fists and fingernails in the 1750s, the priest halted the disturbance by threatening to horsewhip the contestants. Outside the normal Guaycuruan social order, priests could interject themselves in these formerly all-female affrays without upsetting the social balance. Women were reluctant to part with the traditional way of settling disputes, which helped relieve tension, brought excitement to humdrum lives, and unlike men's contests, put no one in mortal danger.[72] But they feared the Christian whip.

PUBLIC RITUALS, OLD AND NEW

Although female participation in rituals declined, Guaycuruan life in missions grew more elaborate and entertaining. Partial fasting on Fridays was not difficult for people who had always recognized such dietary taboos. Chaco peoples in missions saw mass, vespers, catechism, and confession as ceremonies that made life interesting. Baptisms, First Communion, Holy Week, and the fiestas honoring the patron saints of the missions gave a new spark to life. People gathered at religious observances to observe the cloth, ornaments, and jewelry displayed in even the poorest mission churches.[73] As in Mexico, festivals in Chaco missions included battle re-creations, parades, and such customary entertainments as races and archery contests. In San Javier to honor the mission's patron, St. Xavier, fifteen twenty-five-man companies paraded through the village behind standard bearers. The companies were identified by the color of their horses, the distinctiveness of the uniforms of the riders, and the designs on their guidons. New rituals meant new parades and European music, which supplemented but did not replace their own.[74]

Among long-time residents of missions, male drinking habits changed only slowly. In Concepción de Abipones older men refused to give up drinking traditional intoxicants despite the priests' scolding. Missionaries encouraged men to substitute yerba maté for the alcoholic beverage *chicha*. People in San Javier de Mocobis grew maize for fermentation into alcohol, which supplemented such wild sources as honey. Public drinking in the traditional way slowly declined, and the early missionaries thought that the habit of drinking to excess was on the way to extinction. Such native leaders as Cacique Domingo Nevedagnac of San Javier endorsed and practiced moderate drinking. Priests reprimanded adult tipplers, and Mocobi authorities such as Nevedagnac punished youths who drank. In fact, thirsty Guaycuruan men merely removed their revels from public view to avoid the zealous priests. They had horses and could ride off a mile or two to drink. If priests left for a time, the men of the mission resumed public consumption in the old way.[75]

Easily available intoxicants of Spanish origin, produced in large quantities and distributed relatively inexpensively, did more to change Guaycuruan drinking patterns than temperance lectures by priests. The chicha of algarroba, honey, or corn required a cooperative effort to make and was less potent than the sugar-based aguardiente of Spaniards. Raiding and trading with Spaniards had earlier brought strong drink only in small quantities. The men of the missions of Santa Fe began buying aguardiente with hides from their own estancias. Alcohol lost its ceremonial significance, and men drank alone or in small groups. Alcohol abuse became more frequent once such traditional restraints as the lack of honey or algarroba were removed. By the late 1770s, enough Guaycuruans drank aguardiente to contribute significantly to rural crime around missions. The thirst for spirits also inflamed the inter-mission wars of the 1770s, because men from San Pedro de Mocobis, San Jerónimo de Abipones, and San Javier de Mocobis raided one another in part for horses to sell so they could buy Spanish liquors.[76]

Along with Spanish intoxicants, Guaycuruan men also embraced Spanish games of chance, despite the missionaries' opposition. Missionary sermons could not prevent Guaycuruans in reductions from gambling, and they had even less effect on those who settled in non-mission clusters on the outskirts of the white world. At the urging of the missionaries of San Javier, Caciques Nevedagnac and Aletin destroyed all cards and dice in the mission.[77] But all men were mounted, and they simply went outside the mission to play games of chance.

Mission Guaycuruans slowly adopted Catholic rituals. Baptism ultimately displaced the former birth ceremonies. By the second decade of mission life, a majority of Guaycuruans brought sons and daughters to the priest for the sacred ceremony. Even in the earliest days, when the priest threw water on the child, spoke magical words, gave the infant a new name, and congratulated parents, he was doing something already familiar to parents. The new ritual was more elaborate but not outwardly all that different from their earlier practices. Abipones learned empirically that baptism would not hurt children after healthy babies survived the service.[78] Baptisms were special, in part because the European shamans made such a fuss over them. As in the European world, they were occasions for celebration.[79]

Along with baptism neophyte Guaycuruans adopted Spanish practices of ritual kinship. Mission leaders chose elite Spaniards as godparents for themselves and their children. Domingo Crespo de los Ríos of Santa Fe became godfather to Nevedagnac, later known as "the Indian Crespo." Spanish godfathers generally gave Indian godchildren gifts of clothing, knives, hatchets, and livestock.[80]

Marriage and the Family in Missions

First-generation mission Guaycuruans did not normally enter into Christian marriages. Even the Guaycuruan men most trusted by priests, like the Maya schoolmasters in sixteenth-century Yucatan who used new rituals to mask the old ones, preferred established marriage customs to the more demanding new regulations. Some of those who underwent church weddings did so for political gain. After Abipon Cacique Laberequin of San Jerónimo wed his wife in church, he became corregidor. In San Javier, Francisco Nalacolec and Antonio Tiew spurned their old wives and fled with new ones. Encouraged by the priest, Cacique Aletin unsuccessfully led a posse to bring them back. The fugitives had relatives and friends in the Chaco who harbored them.[81]

Traditional Guaycuruan men disliked committing themselves to one woman for life, so priests did not insist on rapid introduction of the marriage sacrament. Sixteen years after the founding of San Fernando de Abipones, only 10 percent of couples (6 of 58) were married by priests. More men in San Jerónimo fulfilled priests' notion of a Christian husband, but even there the number was still less than half (55 of 120, or 45.8 percent) after fourteen years of mission life. The second and succeeding generations married, perhaps because the priests focused on converting them. By 1785 most couples in San Jerónimo and San Javier had been married in the church.[82] In San Javier, the largest mission, young men and women of marriageable age did not normally marry outside the reduction.

Unlike men, women welcomed the new marriage rules. The Christian ceremony promised to secure the "perpetuity of their marriage" and that "their husbands [would be] prevented from changing or increasing the number of their wives."[83] As divorce declined, their security increased. Moreover, Catholic doctrine outlawed forced unions, giving women greater freedom. If a woman's parents contracted a marriage with an obnoxious man, she could seek sanctuary in the church. But certain old ways endured. When Abipon non-Christian Panzonoirin contracted marriage with the parents of an unwilling Christian woman, the bride hid in the woods, as her grandmother might have done, without appealing to the priest.[84]

Old and new ways merged. In San Javier the father of Cacique Ariacaiquin wanted to marry a mature woman, who spurned his overtures. When the old man persisted in importuning, the woman relented. She said, "I will start to run, and if he overtakes me, I will marry him. If he does not overtake me, he must cease pestering me."[85] The cacique arranged the contest, and his father won the race and the bride. The woman had assured herself of a husband who was still fit enough to hunt and who had proved that he wanted her. They accepted baptism, new names—Simón and Ana—and a church wedding.

Guaycuruan men in missions largely discontinued plural marriages, although a few were defiant. In San Javier de Mocobis, only three plural marriages existed in 1750. Having brought two wives to the mission, Cacique Cithaalin was pressured to renounce one. The woman he discarded, then raising their two sons, was disconsolate. She and other superfluous wives now lived as widows, depending in large part on their own families and welfare from the common stores of the mission. In San Pedro de Mocobis in 1765, fifteen Guaycuruan men took the missionaries' advice to give up second wives.[86] Their gestures lightened their economic burden, because they were no longer obligated to provide for a second family. Accepting Christian rules gave many men an excuse to jettison an older, less productive wife, although they were told that they must keep the "legitimate" one, a meaningless notion to them. Backsliding occurred. A prominent Christian in San Javier took a second wife, a non-Christian. A council of mission elders, which included several of the man's relatives, convened. They decided to banish the bigamist. To avoid exile, he gave up the second woman. Adultery also occurred in missions, where adulterers received reprimands from the priest and whippings from Native American enforcers of Spanish rules. In cases of fornication, the couple was separated.[87]

As the Chaco bands were considering joining missions, many Guaycuruan women were giving up the practice of abortion on their own initiative. Abortion by pounding on a pregnant woman's stomach in the fifth month of pregnancy was painful and dangerous. In the 1740s, a few Abipon women refused to abort pregnancies. Some came to missions with three or four children, a number unthinkable in earlier times. The average Guaycuruan family in a mission numbered five persons. Because of permanent cattle herds, fields, and orchards, hunger was less threatening. Women now had less economic incentive to practice abortion than their mothers and grandmothers. As more women contracted Christian marriages, they also practiced fewer abortions, formerly a strategy used to keep a husband. Thus the decline of abortion in missions was the continuation of a trend that Guaycuruans initiated earlier, accelerated by the change in marriage customs, not a new departure. Abortion declined even among Mbayás in the missions of Belén and Refugio,[88] although most Mbayás remained outside missions.

Infanticide also waned. Just as women in missions had less incentive to abort their pregnancies, the same was true of killing infants. Mbayá mothers in Belén gave formerly doomed twins to missionaries. Among Mocobis, who practiced infanticide less often than other groups even before 1743, the execution of newborns was totally extinguished in missions. Priests rescued and then accepted responsibility for rearing deformed children, twins, or those born with unusual marks, who previously would have been killed for religious reasons. Priests now gave women material support and a clear rationale for not doing something that they found difficult, killing their children. Therefore, although the priests' support was a factor, women made the choice on their own to oppose infanticide.[89]

NEW EDUCATIONAL PRACTICES

One abrupt change for mission Guaycuruans was in the education of children, especially boys. Guaycuruan parents and missionaries alike judged the education of youth central to a community. Thus, if a mission had a resident priest, some sort of formal schooling went on. The new ways involved far more discipline. Mocobis accepted the priestly model of children who were respectful, subordinate, and obedient to their parents. Formerly content to teach by example and to accept disobedience, Mocobis now learned that children benefited from beatings, if the force were not excessive. Guaycuruans never had opposed violence; they merely refused to practice it on their own children, although they did violence to the children of outsiders. Now Guaycuruans accepted the notion that corporal punishment was good for youthful souls.[90]

Formal schooling began immediately. In Rosario del Timbó, forty Abipon boys began studying reading, writing, and religion from Father Lehmann soon after the mission commenced. They also learned that farmwork was acceptable male behavior. In San Javier, many boys attended two schools. In one they learned to read and write. In the other those with talent studied European vocal and instrumental music. The most gifted became accomplished performers, whose music drew people to mass and allowed proud parents to boast. After mass and prayers, younger boys in San Javier studied music for two hours in the morning, while the older ones went to work. After lunch, they all spent another two hours learning to read, write, and sum, and studying how Europeans wished them to behave. In addition, they learned trades from priests and Guarani artisans.[91]

Girls participated in lessons in religion, although sexual segregation in education was the preference of both Guaycuruans and Catholics, and few saw utility in literacy for females. Thus, girls' education was closer to traditional experience than was that of boys. Throughout the Americas, whites more readily accepted indigenous work habits of females than of males. Therefore, for young females missions meant alteration of indigenous education rather than a radical departure. Girls nevertheless showed aptitude for taking direction from Europeans. In San Javier, for example, Mocobi girls learned how to make clothing by spinning, dyeing, and weaving cloth in a class team-taught by a missionary and a Mocobi widow of the elite class. The priest taught manual arts while the widow enforced discipline. After a few days the young women spun diligently, and priests boasted that they had accomplished wonders; in reality, however, the girls had already possessed many of the necessary skills.[92] They shaped traditional skills to new technology, including larger looms and spinning wheels. What was new and radical was the formal, hierarchical discipline.

Parents' reactions to the new system of education were ambivalent. Many parents sent children to the new teachers. Ambitious mothers sought missionary preference for their children. Mothers welcomed clerical interest in their offspring. They also appreciated a Catholic support system to rear their children after catastrophes. At the same time, parents regretted the loss of traditional ways, and some worked hard to resist the lure of the new. Cacique Cithaalin of San Javier, for example, tried to shield his children from the teachings of the priest. The Mocobi removed his sons from the mission to hunt, frustrating the missionary who wanted them in school. At times father and sons rode off to Santa Fe, challenging the missionary effort to segregate Indians from the undesirable influences of Spanish communities. But even Cithaalin ultimately sent his sons—Devatcaiti, Acanagqui, and Cadiodi—for a European education. In time they became known as Sebastián, Vicente, and Antonio.[93]

Children eagerly investigated European ways. Young Guaycuruans contributed to mission stability because they preferred sedentary life to life on the move. Children, who traditionally had a great deal of influence over family matters, often persuaded parents to remain in or return to a mission.[94] They quickly understood the European ways described by the priests and abandoned tradition more quickly than their parents and grandparents wished. Those new ways that they found useful they adopted eagerly, and they opposed traditional customs that threatened or embarrassed them. Mocobi children regularly tattled on their fathers who prepared an intoxicant for a drinking ceremony.[95] Not only was it embarrassing for children to watch drunken fathers foolishly staggering around the village but the ritual was also potentially dangerous. Drunken fathers might do physical violence to their wives and children, so boys and girls had reason to fear alcohol-induced rages. Cithaalin's children hid with priests when their father was drinking. One drunken Mocobi, Otepandagaiguin, killed his wife with a lance after celebrating too much. In indigenous times her brothers would have sought revenge, but priests in this instance convinced them not to kill the man.[96]

Mission children later in the century learned their lessons in Spanish, because many Franciscans, Mercedarians, and others who replaced Jesuit missionaries after 1767 did not learn Guaycuruan languages. In San Javier de Mocobis, San Pedro de Mocobis, and San Jerónimo de Abipones in the 1780s, the children faithfully attended classes in reading, writing, and religion taught in Spanish, despite years of intermittent war among these three missions. At the same time adults heard lessons in their own languages recited by captive interpreters or by bilingual Guaycuruans. In the Abipon pueblo of San Fernando de las Garzas in the 1790s, Abipon children attended daily classes in reading and Christian doctrine.[97]

Despite the introduction of European schooling, the changes were not wholesale. Much traditional education of Guaycuruan children continued. Boys still needed to know how to hunt and make war, and girls still learned to gather, prepare, and cook available foods. They learned these lessons in traditional ways, at first from their mothers and then, for boys, from their fathers.

AGING AND DEATH

Gender ratios in missions changed as people aged. The number of young males and females was nearly equal. Girls slightly outnumbered boys in San Fernando de Abipones for the first fifteen years. There were only slightly more boys than girls in San Jerónimo de Abipones and San Javier de Mocobis in 1785, a profile which resembled San Ignacio de Tobas in 1757 and 1778. Over the years, however, more men died prematurely than women, as combat and hunting accidents killed more men than childbirth killed women. In pre-mission Guaycuruan societies, women generally outlived men. This imbalance continued in missions, where war was still a fact of life and hunting perilous. In addition, men were more likely to desert their families and return to the Chaco than were women. In San Fernando de Abipones in the 1750s and 1760s, widows outnumbered widowers by a ratio of 34 to 1. In San Jerónimo de Abipones in 1762, fifteen widows existed for every widower. In 1785 San Javier de Mocobis had a ratio of eleven widows for every widower. In 1785, a time when all permanent residents had been born in the mission, San Jerónimo's widows still outnumbered widowers by more than 5 to 1, a ratio similar to that of San Ignacio de Tobas in 1757, just after the mission's foundation.[98]

Elderly Guaycuruan women were reluctant to adopt new ways, and because there were many older women, this defiance was formidable. Cacique Cithaalin's grandmother, for example, said that she wished to die like her ancestors. If what the priest said was true, that her ancestors really were in hell, she wanted to join them there. She changed her mind only minutes before her death, when told that she could escape the terrible flames that awaited her by accepting baptism.

Prior to missions, women's influence increased with age. Honor and responsibility were the perquisites of age, and they resented the mission agenda that robbed them of their due. Female shamans, usually older women, clung to their hard-won authority. They lectured others against the innovations. Their opposition was the easiest to overcome, because unlike young men who retained military power, elderly females could summon no force. The few older men of the mission, in contrast, had lost their leadership role and offered little opposition to the mission experiment.[99]

Funeral practices changed dramatically in missions. When priests insisted on Catholic burial in holy ground for Christian Guaycuruans, mission residents protested. Abipones criticized priests for tarrying before burial. Initially, Guaycuruan burial customs blended with Catholic ones. When a three-year-old in Belén died, his mother began to lament, and the other women echoed her. They sang about the child while facing east with their arms upraised. After their song they returned cheerfully to work and allowed a Christian burial. On a hunt, a jaguar killed Florián Connogoiquin of San Javier de Mocobis. His friends stripped his flesh and brought his bones to the mission, as their ancestors had done. There they asked the priest to inter them in a Catholic ceremony. The priest pleased the Guaycuruans by seeming to comply; he buried the remains in ground adjacent to the mission cemetery.[100]

Important changes in Guaycuruan culture altered the disposition of property at death and coincided with the coming of missions. After the livestock revolution, some Guaycuruans amassed substantial property, as compared to their earlier poverty. Independently, they were concluding that property should be passed on after death, not destroyed as before. In San Jerónimo de Abipones, Cacique Ychohake bequeathed his horses and sheep to his daughter, instead of ordering them slaughtered at his grave site, as his father and grandfather might have done. Interested in encouraging Catholic traditions and in building endowments, the priests reinforced this trend, telling Guaycuruans how to bequeath property. Thus, Guaycuruans in missions learned that they must will at least some property to the church and that survivors should make use of the remaining goods. Through his father, Diego Nevedagnac, who died in San Javier during the 1759 smallpox epidemic, left an estate of six horses, two cows, and eight sheep. To one brother he left two cows and to another, two horses, but the bulk of his estate went elsewhere. To the poor of the village, he left eight sheep and his clothing, and to the mission's common herd, he left the remaining four horses.[101]

Conclusions

Guaycuruan society changed in missions, although the continuities are also striking. Guaycuruans accepted missionary instructions that they found useful and rejected those of little value to them. The Guaycuruan class structure leveled in missions, because the captive and servant populations declined. Styles changed, as males and females discontinued body painting, tattooing, and scarification, and most mission residents chose to wear textile clothing instead of leather garments. As priests intervened, fights between women declined, and male drinking became less public. Catholic ceremonials included public naming rituals, but mission Guaycuruans continued to address each other by aboriginal names into the second and third generations. The richness of Catholic ceremonial life, mass, vespers, and church-related festivals, supplanted the simple Chaco rituals. Such church observances as confirmation replaced aboriginal initiations for young men and women. As the one form replaced the other, however, the participation of women in rituals gave way to an increasingly male-dominated ceremonial life.

Women generally were more attached to mission life than men, but they got little relief from their dawn-to-dusk work schedule. In such aspects of daily life as food acquisition and preparation, mission women followed the old ways. The status of younger females improved, though, and they enjoyed a wider range of economic opportunities. They raised livestock in a more stable setting. They also made and sold blankets to whites. Young, unmarried Guaycuruan women, wives in their childbearing years, and women with children became devoted to missions. Adolescent women now had the freedom to reject (with the priest's support) the pain of tattooing and scarification. Married women appreciated Christian doctrines about the sanctity of marriage and the sinfulness of divorce.[102] They looked to priests to protect them from desertion. Similarly, priests supported women who chose to avoid the peril and pain of abortion. Mission women also found that priests reinforced their increasing reluctance to deliver newborns to the executioner. In cases of spousal abuse, women now asked priests for help, although priests could do little more than admonish brutal husbands; formerly, a woman's only alternative was to call on her male relatives for reprisal and seek the protection of her family, not an effective deterrent at any time. Older females were the only ones who did not find their lives improved in missions. They perceived a status loss, especially since their former religious functions were now officially proscribed.

The influence of Guaycuruan political leaders—all males—increased in missions (see chapter 5). Traditional Guaycuruan society was already patriarchal, and Spanish patriarchy reinforced Guaycuruan traditions. Conversely, the status of men who were not caciques or mission officials declined, as the callings of hunter and warrior became less important. Although raids and war declined in the mission setting, the Guaycuruan way of war did not disappear entirely. Guaycuruan women continued to support their men when they went to war and to suffer from the attacks of enemies and rivals.

In missions, as in indigenous Guaycuruan bands, outsiders—including Spanish renegades, Guaranis, and Guaycuruans of other regional and language groups—continued to join local societies. The presence of culturally Hispanized persons likely contributed to the increase in pastimes more common to Spanish than to Guaycuruan society, including games of chance and drinking distilled spirits in private.

Discipline for mission Guaycuruan children increased, and they underwent a more regimented education. Children, nevertheless, preferred the mission to their previous mobile life. Their parents encouraged them to participate in the programs of missionaries, and they willingly complied. Boys attended formal classes in reading, writing, and religion; these tended to be conducted in native languages before 1767 and in Spanish thereafter. Although missions also sponsored formal instruction for girls, especially religious education, their schooling focused on traditional women's domestic arts.

As they matured, Guaycuruans married in Christian ceremonies. Among the first generation in missions, few individuals other than political leaders married in church, but in the second and third generations most did so. Plural marriages, never common, became increasingly rare. Guaycuruans intensified the recognition of private property that began in the post-quadruped era of the 1600s. They now bequeathed their property to heirs and to the church in ways that European Catholics would find familiar. Nevertheless, the social patterns of Guaycuruan missions revealed stronger ties to the past than missionaries cared to admit; the most significant social changes had begun after the acquisition of horses and iron and prior to entering missions. Many social changes that took place in missions were continuations of these earlier innovations. These shifts were themselves reasons why Guaycuruans after 1740 found missions desirable alternatives to life on the move.

Guaycuruan warfare and weapons. [From Florian Paucke, *Hacia allá y para acá (una estada entre los indios Mocobíes, 1749–1767)*, vol. 2, fol. p. 310]

CHAPTER 5

Politics and War

Politics and war among Guaycuruans changed as horses, cattle, and iron remodeled their societies in the 1600s. Their political decision making shifted for several reasons, only one of which was Spanish influence. This chapter will examine Guaycuruan rivalries and politics in the pre-mission period and political developments during the mission era. It will focus on the functions of chiefs, their followers, and their rivals, as well as how leadership changed in missions.

Indigenous Conflicts

In the half-century before missions, Guaycuruan chiefs had many duties. They led economic exchanges, negotiated truces, initiated hostilities, and arranged alliances. Men of the leadership class, including chiefs, war leaders, and aspirants to leadership positions, often competed for influence. When Guaycuruan chiefs dealt among themselves and with the Spanish and Portuguese worlds, they aimed to enhance their own reputations. They had to maintain their authority over their own followers, and they hoped to attract followers from other chiefs. How diplomacy or war affected the Hispanic world was frequently a secondary though important consideration.

Ethnic rivalries and competition for scarce resources led to hostilities among Chaco peoples. Throughout the colonial era, disputes led to periodic warfare between the Mbayás and adjacent peoples, including the Lenguas and Chiquitos of the west bank of the Río Paraguay and Guaranis of central Paraguay. Similar struggles among Mocobis, Abipones, and the Toba spilled over into Corrientes, Santa Fe, and the Guarani missions.

Intra-Guaycuruan conflict and hostilities between Guaycuruans and other Native Americans did not cease with missions. Such hostilities as the war between the Abipon and Mocobi missions of Santa Fe in the late 1770s were continuations of indigenous factionalism.[1] For people in missions, pressures from Spaniards—a company of troops stationed between the villages, for example—might relieve or intensify antagonisms, but the antagonisms themselves were largely traditional and preexisting.

The political choices of Guaycuruans in and out of missions had indigenous sources and were not necessarily of Spanish instigation. In fact, on the Chaco periphery in the mid-1700s, "the roots of many white-oriented political cleavages were indigenous." Like tribal peoples on the northern continent, Guaycuruans were often more concerned with the "political context of their own communities" than with Spaniards.[2] One North American native leader whose political goals and tactics parallel those of Chaco chiefs was Uncas, a Mohegan-Pequot of New England. Uncas was a subordinate Pequot sachem who in 1634 claimed the office of grand sachem. When the post was awarded to his rival Sassacus, Uncas was bitter. The ensuing feud between the two leaders grew out of dynastic politics, reflecting "a deep-rooted conflict in Pequot society, relating to a usurpation of position by a previously subordinate kinship group." In 1637 war between Puritans and Pequots gave Uncas the opportunity to join the whites and vanquish a rival. Uncas helped drive away Sassacus, who was killed. "From Uncas' point of view, the white men proved a handy tool" to help him achieve his aims.[3] Like Uncas, Guaycuruan leaders in missions, including Caciques Ychoalay (Abipon) and Nevedagnac (Mocobi), used Europeans to advance their own interests.

For Guaycuruans, settling in a Catholic mission was a way to gain ascendancy in a conflict with their traditional rivals. The Abipon band led by Ychoalay strengthened its military potential with mission support. In response in 1774 Mocobi chiefs Paikin, Lachiriquin, and Coglocoyquin, who had until then spurned missions, led their followers to confer with Governor Gerónimo Matorras of Tucumán, and these bands agreed to live in missions, as relatives and rivals in other Guaycuruan bands had already done. Spaniards hoped that their diplomacy and evangelism would relieve Tucumán from hostile Mocobi raids, but the Mocobis had a very different agenda. Paikin hoped that a peace with Tucumán would facilitate raids on Santa Fe and Corrientes. His principal object, however, was to acquire a margin of victory in the Mocobis' struggle with the Abipones of the San Jerónimo mission and their leader Ychoalay (Cacique José Benavides).[4] By the 1770s, the Abipones of Cacique Benavides had lived in their mission for twenty-five years and they possessed firearms.[5] Although these were not decisive in Chaco warfare, Paikin envied the many advantages of Benavides-Ychoalay, his principal enemy.

Even people of the same language group fought each other. Men owed greater allegiance to regional bands than to the larger language group—once mistakenly called a "tribe," a designation without political significance. Guaycuruan conflict between rival Abipon missions escalated into war in the 1760s. Ychoalay–José Benavides of San Jerónimo and the Abipones of San Carlos y Rosario del Timbó south of Asunción were enemies. When the Abipones of San Carlos settled with Jesuit priests along the Río Paraguay in 1764, they sought not only accommodation with Spanish Paraguay but also a refuge from the hated Ychoalay.[6]

Guaycuruan politics, defined as "competition over public goals and the distribution of power,"[7] never occurred at the level of a "tribe," because there were no Guaycuruan tribes. Abipones, Mocobis, Toba, Mbayás, and Payaguás felt little political solidarity, although they recognized a cultural affinity. They made political and military decisions at the level of the band. They also decided policy matters in such subgroups as a cluster of extended families led by minor chiefs whose prestige was inferior to that of band leaders. Family groups periodically met as bands, whose cohesiveness and ability to remain together were limited by scarce resources. A major variable in Guaycuruan politics was kinship, which usually brought alliances but sometimes sparked rivalries. A family group often constituted "a miniature state,"[8] and close relatives, such as nephews, cousins, and brothers-in-law, were more often allies than adversaries.

Leaders and Decision Making

Three types of sometimes conflicting, sometimes allied leadership existed in Guaycuruan society. The leader of a band was a chief. Because Guaycuruans aimed at (although fell short of) ethnic exclusivity, a chief's descendants could retain leadership over several generations through birth, prestige, and example, but not hereditary privilege as in European society. Unlike chiefs, who inherited their positions, most Guaycuruan war leaders' status was intermittent and limited to periods of conflict. War leaders depended on followers' recalling their great exploits and rich booty. The third level of leadership came from religious leaders, or shamans. At times shamans reinforced a chief's authority; at other times chiefs and shamans might be rivals. Competition between shamans and chiefs intensified in the mission environment, with chiefs becoming dominant[9] as Christian influences eliminated the public duties of shamans.

Political decisions in this leadership system began with discussions among adult males of the warrior class. The final decision was deferred to the political elite, including the chief. Chiefs generally followed the counsel of elders and the opinions of all initiated adult men. In Guaycuruan communities, therefore, chiefs' authority in peace and war was weaker than that of Spanish political and military leaders. If they were unconvinced of a chief's magic, followers would move away, explaining that they had to hunt, so as not to be thought cowards. They then might join another chief, and in time might tire of him too and return to the first.

When chiefs failed to meet expectations,[10] followers selected other leaders. When Mocobi Chief Amaquin came to San Javier to request a mission, his following was considerable. After a long wait, his people returned to the Chaco. When Amaquin reappeared in San Javier, he had far fewer followers.[11] In the Chaco, it is clear, one faction had rejected him. The faithful were ultimately rewarded, however, for Amaquin and his people settled the mission of San Pedro.[12]

Hereditary chiefs spoke for most Guaycuruans but lacked coercive powers. The influence of a Guaycuruan chief was proportional to his skill in war and hunting and the persuasiveness of his oratory. Political and military leaders in Guaycuruan societies led by example, and they moved others by persuasive oratory, backed up by their personal reputations for success in war and peace. Thus, a chief's status was tenuous. Some leaders lost followers as they aged; others, even while young, lost the knack of persuasion. Abipon chiefs Kaapetraikin and Kebachin attracted numerous followers in their youth, but as they aged, many adherents lost confidence in their abilities, and their followings dwindled. Finally, only close relatives sustained them.[13]

Chiefs before the mission era lacked personal wealth; thus they had little economic power. Those with surplus goods redistributed them to followers, a mark of nobility. Because they gave away their nice things, chiefs often dressed more shabbily than followers.[14] Both chiefs' economic position and their mode of dress improved substantially in missions.

Before entering missions, Guaycuruan leaders also lacked judicial authority. Leaders who intervened in disputes faced trouble, because people opposed their acting as peacemakers. Men offended by a chief's meddling would wait for a drinking festival, on which occasion they thrashed any leaders who had interfered in private disputes. Such beatings befell Abipon chiefs Ychamenraikin and Naré.[15]

At the same time, however, a chief's duties were essential, and his followers honored him. As Dobrizhoffer observed, "The name of cacique is certainly a high title amongst the Abipones. . . ."[16] A chief's sociopolitical prestige often unified a group. Guaycuruan leaders made life-and-death decisions. They oversaw their people's security, ensuring the group's defenses and establishing an avenue for flight in case of attack. They posted scouts to warn of danger. They decided where to pasture horses and when to bring them to the settlement. Guaycuruan chiefs also decided when to break a peace. Leaders in all Guaycuruan societies invited male followers to join them in expeditions for gain and glory. Mbayá chiefs, who personified the limits of the lands that the group claimed, issued safe-conduct passes to outsiders who wished to travel through their territory.

The most important policy decision was war. The leaders who rallied men for war had few command functions and were not necessarily chiefs. In fact, conflict often occurred between ambitious war leaders and hereditary chiefs. In the 1760s, Chief Caminigo of the Enacagas and Chief Napidrigi of the Lichagotegodis, both non-mission Mbayá bands, were wary of a young factional chief, Antonio, known as "the Portuguese," once a captive in Cuyabá, Brazil. Throughout the 1760s Antonio sought to sway men of his generation to follow him, and his ambitions threatened older authorities. Thus, Caminigo tried to destroy Antonio's reputation. Napidrigi even offered to lend a priest his warriors to kill the upstart.[17]

Spanish accounts reveal details of the leadership process in various groups. Like Abipones and Mbayás, Mocobi leaders "invited" volunteers to seek economic reward and glory through war. Because chiefs sent scouts to the territories of adversaries, they got intelligence first. In war, chiefs risked their lives in the vanguard of an assault.[18] Toba chiefs were generally less influential than Abipon, Mocobi, and Mbayá chiefs. A few Toba chiefs, such as Keebetavalkin, were also shamans. The peacetime influence of men who combined political and religious duties was greater than that of their counterparts, but their authority remained fragile.[19]

In Mbayá bands, eligible adult men decided policy while sitting in a semicircle. They passed a pipe as the women stood behind them. Discussions were so tumultuous that Spanish observers incorrectly concluded the participants lacked respect for their chiefs.[20] In fact, Mbayá chiefs customarily enjoyed more influence and freedom of action than other Guaycuruan leaders because of their patronal relationship with neighboring Guanás. The Guanás were Arawakian-speaking sedentary agriculturalists of the northern Chaco, who paid tribute by supplying Mbayá chiefs with wives. Mbayá chief Caminigo, for example, claimed the loyalty of the nine-hundred-family village of his Guaná wife. Mbayá leaders protected their Guaná tribute-payers in exchange for a share of their harvest and a mutually acceptable amount of labor. An Mbayá leader gave "his" Guanás goods on request, often knives, and was also expected to let them steal from him. If he deviated from this code, he ruined his reputation. Mbayá men of the warrior class had no claim to the loyalty or tribute of Guanás, who thought of Mbayá chiefs as "lords" but of those beneath them as "brothers." Because of this relationship, some Mbayá chiefs acquired limited powers of command,[21] although this fell far short of the authority of European leaders.

Chiefs and followers connected by elective loyalty and kinship formed a "factional political system" in which conflict as much as consensus characterized political relationships.[22] Outsiders who have mislabeled Guaycuruan and other traditional societies as polities operating by consensus have failed to recognize that the consensual decision making was often merely group aspiration, not a description of political behavior.[23] Far from achieving consensus, factional politics "involves a small number of people competing . . . in a large number of weak, transitory alliances . . . [with] little durability and no structure. They are typically the projections of individual ambitions in the context of personal and family rivalries."[24] Prime examples were Mocobi Chiefs Aletin and Cithaalin, the latter of whom was married to Aletin's sister Cainet. The two chiefs frequently differed, both over Cithaalin's abuse of Cainet and over their degrees of attachment to traditional ways. These disagreements became policy disputes about Mocobi culture. The more traditional Cithaalin resisted missionary guidance in San Javier. He frequently led followers away from the mission to hunt and raid, causing the priests no little anguish. Aletin, on the other hand, was able to please the priests without betraying Mocobi traditions, and he became foreman of the mission estancia, where he extended his influence and prevailed over other Mocobis, even Cithaalin, whom the Mocobis recognized as having a more illustrious lineage.[25] Like Uncas, Ychoalay, and Paikin, Aletin took advantage of European systems to gain ascendancy over a traditional political rival.

Status and Succession

Indigenous chiefs revealed their importance not by wealth but in other ways. Mocobi Chief Nezeleagnac lived in a home resembling others, but his was in a more honored location. Similarly, Mbayá groups built their settlements in a semicircle and placed the chief's dwelling at the honored center.[26] A chief's home was a place of sanctuary for fugitives, just as Catholic churches were.[27] Pursuers were honor bound to preserve the safety of the chief's dwelling.

Guaycuruan traditions of inheritance led to dynastic politics like those of Pequot society. Children of chiefs merited special consideration as leaders. Worthy sons inherited chieftainships, unless their fathers had repudiated their mothers.[28] Worthless sons, however, did not acquire their fathers' duties, because Guaycuruans would not follow "indolent, ill-natured, and foolish" men, even if well-born. Abipon chief Debayakaikin, for instance, had four sons. None, the other men of the band decided, was worthy to succeed his father,[29] and all joined different bands after Debayakaikin's death.

Such a situation was unusual, however. Normal patterns of political inheritance were exemplified in the five Mocobi leaders who petitioned Tucumán authorities for a mission in 1770. The spokesman, Chief Raboykin, then thirty, was the son of a previous chief but also evidently possessed a talent for leadership, as he had many followers. The second chief, Aleogtrigkin, was also thirty and a chief's son. The father of Chief Anteoakin, the third emissary, had recently died and left his son the leadership of his sizable band. The remaining Mocobi ambassadors, Antreyok and Echgreyk, were sons of elderly chiefs. In return for tools and cattle, these five Mocobis granted Spanish merchants rights to do business in their lands, although Guaycuruans and Spaniards had different understandings of the extent of the territories in question.[30]

The strength of leadership inheritance rights in Mbayá bands was evidenced in the case of Epilig Iyegi, the ethnically mixed son of Chief Epaquini. Until age ten, Epilig lived at Asunción with his mother, a Payaguá woman.[31] Ethnic mixture was scorned by Mbayás, who professed racial purity, or at least marriage with Guanás of the chiefly class, for the upper classes. Still, Epaquini fetched the boy home and raised him as his political heir, and other Mbayás recognized Epilig's right to succession. The son's leadership ability overcame Mbayá ethnocentrism and concern for purity of lineage. As an adult in the 1760s, Epilig-Lorenzo was useful both to Mbayás and to whites, often mediating between Paraguayans and Mbayás.[32]

Exceptions to the principle of leadership by inheritance were not uncommon, however. Ambitious war leaders frequently competed for prestige and influence with chiefs by birth. An example is Abipon leader Ychoalay, who began his public career in pre-mission society as a war leader, not a chief. Ychoalay was related to Debayakaikin, "who taught him, when he was a boy, to sit a horse," but he grew into a feared adversary of his tutor. Ychoalay and Debayakaikin frequently led their followers to battle against each other. Their political and personal rivalry ended only when Ychoalay and his troops killed and decapitated Debayakaikin. Ychoalay suspended the enemy heads in the center of his settlement, and there he orated before them. In the ceremonial language of the Abipones, the victor praised his men and his rivals, an essential ritual for a victorious leader.[33]

Only those of elevated status in Guaycuruan culture had the right of oration. Among Abipones, for example, only the initiated warrior nobles, hĕcheri, who had earned status by deeds, could boast of their valor. Similarly, Mbayás expected each "captain" to boast of what he had taken from enemies before distributing it to his followers.[34] These discourses served both speakers and audiences, because they increased the prestige of the speaker and reinforced the audience's sense of virtue.

Social Class and Political Allegiance

After acquiring cattle and horses in the early 1600s, three of the Guaycuruan groups that eventually chose missions developed well-defined class structures. Mbayás, Mocobis, and Abipones recognized clear distinctions among chiefs, commoners, and servants, while the Toba enjoyed more social fluidity.[35] Guaycuruan chiefs, unlike shamans, did not display their rank through distinctive dress. In societies with few clothes, especially during torrid Chaco summers, and without economic surpluses, distinctive dress and conspicuous display of possessions would have been ineffective ways to display status. Instead language served a function similar to European sumptuary laws. Distinctive dialects separated chiefs and commoners, men and women, creating social distance.

Class[36] distinctions were most pronounced in Mbayá bands, where even commoners kept multiple slaves (mostly war captives) for menial chores. This caste system was a different type of relationship from that between chiefs and Guaná servants.[37] Mbayás had two categories in the chiefly class: those who inherited and could bequeath status and those who received it as a lifetime-only honor. Life nobles were subordinate to chiefs-by-birth. On a march, blood nobles commanded their own retinues[38] and honorific chiefs attended them.[39]

The size of a chief's following varied according to his charisma, the bounty of the area that he could control, and who his friends and enemies were. The basic social unit was the extended family, and the male head of each family chose which chief the family would follow. Leaders claimed from fifteen to five hundred followers. For the most part a chief's followers constituted a relatively small politico-military unit, but there were exceptions. In 1763, for example, Mocobi Chief Elebogdin represented two subordinate chiefs and four hundred followers. Other groups of similar size existed. The size of political units was highly variable, but with the introduction of iron weapons, horses, and cattle they tended to become larger. The increasing size of basic units probably led Guaycuruans to investigate missions, because larger groups found subsistence increasingly difficult.

Political behavior in missions helps us understand pre-mission Guaycuruan politics. In San Javier de Mocobis, Cacique Nevedagnac claimed the allegiance of four lesser caciques, who led from three to six families each, a total of eighteen families. When Nevedagnac arrived at the mission, however, he had led forty families, about two hundred people. In the mission, twenty-two families chose another leader.[40] An earlier arrival, Cacique Aletin claimed the fealty of no other chief, but still led twenty-four families, roughly 120 people. When Aletin helped found the mission in 1743, he had led about one hundred persons. Cacique Cithaalin himself claimed only three families who directly paid him allegiance. But Caciques Canatnodin and Pahsodin also favored his party, and their followers bolstered Cithaalin's standing. Other San Javier caciques led about twenty-five to fifty people each.

Mbayá regional chiefs customarily represented more people than did Toba, Abipon, or Mocobi chiefs. The Lichagotegodis, an Mbayá band named for the red clay of their habitat, had political units that ranged from two hundred to five hundred persons.[41] The Mbayá band of Chief Epaquini numbered more than six hundred. The larger band size intensified dynastic politics among the Mbayá. Chief Napidrigi assumed his post after caimans ate his brother Conelicogodi, who had no adult son. Another band, the Guetiadegodi, was led by Chief Atenogodi. When he died, his son Golanigi succeeded him. These and other chiefs kept only families, captives, and servants as permanent companions, while ordinary Mbayás lived in the more dispersed fashion of nonsedentary peoples.[42]

The Functions of War

Guaycuruan decision making demonstrates Clausewitz's observation "that war is not a mere act of policy but a true political instrument, a continuation of political activity by other means,"[43] a statement as true of Guaycuruan societies as of European monarchies. Scholars debate causes of "primitive war." Some, such as Alfred Métraux, speculate that Chaco peoples did not really go to war to dominate an enemy or for spoils. Instead, their aims were glory and vengeance. This mistaken argument makes of Guaycuruans and others exotic primitives. Guaycuruans did, as Métraux says, initiate hostilities to avenge wrongs;[44] but as "materialist" authors have shown, Guaycuruans and other preliterate peoples also conducted offensive and defensive war for political and economic reasons. They fought for vengeance and the honor of a war chief and his followers, and for the integrity of their hunting areas. They fought for economic gain, because war brought captives, cattle, and horses. They encroached on neighboring hunting areas while protecting their own, and they fought over the valuable lands closest to creoles. In other words, they fought for territorial reasons. Conflict between Guaycuruans and creoles and between Guaycuruan bands was thus truly warfare, although violent conflict within a band itself was more like a feud, a long-lasting, violent conflict between intimate groups.[45]

Choosing Reductions

Chiefs performed essential services as their bands negotiated for missions. Most risked and some gave their lives as diplomats. In the early 1700s Abipon Chief Chilome went to Corrientes to do business with the city's teniente; there he fell victim to a fearful mob. Similarly, in Paraguay in 1776, Mocobi Chief Etazorin fell afoul of the Paraguayan militia officer in the southern region, whom the chief's independence enraged. The teniente sent him in fetters to Asunción, where he died on the cold bricks of the jail.[46]

In the bands that chose missions,[47] chiefs were central to the decision making. Chiefs and war leaders, as the most persuasive orators in the band, framed the debate and argued their cases. Although the males of the band collectively determined policy, it was the chief who then negotiated with Spanish authorities to realize their followers' wishes, first for peace and later for a mission. No chief could impose a treaty on unwilling followers, but once a band decided to approach Europeans, chiefs were essential brokers.

Among the Toba, too, men delegated to chiefs the duty of negotiating for a mission. In 1776 Toba chief Quetaidy journeyed to Salta and persuaded the governor to promise another Toba reduction. In the interim he convinced his people to be content with staying at the reduction of Macapillo, with whose Pasaínes Quetaidy had a "personal alliance."[48]

The decision to choose missions was a highly contested one. Abipon leaders and elders from the Chaco came to San Jerónimo to discuss peace with Spanish officials. Speakers included Ychoalay and Ychamenraikin from San Jerónimo and visitors Debayakaikin, Kevachichi, and Alaykin. The non-mission faction favored continuing the strategy of making selective truces with certain regions while directing hostilities elsewhere. They argued that a universal peace with Spaniards would sap the vigor of Abipon men. Spaniards could easily subjugate men who forgot martial skills. War brought greater rewards than peace.

The peace faction disagreed. Abipones in missions, they argued, had abundant opportunities to prove their manhood by hunting deer and great cats. The requisite skills for these dangerous pursuits were identical to those needed in war. Beyond the hunt, mission Abipones still had potent enemies. A general peace with Spaniards, its supporters counseled, would let Abipones sleep soundly. Continued war with Spaniards would doom Abipones to extinction. In fact, peace proponents argued, Abipon and Mocobi war prisoners now enslaved on Spanish estates proved exactly this. Courageous in war, Abipones now must be bold enough to conclude a general peace, which is the course most decided on.[49]

Among the bands that chose missions, both chiefs and ambitious, able non-chiefs who pleased priests and civil officials benefited. Spaniards appointed Guaycuruan leaders caciques and called them "Don," giving them greater power than aboriginal chiefs had enjoyed. Most chiefs became caciques, as did non-chiefs with leadership skills and the ability to please Europeans. Cacique Oahari of San Carlos de Timbó, "of mean extraction," nevertheless became a cacique because Europeans saw him as "politic, intrepid, courteous to his own countrymen, and formidable to strangers . . . superior to most of the Abipones in dignity and beauty of person, in dexterity in horsemanship and the handling of weapons, in contempt of danger, and in greatness of mind." His people recognized his talent for leadership, but his cordial relationship with the missionary was the decisive factor. From this, Guaycuruans saw that priests favored certain leaders and neglected others. They recognized priests as political forces in missions and a new element in their lives. They respected priests as they had chiefs and expected priests to redistribute material goods on request, as chiefs had done.[50]

Politics and Governance in Missions

Guaycuruans found their once-simple political system became more complex when they entered missions. The mission village, modeled on Spanish municipalities, gave Guaycuruan leaders a political structure with opportunities for promotion. Spaniards appointed Guaycuruans of the aboriginal leadership class to a variety of civil offices, including corregidor, alcalde, and *regidor.* It is unlikely, however, that Guaycuruan *cabildos,* or town councils, ever took on the complex functions of their counterparts in central Mexico,[51] owing to the differences in indigenous political traditions. In the new Mocobi reduction of Ispín (or Inispín) in 1799, as was characteristic of other missions, one Mocobi became *fiscal* and two others were *alcaldes.* These judicial and political offices had no counterparts in the indigenous world.

The Spanish monarchy required local elites to assist in ruling their far-flung empire. Therefore, Spanish officials adopted the term *cacique,* actually a West Indian title, and awarded it like a title of nobility to the Indians they recognized as having the highest level of native authority in a mission. In missions, caciques exercised civil authority in the name of the king,[52] and the monarch's prestige reinforced their own. Spanish policymakers assumed that in awarding this title, they were legitimating preexisting aboriginal leadership and introducing Indians to the concept of a European-style hereditary aristocracy. In fact, this policy had unintended effects. Guaycuruans already recognized hereditary succession; their leaders simply did not have the material trappings that were symbols of leadership to Europeans. Partly because Spaniards did not differentiate war leaders from hereditary chiefs, and partly because they used mission offices as a tool to promote acculturation, they frequently promoted ambitious war leaders who were willing to accommodate European interests over more independent-minded traditional chiefs. Thus, Spaniards frequently undermined rather than reinforcing aboriginal hereditary leadership.[53]

Most Guaycuruan missions contained several caciques. In San Ignacio de Tobas in 1778, two caciques shared the leadership. Cacique Juan Manuel Tesodi had 191 followers. The other 192 were led by Cacique Santiago Quimadin.[54] In Nuestra Señora de Concepción de Abipones, Cacique Alaykin, a war leader of non-noble birth, became the first cacique in the new mission. Later the hereditary chiefs in the mission—Malakin, Ypirikin, Oaikin, and Zapanche—were all named caciques.

Among the caciques in a mission, Spaniards selected one as the main leader, or *cacique principal,* and considered the others lesser leaders, a hierarchy that was completely foreign to Guaycuruan understanding. Spaniards awarded the caciques thin, short staffs known as *bastones de mando* (or *varas*) as symbols of office. The cacique principal typically received a silver-tipped staff, while staffs tipped in base metals were given to those the Spaniards considered lesser leaders.[55] In the 1770s, Chaco Mocobi chiefs Paikin and Queyaberi treasured silver-tipped staffs, while those receiving ones with tips of base metals were insulted. Since the hierarchy of leadership among caciques was of Spanish imposition, it probably had little meaning to Guaycuruans, and in part silver staffs were valued simply because they were rarer.[56]

Caciques' personal status symbols were omnipresent. In San Javier and other missions, the male mission elite alone received not only staffs but also Spanish hats. They developed personal ties to Spanish elites. At Cithaalin's baptism, for example, Lieutenant Governor Vera Múxica of Santa Fe became his godfather. Corregidor Nevedagnac became godson of Francisco de Echagüe, and the corregidor's brother was the godson of Narciso de Echagüe, members of a leading family of Santa Fe. These ceremonies linked important Mocobi and Spanish families.[57]

Native leaders in missions welcomed their elevation to cacique status and enhanced power. Most enjoyed improved economic status, reinforcing their new political role. In San Javier, for example, previously poor Mocobi chiefs became caciques who owned ranches and fields. Although the mission had its own common fields and ranches,[58] Caciques Nalaguin, José Nedlaniguin, Quevagij, Domingo Nevedagnac, Juan Canotdin, and Passodin had their own estancias.[59] Abipon Cacique Laberequin in 1759 maintained a personal estancia with ten thousand head of cattle.

Caciques also gained limited powers of coercion. Their once merely persuasive oratory became more forceful. During an epidemic, Cacique Aletin ordered men to dig graves for the dead, and they complied. Caciques also convinced women to spin and dye cloth, as missionaries urged, whereas men never would have interfered in women's occupations previously. Militarily, caciques in San Javier resembled white commanders, as their forces became more hierarchical. Two twenty-man patrols under lesser caciques regularly protected the mission. These secondary commanders served under an overall Mocobi head.

The careers of Cithaalin, Aletin, and Nevedagnac of San Javier de Mocobis showed the new opportunities for leaders in missions. Cithaalin arrived at San Javier first, next came Aletin, and finally Nevedagnac joined the mission. Although all three became caciques, Aletin learned most quickly how to please priests and elevated his position over Cithaalin's, despite his humbler lineage. Aletin's attendance at religious services and his respectful attitude toward whites caused priests to think of him as a "noble Indian." This favoritism was significant, because priests had patronage to dispense. Aletin's first reward was the vara, the symbol of nobility, and the next was his appointment as foreman of the mission estancia. In his new capacity, he directed and coerced subordinates, something pre-mission Guaycuruan chiefs could not have done.

Cithaalin, on the other hand, was less willing to mold himself to the priests' expectations. A famed warrior, he irritated priests by expecting them to pay his children for their work. He often withdrew his own children from the mission school to hunt, which missionaries considered frivolous. Cithaalin also regularly met with lay Spaniards, whom priests considered corrupting influences. He disrupted the mission by quarreling with his former brother-in-law Nevedagnac, whom Mocobis and Spaniards alike eventually recognized as the highest Mocobi authority in San Javier. Furthermore, Cithaalin kept two wives. For a time, therefore, priests withheld from him the silver vara. In time Cithaalin learned to please priests, and he too got the prized staff, symbolizing his status as a "co-captain" of San Javier.[60]

Nevedagnac, now Don Domingo Nevedagnac, ultimately became the leading Native American official in the mission. For years he had resisted mission life and had continued raiding around Córdoba. When he joined San Javier, probably in the early 1750s, the respect of Mocobis and his pleasing demeanor earned him the staff of command. Ultimately, the governor appointed Nevedagnac corregidor of San Javier.[61] Nevedagnac also won a Spanish militia appointment as *maestre de campo* commanding Mocobi troops. He spoke for Mocobi interests and increasingly decided Mocobi issues in San Javier. By 1780 he had learned the forms of Spanish municipal government and could deal effectively with the Spanish bureaucracy.[62] Teniente Riva Herrera of Santa Fe, for example, communicated with Mocobis who aspired to join a mission through Cacique Domingo.[63]

In San Jerónimo, Abipon war leader Ychoalay, who later took the name José Benavides, showed how men of humble birth could rise. Not an indigenous chief, he won from Spaniards the title of cacique and later became corregidor, the highest Indian office in Platine missions.[64] As Spanish accounts record, Abipon leaders "Ychoalay, Kevachichi, Tannerchin, and others . . . the most fortunate chiefs of the whole nation, became diligent above the rest in ploughing and building . . . ."[65] Ychoalay assisted secular authorities and pleased the priests by encouraging Abipones to honor Catholic rituals. In 1752, for example, he helped recover horses stolen by his long-standing enemies, Abipones of Concepción. In contrast, the first cacique of the new mission, Ychamenraikin, a chief by birth, was uninterested in pleasing priests and never prospered in the new setting. Ychoalay's courting of the priests of San Jerónimo and civil authorities in Santa Fe raised him above the more traditional Ychamenraikin, who had inherited status but was too attached to Abipon traditions to grasp new opportunities. He divorced several wives and frequently drank to stupefaction. Ychoalay, although an enthusiastic militarist to the end of his life, kept but one wife, avoided drinking rituals, attended Christian services, and urged others to follow his example.

Perhaps one reason for Ychoalay-Benavides' success was that he respected traditional customs of leadership even as he increased his authority in the mission. He carefully avoided presuming to ape the Abipon upper class, always using the dialect of commoners,[66] to avoid giving offense. He distributed some of his own cattle to other Abipones and customarily was more generous with his own possessions than with those of the mission. This echoing of the redistribution policies of indigenous chiefs was one reason why he was able to maintain leadership.[67] When he got a hat decorated with silver, for example, he gave it to the first man who asked for it properly. By combining traditional and transitional behaviors, Ychoalay managed to please both Spanish officials and Abipon followers.

Even as non-hereditary leaders were appointed caciques in missions, Guaycuruans invented new means of distinguishing traditional hereditary leaders from others. The Mbayá borrowed Spanish honorific terms, including the designation *capitán*. Among the Mbayá chiefly class (*niniotagi*) at Belén, about twenty men were "captains," an honor open only to those inheriting chieftainships or paired at birth with a chief's son. No one else received the title, no matter how valorous.[68]

Although Guaycuruan caciques were subordinate to the imperial government,[69] how much direction they actually took from priests depended on the wishes of the people of the mission, who continued to exercise considerable influence. If they were offended by mission policies the people were willing and able to leave. Mission caciques who represented their people blended old traditions of persuasion by oratory and reputation with a sensitivity to the increased leadership responsibilities in missions. As a result Guaycuruan leaders often found it in their personal interest to support Spanish imperialism, but they did not always promote Spanish interests over the interests of their own people. At San Fernando, Debayakaikin slaughtered cattle that priests wanted left alive.[70] When young followers of Abipon Cacique Alaykin in Concepción conducted raids against Santa Fe, Alaykin claimed these hostilities were beyond his control, even though his son Pachieke had led the attacks.[71] Similarly, in 1775 authorities rode from Santa Fe to San Jerónimo to stop contraband exchanges on mission lands, but the alcaldes and caciques refused to help.[72]

Even Ychoalay, who appeared to be the model of Indian assimilation, was far from a pawn in Spanish hands. Spaniards assumed that in casting his lot with theirs, Ychoalay had renounced Abipon ways. In fact he had not done so, and his reality was more complex than a syncretic progression from indigenous to Spanish. As cacique, Ychoalay continued to champion the interests of his Riikahés. Many later battles ostensibly fought on behalf of whites were really contests with his own Native American enemies. Their threat had pushed him to San Jerónimo.

Guaycuruans carried to missions the conviction that they should select their own leaders. When they opposed a mission's leadership, whether Guaycuruan or European, they left, especially in the early years. In the 1750s, Chief Debayakaikin and his people came to San Fernando. When the chief chose to quit the mission, his group split into three factions. Some stayed in the mission. Others switched their allegiance from Debayakaikin to Chief Oaherkaikin, whose people still traveled but at times lived within sight of San Fernando, and others followed Debayakaikin. In April 1786 Abipon families fled Concepción to Fort San Nicolás in Santa Fe. They wanted a mission but did not wish to stay at Concepción. They elected to follow the Mocobi cacique of San Javier, instead of the Abipones of San Jerónimo, whom they feared. They remained at San Nicolás for years because Spanish notions of ethnicity failed to comprehend Guaycuruan reality. The viceroy prevented them from joining the Mocobis, because they were Abipones.[73]

When mission conditions outraged only a few, they retained the option of flight, because the Chaco remained unconquered until the late nineteenth century. Although environmental changes made the Chaco less hospitable after 1740 than earlier, it still provided refuge. At times, entire populations of missions departed. Hostilities pushed all Abipones from Timbó in 1767 and from San Fernando in the 1770s. At other times, only one faction fled. On June 30, 1808, for example, the San Ignacio Toba of Cacique Feliciano Juárez departed because they opposed the mission leadership, including the priest and the Toba corregidor. They objected to the labor policy of the mission leaders and the interim governor-intendant of Salta. The remaining faction advised the authorities on how to capture the runaways, but two and a half months later they were still missing.[74]

Spaniards hoped that hereditary succession to mission offices would promote European notions of aristocracy. Sometimes it did. In 1758, the cacique principal of San Fernando de Abipones, Neriguey, died, leaving the office to his son, Fernando.[75] In San Fernando and San Javier, Abipones and Mocobis also continued the tradition of family leadership. In San Javier de Mocobis, Cacique and Corregidor Don Domingo Nevedagnac bequeathed both honors to his son, Don Manuel Nevedagnac, who headed the mission in the late 1780s. Descendants of founder Cacique Naré filled important positions at San Fernando at the turn of the nineteenth century. Don Gregorio Naré was the leading cacique of the reduction, and his assertiveness caused the Corrientes cabildo to request his removal. The family also presented Pedro Naré as regidor to the San Fernando cabildo in 1800 and 1803.[76]

At other times, hereditary succession did not take root, at least not immediately. Though influential, Ychoalay–José Benavides could not impose a dynasty. After his death in 1776, the aged Laberequin, a successful Abipon rancher with an estancia of ten thousand cattle, was appointed the next corregidor. He gave Spaniards no trouble, but the teniente of Santa Fe removed him from office for ineffective leadership. The next corregidor, Damaso Queran (Kera), was appointed for "his love for the Spanish," but he proved to be independent-minded. He personally asked the viceroy to protect his people from the meddling bureaucrats in Santa Fe.

After Queran died in late 1780, Miguel Jerónimo Benavides, Ychoalay's son, became corregidor. He, like Queran, resisted officials in Santa Fe. The younger Benavides troubled Spanish officials, who wished to remove him from office for his independence and his observance of Guaycuruan ways. Officials reluctantly concluded, however, that removing him from office was more trouble than it was worth.[77] Guaycuruan leaders who held the trust of their people, as both Benavides father and son did, had room for maneuver, despite their dependence on Spaniards.

After Jesuits left in 1767, Guaycuruan caciques became even more authoritative. Many missions were left with ineffective missionaries or with no priests at all, so caciques now mediated directly between missions and the Spanish communities from which they drew subsidies. When the government in the 1780s and 1790s sent subventions of cattle and sheep to San Javier and San Jerónimo, the animals were delivered to the caciques principales,[78] who were also corregidores. In another example, Corregidor Don Damaso Queran (Kera) of San Jerónimo clashed with the missionary, Friar José de Córdoba, and drove the cleric from the mission in late 1770s.[79] When a fire devastated San Jerónimo in 1769, Cacique José Benavides oversaw its reconstruction. He procured builders, peones, and lumber, and approached the teniente of Santa Fe for a subvention. Miguel Jerónimo Benavides took other actions on behalf of the disgruntled Abipones of San Jerónimo. He carried to the viceroy a dispute with José Tarragona, the anti-Abipon administrator of the Guaycuruan missions of Santa Fe. When Abipones hungered in 1788, he brought relief. Knowing that Santafecinos valued the mission as a buffer between Santa Fe and the Chaco, he threatened to move his people away so they could survive. Hearing the cacique's plan, the viceroy quickly ordered Santa Fe to give the Abipon mission what Benavides wanted.[80]

Corregidor Miguel Jerónimo Benavides' position was secure enough he could defy Spanish authorities on noncritical matters. Having married a woman in the mission church, he rejected her in Abipon fashion and took a new wife. His flouting of Christian vows angered the priest, who reported him to civil authorities. When a Paraguayan arrived at the reduction with a Guarani woman he had abducted, Benavides rejected the priest's advice to arrest the felon and instead allowed him to escape. When the priest and the teniente ordered Benavides to a hearing in Santa Fe, he ignored them. The teniente could not enforce his order. Because mission Abipones continued to wield substantial military power on a violent frontier with few Spanish soldiers, Benavides was thus in limited ways able to live a life that suited him and troubled white authorities.[81]

Another mission cacique who dealt directly with Spanish authorities was Corregidor Don Domingo Nevedagnac of San Javier. He petitioned the government of Santa Fe to retain missionary father Julián Obelar, whom Mocobis liked.[82] In San Fernando, Abipon Cacique Naré also appealed unsuccessfully to Corrientes when the mission priest deserted.

The cacique promised to lead his followers from the mission. He and his people did not, however, return to the Chaco. Instead they went to San Jerónimo, the Abipon mission near Santa Fe.[83] Later they refounded San Fernando.

Toba Cacique Pognagari of San Bernardo and Mocobi Cacique Lachitiqui of Cangayé confronted problems of mission survival in 1790. Their mission priests had deserted to Corrientes, eighty leagues away, and unlike Benavides, Pognagari and Lachitiqui were unable to negotiate effectively with Spanish civil authorities. Thus the missions deteriorated,[84] and eventually some of the residents moved to the Chaco bank of the Río Paraguay while others dispersed in the interior.

Despite changes, many political and martial practices remained unaltered or altered only slightly in the mission environment, at least in the first few generations. Personal allegiances and band alliances displayed continuity. The continuity of pre-mission political relationships was revealed when a party of non-mission Mocobis and Toba raided San Jerónimo de Abipones. Two factions in the Mocobi mission of San Javier responded in very different ways. Aletin and his soldiers raced to protect San Jerónimo, whose leaders were then their allies. They counterattacked, saving the Abipones' cattle and horses and taking for themselves enemy heads as badges of honor. The leader of the other faction was Cithaalin, normally a vigorous war leader, who on this occasion dallied in San Javier. That the one cacique responded quickly and the other reluctantly, missionaries suggested, was because of their respective acceptance and rejection of Christianity. It is more likely, however, that the two leaders responded differently because of previous political relationships, not Hispanization in matters of religion.

Many war practices remained unaffected by missionary influences. The leaders of Abipon San Jerónimo and Mocobi San Javier, for example, cooperated during most of the Jesuit period, reflecting the alliances that the peoples brought to missions. Under leaders of the late 1770s, however, the two missions fought bitterly, continuing the Guaycuruan tradition of feuds with reprisals and revenge. Mocobis of San Javier continued to take enemy heads and to kidnap their enemies' children. Victors decorated their horses with trophies, including the ears and noses of fallen foes.[85]

In the end, however, acculturation occurred in war as in other aspects of Guaycuruan life. Guaycuruan political and military leaders increasingly copied their Spanish counterparts. Of the Abipon volunteer members of the company of Santa Fe in 1803, eighty carried muskets. This formidable fighting force showed Abipon acceptance of European discipline. They coordinated their activities with imperial troops and later joined independence armies.[86]

Justice

In aboriginal society, Guaycuruan leaders typically refused to intervene in questions of justice, and disputants settled cases privately. As new leaders in missions involved themselves in disputes, a formerly private process became a public function. For example, when a Mocobi visiting San Jerónimo butchered a cow from Ychoalay's personal estancia, the cacique exiled him, although he could have killed him according to traditional law.

Some caciques became magistrates, a function unknown in Guaycuruan governance, and priests encouraged this enlargement of responsibility. Cithaalin of San Javier even attempted to act as both judge and executioner, which neither Guaycuruan nor Spanish law sanctioned. Cacique Aletin also acted coercively. Once he punished a mestizo peon for having sex with a Mocobi woman. Another time, he ordered a Mocobi girl who had sex with a married man to receive twelve lashes. The girl's father had originally sought justice in the old, private way, by trying to kill her.[87]

War and Diplomacy in Missions

Mission Guaycuruans still regarded war as honorable. War and peace were the most important policy choices in Guaycuruan societies. Local and long-distance contests were waged for domination and trophies and for valuable prizes, including power, female captives, and horses. Whether potential enemies were Christians was unimportant; Guaycuruan bands primarily weighed Native American considerations. First- and second-generation mission leaders accepted Europeans' advice in matters of war only when they had already decided on the course of action.

Ychoalay is an example of a leader focused on war, his main interest. He saw it as a way to increase his own wealth and influence, as well as for Abipon fighting men to remain as proud as those of past decades. Through war, Ychoalay, a new man of the mission culture, preserved his heritage, combating old enemies with new allies.

Missions now became logistical centers for carrying out pre-mission feuds. Building on his aboriginal war leadership, Ychoalay pursued factional quarrels inside San Jerónimo and war outside with other Abipones and with Toba and Mocobi groups. He favored peace with Spaniards in order to make war on rival Native Americans.[88] One old enemy was Chief Oaherkaikin, who was an ally of Cacique Debayakaikin of Concepción. Oaherkaikin had remained hostile after most of his band made peace with Spaniards. He and his men plundered Paraguay, which intensified friction among mission Abipones and infuriated Ychoalay, who had trade relationships with Paraguayan merchants. When Ychoalay sought to liberate captured property from the insurgents, the combined forces of Debayakaikin and Oaherkaikin outnumbered his own. Ychoalay lost the battle and retreated to San Jerónimo. The encounter presaged two decades of war between opposing bands of Abipones in and out of missions.[89]

Enmity between the Riikahé Abipones of San Jerónimo and the San Fernando Abipones antedated missions and characterized their early years there. Strife migrated from the indigenous Chaco to reductions, where new conflicts arose. From 1748 to 1767, Ychoalay's folk fought mostly with other Abipones from San Fernando. This conflict was especially dear to his heart, because San Fernando's leadership included Ychoalay's hated cousins and nephews.[90] In 1762 Ychoalay's people exchanged raids on horse herds with Abipones of San Fernando. Yet in an example of the complex factionalism of Guaycuruan politics, Cacique Naré of San Fernando led a peace party that opposed the anti-Ychoalay warriors. Nevertheless, the war party prevailed, and hostilities between San Fernando and San Jerónimo continued from the 1750s into the 1760s. Naré became a laughingstock in San Fernando for his efforts at mediation.[91]

In missions as before, no political allegiance necessarily attached to an Abipon, Mocobi, Toba or Mbayá identity. In the 1750s and 1760s, San Jerónimo Abipones often allied with Mocobis from San Javier to fight other Abipones. On one occasion, Debayakaikin's Abipon warriors attacked San Jerónimo de Abipones, stealing horses and killing the drovers. While his people defended their homes,[92] Ychoalay asked Santa Fe officials for thirty soldiers to crush his enemies; but he overplayed his hand. Santafecinos refused: they would protect the mission, not conduct offensive operations. Unable to enlist Spaniards in his war aims, Ychoalay persuaded anti-Debayakaikin Abipones from Concepción and Mocobis from San Javier to join him. The allied force pushed the wounded Debayakaikin and followers north, where they took refuge with friends in San Fernando. Jesuits there oversaw Debayakaikin's return of booty to San Jerónimo and arranged a temporary truce.[93]

The hostility between Ychoalay's adherents in San Jerónimo and the residents of San Fernando had been intense in the 1750s even before Naré came to power. Ychoalay and his rival Petizo in San Fernando led men into battle against each other frequently. In the late 1750s, the Abipones of San Jerónimo killed Petizo, and Cacique Naré became leader of San Fernando, ascendant but not unchallenged. Guevachin, Ychoalay's uncle and enemy, tried unsuccessfully to influence policy in San Fernando, but Naré, in time, established his authority. Naré could now deal with Ychoalay unencumbered by factionalism at home.[94]

The Naré-Ychoalay conflict lasted into the early 1760s. Whites usually abstained from the fighting, although the Corrientes militia tried to force raiding Abipones back to San Fernando. One patrol in 1762 tried to reconcile the warring Abipon groups; the fifty-man Spanish unit could not risk a fight, however, because the Abipon military potential exceeded that of the Corrientes contingent.[95]

After the Abipones of Debayakaikin took refuge in San Fernando, they faced attacks from Mocobis as well as from other Abipones. During Debayakaikin's earlier war on the Santa Fe missions, mounted from Concepción de Abipones, his men killed Cacique Ychamenraikin of San Jerónimo. Ychoalay sagely convinced colonial authorities that Debayakaikin's wrath arose from resentment over the friendship between the people of San Jerónimo mission and the Spanish. Although untrue, this explanation was what the Spanish wanted to hear. Believing Ychoalay, the creoles mounted a joint punitive expedition against Debayakaikin. Ychoalay's men obtained Spanish saddles and iron lances, giving them battlefield superiority over an adversary more traditionally armed. Finally, Ychoalay and his men found and slew Debayakaikin and displayed his head in their mission.[96]

The dispute also ensnared Cacique Alaykin of Concepción, who supported Debayakaikin. Alaykin encouraged his followers to rustle from ranchers of Santa Fe, Ychoalay's allies, and ignored priestly protests. In addition to seeking profit, Alaykin wished to embarrass Ychoalay. In response, Ychoalay led a force of Spaniards and Abipones to Concepción. Intimidated, the opponents returned their prizes while Ychoalay rubbed salt in the wound. Priests arranged a brief truce between the peoples, who detested each other. Renewed conflict brought Alaykin's death in 1753.[97]

After the coming of missions, Guaycuruan warfare grew more complex, as disputes among Spanish locales and various Guaycuruan groups took shape. In a military exercise of 1758, Aletin, Cithaalin, and seventy-one Mocobi militia of San Javier protected Abipones of San Jerónimo from attack by enemy Abipones from the Chaco. The men of San Javier simultaneously served their own and Spanish interests, because of the amity between the bands in San Jerónimo and San Javier in the 1750s and early 1760s, a cooperation antedating the founding of either mission.[98]

The bitterest warfare among mission Guaycuruans occurred in the 1770s and 1780s. On the one side, the Abipones of San Jerónimo—followers of Ychoalay and after his death Lachiriquin, Damaso Queran, and Miguel Jerónimo Benavides—battled numerous enemies, including several Mocobi Chaco chiefs, of whom Paikin was the best known. Paikin's followers were connected by blood and interest to the Mocobis of San Pedro and through them to San Javier de Mocobis. The Chaco Mocobis visited relatives in San Pedro and raided San Jerónimo. The aggrieved Abipones always retaliated, usually on San Pedro.

At about the same time, Cacique Ychoalay-Benavides of San Jerónimo pressed his war against northern Mocobi chiefs, including Etazorin, Paikin's son, who inherited the feud with Ychoalay from his father. Benavides allied with Governor Agustín Fernando de Pinedo of Paraguay, where Etazorin raided. Worried officials in Santa Fe begged the Paraguayan governor to appease Etazorin. Facing a two-front war, Etazorin agreed to a mission in the Paraguayan Chaco and to make peace with Jerónimo.[99]

The Mocobi-Abipon war of the missions of Santa Fe in the late 1770s and 1780s was mostly a Guaycuruan not Hispanic episode. It began as a conflict not between Abipones and Mocobis but between groups and leaders across "tribal" lines. In fact, in 1775, Mocobi Cacique Domingo Nevedagnac of San Javier warned San Jerónimo Abipones about a surprise attack by Mocobi Paikin. In early 1775, defenders of San Jerónimo killed Paikin. Although Ychoalay-Benavides died the next year, Paikin's death enlarged the conflict, as Paikin's heirs were linked to both San Pedro and to San Javier.[100]

The combats of the Guaycuruan missions of Santa Fe involved between a score and several hundred warriors and spread to Corrientes and Paraguay. The conflict continued into the 1780s, impoverishing all parties. Although Guaycuruans glorified war, they fought intermittently. War was costly. The death of even a few men or the loss of several women was a calamity. Thus, making peace was also vital. In 1783 the beleaguered Abipones made peace with the Mocobi missions.[101]

The Mocobis of San Javier continued Guaycuruan ways of war—raiding for profit, feuds, and reprisals—but missions slowly altered these practices. Influences included advice of Jesuits, subsidies, and the threat of Spanish forces. The resultant decline in intensity of their war effort convinced Spaniards that Mocobis enthusiastically accepted European ways, a distorted perception, although many traditional Mocobi enemies now became enemies of Santa Fe. Exalting in combat, Mocobis fought old foes and discovered new ones. Between 1743 and 1764, San Javier Mocobis fought their own enemies and those of Santa Fe in twenty-one battles. They gained payment in kind from Santa Fe, usually horses, and booty from defeated enemies.[102] San Javier Mocobis welcomed these assignments because war, man's highest calling, was profitable.

In the northern Chaco, Mbayá warfare differed slightly from that of distant Guaycuruans in missions to the south. The two bands with lands nearest to Spaniards received the missions of Belén and Refugio in their own territories, and after 1760 they had few serious quarrels with each other. Belén Mbayás raided other Jesuit missions, however, including the Guarani and Chiquitos missions. Raiding remained important for mission Mbayás, who fought for captives to bolster their own sagging population and to sell to Paraguayans, who purchased piezas into the late colonial era.[103] Like Abipones and Mocobis, Mbayás in and out of missions allied with Spaniards militarily.

Because Mbayá missions were on the frontier between the Spanish and Portuguese empires, different patterns of politics and war emerged there. The Apacachodegodegis thought of Belén as home, but they were often on the move. The Lichagotegodis continued to live around the defunct Refugio after the short-lived mission disappeared in the 1770s. In the 1790s, four Mbayá bands remained neutral in the Spanish-Portuguese conflict. These non-mission groups profited from the imperial rivalry and won concessions from both sides, including cloth, knives, food, and trading rights.[104]

Conclusion

After Guaycuruans joined missions and while Spanish benefits were still substantial, their assaults declined. Many still took livestock from distant Spanish jurisdictions, and individuals sought meat and hides closer to home. But military efforts against creoles waned as mission peoples traded mobility for subsidies. Mission Guaycuruans who threatened white society courted disaster.[105]

Eventually, the upheavals of the independence period destroyed Guaycuruan missions. North of Santa Fe, many Guaycuruans remained near their old missions, although the institutional structures were shattered. In the organized violence of the wars of independence, however, many Guaycuruans found employment as soldiers. Mocobi Cacique Alaiquin led the men of San Javier into battle behind José Artigas and in 1816 served Governor Vera Múxica of Santa Fe.[106]

In pre-mission and mission settings, Guaycuruans practiced collective decision making. In the volitional and factional Guaycuruan system, adult males chose missions. Those not attracted to mission life kept their families away, and those who came but found missions too confining or emasculating left. For those in missions, their political systems became more complex while still retaining traditional features.

The factional political system of the Chaco meshed with the hierarchical, authoritarian demands of mission life. Old ways of decision making, though, persisted, partly because Guaycuruans were not subjugated with the military finality of the peoples of Mesoamerica and the Andes.

Political elites in missions gained prestige and power. Some became relatively affluent. Leaders by birth spoke with an authority reinforced by European support. They were joined by upwardly mobile "commoners." All exercised more influence, authority, and coercive power than leaders had in the Chaco. As before, they represented their people to strangers and persuaded them to action by oratory, but in the missions they began to give orders and judge transgressors.

At the time of the Plata region's de facto independence in 1810, Guaycuruan political practices were still in transition between the old consensual-factional decision making and the new, Hispanic system, in which the voice of the governed counted less. Guaycuruan military habits changed as well in the world of missions. The major decision groups faced was no longer whether to attack whites. Even bands outside missions were increasingly reluctant to raid white communities. But they still honored war and fought each other. When the winds of independence blew missions away, the Guaycuruan capacity for violence was still formidable.

CHAPTER 6

Religion

Religious beliefs[1] explained the world to the peoples of the Gran Chaco. Their religious complex sanctioned hunting and war. It embodied forces that could either cure or kill. Economic and political alterations triggered by animals and artifacts of European origin gradually altered Guaycuruan religious beliefs. This chapter will explore indigenous Guaycuruan religious beliefs and how they changed with missions.

Guaycuruans in missions revitalized their culture. Although attracted to Catholic concepts, they reacted against the missionaries' attack on their religion. Substantial numbers of people rejected Christianity and departed the missions. Ironically, the missionaries' preaching gave people secular explanations for events formerly understood as supernatural, because missionaries of the 1740s purveyed a partly naturalistic universe. That is, priests often interpreted everyday matters—from writing, to clocks, to vegetable laxatives—in light of the science of the eighteenth century. Naturalistic, or "cause and effect explanations based on natural laws rather than explanations which rely on supernatural powers of intervention in human affairs,"[2] undermined the basis of Guaycuruans' spiritual lives.

Creators and Other Supernatural Beings

Guaycuruans recognized a spiritual creator, or "Great Ancestor," who made the world and pointed the way to a proper life. The Mocobis called him Kotaá, "our father," and conceived of him as a benefactor. The Caduveo, an Mbayá band of the twentieth century, identified Onoenrgodi (Onoenrodi) as the creator of all Indians, Brazilians, and Portuguese.[3]

This ancestor ruled the land of the dead, and believers associated him with the afterworld. The Abipones' Great Ancestor, Queebet, was endowed with positive human and spiritual attributes. More venerated than worshiped, Queebet was affectionately nicknamed Groaperikie, meaning "grandfather." He was, Abipones believed, the benefactor of all. To Spaniards he gave gold, silver, and clothing, and to Abipones courage.[4] Represented in the heavens by the Pleiades, Queebet sickened and left the southern sky each spring but returned in May. The people welcomed him back, saying, "*Quemen naachic latenc! layàm nauichi ena*" ("What thanks do we owe thee! And art thou returned at last? Ah, thou hast happily recovered!"). Abipones celebrated his return with a communal drinking festival. Led by a (sometimes female) shaman, the married men drank to ecstasy, their women attended them and sang loudly, and unmarried adults provided the audience. Queebet, through the shaman, then bestowed on favored men greater skill in hunting and war. The religious professional who officiated at this ceremony was called Queebet as well, meaning "one who made things contrary to what they were and one of superior capacity," a phrase describing the spirit's attributes. His human representatives could know or divine all things, cure diseases, cause great storms, and even detect another person's secrets. Some were called to their profession by Queebet, who gave them their special powers; others got their powers from less-celebrated spirits.[5]

The sky was peopled with heavenly spirits that intervened in the Chaco peoples' world. Some among them protected animals and could assume human shapes. Other spirits possessed human characteristics.[6] Some of these spirits had names, others did not. Shamans could summon both named and unnamed spirits. Most spirits were potentially malevolent, some merely mischievous. Humans, largely defenseless, feared these powers, who had the power to steal souls.[7]

Although Guaycuruans did not invoke supernatural beings in the Christian sense as determiners of man's destiny, they nevertheless struggled for their souls with malevolent spirits. Malign powers were omnipresent. "No place nor time was free from danger and anxiety to the Abipones." Dreams connected the Toba to "levels of nonhuman reality."[8] Their dreams continually foretold attacks from enemy infiltrators who could take the form of insects. "A certain species of beetle, humming at an unlucky moment was . . . a spy belonging to the enemy."[9] The Toba *payak*—hostile spirits living in trees, water, or animals—could plague individuals. Mbayá men feared the *ayamarigodi* and women the *guayemagayego,* evil presences that caused general misery.[10] A favored few humans could magically combat these spirits with powers given them by their Great Ancestor.[11] These magical powers were the most valid and useful sort of knowledge a human could have.[12] They took ritual precautions against sinister powers. The only good spirits were those a person could control with magical powers. Unpropitiated spirits brought illness, death, military defeat, and departure of game.

Guaycuruans were proud militarists. Their beliefs gave religious sanction to combative urges. The Mbayá believed the spirit Karakará awarded choice hunting lands to all peoples except them. Last in line, Mbayás found that no lands remained for them. Instead, Karakará awarded them bows and arrows, the mission of conquering others, and the bravery and skill to take things by force.[13] In the 1940s, Caduveo informants, descendants of Mbayás, said that all Indians were pulled from a hole in the ground by Onoé-noé, both a Caduveo and a god. Later, while waiting for land, the impatient Mbayá went hunting. This lack of deference angered Onoé-noé, and he condemned them to a hunting life forever.[14]

Cosmology

Uninterested in linear history, Guaycuruans acknowledged their origins but did not stress creation. One starry night in the 1750s, for example, Jesuit Father Martin Dobrizhoffer asked Abipon leader Ychoalay to consider the heavens. Must not this majestic scene, the priest inquired, be guided by an omnipotent being? The Abipon, a friend of the priest's, replied that his people were more concerned about water and pasturage for their horses than with knowing who ruled the skies.[15] He probably meant that Abipones were more interested in the spirits that controlled grass and rain than the more remote ones in the heavens.[16]

Myths surrounded the various heavenly bodies. The Guaycuruan sky was a personified being. It had changed places with the earth to avoid getting dirty. Mocobis believed lunar eclipses occurred when celestial dogs ate the moon, bringing pestilence on earth. For the Toba, dogs chased a rhea into heaven and became the stars.[17] Departed shamans announced their descent to earth through meteors or thunderclaps.

Most Chaco cultures conceived of the universe as tripartite, with a subworld, the earth, and a super world. The progenitors of the Notokowit Tobas ascended from a malicious subterranean world to the earth. In the super world, one found good hunting and abundant honey. A tree of union once had connected earth and the firmament, but a vengeful person broke the connection. Heavenly hunters were cut off from earth and became stars. Mocobis had a similar myth: A giant tree once connected earth and sky, but a vengeful old woman destroyed the tree and punished all Mocobis by cutting off their access to the heavenly hunting grounds.[18]

Guaycuruans accounted for the how women arrived on Earth in several ways. Some said a woman existed before other people. Others thought that the Great Ancestor ejaculated into a pot and begot boys. From them he made girls.[19]

Supernatural powers demanded that Guaycuruans maintain an ecological balance and harmonize with their natural environment. North American and Chaco indigenous religions were similar with regard to beliefs about hunting. Both taught that hunting had a spiritual context. Concern and sensitivity for nature characterized the world of hunters. The Toba, like all Guaycuruan peoples, were ecologists long before such a word was coined who were concerned with maintaining a balance with their environment. A reciprocal spiritual relationship between humans and animals characterized the Guaycuruan world. Hunters believed that every animal had a soul that gave it fighting ability. Human souls at death transported themselves to animals' bodies. Animals in turn sacrificed themselves for humankind, but animals' and insects' souls could also be dangerous. Hunters propitiated the spirits that controlled game such as deer and jaguars and protected themselves from the slain animal's spirit through shamanic activity and religious rituals.[20] The Guaycuruans had a weaker but still significant spiritual connection with the plant world. For example, the sun was a female who was the first harvester of the wild algarroba, a dietary staple.[21]

Domestic animals, acquired after contact, remained ideologically insignificant in traditional Guaycuruan belief. They did not join the Guaycuruan spirit world until long after Guaycuruans were in regular contact with them, possibly in the eighteenth and nineteenth centuries. Caduveos in the 1940s knew of two domestic animal spirits. One was Nakotákra, a bull-like creature that lived in water and raped bathing women. A similar spirit, Emariko-kone, appeared as a burro and preyed on pretty girls.[22]

Aboriginal Guaycuruans depended on nature for subsistence and avoided owning animals, although they killed, ate, and wore them. As in North America, people in the Chaco saw themselves as competing with animals, whose spiritual protectors staved off the animals' wholesale destruction. Hunting was governed by rules that limited a hunter's take to what was needed for survival. Only fools irritated the spirit guardians of animals by excessive hunting. Thus, Guaycuruan shamans and hunters curried favor with spirits,[23] who had foreknowledge of calamities and understanding of the personalities of animals that Guaycuruans wanted.[24] These beliefs were very different from the European belief that God created humans to control nature, and the conflict between the two after missionization was a source of tremendous cultural dissonance.[25] Guaycuruans resolved this by concluding that the more powerful spirits of Spaniards had rendered the spirit owners of game animals impotent. They believed that game-animal spirits retired to the far forests in the 1700s, breaking the equilibrium between men and animals. As their commercial harvesting of game depleted the Chaco's animal population in the 1730s and 1740s, Guaycuruans understood this disaster as the terrible consequences of these alien spirits having upset the balance of life.[26]

Pre-Mission Rituals

To appease a spirit who brought illness, Mocobis held an annual service in which men consumed alcohol. They painted their bodies, adorned themselves with feathers, and congregated in a circle. Drinking to the beat of a drum, they danced individually as the spirit moved them. A shaman, painted a symbolic blood red, simulated the symptoms of disease and begged for renewed health.[27]

The Guaycuruan concept of the supernatural origins of disease contributed to missionary successes in the 1700s, but until the mission period, this notion buttressed the influence of the shaman, whose primary function was to cure the sick. Illnesses could be caused not only by the loss of one's soul to malevolent spirits but also by the magical intrusion of a pathogenic substance into a person. For example, a hostile shaman's incantations might supernaturally introduce a bone into a victim's body, causing the person to sicken and possibly die. Most Chaco cultures believed that disease resulted when a "demon" or spirit kidnapped a person's soul, but diseases also struck wrongdoers who violated taboos. Prayer and exorcism were the remedy.[28]

Guaycuruans believed death was usually caused by an evil shaman. To punish the malevolent shaman, and to ward off the dead person's ghost, Abipones removed the tongue and heart from the cadaver and fed them to dogs. They then wrapped the body in an animal skin (by the 1700s a cowhide) and buried it. The bones of men who fell in combat were sacred; survivors retrieved them from the battlefield, cleaned them, and buried them with ceremony.

Death terrified Guaycuruans. An individual death was a calamity for a band, the stress of which was relieved by communal drinking rituals. The Guaycuruan connection of alcohol and religious observance later made aboriginal drinking a target of missionary wrath. When a Mocobi man died, his widow covered her face for months with a veil, which she burned at the end of her mourning.[29] Everybody cried for several days; then the principal mourner, usually a close male relative, played host to a drinking ceremony. Throughout the night, men lamented and drummed. At sunrise, they destroyed the deceased's possessions, including his hut, to prevent his ghost from attacking survivors. If the dwelling were left standing, Death, who knew the way there, would be a threat to neighbors. With the structure demolished, however, Death would conclude that the people had departed. In Belén, Mbayá leaders enjoyed European-style dwellings, superior to traditional huts, especially during storms. The desire for dry homes, though, could not overcome the pull of aboriginal funeral practice. When a resident of a new house died, survivors burned it to avoid Death.[30] After the mourning period Abipones banished a person's death from their collective memory by refusing to speak the deceased's name.

Like other Chaco people, pre-mission Guaycuruans believed in an immortal soul, equated with life. All human beings wished eventually to join the "community of souls" in the afterlife. A mortal's soul departed at death and traveled about before joining the community of souls. During this time of wandering, the soul might whimsically enter an animal or person.[31] Although a playful act on the part of the spirit, it might have disastrous consequences for the creature possessed. Mbayás thought that a recently departed soul hovered about a grave before entering an animal or joining the community of souls; thus they placed weapons, food, and drink nearby. Like other Guaycuruans, Abipones once sacrificed a horse at a warrior's grave but discontinued this practice as property became more important. Female Guaycuruans received similar burials. Mbayás buried women with appropriate objects, including beads, trinkets, and utensils, suspended on poles at grave sites.[32] If an impious person removed an object from a grave, this would anger departed souls and thus endanger others. The soul that lacked food and weapons or necessary utensils in the afterlife might enter the body of a surviving member of the band, a fearsome prospect. In the short-lived seventeenth-century mission of Santos Magos of Codalodis (Mbayás), a dying female shaman accepted a priest's offer of eternal bliss before she expired. As Father

Romero prepared to bury the body in the mission's holy ground, the Indians protested that this was too close to their homes. The woman's soul recently had entered a tiger's body, they said, and might devour them.[33]

Shamans

One Guaycuruan role that eased the transition to Catholicism was that of religious functionaries. Mbayá shamans displayed their station by distinctive dress. They wore a multicolored, poncho-like cloak over the shoulders and usually carried a seed-filled gourd rattle, a small flask, and a cluster of brown rhea feathers. They often toured an encampment advertising their professional skills and soliciting business, for clients compensated them handsomely. In Belén and Refugio after 1760, they met Jesuits and Franciscans, even more distinctively garbed rivals who reviled them as charlatans, inspired by the devil and motivated by personal gain.[34]

Prominent in all Guaycuruan communities, shamans were the only true specialists, although others practiced magic and supplemented formal shamanic activity. Both men and women could become shamans by apprenticing themselves to a master shaman. At the end of this apprenticeship, the novice fasted and received a vision, after which the master certified him or her in an initiation ceremony.[35]

Venerated but feared, shamans saw themselves only as vehicles through which companion spirits worked, not as powerful agents in their own right.[36] In their rituals, shamans could invite temporary soul loss, an event that would cause death or illness for the average person. During a trance the soul left the shaman's body and wandered off in search of knowledge.

Because of their ability to summon companion spirits, shamans had considerable influence. In Abipon bands they performed superhuman acts. Through powers bequeathed by Queebet, they became all-knowing and all-powerful; they could cause or cure illness, bring death, predict the future, see from afar, and conjure up storms or send them away. Respected shamans terrorized their own people by transforming themselves into great jaguar-like cats. Abipon males had little fear of normal jaguars, which they hunted and killed, but these spirit jaguars were both invisible and indestructible.[37] Abipon shamans were believed to have power even in death. When they traveled Abipones carried the bones of deceased shamans as sacred relics.

Abipon shamans mediated between their communities and the supernatural world and could consult ghosts to foretell peril. During such a ceremony, people surrounded the shaman's dwelling. He covered himself with a cowhide curtain to prevent rival shamans or spirits from identifying and killing him. A ghost entered the shaman's body and exhorted the gathering, evidenced by the marked change in the man's voice.[38]

On a hunt or a raid, shamans advised political and military leaders about the location of game or enemies. Before a fray they toured the battlefield threatening foes with a palm branch. After a victorious raid the shaman claimed the choicest booty. If an enterprise failed, the setback was attributed to an opposing shaman of greater power.[39] Abipon shamans were thus essential to warfare and community security. During the night—a dangerous time much to be feared—they would learn of the proximity of enemies from supernatural colleagues and sound the alarm with whistles and flutes. The men rushed to arms, while women and children hid. If no adversary appeared by dawn, it was assumed the shaman's partner spirit had turned away the enemy.[40]

Mbayá, Abipon, and Mocobi shamans generally rejected herbal remedies; instead they practiced purification by sucking the evil from a suffering body. An Mbayá shaman sent the afflicted soul on an errand, sucked the body healthy, and then recalled the soul. If an invalid was past recovery, the shaman announced that the soul was leaving forever.[41] If the patient died, his survivors had the right to kill the failed physician.[42]

Guaycuruans maintained that people died as a result of witchcraft. Diseases were only proximate not ultimate causes. When someone died, survivors suspected that the culprit was a shaman. Among the Mocobis, if the guilty party could be identified, the deceased person's kinsmen might kill him or her in reprisal. If unable to apprehend an offending shaman physically, the kinsmen might seek the services of a cooperative practitioner to slay the offender magically. The shaman took the corpse to open country, placed it on straw, and scorched it by igniting the grass. He then shot arrows into the cadaver's throat and heart. Finally, he secretly pronounced magic words to execute the assassin. This ceremony transported the arrows from the corpse to the vital organs of the malefactor,[43] unless the latter's powers were too strong.

Female shamans also commanded significant power. Abipon shamans made men swift and strong. They rubbed men's thighs with gourds, increasing their potency against human and animal opponents. Abipones and Mbayás often sought the intercession of elderly female shamans to neutralize human and spectral enemies. Female shamans met at nightfall in a large hut. Naked to the waist, they shook rattles and pots, beat drums, and chanted to propitiate hostile spirits. At dawn people of the community reported to the site to pay the women for their services and hear their prophecies. At times conflicting prophecies caused terrible quarrels among shamans. Female shamans injured enemies, protected clients, and conjured up terrible storms, for example, to torment adversaries.[44]

In Mocobi society, female shamans officiated at funerals; an old woman beat a drum and sang, and another shook a rattle, chanted, and danced before the body. Since "great power" was "attributed to chanting and to the sound of the gourd rattle which accompanies it,"[45] we can see how deeply involved women were in Mocobi religious life. Mocobis also believed females with supernatural power[46] could intercede with supernatural forces. Mocobi female shamans dressed distinctively, could cure, cause injury, prophesy the future, or even bring about the dissolution of marriages,[47] but they had lesser social status than male specialists. Evidence from contemporary Toba society can instruct us about the Mocobis, whom they closely resembled. The Toba had three categories of "power specialists": (1) true shamans, who could cure or harm; (2) curers, who could only cure; and (3) sorcerers, mostly women, who did injury.[48]

The Failure of Traditional Faith and the Movement to Missions

Eighteenth-century Seneca in New York state illustrate the phenomenon of societies experiencing increasing stress when familiar "stress-reduction techniques" begin to fail. Among the factors that caused cultural confusion and social stress were "climatic, floral and faunal change; military defeat; political subordination; extreme pressure toward acculturation resulting in internal cultural conflict; economic distress; epidemics."[49] Similar calamities disrupted Guaycuruan societies in the 1730s. Entropy led to increasing individual and societal stress, which ultimately resulted in a "vitalistic movement." This caused the "importation of alien elements" into the Guaycuruan groups that found themselves in Catholic missions.[50]

As a result of the upheavals of the 1730s and after, traditional Guaycuruan religion no longer explained the world satisfactorily. As confidence in old beliefs crumbled, the more culturally innovative Guaycuruans searched for new explanations, and many turned to missions.

In the mid-eighteenth century, Abipon shamans reinterpreted their crumbling world. Once, they said, shamans and other Abipones had been immortal. None would have died but for the superior Spanish magic. Death came not from Spanish firearms but from the magic behind Spanish weapons,[51] and the movement to missions was partly a search for the spiritual source of Spanish power.

Although the decision to accept missions stemmed directly from economic and security considerations, Guaycuruans were aware of Spanish religion. Sixteenth- and seventeenth-century missionaries had penetrated the Chaco; southwestern Chaco missions to the Lules and Vilelas were founded in the early 1700s; and Hispanic captives and repatriated Guaycuruans had introduced Chaqueños to Christian beliefs. Chaco peoples had observed Spanish religious behavior while on journeys for trade and plunder, and they understood it sufficiently to attack when a community gathered for mass.

One incident illustrates the length of contact pre-mission Guaycuruans had with Christianity. Tobas and Mocobis in 1776 fetched Friar Antonio Lapa from his reduction in Tucumán to the Río Bermejo to assist in their quest for missions. They helped him raise a cross, preliminary to erecting a church. When Lapa lamented that acquiring a church bell would be difficult, they replied that they had one in the ruins of the abandoned Concepción del Bermejo, where Spanish vecinos had left it in the 1630s when they fled the ancestors of the present supplicants.[52]

Guaycuruans learned more about Christianity from mission treaties. The agreement between the Mocobis of Chief Etazorin and the governor of Paraguay in 1776, although a late document, is illustrative of the process that began in the 1740s. The supplicants agreed to permit priests to explain the Christians' Holy Law to them, to baptize all infants at birth, and to baptize older children at their discretion.[53] Since Guaycuruan society operated consensually, we know that acceptance of such a contract reflected the wishes of the band.

When Guaycuruans settled in missions, they learned still more. Mocobis who settled at Cangayé on the Río Bermejo in 1780 heard that there was but one deity, whose nature was triune, a concept that certainly confused them if they paid it heed. They now heard how fully the white men with whom they would live condemned their traditional ideas and practices. They would have to learn to live by a new set of rules, called the Holy Laws of God and of Our Holy Mother Church. They apprehended that they must bring their children to priests for baptism and must not oppose the rites and dogmas of Catholicism. They pledged to gather morning and afternoon at the chapel for the catechism and the Angelus. They also were required to recite the Ave Maria and on Saturdays to chant the Rosary. On Sundays and holy days all were to attend mass.

Mission Guaycuruans also began transferring their respect for aboriginal shamans to priests, coming to regard priests with reverence, affection, and respect.[54] This transference was exemplified in April 1782, when about sixty Guaycuruans encountered a Dominican traveling from Córdoba. On discovering his calling, they refused to kill him, their usual practice with Spaniards whom they robbed. Still, they took his money and goods before sending him on his way.[55]

Missionary Christianity and Guaycuruan Responses

Non-mission Guaycuruans without a thorough knowledge of Christianity sometimes welcomed its ceremonies. In 1776, for instance, as Friar Lapa searched for the Guaycuruans who wanted reductions, anxious Mocobis sought his professional services. Chief Lachiriquin had Lapa baptize a dying woman and teach men to pray. The chief wanted to heal the afflicted and to learn the power of Spanish religion.[56] Mocobis joined Lapa in prayer, investigating the spiritual source of the European society's power.

For Guaycuruans who abandoned nomadic lives, as for the priests in Chaco missions, religion was at the core of life. From the missionaries Guaycuruans learned that the central figure in the priests' religion was Jesus Christ, a man from a faraway place who lived long ago, was the son of the true God, and was born to a virgin. They heard that he was crucified, died, and after three days rose and ascended to heaven. They learned that although there was only one God, he existed as three persons, a confusing but central "mystery" of the invaders' faith. Practices called sacraments, chosen by Christ, brought them something called grace. They discovered that a practice called baptism, representing the death and resurrection of Christ, first admitted them to the church and then enabled them, like Jesus, to be reborn after death, a belief for which their aboriginal faith prepared them. Another Christian ritual, marriage, spiritually united men and women, whose ties in Guaycuruan society until then had been loose, in a lifelong bond.[57] Christian Guaycuruans, according to priests, should marry only other Christians, limiting their choice of marriage partners. To Guaycuruans, as to the people of Mesoamerica, European clerics explained biblical monotheism. They brought to missions a host of sacred spirits, including angels, saints, the devil, and various lesser beings.[58]

In another practice, the Eucharist, people ate the body and drank the blood of Jesus to gain salvation. They bragged of past cannibalism but no longer practiced it, so they understood meals of human flesh. The Christian sacrament, therefore, was an act of simulation, consistent with aspects of their own faith. They also learned of confession, usually performed annually, and penance, after which they could be cleansed.

Central to this new religious complex was a new notion, sin, an evil human act that offended God, and seven of these were especially offensive. Those committing a mortal sin, they were told, could set things right by securing the intercession of a European shaman. For other transgressions, venial sins, whose commission did not cost them God's grace, they could seek forgiveness themselves. To please God, they must now behave in special ways every seventh day. Men whose life and religion had revolved around warfare and plunder heard that now they could kill only under radically different circumstances. They also learned that on holy days they must not eat traditional foods. Another message, that they must support their new religious functionaries with material gifts, as they had supported shamans, was familiar and expected.[59]

Guaycuruans observed their new black-robed, light-skinned shamans talking daily to their companion spirit, as their own prophets had done. The new spiritual counselors, however, communicated more frequently, at daily mass and prayers, and held their conversations openly for all to see. Their own shamans at times had performed their rites in secret.

Instruction given by Jesuit, Franciscan, and Mercedarian missionaries in the Chaco resembled that in most other missions in Spanish South America, as it followed religious guidelines for Indians approved by the Council of Lima of 1583. These guidelines were similar to Father Ripalda's *Doctrina cristiana* (published in Burgos in 1591) written for Spanish children, and to the guidelines for instruction of native peoples in Mexico in the 1540s. Indians learned to recite prayers and the "essential verities" in church. Candidates for baptism, confession, communion, and confirmation mastered the Credo, Pater Noster, Ave Maria, Salve Regina, the fourteen Articles of Faith (on Christ's divinity and humanity), "the Ten Commandments of God, the Five Commandments of the Church, and the Seven Sacraments; the seven deadly sins; and the general confession." They also learned of the complementary virtues.[60] The change experienced by Guaycuruans resembled the transformation of religious belief among the popular classes of France in the seventeenth and eighteenth centuries. For both a "hierarchy was imposed on the divine world, and in like fashion sermons [and] missions . . . joined to present a hell that was just as hierarchical."[61]

In the newly established Guaycuruan reductions of Santa Fe José Cardiel began the instruction of Mocobis and Abipones through an interpreter. Cardiel and others gave the Guaycuruans small gifts, usually food or tobacco, at their doctrinal lessons. They listened to Cardiel's explication of the catechism with interest, especially the description of God's punishment for those who refused Christianity or renounced Christian lives after baptism. If they became Christians, they learned, God would reward them in the afterlife. The new power was as vengeful as Guaycuruans' traditional spirits, but unlike them he was also beneficent, giving daily gifts—sun, light, rain, hunting, and all food.[62]

Neophytes responded loudly in Spanish to the missionary's teaching, "Christians are good! Christians are good!" Most Guaycuruans who elected the new religion witnessed priestly tests of their sincerity, because apostasy was worse than paganism.[63] Nevertheless, like the friars who taught Nahuas in postconquest Mexico, Jesuits and their successors "lacked sensitivity to the relationship between language and thought." They expressed concepts new to Guaycuruans in an unfamiliar language.[64] During the transition to mission life, Christian messages sometimes were lost in translation. In the late 1740s Father Nabalón, the *compañero* (companion priest) of San Jerónimo, asked some women a hypothetical question through an interpreter. If they were blind, would they not then thank the one who gave them eyes with which to see the earth and sky? Horrified, they fled to Father Brigniel, the *cura,* to complain. His companion, they believed, wished to pluck their eyes out.[65]

A component of the Guaycuruan amalgamation of Christianity and indigenous beliefs was language adaptation. Abipones and others lacked a word for God,[66] which many Jesuits thought disqualified them from rationality. The priests joined Spanish and Abipon words into *Dios ecnam caogarik,* meaning "God the Creator of All Things." Abipones mixed the priests' concepts and their own ideas. They sometimes called a church *loákal lëëriki,* "the house of images," and referred to it as *natamenriki,* "where thanks are given to God." Souls, shadows, echoes, and images were all identified by the words *loákal* or *ikihi*. Hell was *aalóo labachiñi,* "the center of the earth," or *Keevét lëëriki,* which priests called the devil's house[67] but which had a more positive connotation for Guaycuruans, indicating the dwelling place of their grandfather. This phrase suggests that Abipones connected the Christian God with Keebet.

Syncretism occurred in deeds as much as language. Ychoalay-Benavides, who led his band to Christianity at San Jerónimo, persuaded others in San Jerónimo to accept baptism before he himself did. He wished to postpone the sacrament symbolizing his peace with the Spanish world until he had killed a rival, Oaherkaikin. (A truce eventually sufficed.) He knew that this act of vengeance would be condemned by the new faith, whereas the execution of an enemy was venerated under the old one. As Ychoalay accepted new religious rituals, he proselytized Christian beliefs. He attended daily instruction and rallied others. His encouragement ensured a regularly filled chapel. He urged baptism on dying Abipones and burial in the missionaries' holy ground, rather than their own sanctified forests. As the priests' faith spread among his people, it solidified the aspiring cacique's leadership.[68]

Despite Ychoalay's efforts, fewer adult San Jerónimo Abipones than San Javier Mocobis converted to Christianity. Yet some did choose the Europeans' beliefs and rituals—including Ychoalay himself, a decade after the founding of San Jerónimo. He requested that his baptism be held in Santa Fe, where Teniente Francisco Antonio de Vera Múxica became his godfather. The event was solemnized by the attendance of the cabildo, secular clerics, religious orders, and important citizens.[69]

Although priests welcomed adult baptisms such as Benavides', their principal goal was to convert the second generation, and they concentrated on the children. Benavides' son, Miguel Gerónimo, later corregidor of the mission, exemplified the successes and limitations of the new religious order. Baptized as an infant, he accepted the faith, but as an Abipon not a Spaniard. Once when the missionary asked the boy why he was downcast, Miguel Gerónimo replied that another youth had wronged him, but he could not seek vengeance because worthy Christians repaid evil with good.[70] As an adult leader of the pueblo, the younger Benavides saw himself as a good Christian, although Spanish critics denounced him as too Indian, particularly because of his poorly concealed plural marriages.[71]

Guaycuruan adults in the first mission years commonly resisted Christianity, although they were curious. In a short-lived seventeenth-century Abipon mission near Santiago del Estero, Father Juan Pastor tried to convert a dying religious specialist; he warned that the devil would punish her forever. "She replied with a laugh that she had little occasion to fear 'this spirit,' with whom she had been familiar so many years," and a hundred years later the process would recur. In San Fernando, many Yaaucanigas resisted Christianity because female religious leaders, "thinking it a crime even to touch the threshold of the church," condemned services. Boys attended reluctantly. Nevertheless most Guaycuruans lost their "horror of baptism" and slowly incorporated new ideas.[72]

One Guaycuruan who openly resisted Catholicism was Santiago, a Toba cacique of San Ignacio. After a combat, he awarded the head of a fallen enemy to his daughter. The horrified missionary reviled him as a bloodthirsty barbarian who must spare his children such evil examples. Chastened, the man promised not to repeat the gift, and the missionary, Father Harto, judged that Santiago would now accept Christian doctrine. Harto explained the Christian God and emphasized his triune nature. Confused by the Trinity, a drunken Santiago later yelled at the missionary, "You lie! You lie! There is no God! Where is that God? Tell Him to come here. If He is a man, I want to see Him and meet Him. Why does He not speak? Why does he not let Himself be seen?"[73]

Jesuits on the eighteenth-century Chaco frontier repeated the three-stage attack on native religion of their brethren in Canada a century earlier. First they challenged native beliefs that supported shamans. Next they demeaned native practitioners as tricksters and profiteers. Finally, they convinced Indians that Christian rituals were superior to the shamans' methods, especially new medical practices, although these European introductions were often only herbal remedies. Jesuits were better able than their native counterparts to explain disease and disaster, a major advantage. "God's just punishment of native sin," caused misfortune, they said, allowing missionaries to "take partial credit for the recovery of ailing Indians" and deflect personal blame for native deaths.[74]

At the outset of mission life, adjusting to the peculiarities of those on the other side of the cultural divide was trying for all. Jesuits did not yet regard Indians as catechumens. Instead, as Father Brigniel labeled San Jerónimo Abipones, they were *ergumenos*, persons possessed of evil spirits. The priests, though, were certain that the Indians eventually would elect the Europeans' faith,[75] as many Guaycuruans did, but in their own way. They did not, however, jettison ancient convictions quickly. As the unpacified zones of Yucatan became a safety valve for the colonial Maya,[76] so did the unconquered Chaco for resistant Guaycuruans.

Shamans Discredited

The rituals of Catholicism outshone the shamans' simple practices. Ostentatious religious display in all missions impressed Guaycuruans. Mission churches showed Guaycuruans the magnificence of the Supreme Being, housing statuary, metal crucifixes, altar cloths of fine linen, chalices of silver and gold, and paintings of objects of veneration.[77] The richness of church ornaments contrasted with the simplicity of Chaco religious symbols, gourd rattles, drums, and feathers.

Priests directly undermined Guaycuruan shamans' influence. An effective approach was that of Father Dobrizhoffer in the Guarani mission of San Joaquín, who caught his rival Yaguareté (Jaguar) practicing his vocation. He threatened the shaman with eternal torment, which had little effect. Father Martin then screamed that the shaman should live in the forest with beasts, because he was himself so beastly. This failed to influence the prophet, who boasted of his spiritual connection with animals. Finally Dobrizhoffer promised that if the man persisted, he would drag him through the streets and cover him with cow dung. This drove Yaguareté's professional activities underground, a method repeated in Guaycuruan missions.[78] Priests concluded that shamanic activities ceased, which is unlikely. Although priests influenced behavior and belief on a communal level, they could not eliminate old beliefs or private practices.

Missionaries also ridiculed shamans' methods. Once when Father Dobrizhoffer fell ill in Concepción de Abipones, a celebrated female healer brought a boiling root to speed his convalescence. He refused emphatically, shuddering "at the old hag that prescribed it." His recovery enhanced his reputation and diminished that of native practitioners. To deride the Indian practice of renaming survivors after a death, Father Martin joked that he would have to find a new name for the dog, "to show them that we held their absurd rites in ridicule."[79]

A confrontation between Father Paucke and Pezezeguenac, a Mocobi shaman, reveals the missionary method of discrediting traditional physicians and the old religion's persistence. Blinded by smallpox as a youth, Pezezeguenac commuted between traditional hunting grounds and the Mocobi-Jesuit mission of San Javier until disease crippled his limbs, confining him to the mission. After two years, the man's health improved enough that he could hobble around with crutches, and he begged from hut to hut, as he had been told handicapped Christians in Santa Fe did.

Happy with his apparent enlightenment, Paucke baptized the man Valentín.

Valentín's mendicancy was profitable. He collected meat, watermelons, squash, knives, hats, and wool. Divorced women volunteered to marry this good provider, until Paucke discovered that the source of Valentín-Pezezeguenac's new wealth was his former profession. When Paucke found Valentín out, he lured his sightless rival into a trap. At a service, he snuck up beside the shaman to puncture his reputation as a visionary. Paucke demonstrated that Valentín was unaware of him and proclaimed that this shattered his claims of magical powers. Valentín-Pezezeguenac, in frustration revealing both an evolving faith and an attempt to maintain his status, insisted that he had spoken with God the Father, who would refuse the arrogant Jesuit entrance to heaven. The caciques, however, allied with the Jesuits, and they ended the healer's activities.[80] Priests, it seems, needed the Guaycuruan elite to counter shamanic activities.

Guaycuruan shamans lost status as religious leaders, partly because they faced more "powerful medicine men." Although Father Sánchez moved cautiously in Belén, he used his literacy, European technology, and audacity to discredit Mbayá shamans. A sojourning compañero once wrote Sánchez of his impending arrival in Belén, and Father José said nothing. When that night Mbayás asked whose campfire glowed in the distance, Sánchez remained silent, hoping to snare a rival. Since such sightings often warned of an enemy, the people asked the shaman (*nigienigi*) for the newcomers' identity. The prophet consulted his companion spirit (*latenigi*) who erroneously reported that those on the horizon were enemies. Sánchez saw his expected visitors through his telescope and crowed that his spyglass saw farther than the shaman's ignorant companion spirit. Mbayás thus doubted the nigienigi's prophesies.[81]

Occasionally, priestly efforts to discredit a Guaycuruan rival misfired. The people of Belén were awaiting the arrival of a new priest, worried about his safety. A shaman who predicted the man's arrival that day was denounced by Sánchez as an imposter. The priest did arrive that afternoon,[82] bolstering the shaman's credibility. In another example of Catholic efforts backfiring, Guaycuruans in San Javier de Mocobis withdrew when a priest overplayed his hand. As a Jesuit compañero tried to cure a cacique, an indigenous healer entered the hut with her rattles and drum. The missionary insulted her, infuriating the patient and his family, who returned to the Chaco.[83]

Shamans resisted priests' attacks on their authority. Abipon religious leaders warned against entering the mission church, receiving baptism, or observing Catholic doctrine, threatening people who rejected the old religion with death and ruination.[84] The failure of these calamities to occur convinced former followers that the priests had better contacts in the spirit world, coincided with the priests' naturalistic explanation of everyday life, and contributed to the breakdown of aboriginal belief.

Guaycuruan shamans persisted into the twentieth century, however, continuing to mediate between their people and the supernatural world. One example is Polinari, a "Christian shaman" of the Caduveo, descendants of the Mbayá, in the 1940s. Polinari received baptism from a priest, and his ritual combined Christian and Mbayá forms. Like his professional ancestors whose powers came from aboriginal companion spirits, Polinari "received the power to cure from Saint John and Saint Anthony who appeared to him in a vision." Instead of the gourd rattle and feather baton favored by colonial shamans, Polinari cured with "holy water, prayers to the saints, medicines made from herbs, and blessings." He enlisted Saint Mark for snakebite and Saint Anthony for bodily pain. His companion spirit, Saint John, came to him in dreams to reveal the correct herb or root.[85] Such Guaycuruan melding of Christianity with aboriginal beliefs was usually hidden from priests in the missions of the 1700s.

The Persistence of Indigenous Faith

Old beliefs survived. No mission was ever isolated from non-mission Guaycuruans in the Chaco. Thus contact with people who practiced the old rites continued. Mission Abipones continued to communicate with their grandfather. One day Father José Brigniel saw inhabitants of San Jerónimo riding to a nearby field, and followed them. There he found a shack of palm branches, a home they had built for their grandfather. Celebrants warned him to avoid the deadly claws of their grandfather, who was in the shack with the shaman Haanetrain. Through the shaman, the spirit roared like a tiger and addressed the assembly.[86]

Mission Guaycuruans continued to recognize phenomena like comets as harbingers of evil foretelling calamities. When storms approached, Abipon women still threw ashes to the tempests in a circular fashion so that the storm would eat the ashes, be sated, and travel elsewhere. Bees killed inside one's house prevented the collection of honey and the ecstasy of its fermentation,[87] so Abipones avoided bee killing indoors.

Guaycuruans in missions continued to believe in supernatural causes of death and disease.[88] They might kill a man alleged to be a murderous shaman by summoning their own spirit powers. Abipones experienced an illness of magical origin that infected its victim with murderous delirium, usually at night; he suffered rapid changes in temperature and assaulted whomever he encountered. One cure was to kill female shamans.[89]

Abipones encountered familiar specters. In San Jerónimo, men often saw the ghost of a Spanish employee of the mission slain by enemies; he toured the countryside whistling sadly.[90] Such belief in an afterlife convinced priests that Guaycuruans understood the Christian notion of an immortal soul.[91]

Mission Guaycuruan views of illnesses and cures remained supernatural. Abipones judged themselves a healthy people, a notion with which Jesuits agreed, and said that none would die were it not for supernatural intervention. In Concepción de Abipones, for example, two Chaco visitors quarrelled drunkenly over a horse. A sober mediator accidentally received a fatal lance thrust for his trouble. The community concluded that the real perpetrator was a spiteful old woman with magical powers, and they beat her to death.[92]

Guaycuruans later heard from missionaries the European cause-and-effect interpretation of death by violence. Interpreting aboriginal belief as an absence of religion,[93] priests concluded that devout Abipones were either deranged or misguided. In San Fernando a famous Abipon war leader, grief-stricken over the death of his daughter, learned from the village women that the executioner was an outsider, the wife of a village man not of the (Yaaucaniga) group that settled the mission, and the grieving parent speared the alleged poisoner through the breast. Jesuits, however, nursed her back to health with nourishing meals, liberal daily washing of the wound, and lectures on the naturalistic origin of death.[94]

Guaycuruan theories of the spiritual origins of disease and shamanic efforts to drive disease from the afflicted body enraged priests. They accused shamans of being rogues and knaves whose fame rested on their ability to deceive. Yet shamans intoned their magic powers in the first generation or two of mission life. When a person contracted a disease such as smallpox or measles, four or five shamans might cooperate in the cure. Shamans, mission Abipones insisted, contributed to healthy lives. Thus, they paid shamans promptly for their services to prevent return of the disease. When patients died, the Abipon explanation that the shaman's abilities were overcome by those of a more powerful practitioner provided an opening for priests.[95] To discredit them, priests exposed shamans who asked missionaries for cures. Consulting priests, however, was not a sign that shamans rejected their own beliefs, but rather that they recognized the black-robed practitioners as shamans connected to a more powerful deity.[96]

Merging of Two Systems

Mission Guaycuruans slowly accepted Catholicism. The advantages of European over aboriginal medicine undoubtedly convinced wavering Guaycuruans that the newcomers knew more powerful spirits than their healers did. Especially noteworthy was nursing care. Preconquest natives did not care for their sick,[97] whereas priests attended the ill, the weak, and the feeble. Their medicines—sugar water, figs in juice, a piece of hardtack—had no curative powers, but nursing techniques, including daily meals, increased the survival rate among their patients.

As the new power specialists of Guaycuruan bands, Jesuits and later Franciscans and Mercedarians frightened people toward Christian doctrine, as seen in an exchange between Father Paucke and his charges in San Xavier. Mocobis maintained that a gray heron's cries presaged someone's death. One day Father Paucke was conversing beside the chapel with Anselmo Pelegzonguin when a shrieking heron flew to the cross. When Anselmo predicted that a mission Mocobi would die, Paucke replied that a man should be ashamed to repeat the tales of women. God was more likely, the priest said, to punish Anselmo for being faithless. The next day Anselmo's five-year-old son, Pantaleón, died from a blow suffered while playing, and Anselmo concluded that this fulfilled Paucke's prophecy. God had punished Anselmo by killing his beloved son for following the older, weaker religion. From then on, he said, he would trust the priests.[98]

A cacique ally of Father Paucke's herded shamans to church, where the priest branded them false prophets. From his own arsenal, Father Paucke brought the written word, threatening to write his adversaries' names on a paper placed under the image of Saint Francis Xavier. The intimidated shamans told Paucke what he wanted to hear: They possessed no "black magic" but merely deceived their followers for personal gain. They promised, surely insincerely, to stop their old rites. Caciques, who challenged shamans for influence, tried to stop shamanic activity by reporting transgressions to priests. Frequent contact with relatives from the Chaco, though, sustained older notions,[99] of which missionary accounts give us too few examples.

Spanish missionaries often suppressed information about such heresies.[100] Yet the fact that the Indians conceived of the missionary priests as shamans reveals a "spontaneous syncretism," in Hugo Nutini's words, of old and new beliefs.[101] Once when Father Dobrizhoffer adorned the mission chapel to represent nature, Abipones exclaimed, "The father is either a magician or is born from a prophetic mother."[102] Others thought that a Jesuit carpenter who worked with a lathe and chisel, unfamiliar tools, was similarly a magician.[103] From their own magic-filled perspective, they saw these acts as divination.

To the Guaycuruans religion meant power, and they interpreted the Spaniards' connection with the spirit world as the source of the latter's strength. They hoped that learning the secrets of the European religion could provide the potency that their failed faith once had offered. In 1757, before his baptism, Ychoalay tested the new religion as he prepared to lead San Jerónimo Abipones, some now Christians, against a force of enemy Abipones. He said, "Now we will see if God helps Christians." God apparently did help, because the mission Abipones returned victorious, and Ychoalay acknowledged that God had willed the triumph. Abipon women celebrated traditionally, by breaking their pots,[104] demonstrating that in family settings traditional observances survived. As the public sphere moved toward Christianity, the private sphere remained Abipon.

Upon joining a mission, unbaptized Guaycuruans adopted selected Christian practices. Mocobis of the new reduction of San Pedro in 1765 often attended evening church services and enthusiastically chanted the Rosary. After dinner, there came from the hut of Cacique Amaquin the unmistakable sound of a Mocobi intoning Christian doctrine.[105]

The Mocobis who founded San Javier in the 1740s were the most culturally innovative of the Chaco equestrians and the quickest to subordinate their beliefs to the Europeans'. After only twenty years, the Mocobis so embraced the new ideas that they implored Father Paucke to be more zealous with new arrivals. By 1780, the people of the mission boasted of how Christian they were.[106] They now depended on priests to mediate not only with God but with the Spanish world.

New Generations, New Christians

The most complete surviving indications of religious change come from the Abipon missions of San Jerónimo and San Fernando in the 1750s and 1760s. The best measures are adult baptisms, church marriages, and baptisms of infants and children (see Appendix B, tables 1 and 2a, b, c).

First-generation adults usually rejected Christian rituals, although most accepted isolated tenets of the religion. Resisting baptism made them ineligible for other sacraments. In San Fernando de Abipones in

1766, for instance, sixteen years after its foundation, of the fifty-eight married couples in the village, only six (10.3 percent) were married *in facie ecclesia*. In that year priests heard but twenty-four confessions and officiated at only twenty communions in a population of about three hundred. The number of baptized adults, twenty-one in 1762, rose to thirty-six four years later, as children born in the mission and raised with Christian ritual grew to maturity. Unbaptized first-generation adults attended services only sporadically, and Father Klein lamented that they were not more enthusiastic.[107]

Demonstrating the adults' reluctance to embrace fully the missionaries' faith, only ten adult Abipones in San Fernando accepted baptism in the decade 1753–62, when the mission's population fluctuated between 151 and 677 (averaging 358). In six of these years, no Yaaucaniga man or woman received baptism. Similarly only four couples married in church. Because adults were baptized only after a priest concluded that they understood the ceremony, the low baptism rate indicates slow acceptance of Christianity.[108]

Less culturally innovative than southern Mocobis or Riikahé Abipones and more reluctant to accept Christian ideology, the Yaaucanigas of San Fernando nevertheless drifted toward the new faith. When Father Klein complained in 1763 that only five of the fifteen adults who chose baptism lived truly Christian lives, he could as easily have been speaking of Santafecinos or porteños. Although only a minority of adults accepted Christianity, others feared the same hell as other eighteenth-century Catholics. The transition from indigenous ideas to belief in hell was easier than the change from customary behavior to imitating the life of Christ. When Christian Abipones behaved humbly, friends often called them cowards and slaves.[109]

Mission census figures also show another trend in stable missions, however: a largely Christianized second generation. Since adults wanted Spanish secrets, they entrusted their children to Jesuit teaching. In each year of the decade 1753–62, an average of ten young San Fernando Abipones received baptism. The high was eighteen in 1754, and the low was three in 1758, a demographic nadir after the Guarani War, which disrupted the region. Priests hoped that baptized youths would grow to maturity as Christians. This outcome was never certain because Guaycuruans moved in and out of missions.

A different picture emerges at San Jerónimo de Abipones (see Appendix B, tables 1 and 2a). The Riikahés accepted the mission experience enthusiastically. More first-generation adults accepted Christianity in San

Jerónimo than in the other Abipon missions, such as the Yaaucanigas in San Fernando or the Nakaiketergehes of Concepción in Santiago del Estero. Nevertheless by January 1762, almost fourteen years after San Jerónimo's establishment, only 40 percent of the adults (121 of 304; total population 570) were Christians, including those baptized as youths who grew up in the new faith. During 1761 there were five adult baptisms and five church marriages, surely no coincidence since baptism was a necessary preliminary to marriage.

On the other hand, the adults who themselves avoided baptism overwhelmingly sent their offspring to baptism and daily instruction. In 1761, twenty-five boys and girls received baptism in San Jerónimo, five times higher than the adult rate. By January 1762, 90.6 percent of the children (232 of 256) in the fourteen-year-old mission were Christians; most others were recent arrivals from the Chaco.

These figures show that conversion was eventual but not immediate for the people who stayed in reductions. After the first few years, the number of baptized children usually approached 100 percent of regular residents. In the census for San Jerónimo in 1785 (Appendix B, table 2c), for example, all the children were baptized. Only 8 percent of inhabitants (54 of 681) were unbaptized, and most (36) were catechumens. In other words, 92 percent of Abipones and their culturally Abipon captives and slaves had publicly accepted Christianity.

The preceding comparison of the behavior of the Abipones of San Fernando and San Jerónimo illustrates the variation in acceptance of Christianity among the various missions.[110] In 1785, when 92% of San Jerónimo residents were Christians, many residents of the Corrientes reduction were still indifferent Christians, and some refused to convert. Their resistance was due partly to disruptive attacks from rivals and partly to the group's cultural peculiarities. For reasons as yet unclear, the Yaaucanigas of San Fernando, once a separate people who became Abipones after military defeat, had a more persistent attachment to aboriginal culture than many other Guaycuruans. When clerics asked men with two wives to reject the "illegitimate" woman, many in San Fernando refused. Relations in the Corrientes mission lacked the accommodation between Indians and priests characteristic of the Santa Fe missions.[111]

Several missions followed a pattern similar to San Jerónimo. In the mission of San Ignacio de Tobas in 1757, a year after its foundation, only one Native American resident, a captive, was Christian. Fourteen years later, in 1771, 82 percent of Tobas there (272 of 332) identified themselves as Christians, and in 1778 the number rose to 87 percent (334 of 383), when all children were baptized (see Appendix B, tables 3a–d). The second generation, therefore, was completely Christian in the Toba sense of the word and also according to Catholic designation. This does not mean, however, that they forgot their aboriginal religion.

Another case that reveals religious change in Chaco missions is San Javier de Mocobis, whose people accepted Christianity the quickest. After a decade, 86 percent (613 of 716) of these Mocobis were Christians, and by 1767 they all were (Appendix B, tables 4a and 5). The arrival of Franciscan and Mercedarian missionaries after 1767 caused no Mocobi defections, because all the 1,041 residents of San Javier in 1785 were still Christians, unusual unanimity.

A later example comes from San Pedro de Mocobis. In 1767, after two years of mission life, more than half the people (80 of 140 or 57 percent) were Christians (Appendix B, table 5). In 1785, after twenty years, most were Christians; only 119 of 674 mission residents (18 percent) rejected public adherence to the Spaniards' faith (Appendix B, table 6). The overwhelming majority of San Pedro residents (82 percent) classified themselves as Christians.[112]

In the tiny, short-lived mission of Santiago at Fort San Nicolás in 1793 lived fifty-eight Abipones, fifty-two of whom (90 percent) were baptized, practicing Christians. Of the six non-Christians, five were between sixty and seventy years old, reflecting the generational process of religious adaptation. The only young non-Christian was Qatequin Reetcaren, 28, wife of Christian Anselmo Buenagrin, 30, and mother of María Carmen, 12, also a Christian. The wife was surely newer to the Hispanic world and thus to Spanish religion than her husband, who had been reared in another mission.[113]

A different picture, more like the San Fernando pattern, emerged from Concepción de Abipones, where a majority (50 percent or 114 of 227) still rejected the Catholic religion in 1777, twenty-seven years after the mission began (Appendix B, table 7). This failure to approach European religious expectations was extreme but conforms to the behavior of these Abipones in politics and war. They competed with Spaniards and were more resistant to the Catholic religion. Concepción was located along the commercial route from Santa Fe to Santiago del Estero, and its residents seized opportunities for collective gain. The men preyed on Spanish merchants after most Riikahés of San Jerónimo had focused their aggression on rival Indians.

In the first mission generation, Guaycuruan culture opposed adult acceptance of Catholicism, but deathbed conversions were not uncommon. One of these happened when the Toba Illiri, alférez real of San Ignacio, took sick. Hoping to save the man from perpetual torment, the missionary offered him baptism, but Illiri refused on his mother's advice. When the mother withdrew her opposition, the Toba leader accepted the sacrament. To the Jesuit's disappointment, however, Illiri spent his last days contemplating hunting and war, not his narrow escape from hell.[114] Illiri's thoughts were of a Toba, not European, reality.

All missionaries condemned alcohol use, but priestly opposition was neither essentially a puritanical denial of Indian pleasure nor a campaign for public health. Their objections were fundamentally religious, because Guaycuruans recalled the old order when intoxicated. When drunk, Guaycuruans insulted the Christian God. Drunken mission Tobas, from the missionaries' point of view, practiced pagan heresies.[115] Priests wished to be religious revolutionaries who would extinguish the old order, but they actually oversaw a merger of two belief systems. In San Javier, an elderly Mocobi had a religious experience that combined the soul loss of aboriginal religion with a Christian vision. He traveled in a dream along a wide, beautiful road to heaven, where he met God. The Lord reproved him for drinking and accepted the man's pledge to abstain.[116]

Guaycuruan Strategies in the Mission Environment

For mission and non-mission Guaycuruans, religion was as necessary to survival as food and drink. They thus vitalized their faith with Christian concepts and validated them with Christian rituals. In San Fernando after twenty years of baptisms and lessons, the Abipones so desired Catholic rituals that they threatened to move elsewhere when priests were inattentive or absent. Disagreement resulted from the differing Spanish and Abipon understandings of Christianity, as occurred in a missionary's rejection of Cacique Naré's request for baptism.[117] The public, communal level of Guaycuruan religion gave way to Christian ritual. Because the Christian message was still transmitted through the Guaycuruan languages, however, the meaning of the ritual was as much Guaycuruan as it was Christian. In San Jerónimo in 1785, Abipones communicated among themselves in their own language but with their priests and outsiders in basic Spanish. Similarly, Mocobi adults in San Javier and San Pedro heard lessons from captive interpreters or bilingual Mocobis, because the missionaries spoke no Mocobi. Because priests were ignorant of native languages while many Guaycuruans knew Spanish, the Indians had the advantage in small daily contests. This facilitated the survival of the indigenous faith, because evangelists could not challenge Guaycuruan ideas of which they were ignorant.[118]

Unlike the conversion process in sixteenth-century Mexico, where priests imposed Christianity with physical abuse, the Chaco peoples rarely faced direct coercion. Seldom were adults physically disciplined for spiritual reasons, even by other Guaycuruans, although missionaries generally withheld food, tobacco, and sweets from resisters. Since Guaycuruans lacked traditions of subservience, their chiefs were constrained from disciplining followers in new missions. Thus in the early years of missions, when Guaycuruan ways were strong and Spanish ones weak, there was little coercion of Native American adults. Threats of violence often went in the other direction, with Guaycuruans bullying priests. One reason Timbó failed in 1767 was that Abipones threatened to kill the priest who replaced the Jesuit missionary. The terrified man fled, and the mission dissolved. In San Fernando a doubter socked Father Klein, saying, "'It is a fable what you tell us about a God who created all things.'"[119] Another man clubbed Klein for preaching Christian love between Spaniards and Indians, causing a head injury, and Father Ramón Harto was beaten by a Toba in San Ignacio. Some Guaycuruans even plotted to kill missionaries. Most who planned to harm priests, however, were restrained by their own people.[120]

After the expulsion of the Jesuits in 1767, the advancement of the Europeans' religion suffered, as did other aspects of the mission endeavor, but not as greatly as Jesuit exiles had imagined they would. If Franciscans and Mercedarians were less able than their predecessors, it could hardly have been otherwise, because clerical manpower was finite. Nevertheless the Chaco peoples supported existing missions and founded others. Sooner or later missions found worthy friars. Guaycuruan acceptance of a missionary depended on his personal qualities, not his order, and natives influenced the selection of their priests. In San Javier in the early 1770s, for example, Mocobis disliked the inattentive and often absent Mercedarian Friar Matías de Ziburu. They longed for the revered Jesuit Father Paucke and would neither confess to the replacement nor let him baptize their children. Their truculence contributed to his departure. In 1772 they finally accepted Mercedarian Friar Julián de Obelar. They noted but forgave his ignorance of their language. Later they welcomed another sympathetic and conscientious Mercedarian, Friar Pedro Morales, as well.[121]

Many Guaycuruans welcomed Christian iconography, especially holy images. Mocobis in San Javier were devoted to the Virgin Mary, calling her Gdaté, Our Mother. Once when the pueblo was being relocated, Mocobi women spontaneously escorted the representation of the Virgin from the chapel to the boat that would transport her to the new site. As the figure arrived in its new home, they surrounded it, kneeled, rose together to kiss the statue's hands, and kneeled again. They often begged her for favors.[122] In the 1800s they carefully wrapped the images of saints to protect them when they departed the mission. They also respected the ciborium containing the Host.[123]

The Christian rituals in San Javier were typical of the Guaycuruan missions. The day began with mass; adults went to work after services, while boys and girls recited doctrine, attended music lessons, and sang the Bendito. After lunch, adults returned to chores and children to instruction in religion, reading, and writing. In the evening, the whole mission assembled at church for the Rosary and the Angelus. On holy days, they heard a sermon.[124]

Adults who became Christians willingly confessed their sins. Having no prior knowledge of sin, most carried knotted threads or numbered sticks as mnemonic devices to record and distinguish among sins. Those eligible took communion enthusiastically.[125] Mocobis and other Chaqueños, who earlier had spurned corporal punishment in child rearing or sanctioning transgressors, readily took to religious flogging. Inspired mothers beat their offspring so enthusiastically that missionaries had to restrain them to protect the young. Once several children were discovered giving each other twenty-five lashes so that God would have compassion on them.[126] These adaptations resembled the situation in sixteenth-century Mexico, where Nahuas requested stronger penances because "to flog oneself until the blood came showed devotion to Christ."[127]

Although they eagerly adopted the practices of the new religion, Guaycuruans usually had their own interpretation of the concepts behind them. Most mission Guaycuruans requested baptism for their newborns. Newcomers assumed that baptism could heal, a natural supposition for people who connected religion with the curing of disease. This message spread to friends and relatives still on the move. When the son of Mocobis living outside San Javier suffered a poisonous snakebite, his parents sent for a priest. They assumed that baptism would immunize the youth against the snake's venom, their principal concern. After baptism, they said, "Now you can return, Father, because our boy has the cure."[128]

Despite the contrasts between Catholicism and Guaycuruan religion, certain aboriginal beliefs prepared the way for Christian ones. Living in a world of hostile spirits, many Guaycuruans accepted the concept of hell. Mocobis were especially impressed by the devil's eternal fires. One sick Mocobi woman in San Javier visited an *hechicera* for a cure. The priest told her that this consultation prevented her from receiving baptism; therefore, her soul would roast forever in endless fire, and vultures and jaguars would eat her. After the tormented woman suffered a sleepless night, she convinced the priest that she was repentant, and baptism brought her a peaceful death.[129]

Guaycuruans invested crosses and crucifixes with magical powers. Mocobis concluded that the devil feared rosaries and avoided those who wore them. When Christian Mocobis were ill, they applied a crucifix to the afflicted part of the body for relief,[130] a legacy of shamanic sucking. A woman of San Javier, troubled by temptation, found tranquility in a bed filled with crucifixes. A man in the same mission reportedly knew two cures for illness: a special grass from the Chaco and the cross.

Despite having resided in missions for two generations or more, mission Guaycuruans at the end of the colonial era retained aboriginal beliefs that they hid from missionaries. The pull of aboriginal religion remained strong for years, often embedded in Guaycuruan Christianity. Guaycuruans conveniently pled ignorance of Catholic doctrine or ritual when they chose to observe ancient ways. Many turned to old practices after 1767, when some missions were without priests for a year or more at a time. After the expulsion of the Jesuits, royal officials and missionary allies looted San Ignacio de Tobas and exploited its people. Lacking funds and the willingness to maintain adobe, villagers allowed the rains to dissolve the church. Thus the Toba had no place to hear mass, pray, or learn Christian values between 1775 and 1778. They professed to have forgotten the simplest Christian rituals, not a credible claim for members of a culture that had always memorized and transmitted information orally.[131]

Nevertheless, the majority considered themselves Christians and their priests concurred, although the two groups disagreed about what being Christian meant. In the early nineteenth century, the curate called the Abipones of San Jerónimo "a faithful and Christian people," a far cry from the denunciations of Santa Fe authorities a generation earlier. The Mocobis of Remolinos also saw themselves as good Christians, with ninety-three of the couples having been married in church ceremonies. They would have raised their children as Christians but for Dr. Francia's destruction of the regular orders. As in postconquest Mexico, a continuity had been established between indigenous thought and Christianity.[132]

Fugitive priests deprived Indians of sacraments, now essential rituals. In San Jerónimo in the 1790s, the people lacked a resident cleric. Thus the teniente of Santa Fe occasionally brought his own chaplain to baptize the young and to prepare the dying for eternity. The shortage of clerics forced the authorities to send lay missionaries to some missions.[133] Without a priestly presence, Guaycuruan ceremonies reappeared even in San Javier, the oldest and most thoroughly Catholic of all the missions.[134] The resurfacing of old customs surely meant the reemergence of aboriginal practitioners as well.

Guaycuruan Christianity

Shamanism surely survived at varying levels of practice for several generations after Guaycuruans moved to missions and in the post-mission years of the Independence period. Faced with documentary silence, however, we might recall the case of Polinari, the "Christian shaman" of the Caduveos in the 1940s. His activities let us conjecture on the role shamans might have played in missions without priests.[135]

In San Fernando in 1792, the old ways, although increasingly subordinated to the new, remained influential. When the priest threatened to force Abipones to attend mass, a threat reinforced by the mission's new proximity to militia outposts, the Abipones threatened to kill him. These Yaaucanigas, still less ardent Catholics than other Abipones, responded to gentler methods. They attended mass and lessons in doctrine for presents, and they sent their children to the priest for instruction and baptism because the youngsters received gifts of clothing.[136]

Cacique and corregidor Don Miguel Jerónimo Benavides of San Jerónimo was both thoroughly Catholic and culturally Abipon. He naturally adorned a missive to the viceroy with Christian imagery, referring to the "cross on which our Lord died for all the living to facilitate our road to glory." Though written by a Spanish employee, these words accurately reflected the second generation's faith. It was God, Don Miguel added, who gave Abipones business ability,[137] just as their spiritual grandfather gave their ancestors courage.

Guaycuruans were never indifferent to Christianity. Religion was too central to their lives. They investigated it, feared it, resisted it, and accepted it; but they never ignored it. For Guaycuruans, as for the colonial Maya of Yucatan, religion was something "personal and public, intellectual and emotional, as well as spiritual." As in Yucatan, Guaycuruan religion operated on at least three levels: the universal, the parochial, and the private. At the universal level, people recognized an all-encompassing deity. At the middle or parochial level, public but somewhat particularistic, the welfare of the group was under the control of corporate deities, which might include patron saints or spirits who advised a group to move for the hunt or protection. At the private level, seen by missionaries as "superstition" but by believers as magic, local nonhuman forces might hurt or help an individual or family.[138]

In Chaco missions as in colonial Yucatan, it was at the middle level that Christianity and native religion found the most conflict, as priests and shamans struggled to gain the allegiance of believers. Nevertheless, people in missions embraced Christian symbols at this level, in particular physical representations such as the images of the patron saints of the missions. At the universal level, the Christian God replaced the Great Ancestor. Catholic rituals dominated; Guaycuruan ones were hidden. At the private or family level of magic, the religion of the Chaco continued to influence some believers in missions. These beliefs were the hardest for priests to discover and eradicate. At this level, Guaycuruan religion even impressed the popular classes in Spanish society, who thought that Indians had special powers. When they could, they patronized magical healers believed to have special Indian knowledge. In religious matters, Guaycuruans found new ways to interpret the radical changes in their lives.

CHAPTER 7

The Nineteenth and Twentieth Centuries

In three Platine intendancies bordering the Gran Chaco—Paraguay, Buenos Aires, and Salta del Tucumán—the end of Spanish rule terminated the colonial missions to Guaycuruans. To the south and west of the Paraguayan Chaco settlements, mission Guaycuruans watched creoles abandon them. In 1811 General Manuel Belgrano of Buenos Aires marched through Santa Fe on his ill-fated expedition to Paraguay. He incorporated into his force the blandengues of Santa Fe, the city's only reliable military unit.[1] It had only seventy soldiers, but to Native Americans in and out of missions it symbolized stability and the authority of the crown.

Guaycuruans understood at once the significance of Hispanic factionalism that followed the declarations of provincial autonomy in 1810 and of independence in 1816.[2] They took the disintegration of Spanish authority as a signal to renew the predatory economic activity that had provided sustenance before missions. They helped themselves to the cattle of local ranchers and to goods from cart trains.[3] As in an earlier era, Guaycuruans sought captives and burned settlements with relative impunity. Because the frontier forts were now deserted, the Guaycuruans, especially Mocobis and Toba from the Chaco, dominated the countryside around Santa Fe intermittently into the 1820s. War alternated with uneasy truces, and pampas groups from the south took advantage of the instability to conduct raids as well. Peaceful Guaycuruans who visited Santa Fe to trade risked their lives.[4]

Interracial homicide returned to the frontier. Except for the Mocobis of San Javier, all the missions lost their priests, who fled to the city of Santa Fe. Residents of the defunct missions, abandoned by priests and protectors, were exposed to attack from other missions, from Chaco raiders, and from whites. The government of Santa Fe attempted to replace the departed blandengues, but the force they put together was ineffective. Estanislao López, returned from defeat and captivity in Paraguay, tried to bring order to the province. A unit under López's command massacred Mocobis working peacefully at three estancias in the Santa Fe area. When Mocobi Cacique José Tarragona of San Pedro traveled to Santa Fe to discuss peace, Santafecinos murdered him and his retinue. In response, men of the three Mocobi missions, San Javier, San Pedro, and Ispín, assailed not only Santa Fe but also the Abipones of San Jerónimo.

Many Guaycuruans, including Corregidor Manuelito and other caciques of San Javier, fought with the armies of José Gervasio Artigas, patriot leader of the Banda Oriental. Abipones from San Jerónimo joined a different insurgent, General José Viamonte, who appointed them his personal escort. Even during the upheaval, however, missions beckoned. Cacique Nancul asked Viamonte in 1815 for a new reduction for his people. Nancul was both a Christian and a traditional Guaycuruan leader whose political decisions reflected the wishes of his people, so we can assume the decision was consensual.

In 1815 Guaycuruans welcomed the peace overtures of Governor Francisco Candioti of Santa Fe because many had worked and lived on his ranches in Santa Fe and Entre Ríos. They underestimated the murderous rage of Santafecinos against allies of their enemy Artigas, however. At dawn of the day after San Javier Mocobis visited Candiotti, Santafecinos slaughtered the men of the delegation and the government rounded up the women. Not surprisingly, errant Mocobis retaliated with similar violence.[5]

Internal strife in the United Provinces of the Río de la Plata occasioned a brief renewal of Guaycuruan strength. José Artigas encouraged Guaycuruans to attack Córdoba and Santiago del Estero. In Corrientes frequent Guaycuruan attacks made the countryside around that city too unsafe for settlers.[6] Guaycuruan men extorted yerba, tobacco, aguardiente, and clothing from those municipalities. The mounted Chaqueños faced only an ineffective force financed by landowners of Córdoba and were able to push the frontier south again in 1816–17. Yet Guaycuruans in the 1810s were still unable to surmount the limitations of their own factional political culture. When Córdoba's forces under General Juan Antonio Arenales marched against Chaco enemies, Guaycuruans fought on both sides.[7]

Another example of factionalism occurred in September 1818, when previously hostile Guaycuruans agreed to peace with the new governor of Santa Fe, Estanislao López. They accepted two thousand pesos' worth of gifts, and most who had once lived in reductions returned to their villages. They still lacked central decision-making authority, however, and factions disputed war and peace. One leader, a cacique known as Mateo el Grande, even tried to kill López. Mateo failed, fled, and finally fell during an attack on Rincón.[8]

Although it appeared on the surface that Guaycuruans had reestablished their once-advantageous relationship of conflict with their Platine adversaries, these hostilities were different from those of the early eighteenth century. The Toba and Mocobis, groups which had often allied at local levels in the 1700s, characteristically hated each other from the 1820s to the 1850s, and Abipones and Mocobis were often mortal enemies as well. Native American forces were sufficiently powerful to keep Argentines from the Chaco by force from the 1810s to the 1840s. Still Guaycuruan culture had changed significantly during the era of missions, and many aspects of Chaco life resembled the late colonial period. Though suspicious of each other, creoles and Guaycuruans were not so culturally dissimilar as before. In the central Chaco along the Río Bermejo, the Toba and Mocobis still lived near the abandoned missions of San Bernardo and Cangayé. Even these Guaycuruans relatively remote from Argentine, Bolivian, and Paraguayan population centers depended on white tools such as knives and hatchets, lived or camped where they had access to these goods, and cultivated commercial relations with Argentine merchants.[9] When the Mocobis of San Javier departed their mission, they covered the images of the Catholic saints, whom they revered, with protective skins.

Unlike the chaos in the southern Chaco, in northern Paraguay and the Mato Grosso of Brazil, independence caused little immediate shift of Mbayás' divided allegiances of the late colonial era. Guaycuruans on the Chaco bank of the Río Paraguay between the mouth of the Bermejo in the south and Concepción, Paraguay, in the north took fewer liberties with the stable Paraguayan republic, bristling with defenses, than did Guaycuruans in the volatile United Provinces. Recalling the Paraguayan massacre in 1796 and the later punitive expedition under José Espínola, many still-neutral Mbayás moved into the Portuguese orbit. The northern Guaycuruans accompanied Portuguese attacks on Paraguayan outposts. In 1812 Mbayás stormed Fort Borbón, which guarded the northern approach to Paraguay, and they handed it over to the Portuguese. In 1815 they besieged Concepción.[10]

After independence, southern Mbayás felt the persecution of the Francia government, which tried to annihilate hostile Mbayás. A few Mbayá groups, however, searched for a working relationship with Dr. Francia. In 1821 several Caduveo caciques agreed to peace with the Francia government and sided with Paraguay against Brazil, but they balked at behaving in the submissive way Francia demanded. In particular, they refused to surrender their firearms. They stole livestock from Paraguayans and sold them to Brazilians for alcohol, which precipitated Francia's decision to deport them. He sent his soldiers to burn the palm groves on which Mbayá material life and cultural identity still depended, took Mbayá captives, and sent them south to the Guarani villages, hastening the Mbayá cultural decline.

Around Cuyabá, Mbayá commoners increasingly mixed with Brazilians. Periodically those who were still culturally Mbayá staged minor raids into northern Paraguay into the early 1850s. Mbayá members of the Brazilian military patrolled the Río Apa region, and Caduveos served imperial Brazil in the great war of the 1860s. During that terrible conflict, known as the War of the Triple Alliance or the Paraguayan War, fighting raged over lands from which Mbayás had pushed Guaranis two centuries earlier. Many received rewards for their participation in the War of the Triple Alliance, including land grants from Brazil, weapons, tools, and clothing, but the war devastated Mbayá society. Mbayá combatants suffered heavy casualties, and their widows and daughters took non-Mbayá partners and bore non-Mbayá children. By the late 1800s, surviving Mbayás lived in small, marginal groups that were steadily declining in numbers. Infanticide and abortion combined with alcoholism and disease took a heavy demographic toll. Now too weak to repopulate their bands by taking captives as they had done in the colonial era, Mbayá population dwindled.[11]

In the southern Chaco, Guaycuruan martial successes were temporary. Chaco Guaycuruan factions hostile to Santa Fe forced the province to spend a great part of its revenues defending the Chaco frontier. At the same time other Guaycuruans of the former reductions of Santa Fe often fought alongside the army of Governor Estanislao López in the civil wars of the early 1820s. The three Mocobi groups of the old missions of San Javier, San Pedro, and Ispín cooperated with each other and Argentines during raids but quarreled on other occasions.

The Abipones of San Jerónimo struggled unsuccessfully to remain aloof, but Mocobi attacks forced them to flee to Corrientes in 1824 and take refuge in the old Guarani pueblo of Santa Lucía. Caciques Benavides, Sira, and their followers conducted commercial exchanges outside Corrientes. In 1822 Abipon Caciques Lorenzo and José Ignacio fought with Correntinos, while other Abipones fought against them. Playing off Corrientes against Santa Fe, Cacique Patricio Ríos and the Abipones of San Fernando opened negotiations with Estanislao López of Santa Fe. They then renegotiated a treaty with Corrientes, which recognized Abipon sovereignty in the Chaco but stipulated that they leave Corrientes. They also promised to allow investors from Corrientes to exploit Chaco forest resources, a concession they had no right to grant.

Meanwhile Governor López summoned the Abipones of San Jerónimo home, and they were joined by the San Fernando Abipones of Cacique Patricio Rios. About five hundred Abipones moved to El Sauce, about ten leagues west of the city of Santa Fe. They were loyal to López and, as in the 1770s, protected Santa Fe from enemy attacks. López's wars stunted the economic growth of their pueblo, however.[12] A rapidly shrinking culture and language group whose members had been drifting into the larger society for decades, by the 1820s the Abipones were on their way to extinction. Many spread out in nuclear families in Corrientes and Entre Ríos. Having lost their land and their language, their children lost their Abipon identity.[13]

The Toba might have numbered fourteen thousand people in the 1820s, but they were widely dispersed along the banks of the Bermejo, the Pilcomayo, and the Río Paraguay. They lived in a variety of ways. Toba and Mocobis of the Bermejo near the former missions of San Bernardo and Cangayé tended horses and mules rustled from Córdoba, Santiago del Estero, and Santa Fe. Still guardians of their territories, they opposed people who entered their lands without permission. For example, Toba males led by chief Teculqui chased the expedition of Pablo Soria down the Bermejo in 1826.[14]

When San Antonio de Tobas and the nearby Naranjay disappeared during the independence period, the Toba began directly trading Chaco products with buyers in Asunción. Like other Guaycuruans, they continued to settle along the Río Paraguay.[15] Independent Toba bands also lived along the Río Pilcomayo between the Andes and Paraguay. These relatively traditional groups now dwelled in small, semipermanent villages instead of the mobile encampments of old, sallying forth from there to attack the northern frontier of Córdoba. The most traditional groups still lived semi-nomadic lives, while others had added agricultural and pastoral pursuits to hunting and gathering. They sowed maize, sweet potatoes, and manioc and attended livestock. When they stopped for long periods of time, some Toba built large, communal houses, closed on the southern end. When they tarried briefly, they lived in more fragile single-family dwellings. The women wove wool from their own sheep and cotton acquired through trade. They also made coarse pots. Both men and women did agricultural work and tended animals, but only the men hunted and fished. Men close to the new lumber enterprises worked as laborers, carrying sawn wood to rivers and streams for transport.[16]

The Toba of the upper (western) Pilcomayo in the early 1800s were still sufficiently powerful to intimidate the more numerous Guarani-speaking Chiriguanos of eastern Bolivia. They traded wild animal skins for industrial goods and accepted Argentine merchants into their midst. At least one merchant was formally adopted as a Toba. A native of Santiago del Estero, he took a Toba wife, the prettiest woman in the village, and the Toba awarded him monopoly rights to their commerce. When he had made enough money, this "Toba" merchant intended to move to Corrientes, where his business was headquartered, abandoning his Toba wife.[17]

Mocobis were still the dominant language group in the southern Chaco. Independent Mocobis lived on elevated plains toward the Chaco interior, in the scrub forests of the southern Chaco, and along the swamps near the Río Paraná to the east.[18] In 1834 Estanislao López defeated groups near Santa Fe. Some Mocobis remained hostile, while others moved to Los Calchines to refound San Javier with a priest, a chapel, houses, and lands. Since these Mocobis had served as peones at the chacras of the Rincón area and farmed their own lands, they now were able to survive without a government subsidy. Mocobi alumni of San Pedro and Ispín, who had fled their missions between 1810 and 1818, settled into San Pedro Chico at Añapiré in 1834, where López brought them a Franciscan lay brother. Others moved to Pueblo del Rincón and San Martín Norte.

Guaycuruan allegiances remained largely factional, personal, local, and temporary throughout the nineteenth century. After López died in 1839, the Abipones of El Sauce for a time in the 1840s supported Governor Ferré of Corrientes, while the "Tobas of Corrientes" (actually Mocobis) allied with non-Guaycuruan Matarás and Chunupíes. At the same time the true Toba of the region cooperated with Argentines. Simultaneously, other Guaycuruans were rustling cattle from Córdoba to sell in

Corrientes. In the civil wars of the Federalist Era, some joined Unitarios while others supported the Federales. Many years later one cacique proudly wore a federal uniform bearing the motto "Death to the Savage Unitarians."[19]

By the 1850s, when new Franciscan missionaries arrived from Italy, the only Guaycuruans living in missions were the Mocobis and Abipones of San Javier, San Pedro, and San Jerónimo, in the vicinity of Santa Fe. At about this time, non-mission Mocobis entered two new pueblos, Cayastá and Santa Rosa. In 1864 the population of these five missions was 3,026 of which 2,524 were Guaycuruans. These included 1,940 Mocobis in Santa Rosa, Cayastá, San Javier, and San Pedro and 564 Abipones in San Jerónimo.[20]

The residents lived by agriculture, sheepraising, and the sale of wool. They hunted wild horses, caught nutria for their soft and pliable skins, and stalked deer and jaguar, whose skins were also valuable. Existing in a more secular world than colonial reductions, the national-period missions lacked the stability of their predecessors. Security remained a problem, because non-mission Mocobis and errant Toba still attacked the missions. Moreover, the government relocated the missions of San Javier, San Pedro, and San Jerónimo several times in the mid-1800s, for reasons that to Guaycuruans appeared mere whim.[21]

The Mocobi missions of Santa Fe at midcentury centered around the *estancia grande*, originally a colonial property whose structural skeleton Mocobis and priests once again fleshed out. Mission San Javier extended over five leagues, smaller than the sprawling colonial missions, but still a substantial property. Having received subventions of food, mares, cows, and oxen from Governor Crespo in the early 1850s, residents expected a monthly allotment of horses from the national government of Justo José de Urquiza. Although the Santa Fe mission Guaycuruans had space enough to survive at midcentury, Argentine land hunger would soon drastically reduce their territories and thus impoverish them.[22]

Men in national-period missions still thought of themselves as hunters. They risked stealing cattle from ranchers, while the women butchered domestic animals and game. They worked and traded for silver, especially to purchase aguardiente, but scorned gold, which traditional Guaycuruans considered a dirty metal. Nineteenth-century Mocobi women wove fine wool fabrics of multicolored threads with indelible dyes and sold them for cash. They made earthenware jugs fired in the ground. Other tasks included gathering firewood; caring, bridling, and saddling horses; and gathering algarroba and honey for the traditional intoxicants their husbands, fathers, and brothers still drank. Priests lamented hyperbolically that the Indians sought ingredients for intoxicants daily, but in fact the limited supply of honey and the seasonal availability of algarroba prevented frequent use of indigenous beverages.

Guaycuruans in reductions largely cooperated with missionaries. During their years without priests, they had continued such Christian practices as abstaining from meat on holy days, and they still valued Christian religious forms. On the other hand, they remained eclectic in choosing which Christian symbols and practices to accept and which to reject. They supported their own religious specialists, who deciphered the future and cured the sick using magic, songs, applications of saliva, and bloodletting. To the dismay of priests, shamans now baptized newborn Mocobis, using priestly practices as models. They recited fragments of the Christian liturgy by heart as they celebrated the birth of a child. When men gambled with cards, they lighted a candle for good luck, a practice learned from the Jesuit and Franciscan fathers, while betting skins, horses, and even captives, a most un-Christian practice.[23]

In the 1850s Guaycuruans watched the Argentine reentry into the Chaco. Military penetrations preceded merchants, farmers, and loggers. Soldiers moved to new frontier forts, encouraged by government grants of nearby lands, which Guaycuruans resented and resisted. In 1862 Mocobi Cacique Javier, Toba Cacique Mariano el Grande, and a renegade called "The Paraguayan" died during a surprise attack by an Argentine army contingent on their force, which was camped on the northern frontier of Santa Fe. Chief Naponarí consulted with other Toba leaders, including Vicente Sarabia, Leoncito, Satigui, Hagañate, and several more, and they formalized a compact in February 1864 to allow an Argentine road through the Chaco. Lacking a binding "principle of authority" or even a vision of a Toba cultural collectivity uniting eastern and western Toba, many Toba disregarded the pact. The more acculturated among them worked as lumberjacks in the forests and laborers in the sawmills of the Chaco, while the more traditional Toba executed Argentines and other people who invaded their territories.[24]

At the other extreme, after decades of forced, voluntary, and incidental assimilation, the eight hundred Abipones at El Sauce were virtually the only members of their language group left in Santa Fe, although a smaller group still held out in Santiago del Estero, survivors of the five thousand Abipones of 1750. Some were now hardworking agriculturalists, growing maize, pumpkins, and peanuts. More traditional males complained of this labor, preferring to hunt jaguars and rheas, whose skins and feathers fetched good prices. Like other Guaycuruans, they gambled and drank the now easy-to-obtain alcohol of the whites as well as yerba maté from Paraguay and Brazil. In a country where horsemanship was important to all males, they were magnificent horsemen who wielded bolas and lances with dexterity. Horsemeat, customarily eaten in a stew but sometimes dried in the sun, was a mainstay of their diet. Living in a village with a brick church and school, they felt little hostility toward Argentine society and cooperated with Argentine authorities against Chaco Guaycuruans. Their homes mostly resembled those of the lower class of Santa Fe, being made of logs and cornstalks covered with leather; a few people lived in dwellings constructed in an older but not aboriginal fashion with sides open to the weather. Few had married in church, but most were as monogamous as their great-grandfathers had been. Men who could afford to dressed like Argentine gauchos. A few women dressed in Argentine fashion, but most wore a skirt from waist to knees and a pullover-style cotton or woolen blouse. They also wove woolen ponchos. Cacique Antonio Crespo could sign his name but employed a mulatto secretary to handle his correspondence, a sign of the changes in Abipon life. He maintained a mutually respectful relationship with Santa Fe Governor Patricio Cullen.[25]

Two small groups of Mocobis lived among the Abipones of El Sauce. Whites called them *indios montaraces* (wild Indians), because they periodically emerged from the Chaco to raid persons and property. The acculturating Mocobis wore clothing from an earlier era, such as bone jewelry and rhea feathers, and the Mocobi women made ponchos that were valued in the upper Plata region for their durability and beauty.[26]

In 1865 the Argentine conflict with Paraguay began. Guaycuruans of Santa Fe enlisted in separate units, the Abipones in the Lanceros del Sauce and the Mocobis in the Lanceros de San Javier and the Lanceros de San Pedro. All officially units of the forces of Santa Fe since the 1830s, they were attached to the regiment Blandengues de Belgrano. In the same year Toba Chiefs Pagnari, Agustín, and Leoncito from the Chaco interior signed a peace that secured the left flank of the Argentine army. The martial aspects of Guaycuruan culture remained strong, and after the war a number of Guaycuruan veterans joined the ranks of Chaco raiders, the indios montaraces. Led by Cacique Mariano López Lanchi, they attacked the Argentine unit stationed at the Arroyo del Rey in 1872, the site of colonial San Jerónimo de Abipones and now the city of Reconquista. The next year, though, several of their leaders, mostly Toba and Mocobis, including Ventura Tarragona, Mateo Villalba, and José Domingo, asked to live in reductions.[27]

In the 1850s and 1860s, Mocobis drifted from San Javier to Santa Rosa de Calchines. They obtained a missionary there in 1861 but had to wait another twelve years for a suitable church. Cacique Mariano Salteño and his five hundred Mocobi followers colonized a similar settlement at San Martín Norte. Another three hundred represented by Cacique Valentín Tiotí and their priest settled at Cayastá Viejo, the location of the old Charrúa mission. Known as Pueblo Dolores, this settlement was devastated by smallpox in 1872–73.[28]

As in the colonial era, the proximity of Argentines, Paraguayans, Brazilians, and Bolivians influenced Guaycuruan lifestyles. The more secluded a Guaycuruan band was from mainstream society—and by the second half of the nineteenth century only the Toba and Pilagás enjoyed isolation in substantial numbers—the more the people retained traditional characteristics. The closer their contacts with national populations, the more rapidly their groups lost identity and cohesiveness. Having virtually lost contact with the Chaco after 1800, Mbayás received lands in the Mato Grosso from Brazil for their efforts against Paraguay. Young Mbayás became Paraguayans and Brazilians.

In the 1870s Guaycuruans of the Argentine Chaco also were losing their identity. As the Argentine government stabilized after 1870, it took control of the Chaco. Into Guaycuruan territories came colonists from Europe, attracted by "free lands," actually Guaycuruan hunting areas. In the early 1870s, Chaco peoples evaded army penetrations from Salta and Santa Fe. Argentine forts pushed deeper into the Chaco and removed 600,000 hectares of land from Guaycuruans.[29]

Mocobis used four strategies for survival. Some settled into the new reductions of Santa Fe. Others moved in family groups and as domestic workers and peones into the expanding Argentine populations of Corrientes, Santa Fe, and Entre Ríos. In June 1872 a few of those still on the move counterattacked against Reconquista, founded the previous April. Others joined Toba bands. When a large number caught smallpox, their caciques, who had served with the Blandengues de Belgrano in the Paraguayan War, capitulated. They led 424 Guaycuruans to settle among immigrants and creoles in the barrio of Purísima Concepción in Reconquista,[30] where maintaining their cultural identity became increasingly difficult.

In the 1870s and 1880s, the Chaco Toba and the Mocobis with them watched as Argentines assembled a final conquest. Traditional Toba bands dominated the interior of the Chaco, while defeated ones and those interested in or forced into acculturation moved toward Spanish employment. Argentine officers estimated that twenty thousand Toba lived in the Chaco, probably too high an estimate. Toba weaponry was a mixed bag of bows and arrows plus firearms, purchased individually and in small lots from merchants. In the 1870s Toba chiefs such as Inglés and Hilarión Lanche still spoke for independent-minded followers, but maintaining a separate existence was becoming increasingly difficult. In 1879 the city of Formosa rose from the former mission of Timbó on land that eastern Toba now considered theirs.

In their battles against Argentines, the Toba faced the superior discipline of a modern army. With their avenues of retreat reduced, their traditional guerrilla-style warfare lost its effectiveness. In 1880 three Toba groups clashed with an Argentine expedition at La Cangayé, and their losses were overwhelming. The conclusive Guaycuruan defeat was the campaign of General Benjamín Vitorica in 1884, which broke the armed resistance of Chaco peoples. Defeated Toba agreed to live in a new reduction, San Antonio de Obligado, under a Franciscan missionary. Others went to Concepción de Reconquista or San Francisco Solano to live among creoles and immigrants, where they gradually lost their language, land, and identity. Some boycotted the agreement. Chiefs of mixed groups were among the last Guaycuruans in Argentina to resist the superior force that had encroached since contact.[31]

In western Formosa territory and the Chaco of Bolivia, some three thousand to four thousand Toba still lived along the Pilcomayo. They retained a culture reminiscent of the 1700s, raising cattle, sheep, goats, and a few crops. Men and women cropped their hair short using scissors or fish teeth. All women and a few men still painted their faces for decoration. Men often went naked in hot weather, while women painted their skin from waist to knees. Men still searched for algarroba for chicha drinking sprees, engaged in bloody fistfights, and occasionally practiced scalping. They practiced infanticide on deformed children and those whose mothers died. Marriage customs were simple, and most couples were monogamous. Shamans commanded respect. They magically cured and killed. Between 1860 and 1873, a sizable number of Toba joined the mission of San Francisco Solano of the Bolivian Franciscans. A Toba mass departure dismayed the priests, who abandoned the mission in 1879 but refounded it in 1884 with Chiriguano additions, despite the indifference of neighboring Bolivian landowners.[32]

The Bolivian Toba and a few to the south and east in Argentina and Paraguay maintained a degree of cultural autonomy into the twentieth century, even as Argentines and Europeans dominated their economic and political lives. Lumbermen, cattlemen, and farmers penetrated the Chaco, and Toba and Mocobi men worked for them. Entire Toba families migrated seasonally to harvest sugarcane in Tucumán and Jujuy, working industriously for low wages at the expense of their traditional subsistence economies. They also picked cotton on their own land and the lands of others in the Chaco province of Argentina. The demands of cotton cultivation and the modern labor market wore down Toba values. Some Toba joined the missions of Laishí and Tacaagle in Formosa, whose organizing principles were neocolonial. Many recalled that they had learned reading, writing, and the value of money in those institutions, but alcohol abuse was a problem in the modern missions.[33]

In the early twentieth century, Guaycuruans in the eastern Chaco experienced a millenarian revival not unlike the Ghost Dance in the western United States a decade or two earlier. In 1904 they suffered the same disastrous defeat that the North American followers of Wovoka did at Wounded Knee. Toba leaders proclaimed that white bullets would not penetrate their followers, and considerable numbers responded to the cry to do battle. When five hundred believers attacked San Javier, Argentine bullets taught them how wrong their prophets were.[34]

By 1912 Pilagás and the western Toba of Argentina and Bolivia, who had guarded their lands from whites until only a few years before then, worked in sugar factories of Jujuy. In Argentina, "The Toba were the only natives at the beginning of the twentieth century who had not been incorporated into the labour market in a permanent way," but in the 1930s, even they participated in the economy.[35] Several factors shoved the Toba into the economic mainstream, including cattle ranchers from Salta expanding to the east, new railroads, and the Chaco War between Paraguay and Bolivia from 1932 to 1935, which forced Tobas from Bolivia and Paraguay to take refuge in Argentina.

Many Toba social and political traditions still resembled those of two centuries earlier, including men's and women's work, menstrual taboos, consensual political leadership of chiefs, fear of the dead, and burial customs. Newer influences included agriculture. The Toba grew maize, pumpkins, watermelons, and beans. They traded with their neighbors the Chiriguanos. They ate both game and fish, but more of the latter. They raised sheep, goats, dogs, and horses. Like much of the rest of their material culture, their weapons were both traditional and modern:

clubs, bows and arrows, and a variety of firearms. They still loved to travel and followed the ripening algarroba. Having less experience with missions than Abipones, Mocobis, or the Toba of eastern Formosa, the Lañagachek, the Toba of the north, and the Takshik practiced a religion that was mostly traditional.[36]

In the middle decades of the twentieth century, Guaycuruan populations fell to minuscule size for all groups save the Toba and the Pilagá. By 1950 the Toba of Argentina typically lived in extended families in semi-sedentary agricultural settlements on lands they worked but did not own. They grew their own cotton and picked cotton for others when they had to, but they lacked the necessary equipment and capital to be competitive. When the Toba got land, as some did, hard times eventually forced them to sell it.

In the 1940s Mocobi small farmers lived in San Javier and Santa Rosa in the Santa Fe province of Argentina. A larger group lived in the civil reduction of Napalpí in Chaco territory, where they also grew cotton and worked in forest industries. About three hundred descendants of the Mbayá lived in settlements around San Juan Nepomuceno in Paraguay. The Caduveos, other descendants of once-powerful Mbayás, occasionally talked with anthropologists from the 1930s to the 1970s. Numbering less than four hundred, they lived in Brazil on lands that their ancestors won fighting in the Paraguayan War. They dressed like Brazilian peasants of the Mato Grosso. Their homes without walls—housing from one to six families—revealed traditional and Brazilian influences. They cultivated manioc, helped themselves to the livestock of neighbors, hunted, sold hides and skins, gathered wild fruits, and worked on neighboring *fazendas*. They exploited palms in the manner of their ancestors. Women made and decorated pots. Shamans were still active.

By this time neither the Abipones nor the Payaguás existed as a cultural group. The Great War of the 1860s had occasioned the demise of the Payaguás, as the widows and daughters of Payaguá soldiers found other fathers for their children. As alcoholism rendered male Payaguás impotent, females began to seek other partners as early as the 1700s. By 1940, only four Payaguá women survived in the Chacarita barrio of Asunción.[37]

By the last third of the twentieth century, only the Toba and Mocobis survived in Argentina, and handfuls of Guaycuruans, mostly Toba, lived with difficulty in Paraguay. By one reading of data from the 1968 census, 16,548 Toba and 1,202 Pilagás lived in Argentina. Another count lists 19,500 Toba in Argentina and 2,600 more retaining a Toba identity in Bolivia. In the process of moving from rural to urban environments, they were dispersed from Buenos Aires to the Río Pilcomayo and from Bolivia to the Paraná-Paraguay river system. The Toba of Buenos Aires lived in the *villas de miseria* on the outskirts of that metropolis, with low incomes, inadequate medical care, and few educational opportunities.[38] In 1968 between 3,000 and 6,246 Mocobis lived in some twenty-five localities in the Argentine provinces of Chaco and Santa Fe, where they worked as "lumberjacks, sawmill laborers, ranch hands, harvesters, and domestics." Only half knew the Mocobi language.[39] Thus the descendants of the peoples who made colonial Spaniards quake had been brought low but had not yet succumbed. How different would their lives have been had the brief mission experiment of the Jesuit period been extended into the national period?

El indio que pereció vive en el gaucho; el gaucho, que está pereciendo, sobrevive en el criollo actual y los tres vivirán en el argentino futuro.

—ATTRIBUTED TO RICARDO ROJAS[40]

CHAPTER 8

Conclusion

A 1995 study by David Sweet, "The Ibero-American Frontier Mission in Native American History," offers a standard by which to measure the eighteenth-century Guaycuruan missions. Able, angry, and grim, Sweet appropriately views missions "from the vantage point of the 'missionized' Indians" (p. 1).[1] He revises Herbert Eugene Bolton's classic *Mission as a Frontier Institution in the Spanish-American Colonies,* in light of how postcolonial attitudes have altered our view of conquered peoples. In an ambitious argument, Sweet surveys two continents and several centuries.

Several of Sweet's most telling allegations do not fit the Guaycuruan missions comfortably, however. The most characteristic mission experience, Sweet claims, was "premature death." Another mission constant, according to Sweet, was "chronic illness." Where missions were in the vanguard of Spanish penetration of new areas, missionaries brought deadly microbes that sickened and killed Native Americans wholesale. Mass death by epidemic disease and chronic illness, however, was not characteristic of the eighteenth-century Guaycuruan missions. Guaycuruans in and out of reductions saw themselves as a healthy people, and their priests concurred. The statistical information is fragmentary. Mission Guaycuruans did suffer epidemics, including the trans-Chaco smallpox and measles tragedy of the 1730s and the smallpox outbreak that hit the Mbayás of Belén in the 1760s, but no evidence indicates that mission Guaycuruans died in greater numbers than residents of the adjacent Spanish settlements. In fact, as late as the 1850s, European observers continued to regard Guaycuruans as healthy people.[2]

The disease histories of the Chaco missions contrasted from those of

California or the Amazon because of chronology and propinquity. Two centuries elapsed between Guaycuruans' first exposure to European diseases and the eighteenth-century foundation of missions. These were centuries of interaction between Guaycuruans and Hispanized persons. This lengthy pre-mission period was undoubtedly when new diseases took their heaviest toll.

Although the sources necessary to establish precise population trends in the Chaco in the sixteenth and seventeenth centuries[3] are nonexistent, the greatest devastation was surely between first contact in the early 1500s and 1700, probably particularly in the earliest years. In this period, virgin soil epidemics, "characterized by an immunologically defenseless host population . . . extremely rapid spread, and almost universal infection"[4] must have taken place. Chaqueños gained partial immunities to these diseases over the next six generations.[5] By 1743, when the first Mocobis joined San Javier, most Chaco peoples presumably possessed the same level of immunity as their Hispanic neighbors. Guaycuruans and Europeans had visited, traded, fought, captured, and incorporated each other into their societies. Such diseases as smallpox and measles were probably endemic by the mission era. It is unlikely that any "virgin soil populations," the isolated groups most devastated by Old World diseases, still existed in the Gran Chaco by the 1740s.

Departure from a mission was more likely than disease to cause population decline, but as in the missions of Sonora, Mexico, complex processes were at work. Guaycuruan missions were not synonymous with Guaycuruan communities, because mission populations fluctuated and group and kinship ties extended beyond them.[6] In the Guarani missions of Paraguay, which bordered the northeastern Chaco Guaycuruan missions, few people were recruited after 1700, yet the population trends there reflect a notable stability. Fluctuations typically occurred when outside pressures disrupted Guarani life. For example, when the epidemic of the 1730s swept the Chaco and the Guarani missions—then vulnerable because of the rebellion in the rival civil province of Paraguay—losses from disease were followed by demographic recovery.[7] Until the development of the smallpox vaccine at the end of the colonial era, missionaries lacked effective cures for infectious diseases. Yet, ill Guaycuruans were more likely to recover in a reduction than in an indigenous setting because missionaries fed and nursed them, whereas their own people shunned them and withheld food.

In most missions, argues Sweet, the Native American inhabitants experienced a "general decline in the level of their nutrition brought about by the mission regime" (pp. 15–16). Before missions, Guaycuruan men and women spent most of their time finding and preparing food. They ate most of what they caught or gleaned immediately to prevent its spoiling. Sedentary agriculture, practiced in the missions, supported larger populations than did hunting and gathering. Many native foods, Sweet points out, disgusted missionaries, and they urged Indians to produce fewer types of foods than before and to eat at regularly scheduled mealtimes. They encouraged their parishioners to avoid what they called gluttony. Jesuits in the Chaco gave or withheld sugar, yerba, and tobacco to induce cooperation. Nevertheless, mission Guaycuruans continued to eat such traditional foods as the fruit of the algarroba and game, and often left missions to obtain them. Thus, Guaycuruans typically did not suffer the restricted diet and withholding of food for social control that Native Americans on the northern frontier experienced.

Like other Native Americans, Guaycuruans suffered when they lost access to accustomed foods. In a departure from Sweet's chronology, however, the most significant dietary changes occurred before missions. In the seventeenth century, Guaycuruans became dependent on cattle, and the increasing difficulty of obtaining foods of European origin, especially beef, in the 1700s was one factor prompting them to request missions. Another was the depletion of such vegetable foods as the palm and the algarroba, which succumbed to the onslaught of iron tools. Thus, for Guaycuruans the causal relationship between nutrition loss and mission life is the reverse of Sweet's model. In the Chaco hunger and malnutrition brought the Indians to missions.

On the other hand, some features of Sweet's arguments capture the Chaco experience: priests attempted to regiment food habits, prompting protest. Guaycuruans initially devoured immense quantities of beef in one meal, horrifying priests. The Mocobis of San Javier, for example, grumbled when the missionary rationed each six families to one cow a week.[8]

As in other areas, missionaries in the Chaco introduced "a new conception of time" (p. 16), and mission Guaycuruans lived more regimented lives than before. The clock, which missionaries in the Chaco used to impress newcomers, was a technological innovation initiating sweeping changes. But this development was surely more revolutionary for remote Guaycuruans than for those with lands bordering on Spanish properties. Most Guaycuruan bands contained at least a few people who had prior contact with European schedules.

In introducing adult Indians to European work habits, the missionaries significantly altered only the habits of hunter-warrior Guaycuruan males, less than half the adults of most bands. Captives and servants, a significant minority of most bands before missions,[9] already faced the kinds of demands that missionaries hoped to impose on all.[10] Guaycuruan women, moreover, brought a European-like work routine to the missions; that is, they toiled most of the time. Sweet says that missionaries tried to make Indians into "unwaged rural proletarians" (p. 17), and indeed many ordinary Guaycuruan males fit this pattern. Caciques, in contrast, went from impoverished chiefs on the move to property owners in missions.

Sweet states, "Mission Indians were by definition deprived of the freedom to live their lives and procure their subsistence as they saw fit" (p. 18). A number of Guaycuruans, especially in the period when missions were being established,[11] resisted Spanish demands and the discipline of reduction life. They simply departed and returned to the Chaco.

Although missions "involved a new division of labor for most native people," (p. 19), the changes were less dramatic in the Guaycuruan settlements than Sweet's model would predict. Women continued to gather, prepare, and cook foods; tend to young children; and make clothing much as they did before. One change in women's work was production for sale, particularly the weaving of textiles. Nevertheless, the changes in women's work habits in missions were not dramatic. In the same way, men continued to exploit cattle and horses—chasing them, rounding them up, driving them, subduing them, and skinning them—as they had done in the century prior to joining missions. They frequently hunted and fished as before. They had been using iron tools and iron-tipped weapons for a century; iron implements were simply more accessible in missions. Agricultural fieldwork changed men's lives, but they continued to identify themselves as hunters and warriors and to revel in combat. Agricultural rhythms provided slow periods for hunting and fishing. Thus, as Sweet might predict, Europeans thought male Guaycuruans lazy, because the former interpreted hunting and fishing as leisure pastimes appropriate to aristocratic Europeans, not as occupations.[12]

The lives of Guaycuruan children in missions changed more drastically than those of their parents. Children attended lessons in subjects that priests thought valuable, and their parents now whipped them. Despite these disadvantages, they preferred the mission to life on the move. When their parents took them from the mission, they begged to return.

The missionaries did indeed seek to train Guaycuruans for work as "domestic servants and ranch hands" (p. 20), but those were occupations in which Native Americans were most likely to find employment beyond the mission's boundaries if they chose or were forced to join the Hispanicized world.[13] Nor were Guaycuruans limited to menial labor: in missions they learned trades as well: making tiles; building carts; and practicing carpentry, smithery, weaving, and music.

Church and state abandoned the Guaycuruan missions at independence, rather than following the route to secularization of eighteenth-century central Mexican parishes.[14] Even in this regard, the Chaco missions contradicted the assertion that no "ex-mission frontier population succeeded in retaining its local economic and administrative autonomy" after the departure of missionaries (p. 21). Because of the weakness of local forces, the vast distances, and the small Hispanic populations, the Chaco mission natives had limited but real autonomy.

Sweet censures missionaries for bringing flogging and other European punishments to Indian society (p. 22), punishments of which Guaycuruan society knew nothing. If the point of his criticism is to show that aboriginal societies were less cruel than European ones, however, he misses the mark. Guaycuruans inflicted all sorts of cruelties on their enemies and on their own young people, through infanticide, tests of manhood, and scarification rituals, which disappeared in missions. Guaycuruans themselves did not protest significantly when priests taught them that corporal punishment was a blessing. Guaycuruan parents themselves came to see whipping as an effective way to raise children and were enthusiastic about self-flagellation.

Flogging, as Sweet says (pp. 20–21), revealed "a harsh social inequality" in missions, because men of the leadership class were not whipped. Guaycuruans recognized sharp social distinctions before missions, however. Because they visited innumerable cruelties on others, Guaycuruans did not find "physical punishment . . . hard to understand," as other native peoples in missions might have (p. 22). For people who regarded war and the forcible acquisition of children and women for servitude as natural, "the pain and humiliation of harsh physical punishments" (p. 22) was not a revolutionary departure. What Guaycuruans did object to so strenuously as to cause suicidal depression was incarceration in a jail in a nearby Spanish town,[15] or even worse, exile to a far-off place such as Montevideo. The physical punishments with which Sweet is familiar—for theft, open sacrilege, or concubinage—occurred only with the endorsement of Guaycuruan leaders, who were the men most likely to take second wives.

Insofar as missionaries achieved their purposes, they were agents of "deculturation," as Sweet rightly says. Jesuits who witnessed the maturation of two generations of Guaycuruans,[16] however, lamented that insufficient deculturation (although they never used this word) took place. In the mid-nineteenth century, Europeans remarked that Guaycuruan customs still dominated the ways of the descendants of mission residents. Yet, Sweet is correct that Hispanic customs replaced native (but among Guaycuruans not aboriginal) ones in missions, and he criticizes the cultural imperialism of imposing the Spanish language or "an Indian lingua franca" such as Guarani (p. 23) on Guaycuruans. Jesuits and Guaycuruans conducted mission business in native languages. Their mostly Franciscan replacements spoke Spanish, occasionally Guarani, but seldom Mbayá, Mocobi, Abipon, or Toba. In neither the eighteenth nor twentieth centuries, the centuries for which documentation is available, was using Guarani a way of "maintaining a desirable isolation of the mission community from nearby secular European outposts" (p. 23); north of Santa Fe, more people spoke Guarani than Spanish, even among the elites. Nor was Guarani a new introduction in the eastern regions where a majority of Guaycuruan missions were located. Guaycuruans on the periphery of the civil and mission provinces of Paraguay knew Guarani before missionaries arrived. Therefore, though living in missions required "learning or accommodating one's self to a new language as well as to a new culture" (pp. 23–24), this process of cultural exchange by force and by choice had been going on for a very long time before the establishment of missions. The Guaranis who crossed the Chaco to the Andes before contact must have been able to communicate with Chaco peoples.

As Sweet observes about missions generally, the hoped-for conversion of adults was virtually impossible to achieve. But the missionary categories of "convert" and "pagan" oversimplify the historical reality of religious development. Guaycuruans, for example, had contact with Christianity periodically for two centuries before the 1740s. Once they arrived in missions, some aspects of Christianity—for example, rituals, images, and the spiritual power of the Spaniards—appealed to them, while they rejected many core values of Catholicism. As the priests had taught their grandparents, post-mission Guaycuruan men in the 1800s lighted candles—but for luck when gambling not religious purposes. Even after the missionaries departed, Guaycuruans remained attached to the images of the Virgin and the saints, wrapping them for protection when they left the missions. Shamans incorporated chunks of the Christian liturgy into their incantations.

The Guaycuruan experience with regard to sexual practices has points of agreement with and departure from the Sweet model. All Guaycuruans were not alike in sexual matters. For example, the premarital chastity of the Abipones differed from the more permissive attitude of Mbayás. Sexual segregation of the young in missions, which Sweet criticizes, was not very different from what Guaycuruans themselves practiced. In their pre-mission societies, after all, men and women spoke different dialects, which segregated them from birth. And, in contrast to Sweet's argument, whether or not one finds Native American "resistance against prohibitions in the realm of sexual behavior" (p. 25) depends upon the segment of Guaycuruan society considered. Men in missions, especially those of the native upper classes, as Sweet indicates, strongly resisted the missionaries' attempts to reform such native habits as plural marriages and serial monogamy. On the other hand, women of childbearing age welcomed the added security that Christian rules promised them, especially that a man should remain faithful to one wife and not divorce her. Missionaries' quest to eliminate abortion and infanticide coincided with the inclinations of many Guaycuruan mothers. Culturally innovative Guaycuruan women had begun to reject these practices on their own, as evidenced in the size of the families they brought to missions. Most were larger than the traditional ideal of one or two children.

In the Chaco, as elsewhere in Latin America, "missionary interventionism was especially active in the area of childrearing," and missionaries hoped to replace Indian family practices with their own (p. 26). Priests in Chaco missions raised abandoned children and the twins and deformed children whom parents otherwise would have executed. Missionaries were no more "demeaning, deemphasizing, and discouraging" of women's roles than were indigenous Guaycuruan men (p. 26). Despite "gender complementarity," Guaycuruan men, like missionaries, admired "patriarchal theocracies" (p. 26). In reality it was not always easy for missionaries to implement patriarchal and misogynistic policies. Father Cardiel, for example, compared women to domestic animals: they both should stay away from his patio. He could ensure that the cows and horses of San Javier stayed away from his patio, but Mocobi women resisted such treatment.

An important aim of missions was the "infantilization of adult Indians" (p. 27). It might equally well be argued that the Roman Catholic Church, a proudly authoritarian institution, sought to "infantilize" its European flocks. Priests were "fathers" and parishioners their "sons" or "daughters." European Catholics could at least become priests, whereas Guaycuruans had no such opportunity.

Missions in the Chaco did not necessarily destroy Guaycuruans' opportunities "for achieving excellence, success, and esteem in the eyes of their neighbors," as happened in the missions with which Sweet is most familiar (p. 27). Large numbers of Guaycuruans in the Chaco interior coveted the advantages of their rivals in missions. Mocobi Chief Paikin, for example, was jealous of the military benefits his bitterest rival, Abipon Cacique Ychoalay–José Benavides, gained at San Jerónimo. For years Paikin sought his own mission to counter the strategic advantages of the Riikahé Abipones.

When Sweet asserts that it was impossible for Indians to be familiar enough with European Christianity to adopt it consciously and become "morally self-sufficient" people (pp. 27–28), he establishes a very high standard for religious change. It is doubtful that the subjects of German princes who chose Protestantism in the sixteenth century could have met this test. As elsewhere, Indians in the Chaco were expected to "memorize formulae they did not understand" in their daily lessons (p. 28). But Guaycuruans were curious about Christianity, and they desired knowledge of the secrets of the religion that gave Hispanics such power. "The oft-cited docility" (p. 28) that characterized mission subjects elsewhere was not a prominent feature of Guaycuruan missions. Even after decades of mission life, Guaycuruans retained minds of their own and the ability to resist intolerable missionary demands by simply leaving. Horses gave them mobility, and the Chaco was vast enough that many individuals could retreat there.

Missionaries in the Chaco, as Sweet claims for other areas, did replace "the Indians' vital sense that the self and community existed and acquired meaning through their intimate relationship with nature," with a concept of nature as a "storehouse of resources disposed by . . . God for Europeans to exploit" (p. 29). Like Spanish merchants and agents of the king, clerics thoughtlessly advocated the "exploitation of nature and its products for commercial purposes" (p. 29). Guaycuruan ideals and practices had already been altered in the preceding century through contact with Hispanic society, and Guaycuruans had participated in the destruction of their own environment for more than a century before they chose missions. They chopped down palm and algarroba trees on which they depended, depleted the supply of game animals, and brought destructive grazing livestock to their Chaco homes. Despite its European origins, environmental degradation on the Chaco frontier preceded rather than followed the coming of missions. It was in fact an important reason why Guaycuruans requested missions. Thus Guaycuruans' "alienation from nature" (p. 31) began when they acquired iron tools and animals of European origin two centuries before the coming of missions.

If, as Sweet says, "from an Indian point of view, the frontier mission experience on balance was surely a catastrophe" (p. 31), most Guaycuruans were unaware of this. The argument that missions brought new evils to the frontier is hard to apply to the Chaco. Most of the damage originated with the Spanish and Portuguese invasions. It was not the particular baggage of the missionaries.

As elsewhere, some Guaycuruans chose missions for "mere physical survival," although their descendants survived after missions disappeared in 1810. During the first two centuries of colonial contact, they rejected missions. Like their Guarani enemies, Guaycuruans in missions retained a significant cultural identity, even though their culture did change. Any culture is more or less dynamic, however, and Guaycuruans made significant cultural changes before the mission period.

Guaycuruans were rarely willing "to risk armed resistance against the missionaries themselves" (p. 33), as did the Tarahumara and the Yaqui of northern Mexico and the Chiriguano of Bolivia. The most common Guaycuruan form of resistance was departure, or desertion from the Spanish point of view, easier in the vast Chaco than it was for the colonial Maya of Yucatan or other peoples. Guaycuruan natives left missions and joined other bands, a traditional practice. But the fugitives once again faced the conditions that they had come to missions to escape. The carrying capacity of the Chaco could not accommodate a large nonagrarian population. Chaco missionaries knew that their charges were potentially dangerous, but seldom did departing Guaycuruans actually harm their missionaries. Father José Sánchez Labrador of Belén recalled that a jealous Mbayá chief tried to assassinate him, and Father Joseph Klein of San Fernando almost died from a blow to the head from an Abipon parishioner. These were isolated and atypical cases, however; no large-scale armed rebellion occurred in the Chaco.

The "previous experience of sedentary agriculture and town life" (p. 33) that contributed to long-lasting missions in northern Mexico and Bolivia was not a precondition of the Chaco experience. Indigenous Guaycuruans lived nomadic lives at the edge of a Spanish cattle frontier. They scorned "corn-growing" Native Americans such as the Guarani of Paraguay and the Omaguaca of Jujuy. Conforming to Sweet's general pattern, Guaycuruans experienced "a gradual rather than an abrupt . . . adaptation to European ways" (p. 33). Adaptation began in the 1540s, however, rather than beginning in missions in the 1700s. Neither did mission Guaycuruans experience the "revolution of the ax" that Alfred Métraux identified.[17] That too had begun long before. In the Chaco, as in the Californian and Brazilian missions that Sweet knows best, missionaries introduced "fruit trees, melons, grapevines, European vegetables and grains" (p. 34), and they also provided the steady supply of iron tools that kept many Guaycuruans tied to missions. Missionaries in the Chaco, however, were not responsible for introducing European livestock. On the eve of the mission era, Guaycuruans depended on cattle and horses for food, transportation, war, and plunder. Mbayás began raising sheep in an innovation predating and unrelated to the mission system.

Another evil that Sweet identifies in missions was the drinking of distilled spirits. Living in territories adjacent to Spanish settlements for two centuries, however, Guaycuruans had access to distilled alcohol many decades before missions. Alcohol was, as Sweet says, "ominous," and contributed to the extinction of many groups, including the Guaycuruan Payaguás. Jesuits in the Chaco were determined enemies of alcohol abuse. They tried to persuade Guaycuruan men to abstain from alcohol misuse, rewarding men such as Mocobi Cacique Aletin of San Javier who spurned even native intoxicants.

As in other areas, Guaycuruans developed new forms of government by "native officials" in missions. Yet Guaycuruan leaders were not as "closely supervised by the missionary" as were the Guarani (p. 37). Priests in Chaco missions had no nearby Spanish forces to summon until the late mission period, and even then presidial militias were heavily outnumbered by Guaycuruan forces. Even had Spanish forces been larger, relations between presidios and natives in missions were not necessarily adversarial. Thus missionaries were often as dependent on native leaders as the leaders were on the clerics. Unquestionably, implementation of new ways "worked best under the guidance of native leaders" (p. 37), as can be seen in the changing work habits of mission Guaycuruans. The authority of Indian leaders was "indispensable to a viable community life," as Sweet says (p. 37), partly because Guaycuruan leaders became more authoritarian in the mission environment compared to premission years.

From the Spanish point of view, missions were fundamentally religious institutions, and indigenous Guaycuruans were deeply religious. As they acquired Christian religious ideas and participated in rituals of the church, some Guaycuruans conformed to the Sweet model while others did not. Although Jesuits asked Guaycuruans to obey their rules, few first-generation mission residents did. The missionary recourse was persuasion, not punishment; it would have been hazardous for missionaries to punish Guaycuruans for "transgressions against them" (p. 39). Occasionally Guaycuruan offenses against Spanish society were serious enough to bring retaliation. These provocations were usually military, but also included threats to property—especially cattle rustling and horse theft. Such merely irksome Guaycuruans as Cacique Miguel Benavides, who resisted Spanish controls, criticized bureaucrats, insisted on Guaycuruan marriage, but caused no harm to most Hispanized residents of the upper Plata region nor to missionaries, simply were tolerated. Harsh punishment of Guaycuruans for resistance to Christianity was beyond the capability of Spanish authority in the Chaco, where flight was easy. When Guaycuruans fled in large numbers, however, as did the Toba of San Ignacio who joined the Jujuy conspiracy of 1781, Spanish forces or Guaycuruan auxiliaries might apprehend them, because the late-eighteenth-century Chaco did not accommodate large refugee groups.

Resistance, "the insistence of individual Indians precisely on being themselves" (p. 41) was characteristic of the Guaycuruan experience with missions. There, Guaycuruans continued speaking their own languages for generations, even as they spoke Spanish, Guarani, or Quechua outside the missions. They spoke Spanish with Franciscans and Mercedarians, who infrequently learned a Guaycuruan language, but spoke their native languages among themselves to prevent missionaries from interfering in their lives. Mission residents continued to consult shamans and rode off to hunt and gather traditional foods, even though missionaries would have preferred that they be sedentary. Sweet claims that resistance was "greatest among the least sedentary and least 'political' of the missionized peoples," and the Guaycuruans prove this point (p. 42). But Sweet also says that such peoples "were most effectively broken" by the mission system (p. 42), which was not a characteristic of the colonial Guaycuruan mission experience. Missionaries had no forces with which to break Guaycuruans, except Guaycuruan ones. Relationships between Spanish soldiers of the presidios that dotted the Chaco frontier and mission natives were occasionally antagonistic in the late eighteenth century; examples were the case of Remolinos for Mocobis and the forts of the Río Negro region that the Toba attacked in 1781. As Bolton remarked, though, presidios existed to protect as well as to control Indians. The Abipones of San Jerónimo in the early 1780s, for example, feared other Guaycuruans more than Hispanic forces, and they welcomed the establishment of a presidio.

As Sweet says, the true enemy of Guaycuruan cultural resistance was demographic decline, which occurred differently on the Chaco mission frontier than in, for example, California. By the 1700s epidemic disease was insufficiently powerful to obliterate mission Guaycuruans, whose ancestors were the true victims. Instead Guaycuruans in and out of missions continued to assimilate into Hispanic Platine society by coercion and choice, as they had been doing for generations. Each Abipon (the group that declined to extinction first) who went to work on a ranch in Paraguay, Corrientes, or Santa Fe left one less member of the band to maintain the cultural identity of the group.

By the mid-nineteenth century, most of the reconstituted national-period missions of Abipones and Mocobis were places where Guaycuruans could maintain their identity, rather than places of assimilation. The Toba, who founded only three or four colonial missions[18]—San Ignacio and San Bernardo of the western Toba in Tucumán, and San Antonio (and possibly Naranjay) of the eastern Toba in the then-Paraguayan Chaco (now Formosa, Argentina)—moved in small numbers to other reductions. The western Toba, the most distant spatially and culturally from the Hispanic world, retained their identity the longest. Like all the rest, however, they were finally overwhelmed in the nineteenth century by the advance of the frontier and the economic pressures that preceded it.

Missionaries aimed at ethnocide, not genocide, as they "sought to exterminate Indian cultures, not Indian peoples" (p. 43); in contrast, secular Spanish bureaucrats and military leaders in the seventeenth and eighteenth centuries had hoped to exterminate Guaycuruans. This proved impossible in the colonial period, and missionaries were equally unable to extinguish Guaycuruan cultures.

The central problem with Sweet's argument is he conflates the establishment of missions with conquest. The two processes must be separated. The founding of missions coincided with conquest in some locations but not in others. The fact of conquest confounded efforts to treat native peoples fairly. To deal justly with peoples whose liberty one has reduced and whose lands one has seized is impossible. This can be seen in the efforts of the United States to provide justice for the Plains Indians. After the Civil War, North American reformers hoped to protect the Plains Indians, but the Indians were prisoners of their time and constrained by a policy of conquest. President Grant's misnamed Peace Policy of the early 1870s was a carrot-and-stick approach to settlement. Words of hope masked the reality of conquest and subordination. Indians were ordered to live on reservations to learn "civilization" and become self-sufficient in agriculture.[19] Instead, the Plains Indians chose hostilities against encroaching whites. Their resistance reached its peak with their defeat of George A. Custer and the Seventh Cavalry at Little Bighorn in 1876. After this, the power of the Sioux, Cheyenne, and others dissipated. With their main food source, the bison, nearing extinction, and with whites overrunning their lands, they had little choice but to accept the humiliation and deprivation of reservations. Their power and their mobility were gone.

In the following decades, white policy continued to be destruction of Indian culture, identified as "savagery," and its replacement with the "civilization" of white America. Indians were immersed in off-reservation schools such as that at Carlisle, Pennsylvania, to change their ways. In addition, the federal government decided to "give the Indians a system of law to replace . . . traditional society."[20] The Dawes General Allotment Act of 1887 was intended to turn them into self-sufficient farmers. Instead, it more than halved their holdings between 1887 and 1934. The religious reformers who pushed education, Christianity, private ownership of land, and Anglo-American law on Indian peoples were filled with "high-minded motivation."[21] They conceived ineffective policies because they, like Spanish conquerors and missionaries, devalued Indian cultures. They were prisoners of their conquest mentality. It was not their remedies that were malign, it was their culture of conquest that afforded them few alternatives.

After the subordination of indigenous peoples of the United States and Latin America, only limited help was available for Native Americans. Missionaries in the Gran Chaco in the 1700s followed their best instincts as they instructed Guaycuruans. Sweet blames missions for problems created by conquest. Some European institutions were less harmful to Indians than others. "Seen," as Sweet recommends, "from the perspective of Indian experience" (p. 45), the Chaco missions were a positive alternative for the Guaycuruans of the Gran Chaco, who welcomed them. Bands wanted more missions than Spanish authorities could provide. Guaycuruans perceived life in missions as preferable to survival in the degraded environment of their old territories.

Eighteenth-century Guaycuruan missions were not utopias. No institutions of foreign invaders were. Nonetheless, in missions many Guaycuruans developed new ways to deal with the economic, security, and environmental problems that threatened to overwhelm them, and they also found satisfactory explanations for the disasters that had befallen them. They succeeded in remaining culturally Guaycuruan while establishing a fragile peace with the dominant culture. As in southern Mexico, when Guaycuruans lost their land and language, their culture disintegrated.[22] A significant but unknown number of Guaycuruans never joined missions. Some could not find room in missions, others encountered adversaries already settled there, and still others preferred the Chaco interior. A large number moved to Spanish ranches, farms, cities, and later factories to work. Some Guaycuruan women took non-Guaycuruan mates. They were less able to retain an indigenous identity in secular settings than in missions. As the culture of conquest that first arrived in the 1500s threatened to engulf them, Guaycuruans chose the missions of the 1700s to enable their cultural survival. Missions were the grounds on which they chose to confront the awful challenges of conquest.

Although the culture of the nonsedentary Guaycuruan peoples differed from that of the semisedentary peoples who joined most other missions in Latin America, the history of the Guaycuruan missions and the methodology of this book in examining them can shed light on the experience of frontier missions elsewhere. Future studies of the mission experience should reconstruct how indigenous society functioned on the eve of the mission experience; without doing so, attempts to assess the impact of missionary practices risk degenerating either into "victimology" or Eurocentric triumphalism. Native Americans were truly victims of European invasions, but they usually were more than just victims.

For purposes of analysis, historians of missions should isolate and investigate the Native American experience before reattaching it to the experiences and ideologies of the missionaries and the state. Native American societies should be considered holistically. To treat them respectfully one should attempt to identify how they saw themselves, without idealizing them or demonizing them. One key issue is the role of war and the warrior. What kind of societies produce warriors and hunters and what social values did hunters and warriors promote? Another is the role of violence in indigenous society. For example, the much-discussed "whipping of Indians" in frontier missions, often foreign to the indigenous experience, should be seen in the larger context of violence within and without a society.

Another concern should be to determine which subgroups in Native American society suffered and which benefited from missions. Did men and women have parallel experiences in the mission environment, or did they suffer or benefit differentially? How did women's and men's work habits change in missions? Did the experiences of the oldest and the youngest members of mission societies differ from those of adults in their childbearing years? As the Spanish Empire governed through local elites connected to local constituencies, how did native elites function before and during the mission experience? How was policy made? What was the role of justice in indigenous and mission cultures?

Since missions were institutions designed to promote European religion, one should first understand how religion functioned in indigenous society. What was the role of native religious specialists? What did belief systems entail? What was the relationship of religion to hunting, war, agriculture, nature, relations between men and women, and a host of other issues? How did religious ritual form a part of pre-mission life? How and how quickly did these ideas and behaviors change in missions? What sectors of native society accepted and which resisted Catholic precepts? How and why did they do so? Addressing these questions will provide a new perspective on the history of missions in the Americas.

APPENDIX A
Guaycuruan Missions in the Río de la Plata, Date of Establishment, and Group

JURISDICTION OF SANTA FE

San Javier, 1743 (Mocobis)[a]
San Jerónimo, 1748 (Abipones)[a]
San Pedro, 1765 (Mocobis)[a]
San Francisco Solano, 1783 (Mocobis)[b]
Las Lomas, 1783 (Mocobis)[b]
Santiago, at Fort San Nicolás, 1793 (Abipones)[b]
Ispín (or Inispín), 1794 (Mocobis)[a]

JURISDICTION OF CORRIENTES

San Fernando, 1750 (Abipones)[a]

JURISDICTION OF SANTIAGO DEL ESTERO

Concepción, c. 1749 (Abipones)[a]

JURISDICTION OF JUJUY

San Ignacio, 1756 (Tobas)[a]

JURISDICTION OF GOBIERNO OF TUCUMÁN

San Bernardo el Vertiz, 1780–81 (Tobas)
Nuestra Señora de Dolores del Cangayé, 1780–81 (Mocobis)

JURISDICTION OF GOBIERNO OF PARAGUAY

Belén, 1760 (Mbayás)[a]
Refugio, 1769 (Mbayás)
San Carlos y Rosario del Timbó, 1764 (Abipones)

Remolinos, 1776 and 1778 (Mocobis)[a]
San Antonio, 1782 (Tobas)[a, c]
Naranjay, 1791 (Tobas)[a, c]
Mission of unknown name (Pilagá)

a. Lasted to end of colonial period
b. Known to have existed in year shown
c. Naranjay and San Antonio might have been the same mission. A separate mission is listed in Durán Estrago, *Presencia franciscana en el Paraguay*, 182–84. Her source is Benjamín Aceval, *Chaco paraguayo*. Naranjay, founded around 1790 and refounded in 1791, welcomed the incorporation of bands of Toba chiefs Hemechon and Guenogiri in the early nineteenth century. A church official active in Chaco mission affairs referred to San Antonio as "Naranjaí de San Antonio de Tobas" in 1788. Lorenzo Suárez Cantillana al virrey, Corrientes, Feb. 25, 1788, AGN, IX, 3-1-4.

APPENDIX B
Mission Censuses

TABLE 1. *Reduction of San Fernando de Abipones, 1753–1762 and 1766*

DATE	FAMILIES[a]	BOYS	GIRLS	WIDOWERS	WIDOWS	TOTAL POPULATION	ADULT BAPTISMS	NEAR-DEATH BAPTISMS	CHILD BAPTISMS	CHURCH MARRIAGES	ADULT DEATHS	CHILD DEATHS
1753	156	134	142	2	89	679	3	1	12	1	1	1
1754	104	83	102	2	60	455	2	0	18	0	0	5
1755	80	65	69	1	49	344	4	3	12	2	1	5
1756	82	66	74	1	50	355	0	1	8	0	1	2
1757	82	69	79	1	50	363	0	2	6	0	1	3
1758	39	21	33	1	18	151	0	1	3	0	1	2
1759	76	65	72	1	48	338	0	0	9	0	0	3
1760	74	68	74	1	48	339	0	3	16	0	2	1
1761	56	62	69	1	39	273	1	2	10	1	0	2
1762	48	67	75	1	45	284[b]	0	0	6	0	0	2
1766	58	70	47	4	50	287[c]	–	–	–	–	4	2
						Total	*10*	*13*	*100*	*4*		

Sources: Annua del Pueblo de San Fernando desde 1753, AGN, IX, 6-10-5; Certificación del P. José Clain, San Fernando, año de 1766, AGN, IX, 6-10-7.

a. Couples married with and without assistance of clergy.

b. Of these 284, baptized adults numbered 21. There had been only 10 adult baptisms in 10 years in the mission. The 21 baptized adults thus included at least 11 who became Christians as children and grew to maturity. Baptized children numbered 62. Thus, 29.2% of 1762 residents of San Fernando were formally Christian and 4 couples participated in church marriages, the same number who confessed and took communion. Of the adults, only 14.7% were baptized, but 42.6% of the children had received baptism.

c. Of these 287 people, 36 adults and 72 children (37.6%) were baptized and 6 of the 58 couples (10.3%) were married by priests. There were 24 confessions and 20 communions in 1766.

TABLE 2A. *Reduction of San Jerónimo de Abipones, January 1, 1761, to January 1, 1762*

	MARRIED COUPLES	BOYS	GIRLS	WIDOWERS	WIDOWS	CAPTIVES (M & F)	TOTAL POPULATIO
Christians	55	142	91	1	10	9	363
Non-Christians	65	16	8	3	50	–	207
Total	*120*	*158*	*99*	*4*	*60*	*9*	*570*

	ADULT BAPTISMS	CHILD BAPTISMS	COMMUNIONS	ADULT BURIALS	CHILD BURIALS	CHURCH MARRIAGES
Christians	5	29	86	2	8	5

Source: Annua enumeratio reductionum fluminis paranensis, Anni 1762, p. 3; AGN, IX, 6-10-5.

TABLE 2B. *Reduction of San Jerónimo de Abipones, 1766*

	POPULATION
Christians	450
Catechumens	278
Total	*728*

Source: Muriel, "Breve noticia de las misiones vivas," 175.

TABLE 2C. *Reduction of San Jerónimo de Abipones, 1785*

	CHRISTIANS	SPANISH CAPTIVES	GUARANI CAPTIVES	SLAVES	CATECHUMENS	NON-CHRISTIANS	TOTAL
Husbands	93	1	3	1	7	2	107
Wives	93	1	4	2	7	1	108 [107][a]
Widowers	9	0 [9]	1	1	1	1	13 [12]
Widows	56	0 [56]	1	1	2	1 [2]	61
Unmarried adult males	52	2	1	2	4	8	69
Unmarried adult females	66	1	8	1	15	5	96
Boys	107	1	10	0 [10]	0 [10]	0 [10]	118
Girls	95	4	9	1	0 [1]	0 [1]	109
Total	*571*	*10*	*37*	*9*	*36*	*18*	*681 [679]*

Source: Urbano de Iriondo, "Apuntes para la historia de Santa Fe," 115.

a. Square brackets [ ] indicate a copying error by Iriondo or a misprint by the editor who prepared his nineteenth-century manuscript for publication.

TABLE 3A. *Reduction of San Ignacio de Tobas, 1757*

	NUMBER
Husbands	47
Wives	47
Widowers	5
Widows	33
Boys	86
Girls	88
Total population	*306*
Child baptisms	94
Adult baptisms	4
Adult deaths	2
Marriages	0
Communions	0

Source: Catálogo annuo de la reducción de San Ignacio de Tobas de 1757, AGN, IX, 6-10-2.

TABLE 3B. *Reduction of San Ignacio de Tobas, 1761*

	NUMBER
Adult Christians	42
Child Christians	163
Non-Christians	160
Total population	*365*
Infants dying baptized, 1756–61	52
Adults dying baptized, 1756–61	7

Source: Muriel, "Breve noticia de las misiones vivas," 159.

TABLE 3C. *Reduction of San Ignacio de Tobas, 1771*

	NUMBER
Males	160
Females	162
Total population	*332*
Christians	272
Non-Christians	60

Source: Testimonio de auto de vista de las reducciones de los indios de las fronteras del Chaco, August 19, 1771, AGI, BA, leg. 468.

TABLE 3D. *Reduction of San Ignacio de Tobas, July 1778*

	ADULT MALES	ADULT FEMALES	BOYS	GIRLS	TOTAL
Christians	104	83	76	71	334
Non-Christians	18	31	0	0	49
Total	*122*	*114*	*76*	*71*	*383*

Source: Resumen general de la reducción de San Ignacio de Tobas, July 23, 1778; Expediente de visitas practicadas en la frontera de Salta y Jujuy por Don Andrés de Mestre, AGN, IX, 30-1-8.

TABLE 4A. *Reduction of San Javier de Mocobis, 1753(?)*

	NUMBER
Christians	613
Catechumens	103
Total population	*716*
Men at arms	162

Source: "Relacion del estado, en que'se halla el Pueblo de San Xavier, de Yndios Mocobis . . . de Santa Fe," in Cortesâo, *Manuscritos da coleçao de Angelis,* vol. 7.

TABLE 4B. *Reduction of San Javier de Mocobis, 1785*

	CHRISTIANS	NON-CHRISTIANS	SPANISH CAPTIVES	GUARANI CAPTIVES	TOTAL
Husbands	191	0	1	2	194
Wives	192	0	0 [192][a]	2	194
Widowers	6	0	0 [6]	0 [6]	6
Widows	66	0	0 [66]	0 [66]	66
Unmarried males	50	0	1	2	53
Unmarried females	104	0	1	1	106
Boys	215	0	1	1	217 [218]
Girls	203	0	1	1	205 [206]
Total	*1,027*	*0*	5	9	*1,041*[b]

Source: Urbano de Iriondo, "Apuntes para la historia de Santa Fe," 115.

a. Square brackets [ ] indicate a misprint or error.

b. M. Cervera (*Historia de la ciudad y provincia de Santa Fe*, 576) records the total population as 1,049. Cervera used the original manuscript from 1785. By 1988, when I worked at the Archivo General de la Provincia de Santa Fe, these records had so deteriorated that they were unavailable to scholars.

TABLE 5. *Guaycuruan Missions, 1767: Counts and Estimates*

MISSION	GROUP	POPULATION	CHRISTIANS	YEAR FOUNDED
Rosario y San Carlos (Timbó)	Abipones	350	[A few][a]	1763
Nuestra Señora de Belén	Mbayás	260	[A few]	1760
San Javier	Mocobis	982	982	1743
San Pedro	Mocobis	150 (300)[b]	80	1765
San Jerónimo	Abipones	823	593	1748
San Fernando	Abipones	440	–	1750
San Ignacio de Ledesma	Tobas	600	300	1756
Concepción	Abipones	400	[A few]	1749

Source: Jolís, *Ensayo sobre la historia natural del Gran Chaco.*

a. Square brackets [ ] indicate an estimate.

b. Parentheses ( ) indicate occasional population.

TABLE 6. *Reduction of San Pedro de Mocobis, 1785*

	CHRISTIANS	SPANISH CAPTIVES	GUARANI CAPTIVES	NON-CHRISTIANS	TOTAL
Husbands	91	1	4	15	111
Wives	96	0 [96][a]	0 [96]	15	111
Widowers	21	0 [21]	0 [21]	0 [21]	21
Widows	17	0 [17]	0 [17]	45	62
Unmarried males	46	1	1	0 [46]	48 [94]
Unmarried females	61	1	1	0 [61]	63 [124]
Boys	101	0 [101]	5	5	111
Girls	107	0 [107]	1	39	147
Total	*540*	*3*	*12*	*119*	*674*

Source: Urbano de Iriondo, "Apuntes para la historia de Santa Fe," 115.

a. Square brackets [ ] indicate misprints.

TABLE 7. *Reduction of Concepción de Abipones, 1777*

	NUMBER[a]
Husbands	48
Wives	48
Widowers	–
Widows	17
Unmarried males	32
Unmarried females	26
Boys	31
Girls	27
Total	*229*[b]
Christians	113[b]
Non-Christians	114[b]

Source: Visita del gobernador de la reducción de Nra. Sra. de la Concepción, Frontera del Gran Chaco, December 2, 1777, AGI, BA, leg. 244.

a. Count of Governor Antonio de Arriaga, who conducted the inspection.

b. The governor or his secretary either miscounted one of the categories or made an error in addition. My total is 229.

TABLE 8A. *San Bernardo de Tobas, Bermejo, Gobierno of Tucumán, 1781*

	NUMBER
Adult males	300
Officials and captains	49
Commoners	251
Adult females	257
Boys	253
Girls	260
Total	*1,070*[a]

Source: Matrícula y padrón de pueblo de Tobas San Bernarde el Vértiz, Jan. 23, 1781, AGN, IX, 2411-1.

a. None of the population was Christian.

TABLE 8B. *Santiago de Cangayé de Mocobies, Bermejo, Gobierno of Tucumán, 1781*

	NUMBER
Adult males	205
Officials and captains	57
Commoners	148
Adult females	277
Boys	96
Girls	124
Children too young to hear doctrine	203
Total	*905*[a]

Source: Padrón de Mocovís de Santiago de Cangayé, Feb. 8, 1781, AGN, IX, 2411-1.

a. Includes one Christian male, a captive.

NOTES

PREFACE

1. Although the literature on Jesuits in Latin America is vast, study of the Spanish Empire would benefit from a counterpart to Alden, *The Making of an Enterprise,* the first of two volumes on the Portuguese Assistancy and a work of great value.

2. The terms *mission* and *reduction* are used interchangeably.

3. Susnik, *El indio colonial,* 3 vols. (Asunción, 1966–1971); Susnik, *Los aborígenes,* 7 vols. (Asunción, 1978–86); Susnik, *El rol de los indígenas,* 2 vols. (Asunción, 1982–83).

4. Mintz, *Sweetness and Power,* xxvi.

5. Muchembled, *Popular Culture and Elite Culture in France,* 3–4.

6. Lockhart, ed. and trans., *We People Here;* Lockhart, *The Nahuas after Conquest;* Lockhart, *Nahuas and Spaniards;* Cline, *Colonial Culhuacán;* Schroeder, *Chimalpahin and the Kingdoms of Chalco;* and Haskett, *Indigenous Rulers,* have all employed indigenous language sources to make impressive contributions.

CHAPTER 1. *The Rise and Fall of Guaycuruan Power*

1. Jones, "Comparative Raiding Economies," 97–114.

2. Mendoza, "Politics and Leadership," p. 24.

3. Dobrizhoffer, *Account of the Abipones,* 2:158.

4. Cabeza de Vaca, "Comentarios," 189–213; Susnik, *El rol de los indígenas,* 2:97–98; Sánchez Labrador, *El Paraguay Católico* (hereinafter SLPC), 2:55–58.

5. The Spaniards' exploding weapons were relatively harmless, especially when it rained, and it rained daily half the year.

6. Métraux, "Ethnography," 217–23; Steward, "Native Population," 662; the figures for the mid-eighteenth century are Mbayá, 7,000–8,000; Abipon, 5,000; Mocobi, 2,000–3,000; Toba, 20,000–30,000, and Pilagá, 200–2,000, but the Mocobis are vastly under-counted, and the Toba over-counted. By 1800, the Payaguá numbered only 1,000. But they had moved to Asunción in two major migra-

tions of the 1700s and were merging into the Paraguayan population. Susnik, *Los aborígenes,* 1:10–11, 64.

7. In this work I use Tucumán to refer to the province, while the city of the same name appears as San Miguel de Tucumán.

8. Rock, *Argentina,* 11–14; Zubizarreta, *Historia de mi ciudad,* 93; Labougle, *Corrientes,* 11; SLPC, 2:59.

9. Jujuy, for example, had a population of 13,519 in 1778, of which 11,081 (82 percent) were Indians; Bidondo, *Historia de Jujuy,* 147. For general population trends see Comadrán Ruiz, *Evolución demográfica argentina.*

10. Santa Fe had 1,076 residents in 1662, about 1,500 in 1698, and between 4,000 and 5,000 in 1793; Gianello, *Historia de Santa Fe,* 142; Azara, *Descripción e historia del Paraguay,* 2:344.

11. Rock, *Argentina,* 15, 26; Cardozo, *El Paraguay colonial,* 118–24; Durán Estrago, *Presencia franciscana en el Paraguay,* 93–151; and Furlong, *Misiones,* 91–107, 110–17.

12. Furlong, *Misiones,* 107–10.

13. Dobrizhoffer, *Account of the Abipones,* 3:8.

14. SLPC, 2:61–74; Paucke, *Hacia allá,* 2:3; Susnik, *El rol de los indígenas,* 2:98–99; Felipe Rexe Corvalán al rey, Asunción, Jan. 28, 1678, CMG, Cal. 766.

15. Susnik, "Dimensiones migratorias y pautas culturales," 89; Susnik, *El indio colonial,* 3:27, 41; Josephy, *Indian Heritage,* 273–74; Canals Frau, *Las poblaciones indígenas,* 299, 315; Palevecino, "Las culturas aborígenes del Chaco," 429–72.

16. Susnik, "Dimensiones migratorias y pautas culturales," 85–88.

17. SLPC, 1:262–63.

18. SLPC, 1:262.

19. The eastern Plata region had one governor until 1617, when it was divided into two jurisdictions with capitals at Asunción and Buenos Aires. Benítez, *Historia del Paraguay,* 92.

20. Zapata Gollán, *El Chaco Gualamba,* 13–28; Monferini, "La historia militar," 311–12; Carta del gobernador al rey, Buenos Aires, July 16, 1664, in Pastells, ed., *Historia de la Compañía de Jesús,* vol. 2; Diego de Góngora al rey, Buenos Aires, Mar. 2, 1620, CMG, Cal. 579.

21. Autos del Gobernador Alonso Sarmiento Figueroa, Asunción, Feb. 20 and Apr. 6, 1660, CMG, Cal. 677 and Cal. 679; SLPC, 2:77. That Guaycuruans visited to trade enraged royal officials new to the region; see, for example, Felipe Rexe Corvalán al rey, Asunción, Jan. 28, 1678, CMG, Cal. 766. Nevertheless, the trade continued, because both cultures benefited.

22. Susnik, *Los aborígenes,* III/1:62.

23. Felipe Rege Corvalán al rey, Asunción, Mar. 28, 1675, CMG, Cal. 826.

24. Francisco de Monforte al rey, Asunción, July 19, 1686, CMG, Cal. 826; Aguirre, "Diario," 19:449–50.

25. D. Angel de Peredo al rey, Oct. 10, 1673, in "Testimonio de autos de Angel de Peredo, gobernador y capitán general del Tucumán en razón de la conquista de los enemigos fronterizos Tobas y Mocobíes de la provincia del Chaco," AGI,

Charcas, leg. 283; Nellar, ed., *Política seguida con el aborigen,* 2:198–99; Informe del cabildo de Jujuy al rey y al Consejo de Indias y al virrey, Jan. 4, 1677, AGI, Charcas, leg. 284.

26. Petición del fiscal a la Real Audiencia de la Plata, Plata, May 15, 1677, AGI, Charcas, leg. 283; Informe del presidente de la Plata al rey, Plata, Jan. 26, 1682, ibid.; Juan, obispo del Tucumán, al rey, Plata, Jan. 7, 1691, ibid.; Fr. Manuel, obispo de Tucumán, al rey, Santiago, June 7, 1691, ibid.

27. Parecer del Mro. Fray Juan Baez, del Orden de Nra. Sra. de la Merced, Convento de San Miguel de Lima, AGI, Charcas, leg. 283; and Parecer del Francisco López, C.J., sobre la guerra de los indios del Chaco, Lima, Oct. 14, 1682, ibid.; the Jesuit maintained that most theologians and legal experts believed that war was justified when infidels refused to receive preachers of the faith. If gentler methods failed, the king was obliged to protect his domain and his subjects.

28. Esteban de Urizar y Arespacochaga al rey, Salta, Nov. 24, 1708, AGI, Charcas, leg. 284.

29. M. Cervera, *Historia de la ciudad y provincia de Santa Fe,* 1:400–16; SLPC, 2:78–79; Labougle, *Corrientes,* 74–80; Aguirre, "Diario," 19:439.

30. Some Spanish accounts boast that the Mbayás came for a fraudulent wedding of the Mbayá chief to Avalos; Lozano, *Gran Chaco Gualamba,* 68–69; Aguirre, "Diario," 19:441–43, says that the false suitor was *Francisco* de Avalos, not José. Later Mbayás did not remember that a wedding ceremony was prelude to the massacre, and it is unlikely that such a ruse took place. Mbayá culture recognized no wedding ceremony. Male social gatherings were usually celebrated by drinking to stupefaction; SLPC, 2:80–81.

31. Esteban de Urizar y Arespacochaga al rey, Salta, Nov., 24, 1708, AGI, Charcas, leg. 284.

32. Urizar al rey, Salta, Nov., 24, 1708, AGI, Charcas, leg. 284.

33. Ibid. Funding was to come from local sources of revenue, including donations from leading citizens, the unpaid salaries of the forty-man garrison at Esteco, from the *sisa,* the *media anata,* the encomiendas of Tucumán, the governor's own salary, and the granting of encomiendas for a third generation. Provincial troops would carry out the assignment; El presidente de la Real Audiencia de la Plata da cuenta, Plata, Mar. 1710, AGI, Charcas, leg. 284; Expediente de junta de Guerra, año de 1710, ibid.

34. Urizar said his objective was "para yntroducir en ellos el Terror"; Esteban de Urizar al rey, Salta, Nov. 24, 1708, AGI, Charcas, leg. 284.

35. Susnik, *Los aborígenes,* III/1: 24; Lozano, *Gran Chaco Gualamba,* 322, 328–29, 345; Lizondo Borda, *Historia del Tucumán,* 407; El gobernador de Tucumán da cuenta, Salta, Aug. 4, 1714, AGI, Charcas, leg. 284; El cabildo de Santiago del Estero al rey, June 6, 1710, ibid.

36. An expedition also went forward from Tarija; Certificación . . . para la entrada a las provincias del Chaco, Campo sobre Valbuena, July 8, 1710, AGI, Charcas, leg. 284.

37. Informe del Gobernador Esteban Urizar de las dos campañas contra las

naciones bárbaras del Chaco, Salta, July 24, 1712, AGI, Charcas, leg. 284; El gobernador de Tucumán da cuenta, Salta, Aug. 4, 1712, ibid.; Susnik erroneously claims that the Mocobis and Toba abandoned the western Chaco and established themselves in the eastern Chaco; *El rol de los indígenas,* 2:116; elsewhere—and more accurately—she says that they found vital interests to the south of the Río Salado; Susnik, *Los aborígines,* III/1: 24. In fact, bands of Mocobis had been raiding Santa Fe for decades.

38. Urizar mendaciously called the Malbaláes "the most valiant warriors in the Chaco," in order to make his campaign appear more successful to superiors in Spain without knowledge of local conditions. One Malbalá, Antonio, who helped guide the Urizar penetration into the Chaco, indicated which were the farms of his relatives; Lozano, *Gran Chaco Gualamba,* 333.

39. Doucet, "Sobre cautivos de guerra," 123–30; Doucet found twice as many Mocobi as Toba captives, reflecting the relative sizes of the two groups in the early 1700s.

40. M. Cervera, *Historia de la ciudad y provincia de Santa Fe,* 1:481; Dobrizhoffer, *Account of the Abipones,* 3:143–47, 213–18, 323–25; Paucke, *Hacia allá,* 2:5–7, Consulta de Josef Lino de Esteban y León al gobernador, Asunción, Jan. 15, 1777, CMG, Cal. 1470.

41. Susnik, *Los aborígenes,* III/1: 11–13, 24, 35–36, 61–62; Dobrizhoffer, *Account of the Abipones,* 2:95–96; see map "Paraguariae Provinciae Soc. Jesu Cum Adjacentibus," drawn in 1722 in Furlong, *Cartografía jesuítica,* and passim.

42. Susnik, *Los aborígenes,* III/1: 61–64; SLPC, 2:255–60.

43. See Socolow, "Spanish Captives in Indian Societies."

44. Métraux, "Ethnography," 224; Susnik, *Los aborígenes,* III/1: 105–20; Aguirre, "Diario," 19:67–102, 472–74; Don Diego de los Reyes al rey, Asunción, July 24, 1719, CMG, Cal. 906; Martín de Barúa al rey, Asunción, Mar. 18, 1730, AGI, Charcas, leg. 217; Ganson, "The Evueví of Paraguay"; Mandato del gobernador Jayme Sanjust, Asunción, Mar. 26, 1753, ANA, SH, vol. 127, no. 7.

45. El cabildo de Córdoba al gobernador, Córdoba, July 12, 1726, AGI, Charcas, leg. 284; Auto del teniente general Mathías de Anglés, Córdoba, Feb. 21, 1727, ibid.; Auto de Anglés, Paraje del Tío, Feb. 26, 1727, ibid.

46. Alonso de la Vega al gobernador, Santa Fe, Mar. 20, 1732, AGN, IX, 4-1-1; Petición del procurador general al cabildo, Santa Fe, Apr. 26, 1732; and Acuerdo del cabildo, both ibid.

47. Gobernador y capitán general Anglés al Marqués de Villa García, Salta, AGI, Charcas, leg. 199.

48. Cabildo de Santa Fe al gobernador, Santa Fe, July 20, 1732, AGN, IX, 4-1-1; Petición del procurador general al cabildo, Apr. 26, 1732, ibid.; Acuerdo del cabildo; and Ignacio Pérez, S.J., al cabildo, both ibid.

49. Cabildo de Santiago del Estero al gobernador, Santiago del Estero, Jan. 12, 1735, AGI, Charcas, leg. 347; Cabildo de San Miguel de Tucumán al la Audiencia de Charcas, San Miguel de Tucumán, Aug. 3, 1734, ibid.; Paucke, *Hacia allá,* 2:12–14.

50. A man named Juan de Aguirre overheard a number of raiders speaking perfect Spanish as they assembled on the outskirts of the city.

51. Immediately after the encounter, Salteños thought that they had lost 250 people, but the next year they recalculated their losses at 400 persons killed and captured by the Mocobi and Toba in the attack of January 5, 1735.

52. El cabildo de Jujuy a la Audiencia de Charcas, Jujuy, Aug. 19, 1734, AGI, Charcas, leg. 347; El cabildo de Salta al virrey, Salta, June 15, 1734, ibid.; Don Ignacio Plazaola a su compadre, Salta, ibid.; Capítulo de carta de José Paez, C.J., al Simón Bailina, C.J., Salta, Jan. 8, 1735, ibid.; Gobernador y capitán general Juan de Armaza a la Audiencia de Charcas, Santa Ana, Jan. 28, 1735, ibid.

53. Mathías Anglés y Gortari a la Audiencia de Charcas, Salta, May 11, 1736, ibid.

54. Mathías Anglés y Gortari a la Audiencia de Charcas, Salta, Dec. 5, 1735, ibid.; El gobernador al Comandante Salvador García, Campo del Saladillo, Dec. 23, 1735, ibid.; Anglés a la Audiencia de Charcas, Salta, Jan. 12, 1736, ibid.

55. Gaspar Suárez Babián al gobernador, Santiago del Estero, June 2, 1736, AGI, Charcas, leg. 199; Mathías de Anglés a la Audiencia de la Plata, Salta, May 11, 1736, AGI, Charcas, leg. 347.

56. Revisionists' assertion that scalping originated with Europeans is inaccurate. Scalping was a pre-Columbian practice; see Axtell and Sturtevant, "The Unkindest Cut," 451–72.

57. Auto del gobernador, Asunción, Nov. 18, 1725, AGI, BA, leg. 48; SLPC, 1:309–11, 2:81–82; Rafael de la Moneda a don Joseph del Cangilo, Asunción, Mar. 11, 1742, AGI, BA, leg. 48; Rafael de la Moneda al rey, Asunción, Nov. 20, 1740, CMG, Cal. 1025.

58. Gobernador del Paraguay al virrey, Asunción, June 25, 1748, AGI, BA, leg. 48; Juan Antonio de Zavala y Miguel Esquibel y Saravia al Marqués de la Ensenada, Asunción, ibid.; Dobrizhoffer, *Account of the Abipones*, 3:22–28.

59. Nellar, ed., *Política seguida con el aborigen*, 1:123; Labougle, *Corrientes*, 192–93; SLPC, 2:82–83; Dobrizhoffer, *Account of the Abipones*, 2:103, 3:128.

60. Smaby, "The Mormons and the Indians," 35–48.

61. Ibid.

62. Gobernador Carlos Morfi al rey, Asunción, Feb. 16, 1769, AGI, BA, leg. 244; SLPC, 1:133–34, 2:82–84; Susnik, *El indio colonial*, vol. 3, pt. 1, 68.

63. Saeger, "Eighteenth-Century Guaycuruan Missions," 59–60; Saeger, "Another View of the Mission," 500–1; Whigham, *Politics of River Trade*, 154–55.

CHAPTER 2. *The Growth of Guaycuruan Missions*

1. Durán Estrago, *Presencia franciscana en el Paraguay*, 98–101.

2. Lozano, *Gran Chaco Gualamba*, 111–21.

3. SLPC, 1:266–67, 2:61–72; Lozano, *Gran Chaco Gualamba*, 141–61.

4. Jesuits in the vast province of Paraguay, which included modern Paraguay, Argentina, and parts of Brazil, Bolivia, and Uruguay then numbered only thirty-eight, and the Society felt that its manpower was better employed with the

more promising Guarani, who would form the heart of the so-called "Jesuit Republic"; SLPC, 2:61–75; Caraman, *Lost Paradise*, 36–81.

5. Saeger, "Another View of the Mission," 495.

6. Paraguayan *criollos* were mestizos. Few Europeans came to the upper Plata after the conquest years.

7. Dobrizhoffer, *Account of the Abipones*, 3:120–25, 102–11.

8. Caraman, *Lost Paradise*, 189–95; Dobrizhoffer, *Account of the Abipones*, 3:102–12.

9. Dobrizhoffer, *Account of the Abipones*, 2:240–46; Nellar, ed., *Política seguida con el aborigen*, 1:123.

10. Susnik, *El indio colonial*, vol. 3, pt. 1, 68–69, 78, 90.

11. Block, *Mission Culture on the Upper Amazon*, 78.

12. M. Cervera, *Historia de la ciudad y provincia de Santa Fe*, 1:489.

13. Acuerdo del cabildo, Santa Fe, June 27, 1741, AGPSF, AC, vol. XI; Acuerdo del cabildo, July 27, 1743, ibid.

14. Santa Fe moved to its permanent location in 1660; Scunio, *La conquista del Chaco*, 92.

15. Auto del teniente del gobernador, paraje del Pueblo Viejo, July 4, 1743, AGPSF, AC, vol. XI; Auto del teniente, Santa Fe, July 21, 1743, ibid.; Ciudad de Santa Fe al rey, Santa Fe, Mar. 6, 1745, ibid.

16. Furlong [Cardiff], *Misiones*, 380–83.

17. Auto del gobernador, Buenos Aires, June 17, 1748, AGPSF, AC, vol. XII; Carta de Manuel Querini, S.J., a Francisco Antonio de Vera y Múxica, Córdoba, Aug. 23, 1748, ibid.

18. Dobrizhoffer, *Account of the Abipones*, 3:128–32.

19. The Jesuit college in Asunción alone had twenty-four thousand head of cattle in 1753. Jesuits in colonial Argentina owned more than 3,400 slaves; Cushner, *Jesuit Ranches and the Agrarian Development of Colonial Argentina*, 133–34.

20. See Bushnell, *Situado and Sabana*, passim.

21. Jackson, *Indian Population Decline*, 160–61; see also Jackson and Castillo, *Indians, Franciscans, and Spanish Colonization*, 41–58.

22. Maeder and Bolsi, "La población de las misiones guaraníes entre 1702–1767," 111–37. From a high of 141,182 in 1732, the population of Guarani missions declined to 73,910, owing to epidemics and political unrest in the civil province of Paraguay. By 1755 the mission population had rebounded to 104,483 on the eve of the Guarani War, which caused another decline.

23. Radding, *Wandering Peoples*, 111, 137.

24. SLPC, 2:107; Extracto de carta de Joaquín Camaño, S.J., al Lorenzo Hervás, May 8, 1783, in Furlong, *Joaquín Camaño S. J.*, 149–50; Muriel, "Breve noticia de las misiones vivas," 175.

25. SLPC, 2:156.

26. Carta de Fray Francisco Méndez a un amigo, Reducción de Refugio de Egvilechingo, June 20, 1772, in Cortesâo, ed., *Do tratado de Madri*, 53–69; Secretario de la provincia al gobernador, Asunción, Apr. 4, 1769, CMG, Cal. 1304.

27. See Appendixes A and B and Saeger, "Another View of the Mission," 517.

28. See Appendix B, tables 8A and 8B.

29. Dobrizhoffer, *Account of the Abipones,* 3:114–15.Ciudad de Santa Fe al rey, Santa Fe, Mar. 6, 1745, AGPSF, AC, vol. XI.

30. Acuerdo del cabildo de Santa Fe, Santa Fe, June 27, 1741, AGPSF, AC, vol. XI; Paucke, *Hacia allá,* 2:7–17.

31. Acuerdo del cabildo de Santa Fe, Santa Fe, June, 14, 1742, AGPSF, AC, vol. XI; Instrucción del cabildo al Sargento Mayor Vera y Múxica, Santa Fe, Aug. 7, 1742, ibid.; Acuerdos del cabildo, Apr. 4 and 30, 1743, ibid.; José de Andonaegi al teniente de Santa Fe, Buenos Aires, Jan. 20, 1746, ibid.; Fray Julián de Ovelar al alcalde don José Arias Troncoso, San Javier, Aug. 30, 1789, AGN, IX, 33-1-2.

32. Auto del teniente del gobernador, Santa Fe, June 27, 1743, AGPSF, AC, vol. XI.

33. Los diputados de . . . Santa Fe al virrey, Buenos Aires, Oct. 2, 1780, AGN, IX, 31-3-5.

34. Los diputados de Santa Fe al virrey, Buenos Aires, Oct 31, 1780, ibid.

35. El gobernador Tineo da cuenta, Salta, Dec. 28, 1750, AGI, BA, leg. 303.

36. Francisco Navalón a Bartolomé Diez de Andino, Santa Fe, Feb. 2, 1752, AGN, IX, 4-1-2; Diez de Andino al gobernador, Santa Fe, Mar. 16, 1752, ibid.

37. El virrey Conde de Superunda al rey, Lima, June 12, 1750, AGI, BA, leg. 199.

38. El gobernador Juan Manuel Campero al rey, Tucumán, Feb. 24, 1767, AGI, BA, leg. 18.

39. Paucke, *Hacia allá,* 3:1, lámina CXIV following 150.

40. Métraux, "Ethnography," 217–18; Susnik, *El indio colonial,* vol. 3, pt. 1, 57–64.

41. SLPC, 82–84, 229; Gobernador Pedro de Ceballos al fray D. Julián Arriaga, San Borja, May 30, 1760, CMG, Cal. 1148; Ceballos a Arriaga, San Borja, Dec. 22, 1760, CMG, Cal. 1062a.

42. SLPC, 2:84.

43. SLPC, 1:6, 2:85–87.

44. Gobernador Pedro de Ceballos al fray D. Julián Arriaga, San Borja. May 30, 1760, CMG, Cal. 1148; Gobernador José Martínez Fontes al R. P. Nicolás Contucci, C.J., Asunción. Jan. 22, 1762, ANA, SH, vol. 133, no. 4; Virrey Manuel Amat al rey, Lima, Oct. 14, 1768, CMG, Cal. 1291; SLPC, 2:242–49.

45. SLPC, 1:6, 2:85–88.

46. SLPC, 2:85–91, 100–2.

47. SLPC, 2:114–15.

48. SLPC, 2:52, 101–3, 118, 276–77.

49. SLPC, 1:257–63, 2:103–7.

50. Francisco Antonio de Vera y Múxica al cabildo de Santa Fe, Río del Rey, Mar. 23, 1753, AGPSF, AC, vol. XV.

51. SLPC, 2:103–6, 130.

52. SLPC, 2:163–64.

53. Blujaki, *Un gran paraguayo;* SLPC, 2:173–74.

54. SLPC, 2:23, 102–9, 116, 173–74, 199.

55. Hemming, *Red Gold,* 385, SLPC; 2:116–20; Azara, *Geografía física y esférica,* 198.

56. SLPC, 1:124–25; José Coene al gobernador intendente, Asunción, Aug. 6, 1795, ANA, NE, vol. 71; Queja de don Casimiro Coene al gobernador intendente, ibid.

57. Serrano, *Los primitivos habitantes del territorio argentino,* 111–12.

58. Sánchez Labrador says that the sheep of the Jesuits were the first in the region but does not claim that they were new to Mbayá experience. In fact, Mbayás appreciated sheep, whose wool provided textiles; SLPC, 2:102.

59. Paucke, *Hacia allá,* 2:20; Dobrizhoffer, *Account of the Abipones,* 2:64–67, 76–80.

60. SLPC, 2:83, 100–1, 110, 137, 169–71, 188–93.

61. SLPC, 2:138–40.

62. SLPC, 2:130–31.

63. SLPC, 2:130–33.

64. SLPC, 2:130–33; 1:113–14, 130–31.

65. SLPC, 2:138–40, 143–50.

66. SLPC, 2:120–30, 138, 263; 1:294–300.

67. SLPC, 1:111–15, 123–29, 228.

68. Aguirre, "Diario," 19:541.

69. SLPC, 1:42–43, 68–69.

70. Viola, *Paraguay, siglo dieciocho,* 35–48.

71. Susnik, *Los aborígenes,* III/1: 83–87.

72. Pedro Antonio Cerviño al gobernador intendente, Concepción, Nov. 11, 1789, ANA, SH, vol. 365.

73. Informe de Pedro de Ceballos, Colonia del Sacramento, Feb. 26, 1763, AGI, BA, leg. 18.

74. In 1778 Friars Hermenegildus Garcete and José Ignacio Arriola served at San Javier, and at San Pedro were Friar Juan Churruca and an assistant. At San Fernando, Friars Francisco Rodríguez and José Bernardo Cabral ministered to Abipones. San Ignacio de Tobas was served by Friars Valentín Ponce and Antonio Castro. At Concepción were Friars Juan de Dios Vilchés and Francisco Albarán. At Remolinos de Mocobis were Mariano Agüero and Francisco Llama; Nómina de los religiosos que al presente tiene esta provincia . . . del Paraguay, Buenos Aires, Oct. 5, 1778, AGN, IX, 7-2-1; Durán Estrago, *Presencia franciscana en el Paraguay,* 176–84.

75. Carta del cura doctrinero Fray Manuel Antonio Fernández al virrey, [San Fernando], May 30, 1798, AGN, IX, 3-4-2; Francisco Antonio de Acuña al subdelegado de Corrientes, Saladas, Dec. 1, 1801, AGN, IX, 3-4-3; Cabildo elections, San Fernando de las Garzas, Nov. 24, 1800, ibid.

76. Gobernador Arriaga al rey, Dec. 23, 1777, Reducción de Miraflores, AGI, BA, leg. 244.

77. Informe de Gabriel de Lasaga al superintendente general, Santa Fe, Oct. 6, 1785, AGN, IX, 4-1-6.

78. Prudencio María de Gastañaduy al virrey, Santa Fe, July 10, 1795, AGN, IX, 30-5-2.

79. Joaquín Maciel al gobernador, Santa Fe, Dec. 2, 1769, AGN, IX, 4-1-3; Gobernador Bucareli a Joaquín Maciel, Buenos Aires, Dec. 17, 1769, ibid.

80. Spanish speakers differentiate horses, *caballos,* from mares, *yeguas.*

81. Visita de la reducción de la Nuestra Señora de la Concepción de Abipones, Frontera del Gran Chaco, Dec. 2, 1777, AGI, BA, leg. 143.

82. Pedro de Gallarreta al consejo, Madrid, Dec. 17, 1778, AGI, BA, leg. 610; Testimonio de auto de visita de las reducciones . . . de las fronteras del Chaco, San Ignacio, Aug. 19, 1771, AGI, BA, leg. 468; Su Magestad al gobernador Juan Victorino Martínez del Tineo, Pardo, Feb. 29, 1776, AGI, BA, leg. 244.

83. Visita de la reducción de indios Tobas, Río Negro, Frontera de Jujuy, Oct. 8, 1776, AGI, BA, leg. 244.

84. Auto del gobernador del Tucumán Andrés de Mestre, Salta, Aug. 25, 1778, AGI, BA, leg. 37; Joaquín de Espinosa al rey, Salta, Oct 3, 1759, AGI, BA, leg. 304.

85. Bushnell, *Situado and Sabana,* 179–80.

86. Joaquín Maciel al gobernador, Santa Fe, Nov. 26, 1769, AGN, IX, 4-1-3.

87. Joaquín Maciel al gobernador, Santa Fe, Mar. 23, 1768, AGN, IX, 4-1-3.

88. Paucke, *Hacia allá,* 2:22; Florian Paucke, S.J., al Visitador Nicolás Contucci, San Javier, Aug. 5, 1762, AGN, IX, 6-10-5.

89. Labougle, *Corrientes,* 284, 303.

90. Francisco Antonio de Vera y Múxica al gobernador, Santa Fe, May 15, 1763, AGN, IX, 4-1-3; Melchor de Echagüe y Andia al virrey, Santa Fe, Dec. 6, 1779, AGN, IX, 31-3-5; Antonio Medina al gobernador de armas, Santa Fe, Sept. 6, 1775, AGN, IX, 32-9-1; Declaración de Dámaso Cazeres, vecino, ibid.; Declaración de José Luis Báez, Asunción, June 26, 1776, ibid.

91. Nellar, ed. *Política seguida con el aborigen,* 2:289; Weber, *The Spanish Frontier in North America,* 212.

92. Durán Estrago, *Presencia franciscana en el Paraguay,* 176–82; Capellán Inocencio Cañete al gobernador, Asunción, Feb. 24, 1782, AGI, BA, leg. 295; Fray José Mariano Bordón al administrador del Ramo de Guerra, Reducción de Remolinos, July 27, 1807, ANA, CVRB, 115, no. 4; Los comandantes de la villa de Remolinos . . . y los pobladores al gobernador intendente, Remolinos, Nov. 30, 1807, ANA, CVRB, 115, no. 6; Benito Villanueva al teniente coronel Gregorio Thadeo de la Cerda, Villeta, Jan. 20, 1809, ANA, CVRB, 138, no. 35; Luis Arevalo . . . a la Junta Gubernativa, Pueblo de Itapé, June 21, 1812, ANA, SH, vol. 219, no. 10.

93. Joaquín Alos al virrey, Asunción, Apr. 19, 1794, CMG, Cal. 2034.

94. Angelis, ed., "Diario de la expedición hecha en 1774 a los paises del Gran Chaco, desde la fuerte del valle por D. Gerónimo de Matorras, gobernador del Tucumán," in *Colección de obras y documentos,* vol. 6.

95. Nellar, ed., *Política seguida con el aborigen,* 1:212–33; Acevedo, *La intendencia de Salta del Tucumán,* 39–40, 387–93; Angelis, ed., "Diario de Francisco Gavino Arias," in *Colección de obras y documentos,* vol. 6.

96. Real cédula, Pardo, Feb. 19, 1785, AGN, IX, 23-10-1, exp. 9.

97. Maeder, *Misiones del Paraguay,* 49–57.

98. Protector de los indios Nicolás León de Ojeda al gobernador intendente, Salta, Feb. 9, 1790, AGN, IX, 23-10-7, exp. 9; El teniente de Santa Fe [al asesor], Santa Fe, Sept. 6, 1785, AGN, IX, 4-1-6; Teniente de Santa Fe al asesor, Santa Fe, Nov. 14, 1785, ibid.

99. Prudencio María de Gastañaduy al virrey, Santa Fe, June 15, 1809, AGN, IX, 4-2-7.

100. In 1810 the Echagüe and Tarragona families were leaders of the local independence movement; Gianello, *Historia de Santa Fe,* 101–3, 179.

101. Riva Herrera al gobernador, Santa Fe, Mar. 20, 1775, AGN, IX, 4-1-5; Riva Herrera a Vértiz, Santa Fe, Apr. 3, 1775, ibid.; Lowie, "Social and Political Organization of Tropical Forest and Marginal Tribes," 343.

102. Juan Francisco de la Riva Herrera a Juan José de Vértiz, Santa Fe, Apr. 13, 1775, AGN, IX, 4-1-5.

103. Riva Herrera a Vértiz, Santa Fe, June 4, 1775, AGN, IX, 4-1-5.

104. European observers criticized Paraguayan forces for their lack of discipline. Compared to Guaycuruans, however, Paraguayan organization was superior.

105. Agustín Fernando de Pinedo al cacique dn. Jph. Benavides, Asunción, Aug. 23, 1775, AGN, IX, 4-1-5; Pinedo a Benavides, Asunción, Nov. 5, 1775, ibid.; Pinedo a Riva Herrera, Asunción, Dec. 26, 1775, ibid.

106. Riva Herrera a Vértiz, Santa Fe, Mar. 2, 1776, AGN, IX, 4-1-5.

107. Melchor de Echagüe y Andia al virrey, Santa Fe, Oct. 9, 1779, AGN, IX, 31-3-5; Melchor de Echagüe y Andia al virrey, Oct. 12, 1779, ibid.; Providencia del virrey, Buenos Aires, Oct. 20, 1779, ibid.; Melchor de Echagüe y Andia al virrey, Dec. 6, 1779, ibid.

108. José Tarragona al teniente Melchor de Echagüe y Andia, Santa Fe, June 4, 1780, AGN, IX, 31-3-5.

109. Melchor de Echagüe y Andia al virrey, Santa Fe, Apr. 29, 1782; Mar. 6, 1783; Apr. 14, 1783; and June 6, 1783, all in AGN, IX, 4-1-6.

110. Socially marginal groups comprised the majority of the 13,519 residents of Jujuy in 1778. Only 5 percent (653) were white, while 82 percent (11,081) were Indians, but they were culturally very different from the Toba. Free blacks, mulattoes, and zambos comprised 11 percent and slaves only 2 percent of the population. Bidondo, *Historia de Jujuy,* 147.

111. Bidondo, *Historia de Jujuy* 153–57; Nellar, ed. *Política seguida con el aborigen,* 2:246ff. The archives of Jujuy yield little information on the rebellion. Much archival testimony from April–June 1781 reposes in AGI, BA, 143, but the documents contain little about Toba involvement. See El gobernador y capitán general Andrés de Mestre a José de Gálvez, Jujuy, June 25, 1781, ibid. The overwhelming number of Indians in the vicinity of Jujuy caused Spaniards to see enemies everywhere. José de Arce al coronel Luis de Mendoza, Villa [de Tarija], July 3, 1781, AGN, IX, 33-2-4. Arce reported that Spaniards killed two hundred Toba, but he was not an eyewitness and certainly meant twenty; Acevedo, *La intendencia de Salta del Tucumán,* 40–45. Acevedo argues that Toba involvement signified

the failure of the reduction system and that the Indians had not been "civilized." It meant no such thing. A Spanish official recalled that he helped escort more than one hundred Toba from the Chaco back to their reduction; Don Pedro de la Vega, natural de España, vecino de Jujuy y ayudante mayor de sus milicias al gobernador de armas, Jujuy, May 4, 1785, AGN, IX, 5-8-1.

112. Fray Sebastián Zapatería al gobernador, Reducción de Tobas, Apr. 20, 1783, AGN, IX, 5-6-6; El fiscal protector al gobernador intendente de Salta, Buenos Aires, Sept. 21, 1807, AGN, IX, 5-7-5; José Francisco de Tineo al virrey, Salta, July 6, 1808, AGN, IX, 5-7-7; Fr. Juan José Ortiz al oidor gobernador intendente José de Medeyros, San Ignacio, Aug. 6, 1808, ibid.

113. Velásquez, *El Paraguay en 1811,* 23, 45; Gobernador Agustín Fernando de Pinedo al rey, Asunción, Sept. 28, 1775, CMG, Cal. 1426.

114. Gobernador Pinedo al rey, Asunción, Sept. 28, 1775, CMG, Cal. 1426; Gobernador Pedro Melo de Portugal al rey, Asunción, July 13, 1778, CMG, Cal. 1560.

115. Azara, *Geografía física y esférica,* 199.

116. Pedro José de Molas al gobernador intendente, Concepción, July 8, 1788, ANA, SH, vol. 365, no. 1; Azara, *Viajes por la América meridional,* 2:137.

117. Aguirre, "Diario," 19, nos. 47–48:23.

118. Molas al gobernador, Concepción, July 8, 1788, ANA, SH, vol. 365, no. 1.

119. José Miguel Ybáñez al Dictador Supremo, Concepción Nov. 16, 1815, ANA, SH, vol. 367, no. 1; Capitán Pedro Domínguez al gobernador intendente, Concepción, Sept. 19, 1789, ANA, SH, vol. 365, no. 1.

120. José Bolaños al gobernador intendente, Concepción, Oct. 30, 1789, ANA, SH, vol. 365, no. 1; Bolaños al gobernador intendente, Concepción, Nov. 11, 1789, ibid.

121. Melchor de Echagüe y Andia al virrey, Santa Fe, Jan. 6, 1785, AGN, IX, 4-1-6; El teniente de Santa Fe al virrey, Santa Fe, Mar. 5, 1799, AGN, IX, 4-2-3.

122. The priest was Friar Andrés Alvarenga; Lorenzo Suárez Cantillana al virrey, Primera jornada del Chaco, Aug, 19, 1784, AGN, IX, 3-3-7.

123. Manuel Gutiérrez al comandante de Corrientes, [Asunción], Apr. 1808, ANA, SH, vol. 207, no. 3.

124. Zubizarreta, *Historia de mi ciudad;* Ganson, "The Evueví of Paraguay," 460–88; Gregorio Thadeo de la Cerda al gobernador intendente, Asunción, Nov. 26, 1808, ANA, CVRB, Cat. 138, no. 6; Susnik, *El indio colonial,* vol. 3, pt. 1, 101–40.

125. Ganson, "The Evueví of Paraguay," 486.

CHAPTER 3. *Economy*

1. Mendoza and Wright, "Sociocultural and Economic Elements," 242–57.

2. Mendoza, "Politics and Leadership," 4.

3. Silverblatt, *Moon, Sun, and Witches,* 3–14.

4. Jolís, *Ensayo sobre la historia natural del Gran Chaco,* 222. The retrieval of honey from the hollows of trees high above the ground was often men's work; Paucke, *Hacia allá,* 2:178, 221.

5. Paucke, *Hacia allá,* 2:180, 221, 233; 3:lámina CVII following p. 150.

6. Dobrizhoffer, *Account of the Abipones,* 2:114.

7. Dobrizhoffer, *Account of the Abipones,* 2:111.

8. Saeger, "Eighteenth-Century Guaycuruan Missions," 59; Métraux, "Revolution of the Ax," 28–40.

9. On food gathering (including locust hunting), food preparation, and tools see Paucke, *Hacia allá,* 2:185–87, 198, 208, and láminas XIX and XXII following pp. 160 and 178 respectively; vol. 3, pt. 2, láminas LIV and LIX; 1:153–60 (also 5, 16); Dobrizhoffer, *Account of the Abipones,* 1:347; 2:111; Susnik, *Los aborígenes,* 4:60.

10. Paucke, *Hacia allá,* 2:láminas XXII and XXIV following pp. 178 and 208 respectively.

11. Paucke, *Hacia allá,* vol. 3, pt. 1, lámina LXXXVII following p. 150.

12. It is now unfashionable to conceive of a Paleolithic Revolution, but *revolutionary* is here appropriate.

13. Susnik, *Los aborígenes,* 4:9, 75, 79; 6:50.

14. Paucke, *Hacia allá,* 2:179.

15. Susnik, *Los aborígenes,* 4:186–87; Dobrizhoffer, *Account of the Abipones,* 2:131–32; Paucke, *Hacia allá,* 2:151–52.

16. Susnik, *Los aborígenes,* 4:85–86.

17. For weaving and pottery see Dobrizhoffer, *Account of the Abipones,* 2:130–31; Susnik, *Los aborígenes,* 4:97; Paucke, *Hacia allá,* vol. 3, pt. 2, lámina XLIV.

18. SLPC, 1:268–70; Dobrizhoffer, *Account of the Abipones,* 2:119–20.

19. Susnik, *Los aborígenes,* 6:8–9.

20. Paucke, *Hacia allá,* 2:179–80; Susnik, *Los aborígenes,* 4:38–43.

21. For jaguar hunting see Paucke, *Hacia allá,* vol. 3, pt. 2, lámina LXXIII following p. 338; and for tunics, see ibid., lámina XVIII following p. 156.

22. Dobrizhoffer, *Account of the Abipones,* 1:251–348; 2:110–26, Susnik, *Los aborígenes,* 4:34–36; Paucke, *Hacia allá,* 2:lámina XIV following p. 140.

23. Dobrizhoffer, *Account of the Abipones* 1:111; Susnik, *Los aborígenes,* 4:33–39; Paucke, *Hacia allá,* 2:lámina XIX and pp. 161–67.

24. Susnik, *El rol de los indígenas,* 2:96; Susnik, *Los aborígenes,* 4:100.

25. Susnik, *Los aborígenes,* 6:65; Paucke, *Hacia allá,* 2:221; Dobrizhoffer, *Account of the Abipones,* 2:64–65.

26. Both quotations from Martin, "European Impact on the Culture of a Northeastern Algonquian Tribe," 4.

27. Martin, "Ethnohistory, 41–56; Martin, "European Impact on the Culture of a Northeastern Algonquian Tribe," 3–26; Cordeu and Siffredi, *De la algarroba al algodón,* 14.

28. Susnik, *Los aborígenes,* 4:26; 6:35; Métraux, "Ethnography," 352.

29. Susnik, *El indio colonial,* vol 3, pt. 1, 23–25 and passim.

30. SLPC 1:193–94; Métraux, "Ethnography," 352; Dobrizhoffer, *Account of the Abipones,* 3:355; Susnik *Los aborígenes,* 6:35.

31. Paucke, *Hacia allá,* vol. 3, pt. 2, láminas XXXVII and XXXVIII.

32. Paucke, *Hacia allá,* 2:lámina XXI and pp. 166–69; Dobrizhoffer, *Account of the Abipones,* 2:113–14.

33. A few males with money bought Spanish saddles; Paucke, *Hacia allá,* 2:265.

34. Dobrizhoffer, *Account of the Abipones,* 3:347; Susnik, *Los aborígenes,* 4:81, 100.

35. Frutos de Palafox al gobernador, letters of July, July 18, July 26, and Oct. 11, 1730, all in AGN, IX, 4-1-1. For Guaycuruan techniques of river crossing see Paucke, *Hacia allá,* vol. 3, pt. 1, lámina CV following p. 150.

36. Susnik, *Los aborígenes,* 4:84–85.

37. Brown, *Socioeconomic History of Argentina,* 2, 7; see also Garavaglia, *Mercado interno,* 381–483.

38. Maeder, *Historia económica de Corrientes,* 220–21.

39. Merrell, "The Indians' New World," 539, 537.

40. Ibid., 549, 551–52.

41. Ibid., 553, 555.

42. Saeger, "Another View of the Mission," 499–500.

43. Cacique y corregidor Miguel Benavides al teniente Melchor de Echagüe y Andia, San Jerónimo, Jan. 26, 1788, AGN, IX, 4-1-7.

44. SLPC, 1:294–300; Dobrizhoffer, *Account of the Abipones,* 2:130–31; Paucke, *Hacia allá,* 2:148, 174.

45. Paucke, *Hacia allá,* 2:272–74; Florian Paucke, C.J., al Visitador Nicolás Contucci, C.J., San Javier, Aug. 5, 1762; AGN, IX, 6-10-5.

46. "Para el Pueblo de Sn. Fernando en el barco de Sn. Ygnacio a dexar en Corrientes en 22 de Sep.re del 1762;" AGN, IX, 6-10-5.

47. Dobrizhoffer, *Account of the Abipones,* 2:130–31.

48. Padrón, Reducción de Santiago en el Fuerte de San Nicolás, June 1, 1793, AGN, IX, 30-5-2.

49. SLPC, 1:308–15.

50. Paucke, *Hacia allá,* 2:269–70, 306; vol. 3, pt. 1, 49 and lámina CXIII following 150; and vol. 3, pt. 2, lámina XXXI following 162; for corroboration of Father Paucke's testimony, see Informe del alcalde ordinario Gabriel de Lasaga a Francisco de Paula Sanz, Santa Fe, Oct. 6, 1785, AGN, IX, 4-1-6.

51. Dobrizhoffer, *Account of the Abipones,* 3:158–59; for a drawing of the buildings and grounds of a typical Guaycuruan mission see Paucke, *Hacia allá,* vol. 3, pt. 1, lámina CXIV following p. 150; for construction techniques, see vol. 3, pt. 2, lámina XXXIX.

52. Susnik, *Los aborígenes,* 4:96–97.

53. Mission residents mostly bought utilitarian items, including hardware, dry goods, and food. They also purchased hats, bridles, cloth, buttons, axes, chisels, needles, and rosaries, as well as flour, salt, vinegar, wine, tobacco, sugar, and yerba. José Clain [Klein], C.J., a José Francisco Carrio, C.J., Corrientes, Feb. 19, 1763, AGN, IX, 6-10-6; El administrador de estas reducciones D. José Tarragona dara para el corregidor y caciques del pueblo de San Jerónimo lo siguiente,

Santa Fe, Nov. 10, 1777, ibid., 30-1-8; Fr. Blas Brite . . . de San Jerónimo . . . pida para el abasto de dho. pueblo . . . Santa Fe, Dec. 22, 1778; ibid.

54. Miller and Hammel, "A New Perspective on Indian-White Contact," 311–28, esp. 316–18, 326.

55. Susnik, *Los aborígenes*, 4:13, 83.

56. SLPC, 1:295–96.

57. Paucke, *Hacia allá*, 2:259–65.

58. Paucke, *Hacia allá*, 2:291, 298, 312; Certificación del capitán Mateo Lencina [Santa Fe], Mar. 9, 1758; AGN, IX, 6-10-5; Florian Paucke, C.J., al visitador Nicolás Contucci, San Javier, May 16, 1764, AGN, IX, 6-10-5; Certificación del sargento mayor Bernardo Garmendia, [Santa Fe], Apr. 15, 1765; AGN, IX, 6-10-6.

59. The twentieth man was the eighty-year-old cacique, listed as infirm. Twelve of these men were propertyless, including the cacique, as was customary for an aboriginal chief. Most others owned only an animal or two, but two were men of substance. Acancainchin had ten cows, two oxen, and four horses; and Joaquín had three herds of mares, eight horses, ten milk cows, ten sheep, and two oxen; Padrón, Reducción de Santiago, June 1, 1793; AGN, IX, 30-5-2.

60. Relación de don Miguel Gerónimo Venavides al virrey, Montevideo, n.d. [1781], AGN, IX, 4-1-6.

61. On cattle see Paucke, *Hacia allá*, 2:176, 269–71; vol. 3, pt. 1, láminas CX, CIX, and CXIV following p. 150; vol. 3, pt. 2, lámina XXX following p. 162; Dobrizhoffer, *Account of the Abipones*, 3:151–60; and Alcalde ordinario Gabriel de Lasaga, Informe de las reducciones del tiempo de los ex-Jesuítas, Santa Fe, Oct. 6, 1785, AGN, IX, 4-1-6.

62. Slatta, *Cowboys of the Americas*, 33.

63. Ibid., 94; Relación de . . . Venavides . . . Montevideo, . . . [1781], AGN, IX, 4-1-1.

64. Some scholars have questioned the "revolutionary" nature of the shift to agriculture; see Salisbury, "American Indians and American History," 50; and Martin, "Ethnohistory," 45–46.

65. SLPC, 2:120–30, 138; Paucke, *Hacia allá*, vol. 3, pt. 2, lámina XXXVI following p. 170; Dobrizhoffer, *Account of the Abipones*, 3:155–56; Susnik, *Los aborígenes*, 4:77; Certificación del José Clain [Klein], C.J., San Fernando, año de 1766, AGN, IX, 6-10-7.

66. Inventory, San Fernando de las Garzas, Feb. 10, 1785, AGN, IX, 30-5-2.

67. After 1810 the Argentine missions were swept away by the chaos of the independence and post-independence wars, and those in Paraguay suffered from Dr. Francia's hostility to the regular orders.

68. The lone Jesuit foundation to disappear was Timbó, an Abipon mission, which foundered because of Paraguayan hostility, niggardliness, neglect, and Spanish settlers' fear of Abipones.

69. Joaquín Maciel al gobernador, [Santa Fe], Mar. 23, 1768, AGN, IX, 4-1-3; Saeger, "Eighteenth-Century Guaycuruan Missions," 61–66.

70. Los diputados de la ciudad de Santa Fe al virrey, Buenos Aires, Oct. 2,

1780, AGN, IX, 31-3-5; Pedro Melo de Portugal al virrey, Asunción, July 12, 1787, AGN, IX, 24-1-3.

71. Fr. Juan Ignacio Ayzpuru al teniente, San Jerónimo, July 12, 1807, AGN, IX, 4-2-6; Prudencio María de Gastañaduy al virrey, Santa Fe, Oct. 8, 1807, ibid.

72. Joaquín Maciel al gobernador, Santa Fe, Nov. 26, 1769, AGN, IX, 4-1-3.

73. Fr. Francisco Rodríguez al alcalde ordinario de primer voto de Corrientes, San Fernando de las Garzas, July 24, 1792, AGN, IX, 31-7-1.

74. See Melchor Echagüe y Andia . . . por pronto socorro de las reducciones de San Francisco Xavier y San Jerónimo, AGN, IX, 33-1-2, exp. 339.

75. Joaquín Maciel al gobernador, Santa Fe, Nov. 26, 1769, AGN, IX, 4-1-3.

76. Sahlins, *Stone Age Economics*, 30–32.

77. José Klein, C.J., al visitador Nicolás Contucci, San Fernando, July 1762, AGN, IX, 6-10-5.

78. Saeger, "Another View of the Mission," 507–12; Informe del cabildo al virrey, Santa Fe, Mar. 25, 1778, AGN, IX, 31-3-5; Fr. Blas Brite al teniente de Santa Fe, Santa Fe, n.d. [1782], ibid.; Pedimento del Fr. Francisco Rodríguez al teniente, Corrientes, n.d. [1798], AGN, IX, 31-7-1; Brite al virrey, San Jerónimo, Oct. 17, 1781, AGN, IX, 4-11-6; José Tarragona a Melchor de Echagüe y Andia (Santa Fe), June 4, 1780, AGN, IX, 31-3-5.

79. Relación de don Miguel Gerónimo Venavides al virrey, Montevideo, n.d. [1781], AGN, IX, 4-1-1.

80. Melchor de Echagüe y Andia al virrey, Santa Fe, Oct. 6, 1780; AGN, IX, 4-1-6.

81. F. Cervera, "Las reducciones indígenas," 89–90 and "Reseña histórica del período hispanico," 35; Urbano de Iriondo, "Apuntes"; Prudencio María de Gastañaduy al virrey, Frontera de Santa Fe, Mar. 11, 1803, AGN, IX, 4-2-4.

82. Fr. Ramón Redrado al virrey, Colegio de San Carlos, Aug. 11, 1803, AGN, IX, 31-3-6; José Francisco de Tineo al virrey, Salta, July 6, 1808, AGN, IX, 5-7-7. Fr. Juan José Ortiz al Oidor Dr. dn José de Medeiros, San Ignacio de Tobas, June 12, 1808, ibid.; Certificaciones del escribano público de cabildo y comercio, Salta, June 20, 1808, ibid. It was rumored in the mission that these youths were to be enslaved and sold in the city. This was not so, although the slavery of Guaycuruans by Spaniards did occur; Fr. Juan José de Ortiz al gobernador intendente interino, San Ignacio, July 3, 1808, ibid.

83. Benito Villanueva al teniente coronel Gregorio Thadeo de la Zerda, Villeta, Jan. 20, 1809, ANA, CVRB, 138, n. 35.

84. Rosario González al teniente coronel Zerda, Yesos, June 4, 1808, ANA, CVRB, 115, n. 2.

85. Tommasini, *La civilización cristiana del Chaco*, 36–37; Informe del comandante don Carlos Sevilla al gobernador de armas, July 22, 1788, Fuerte de Dolores, Río Negro, AHJ, LC, lib. XXVIII, 321–22.

86. Auto del gobernador intendente Andrés de Mestre, Salta, Dec. 14, 1786, Archivo de los Tribunales de Jujuy.

87. Urbano de Iriondo, "Apuntes," 95–96.

CHAPTER 4. *Society*

1. Susnik, *Los aborígenes,* 5:110–11; SLPC, 1:251; Domínguez Ortiz, *The Golden Age of Spain,* 112–61.

2. Métraux initially denies that elite Guaycuruans constituted a "noble" class. Instead, he says, they were members of military societies. Later he gives in and calls them a "military nobility"; "Ethnography," 197–370, quote on p. 309; Dobrizhoffer, *Account of the Abipones,* 2:204–5, 440–45; Paucke, *Hacia allá,* 2:79, 173; Susnik, *Los aborígenes,* 5:112; Furlong, *Entre los Abipones del Chaco,* 64.

3. Sánchez Labrador, SLPC 2:52–53; Muriel, "Breve noticia de las misiones vivas," 213; Saeger, "Another View of the Mission," 501; Dobrizhoffer, *Account of the Abipones,* 2:147–48, 3:349; Josef Lino de Esteban y León al gobernador, Asunción, Jan. 15, 1777, CMG, Cal. 1470. According to the teniente of Santa Fe, the unnamed black Abipon warrior was a "perverse and prejudicial black" whom he sent to the Malvinas as punishment after the man's band joined a mission; Joaquín Maciel al gobernador, Santa Fe, May 17, 1769, AGN, IX, 4-1-3.

4. SLPC, 1:42, 250–51, 308–9, 311–15; 2:28–29; Furlong, *Entre los Mocobíes de Santa Fe,* 90; "Carta de Fray Francisco Méndez, Religioso Franciscano, y Cura que fué de la Reducción del Refugio," in Cortesâo, *Manuscritos de Coleçâo de Angelis,* 7:62; Dobrizhoffer, *Account of the Abipones,* 2:143–47.

5. SLPC, 1:273–74; Furlong, *Entre los Mocobíes de Santa Fe,* 85–90; Susnik, *Los aborígenes,* 5:111–14; Métraux, "Ethnography," 307–8; Paucke, *Hacia allá,* 2:230.

6. Dobrizhoffer, *Account of the Abipones,* 2:17–18.

7. Furlong, *Entre los Abipones del Chaco,* 24; SLPC, 1:246–47, 281; Dobrizhoffer, *Account of the Abipones,* 2:24, 27–28; "Carta de Fray Francisco Méndez," in Cortesâo, *Manuscritos de Coleçâo de Angelis,* 7:64.

8. Furlong, *Entre los Mocobíes de Santa Fe,* 95–98; Muriel, "Breve noticia de las misiones vivas," 135–36; Métraux, "Ethnography," 270–71; Dobrizhoffer, *Account of the Abipones,* 2:129–30; SLPC, 1:279–87.

9. Another kind of women's fight was the *nejetenta,* a conflict between two wives over the same husband. This was much less common than roélakitápegeta. Dobrizhoffer, *Account of the Abipones,* 2:210–11.

10. Furlong, *Entre los Mocobíes de Santa Fe,* 86; SLPC, 1:302–3; Furlong, *Entre los Abipones del Chaco,* 64; Dobrizhoffer, *Account of the Abipones,* 2:154–55.

11. Mbayá women sometimes drank alcohol, but only in private. Elderly women were especially privileged to drink. Female Mocobi shamans also drank, but not at male gatherings.

12. Paucke, *Hacia allá,* 2:197–200, 208–9; SLPC, 1:30–31, 2:3–6.

13. Dobrizhoffer, *Account of the Abipones,* 2:428–39.

14. Paucke, *Hacia allá,* 2:175–76, 209; Susnik, *Los aborígenes,* 5:26–28; Dobrizhoffer, *Account of the Abipones,* 2:443–46; Métraux, "Ethnography," 321. Furlong, *Entre los Mocobíes de Santa Fe,* 82.

15. Dobrizhoffer, *Account of the Abipones,* 2:136–37; Furlong, *Entre los Abipones del Chaco,* 63; SLPC, 1:36–38, 248–49; Métraux, "Ethnography," 311–12.

16. Dobrizhoffer, *Account of the Abipones,* 2:216–18; Furlong, *Entre los Abipones del Chaco,* 33; SLPC, 2:8–12.

17. Métraux, "Ethnography," 324; Susnik, *Los aborígenes,* 5:11–12; SLPC, 1:301–2.

18. Susnik, *Los aborígenes,* 5:17, 23; Métraux, "Ethnography," 317, 319; Paucke, *Hacia allá,* 2:222.

19. Métraux, "Ethnography," 319; "Carta de Fray Francisco Méndez," in Cortesâo, *Manuscritos de Coleção de Angelis,* 7:59.

20. Métraux, "Ethnography," 319; SLPC, 2:14–18.

21. Oberg, *The Terena and the Caduveo,* 55.

22. Mocobis did not reject infanticide completely. They continued to execute babies with blemishes on their faces, those with twisted limbs, those born when the band hungered, and those born to mothers on the move. Men also still demanded that wives put to death children whom they suspected were not theirs. Paucke, *Hacia allá,* 2:135–136, 176; Furlong, *Entre los Mocobíes de Santa Fe,* 95; Métraux, "Ethnography," 319–20; Susnik, *Los aborígenes,* 5:10–12; Dobrizhoffer, *Account of the Abipones,* 3:216, 343; Muriel, "Breve noticia de las missiones vivas," 136, 159–60; SLPC, 2:31.

23. Métraux, "Ethnography," 320; Paucke, *Hacia allá,* 2:243–45; Furlong, *Entre los Abipones del Chaco,* 32; Furlong, *Entre los Mocobíes de Santa Fe,* 91–93; Dobrizhoffer, *Account of the Abipones,* 2:138–39, 214.

24. Paucke, *Hacia allá,* 2:243–45; Dobrizhoffer, *Account of the Abipones,* 2:139.

25. SLPC, 2:8–9, 315–16; Susnik, *Los aborígenes,* 5:33–36.

26. Paucke, *Hacia allá,* 2:243–45; Furlong, *Entre los Mocobíes de Santa Fe,* 93.

27. Muriel, "Breve noticia de las misiones vivas," 162; Furlong, *Entre los Abipones del Chaco,* 25–26; Susnik, *Los aborígenes,* 5:45–48; Métraux, "Ethnography," 323–24.

28. SLPC, 2:90–100.

29. For the modern Toba, "the basic social unit was the extended family, a group of relatives who cooperated and shared resources without a mechanism of centralized authority"; Wright, "Dream, Shamanism, and Powers," 150–51; see also Oberg, *The Terena and the Caduveo,* 61–62. Data from the eighteenth century on extended families are fragmentary.

30. Métraux, "Ethnography," 325; Furlong, *Entre los Abipones del Chaco,* 32; Furlong, *Entre los Mocobíes de Santa Fe,* 89–92; Paucke, *Hacia allá,* 2:219.

31. Furlong, *Entre los Mocobíes de Santa Fe,* 91; Paucke, *Hacia allá,* 2:219–20; "Carta de Fray Francisco Méndez," in Cortesâo, *Manuscritos de Coleção de Angelis,* 7:60, 63; SLPC, 2:25.

32. Dobrizhoffer, *Account of the Abipones,* 2:207–9; Métraux, "Ethnography," 326; Susnik, *Los aborígenes,* 5:71–73.

33. Furlong, *Entre los Mocobíes de Santa Fe,* 107; Dobrizhoffer, *Account of the Abipones,* 2:146–47.

34. Métraux, "Ethnography," 327; SLPC, 2:27, Paucke, *Hacia allá,* 2:200, 204, 224, 232.

35. Furlong, *Entre los Mocobíes de Santa Fe,* 90–92; Susnik, *Los aborígenes,* 5:71–75.

36. Paucke, *Hacia allá,* 2:224–26.

37. Métraux incorrectly claims that "marriage ties are always strengthened by the birth of a child"; "Ethnography," 327; Dobrizhoffer, *Account of the Abipones,* 2:138, 210–11; Furlong, *Entre los Abipones del Chaco,* 62; SLPC, 2:24–25.

38. Dobrizhoffer, *Account of the Abipones,* 2:210–11; Métraux, "Ethnography," 326.

39. Métraux, "Ethnography," 327; Susnik, *Los aborígenes,* 5:11; Paucke, *Hacia allá,* 2:220; Dobrizhoffer, *Account of the Abipones,* 2:210–12.

40. SLPC, 2:26–27; Paucke, *Hacia allá,* 2:221; Dobrizhoffer, *Account of the Abipones,* 2:153–56, 213.

41. Dobrizhoffer, *Account of the Abipones,* 2:152.

42. Paucke, *Hacia allá,* 2:208, 301; SLPC, 1:311.

43. Furlong, *Florián Paucke y sus cartas,* 39–40; Paucke, *Hacia allá,* 2:171–74, 237; Dobrizhoffer, *Account of the Abipones,* 2:273–74; Saeger, "Eighteenth-Century Guaycuruan Missions," 64.

44. Paucke, *Hacia allá,* 2:236.

45. Paucke, *Hacia allá,* 2:237–38; Buffalohead, "Farmers, Warriors, Traders," 236–44.

46. Dobrizhoffer, *Account of the Abipones,* 2:139; see also 2: 268–69, 275–76, 301; and Susnik, *Los aborígenes,* 5:54–56; Métraux, "Ethnography," 328–33; Paucke, *Hacia allá,* 2:240–43, 460; SLPC, 2:46–47; "Carta de Fray Francisco Méndez," in Cortesâo, *Manuscritos de Coleçâo de Angelis,* 7:63.

47. SLPC, 1:289–90, 298; Paucke, *Hacia allá,* 2:174; Furlong, *Entre los Mocobíes de Santa Fe,* 94; Susnik, *Los aborígenes,* 5:12; Dobrizhoffer, *Account of the Abipones,* 2:22, 139–46.

48. Unlike the related dialects of the Abipon genders, Mbayá males and females often used strikingly different words to designate the same thing. For example, men referred to one supernatural being as *Ayamarigodi,* "the one of sorrows," while women called the same spirit *Guayemagayego.* SLPC, 2:54.

49. SLPC, 1:249.

50. Paucke, *Hacia allá,* 2:176; vol. 3, pt. 1, 51–52.

51. Paucke, *Hacia allá,* vol. 3, pt. 1, 45–47.

52. Melchor de Echagüe y Andia al virrey, Santa Fe, Mar. 12, 1781, AGN, IX, 4-1-6; Informe del estado actual de las reducciones del alcalde ordinario al superintendente general, Santa Fe, Oct. 6, 1785, ibid.; Saeger, "Eighteenth-Century Guaycuruan Missions," 65–66, 74–76.

53. Saeger, "Another View of the Mission," passim; Urbano de Iriondo, "Apuntes," 2:115; Dobrizhoffer, *Account of the Abipones,* 3:138–39, 173–76, 223–24.

54. Furlong, *Entre los Abipones del Chaco,* 123; Paucke, *Hacia allá,* 2:71.

55. SLPC, 2:22. In a movement unrelated to mission culture, Mbayás increasingly were unable to hold on to the services of Guaná servants. Not captives, Guanás had worked for Mbayás voluntarily, but this relationship shifted after about 1750. Guanás sought their own missions and endeavored to exchange Mbayá masters for Spanish employers.

56. Muriel, "Breve noticia de las misiones vivas," 161.

57. Dobrizhoffer, *Account of the Abipones*, 3:285–86, 351–54, Paucke, *Hacia allá*, 2:82; SLPC, 2:111–16, 138–40.

58. Clendinnen, *Ambivalent Conquests*, 170–73.

59. Dobrizhoffer, *Account of the Abipones*, 3:200.

60. Diarios ejecutados a los paises del Gran Chaco en los años de 1776 y 1781 por el Rdo. Padre Prior del Orden Seráfico Fr. Antonio de Lapa, cura doctrinero de la Reducción de . . . Macapillo, CMG, Cal. 1676; Agustín Fernando de Pinedo al virrey, Buenos Aires, May 23, 1778, AGN, IX, 30-1-7; Francisco Gavino Arias al rey, Salta, Apr. 24, 1777, AGI, BA, leg. 295; "Catálogo de las Reducciones o Poblaciones, llamadas Misiones, de los Indígenas del Chaco," in Jolís, *Ensayo sobre la historia natural de Gran Chaco*, 324 ff.

61. Dobrizhoffer, *Account of the Abipones*, 3:343–45.

62. Doña María Thomasa de Umeres al virrey, Santa Fe, Aug. 22, 1781, AGN, IX, 4-1-6; Melchor de Echagüe y Andia al virrey, ibid.

63. For a discussion of renegades and social outcasts see Stern, "Social Marginality and Acculturation."

64. Dobrizhoffer, *Account of the Abipones*, 3:213–18.

65. Consulta de Josef Lino de Estevan al gobernador, Asunción, Jan. 15, 1777, CMG, Cal. 1470; Instrucción que debe observar don Francisco Bedoya con el Judío Guaycurú que llevaba en su barco, Asunción, Nov. 22, 1775, CMG, Cal. 1429a.

66. Considerable numbers of Guaycuruans served Spanish men and women on the other side of the cultural frontier. See Doucet, "Sobre cautivos de guerra," 59–152, esp. 123–29.

67. Dobrizhoffer, *Account of the Abipones*, 3: 217–19.

68. Muriel, "Breve noticia de las misiones vivas," 142; Paucke, *Hacia allá*, vol. 3, pt. 1, 6; Juan Francisco de la Riva Herrera al Juan José de Vértiz, Santa Fe, June 4, 1775, AGN, IX, 4-1-5.

69. Dobrizhoffer, *Account of the Abipones*, 3:155.

70. Dobrizhoffer, *Account of the Abipones*, 3:120, 186; Paucke, *Hacia allá*, 2:149–52.

71. SLPC, 1:293–95; Furlong, *Entre los Abipones del Chaco*, 24–25.

72. Paucke, *Hacia allá*, 2:69–70; Dobrizhoffer, *Account of the Abipones*, 2:154–55; Furlong, *Entre los Mocobíes de Santa Fe*, 86.

73. At services at Ispín in 1801, a new and relatively poor mission, attenders could see an image of the Immaculate Conception, yellow metal candlesticks, bells, and fine cloth of various kinds. In Concepción de Abipones, a far more affluent mission with thousands of head of livestock in 1777, the display was lavish.

74. Furlong, *Entre los Mocobíes de Santa Fe*, 143–44; Paucke, *Hacia allá*, 1:lámina IX following p. 138; vol. 3, pt. 1, 157, lámina CXII following p. 150; "Relación de San Xavier," in Cortesâo, *Manuscritos de Coleçâo de Angelis*, 7:20, 22.

75. Dobrizhoffer, *Account of the Abipones*, 3:254, 352; Cardiel, "Carta y relación de las misiones," 197; Paucke, *Hacia allá*, 2:211, lámina XXIV facing p. 208; Informe de las reducciones del tiempo de los ex-Jesuítas, Santa Fe, Oct. 6, 1785,

AGN, IX, 4-1-6; Fray Francisco Rodríguez al alcalde de primer voto, Pueblo de San Fernando de las Garzas, July 24, 1792, AGN, IX, 30-7-1.

76. Informe del estado actual de las reducciones al superintendente general, Santa Fe, Oct. 6, 1785, AGN, IX, 4-1-6; Melchor de Echagüe y Andia a Juan José de Cosío, Santa Fe, Feb. 18, 1777, AGN, IX, 4-1-5.

77. Furlong, *Entre los Mocobíes de Santa Fe,* 138–39.

78. One grandmother in San Carlos de Abipones opposed baptism because of its danger to her grandson's health but was unable to convince the father to oppose the ceremony. The priest secured her consent by promising to bury the boy in the traditional way if he died because of baptism; Dobrizhoffer, *Account of the Abipones,* 3:150–51, 341–42; "Relación de . . . San Xavier," in Cortesâo, *Manuscritos de Coleção de Angelis,* 7:19; see also baptism statistics in Appendix B.

79. San Fernando de Abipones averaged one adult and ten infant baptisms a year between 1753 and 1762. A larger mission, San Jerónimo, celebrated thirty-four baptisms in 1762. See Appendix B, 1 and 2a.

80. Paucke, *Hacia allá,* vol. 3, pt. 1, 27–28.

81. See the marriage figures in Appendix B; Clendinnen, *Ambivalent Conquests,* 89–91, 170–73; Paucke, *Hacia allá,* vol. 3, pt. 1, 43–44, 46–48.

82. Melchor de Echagüe y Andia al gobernador, Santa Fe, June 7, 1776, AGN, IX, 4-1-5; Annua Enumeratio Reductionum Fluminis Paranensis, Anni 1762, AGN, IX, 6-10-5; Certificación del José Clain [Klein], San Fernando, año de 1766, AGN, IX, 6-10-7; Paucke, *Hacia allá,* vol. 3, pt. 1, 66; see also Appendix B, tables 1, 2a, 2c, and 4b.

83. Dobrizhoffer, *Account of the Abipones,* 2:212.

84. Dobrizhoffer, *Account of the Abipones,* 2:207, 212, 3:405; Furlong, *Entre los Mocobíes de Santa Fe,* 90.

85. Furlong, *Entre los Mocobíes de Santa Fe,* 107.

86. Furlong, *Entre los Mocobíes de Santa Fe,* 158; Paucke, *Hacia allá,* 2:108, 120.

87. "Relación del Estado . . . de San Javier," in Cortesâo, *Manuscritos de Coleção de Angelis,* 7:17–18; Paucke, *Hacia allá,* vol. 3, pt. 1, 24.

88. Furlong, *Entre los Abipones,* 48; Dobrizhoffer, *Account of the Abipones,* 3:405; Paucke, *Hacia allá,* 2:315; "Carta de Fray Francisco Méndez," in Cortesâo, *Manuscritos de Coleção de Angelis,* 7:64.

89. "Relación de . . . San Xavier," in Cortesâo, *Manuscritos de Coleção de Angelis,* 7:18; SLPC, 2:310; Paucke, *Hacia allá,* 2:66, 136–37.

90. Furlong, *Entre los Mocobíes de Santa Fe,* 29–30, 93; SLPC, 1:293–94.

91. Muriel, "Breve noticia de las misiones vivas," 176; Dobrizhoffer, *Account of the Abipones,* 3:116–17; Furlong, *Florián Paucke y sus cartas al visitador Contucci,* 49–54; Furlong, *Entre los Mocobíes de Santa Fe,* 158; "Relación . . . de San Xavier," in Cortesâo, *Manuscritos de Coleção de Angelis,* 7:17.

92. Paucke, *Hacia allá,* 2:272–73; Furlong, *Entre los Mocobíes de Santa Fe,* 131–32.

93. Paucke, *Hacia allá,* 2:59–60, Furlong, *Entre los Mocobíes de Santa Fe,* 26–27.

94. Saeger, "Eighteenth-Century Guaycuruan Missions," 67; Furlong, *Entre los Abipones del Chaco,* 147.

95. Paucke, *Hacia allá,* 2:201–10.

96. Paucke, *Hacia allá,* 2:65–68.

97. Fray Francisco Rodríguez al alcalde de primer voto, San Fernando de las Garzas, July 27, 1792, AGN, IX, 31-7-1; Informe del estado actual de las reducciones del alcalde ordinario Gabriel de Lasaga al superintendente general, Santa Fe, Oct. 6, 1785, AGN, IX, 4-1-6.

98. See Appendix B, tables 1, 2a, 2c, 3a, and 4b. I cannot explain why so many more boys than girls lived in San Jerónimo in the 1760s. Some "widows" were actually wives whom Christian rules caused husbands to discard. But plural marriage was not common enough in any of these bands to affect the general picture materially.

99. Paucke, *Hacia allá,* vol. 3, pt. 1, 40; Dobrizhoffer, *Account of the Abipones,* 2:153; 3:254, 399.

100. Paucke, *Hacia allá,* 2:239–40; SLPC, 1:26–28.

101. Paucke, *Hacia allá,* vol. 3, pt. 1, 6–8, 33–34; Dobrizhoffer, *Account of the Abipones,* 3:404–5.

102. Furlong, *Entre los Abipones del Chaco,* 63–64; Dobrizhoffer, *Account of the Abipones,* 2:152–53; Paucke, *Hacia allá,* 2:274; vol. 3, pt. 1, 23.

CHAPTER 5. *Politics and War*

1. See Saeger, "Another View of the Mission," 493–512, esp. 507–12.

2. Metcalf, "Who Should Rule at Home?" 651–65, quote on p. 653.

3. Metcalf, "Who Should Rule at Home?" 655–56.

4. Junta de Guerra, Payses del Gran Chaco, July 28, 1774, AGI, BA, leg. 244.

5. Teniente Melchor de Echagüe y Andia al virrey, Santa Fe, Oct. 12, 1779, AGN, IX, 31-3-5.

6. Dobrizhoffer, *Account of the Abipones,* 3:303, 323–24.

7. Metcalf, "Who Should Rule at Home?" 651.

8. Lowie, "Social and Political Organization of Tropical Forest and Marginal Tribes," 340.

9. Many caciques cooperated with priests against shamans. The Abipon Ychoalay-Benavides assisted priests in San Jerónimo, as did the Mocobis Nevedagnac and Aletin in San Javier, and the Mbayá Epaquini in Belén. Each increased his own authority and reduced that of rival claimants to influence.

10. Many failed to get a mission. Costs to Spanish governments and the Society of Jesus included a heavy capital investment and continuing subventions. Thus petitioners did not automatically win a mission. All eight Mbayá bands in the 1760s wanted missions. Only two received them, and neither reduction thrived because they lacked adequate support (see chapters 2 and 7).

11. Dobrizhoffer, *Account of the Abipones,* 2:105–8.

12. Florian Paucke, C.J., al Nicolás Contucci, C.J., San Javier, May 16, 1764, AGN, IX, 6-10-5.

13. Compañero de cura de San Pedro al visitador Nicolás Contucci [fragment], San Pedro, n.d. [1765], AGN, IX, 7-1-2.

14. Susnik, *Los aborígenes,* 5:105–6, 109.

15. Dobrizhoffer, *Account of the Abipones,* 2:103.

16. Dobrizhoffer, *Account of the Abipones,* 2:102.

17. SLPC, 2:135–36.

18. Dobrizhoffer, *Account of the Abipones,* 2:104; SLPC, 1:249, 255–56, 260.

19. Susnik, *Los aborígenes,* 5:104–5; Paucke, *Hacia allá,* 2:104–5.

20. Susnik, *Los aborígenes,* 5:105; Dobrizhoffer, *Account of the Abipones,* 3:337–45.

21. SLPC, 2:255–67.

22. Winckler, "Political Anthropology," 333.

23. In "Who Should Rule at Home?" Richard Metcalf says, "The belief that aboriginal societies were ruled by consensus is largely a concept of anthropologists, whose native informants often tend to be selfconscious [*sic*] keepers of a tribal heritage which they remember in idealistic terms. This is one area where historians are better off trusting the accounts of early white observers than the scholarly theories of social science" (p. 665).

24. Huntington, *Political Order in Changing Societies,* 412–13.

25. Paucke, *Hacia allá,* 2:18, 31–38, 66; Dobrizhoffer, *Account of the Abipones,* 3:117–18.

26. SLPC, 1:273.

27. Paucke, *Hacia allá,* 2:203.

28. Several sources mention the possibility of female chiefs in aboriginal Guaycuruan society, but I located only one. Dobrizhoffer, *Account of the Abipones,* 2:108.

29. Quote in Dobrizhoffer, *Account of the Abipones,* 2:102; see also 2:108; 3:211.

30. Declaración y contrata de paces, Reducción de Concepción de Abipones, June 29, 1770, AGI, Buenos Aires, leg. 198. The same pattern of succession can be seen in five other Mocobi chiefs: Queyaberi, Nacinquin, Ladinogotin, Cottogorin (son of Cottogorin), and Quidiogorin. All were chiefs by inheritance or men who expected to inherit leadership from their fathers. Parlamento del gobernador con Mocobi caciques, Salta, July 30, 1776, AGI, BA, leg. 244.

31. The high status of Epilig-Lorenzo, the responsibilities inherited from his father, and acceptance of his leadership by other male Mbayás challenge the assertions of Branislava Susnik that Mbayás were in practice an intensely exclusive group. She goes on to attribute the Mbayá demographic decline in the eighteenth and nineteenth centuries in part to their refusal to be more open. Mbayá *ideology* was exceedingly ethnocentric, and they assimilated outsiders less comfortably than other Guaycuruans, but they were also pragmatic. Lorenzo's Mbayá-Payaguá parentage and the marriage of Chief Golanigi of the Guetiadegodis to a Paraguayan woman show the gap between ideology and behavior; SLPC, 1:267, 2:127, and passim.

32. SLPC, 2:82–83.

33. Quote in Dobrizhoffer, *Account of the Abipones,* 3:143; see also 3:207–12.

34. SLPC, 2:23; Susnik, *Los aborígenes,* 5:114.

35. Susnik, *Los aborígenes,* 104.

36. *Class* here is used in the everyday sense commonly used in the United States, to denote simply a category of people.

37. Lowie claims "a caste system develops most readily through war"; "Social and Political Organization of Marginal and Tropical Forest Tribes," 348–49.

38. SLPC, 2:14–20.

39. SLPC, 2:20; Dobrizhoffer, *Account of the Abipones,* 2:100–1.

40. Paucke, *Hacia allá,* 2:107–11.

41. Paucke, *Hacia allá,* 2:12; 3:59; SLPC, 1:32; Acuerdo del cabildo de Santa Fe, Santa Fe, Apr. 4, 1743, AGPSF, AC, vol. XI; Auto del teniente del gobernador, Paraje del Pueblo Viejo, July 21, 1743, ibid.

42. SLPC, 1:255–60; 2:107–8, 127, 131.

43. Clausewitz, *On War,* 87. In *A History of Warfare,* pp. 46–60, John Keegan challenges Clausewitz. The Prussian, however, explains Guaycuruan behavior better than his distinguished modern critic.

44. Métraux, "Warfare, Cannibalism, and Human Trophies," 383.

45. Susnik, *Los aborígenes,* 5:135. War is understudied by anthropologists. Métraux, in "Warfare, Cannibalism, and Human Trophies," and Lowie, in *The Crow Indians,* see primitive war as a contest mostly for prestige, almost like a game. Their cultural interpretation undervalues economic motives. R. Brian Ferguson, though, thinks that "the occurrence and form of warfare are intimately related to processes of material production and other exigencies of survival"; *Warfare, Culture, and Environment,* 2; see also his *Yanomami Warfare.* Although anthropologists are often more concerned about ideal types than historians, Thomas Biolsi's "Ecological and Cultural Factors in Plains Indians Warfare" is a commonsense account that argues "resource competition and large-scale warfare on the Great Plains were multifactorial, the result of the simultaneous effects of ecological and cultural causes" (p. 161). Also debated is the relationship between primitive warfare and feuds, or between intertribal and intratribal violence. See Vayda, "Primitive Warfare," and Pospisil, "Feud," 389.

In *A History of Warfare,* 79–136, especially 121, John Keegan denies that primitive war, especially raiding, is "a true act of warfare." One's definition of warfare depends on whether one's focus is on simple or complex societies. In the Chaco in the last half of the colonial era, war grew out of feuds. But violent conflict between Abipon or Mocobi bands is legitimately understood as war, even though personal rivalries between chiefs often precipitated it.

46. Dobrizhoffer, *Account of the Abipones,* 3:30–31; Don Esteban Huget, cirujano, al cabildo de la Asunción, Asunción, Nov. 9, 1776; AGI, BA, leg. 48; El cabildo de la Asunción al rey, Asunción, Jan. 29, 1777, ibid.

47. Some Guaycuruans, including many Toba, stayed in the Chaco and only infrequently contacted the Hispanic world. Other Guaycuruans approached the white-dominated world in less formal ways than by requesting missions. Some settled on the outskirts of Spanish settlements; groups of Mbayás in the late 1700s camped with increasing permanence in the environs of the northern Paraguayan city of Concepción, and growing numbers of Payaguás came to Asunción. After the failure of the missions of San Bernardo and Cangayé, Tobas and Mocobis drifted to the west bank of the Río Paraguay just north of the Bermejo. Gobernador Pedro Melo de Portugal al rey, Asunción, July 13, 1778, CMG, Cal.

1560; Ganson, "The Evueví of Paraguay," 461–88; Doucet, "Sobre cautivos de guerra."

48. Francisco Gavino Arias, gobernador interino, al rey, Salta, May 24, 1776, AGI, BA, leg. 295. From elsewhere in the Chaco Toba chiefs Asistery, Quiguiry, and others also attempted to negotiate with their former Hispanic adversaries for missions in order to gain advantage over Native American rivals. Carta del fray Antonio de Lapa al gobernador, Gran Chaco, June 22, 1776, AGI, BA, leg. 244; Diligencia del . . . Fr. Antonio de Lapa, Reducción de Macapillo, Nov. 20, 1776, ibid.

49. Dobrizhoffer, *Account of the Abipones*, 3:133–38.

50. Dobrizhoffer, *Account of the Abipones*, 3:381–82, 392–94; quote on p. 382. Priests usually misunderstood the role they were expected to play in Guaycuruan patterns of distribution and consumption. That priests failed to understand how Guaycuruans viewed them politically is curious because they worked hard to contrast themselves to native leaders, in order to discredit the latter. Priests generally interpreted Guaycuruan demands for knives or needles or wages as the result of their greed or childishness. They failed to see that Guaycuruans had placed them in their political structure, investing them with attributes of their own leaders.

51. Robert Haskett, *Indigenous Rulers*, 60–123.

52. Tommasini, *La civilización cristiana del Chaco*, 164.

53. Dobrizhoffer, *Account of the Abipones*, 2:108–9. Dobrizhoffer rationalized the appointment of able war leaders as Guaycuruan caciques by saying that many Guarani chiefs by birth were "more stupid than the common people and less skillful in the public employments of the town."

54. Resumen general de la Reducción de San Ignacio de Tobas, folios. 9–9v of Expediente de visitas practicadas . . . por Don Andrés de Mestre, AGN, IX, 30-1-8, exp. 12.

55. Carta del Fr. Antonio de Lapa al gobernador, Gran Chaco, June 22, 1776, AGI, BA, leg. 244; Parlamento del gobernador y cinco Mocobi caciques, Salta, July 30, 1776, ibid.

56. Fr. Antonio de Lapa, Diario exacto y fiel de los acaecim.tos sucedidos en la entrada al Gran Chaco Gualamba por el mes de mayo del año de 1776, folios 32, 37; Expediente sobre la reducción que solicitan varias naciones . . . del Gran Chaco, AGN, IX, 30-1-7.

57. Paucke, *Hacia allá*, vol. 3, pt. 1, 31–32; 2:109, 123–27, 173, 271, 300.

58. On the mission ranch in the late Jesuit era, 12,000 cattle, 1,000 horses, 1,200 mares, 400 mules, 182 burros, and 1,700 sheep grazed. A second estancia of this mission kept 1,500 horses, 6,000 cattle, and 600 sheep. The third estancia was similar in size to the second.

59. Paucke, *Hacia allá*, vol. 3, pt. 1, lámina CXIV following p. 150.

60. Paucke, *Hacia allá*, 2:18, 36, 59–60, 80–90, 114, 127; Dobrizhoffer, *Account of the Abipones*, 3:117–18.

61. Dobrizhoffer, *Account of the Abipones*, 3:119; "Carta del procurador general

al cabildo de Santa Fe, Santa Fe, Nov. 3, 1774," in M. Cervera, *Poblaciones y curatos,* 359.

62. Don Domingo Nevedagnac, cacique, corregidor y maestre de campo de la nación Mocobi, y alcaldes ordinarios Antonio Dañgoidin y Estanislao Yuniniga al virrey, San Javier, Nov. 1, 1780, AGN, IX, 4-1-6.

63. Instrucción de Juan Francisco de la Riva Herrera de lo que debe observar el sargento mayor Melchor de Echagüe y Andia, Santa Fe, May 15, 1773, AGN, IX, 4-1-4.

64. In Guarani missions corregidores were appointed by and represented the interests of Jesuits. Caciques more frequently articulated the wishes of most Guaranis.

65. Dobrizhoffer, *Account of the Abipones,* 3:403.

66. Dobrizhoffer, *Account of the Abipones,* 3:143–62; see also chapter 6.

67. Dobrizhoffer, *Account of the Abipones,* 3:151–60. Alcalde ordinario Gabriel de Lasaga, Informe de las reducciones del tiempo de la expulsión de los ex-Jesuítas, Santa Fe, Oct. 6, 1785; AGN, IX, 4-1-6.

68. SLPC, 2:19.

69. El virrey al teniente del gobernador de Santa Fe, Buenos Aires, Sept. 30, 1799, AGN, IX, 4-2-3.

70. Dobrizhoffer, *Account of the Abipones,* 3:264–65, 286; Testimonio del teniente José del Barco, Santa Fe, Apr. 10, 1752, AGN, IX, 4-1-2; Testimonio del Capitán Pedro Manuel de Arizmendi, ibid.; Juan Francisco de la Riva Herrera al virrey, Santa Fe, Apr. 7, 1776, AGN, IX, 4-1-5.

71. Dobrizhoffer, *Account of the Abipones,* 3:257–59.

72. Antonio Medina al gobernador de armas Juan Francisco de la Riva Herrera, Santa Fe, Sept. 6, 1775, AGN, IX, 32-9-1; Auto de Basilio Jaques, Santa Fe, Sept. 15, 1775, ibid.

73. Dobrizhoffer, *Account of the Abipones,* 3:299; El teniente de Santa Fe al virrey, Santa Fe, Apr. 19, 1786, AGN, IX, 4-1-7; Respuesta del virrey, Buenos Aires, May 8, 1786, ibid. There is no further record of these Abipones. Probably they eventually merged into the Hispanized population of the area.

74. Oficio del comandante de Ledesma al comandante de Fronteras, Ledesma, July 3, 1808, AGN, IX, 5-7-7; José Francisco de Tineo al virrey, Salta, July 6, 1808, ibid.; Fr. Juan José Ortiz al oidor Don José Medeiros, San Ignacio, June 12, 1808, ibid.

75. Nicolás Patrón al gobernador, Corrientes, Feb. 8, 1759, AGN, IX, 3-3-6.

76. Isidro Martínez y Cires, alcalde ordinario de primer voto, al virrey, Corrientes, Feb. 3, 1799, AGN, IX, 3-4-2; Cabildo elections of San Fernando de las Garzas, Nov. 24, 1800 and Jan. 1803, AGN, IX, 3-4-3.

77. Dobrizhoffer, *Account of the Abipones,* 3:215–16; Juan Francisco de la Riva Herrera al virrey, Santa Fe, Apr. 7, 1776, AGN, IX, 4-1-5; Melchor de Echagüe y Andia al gobernador, Santa Fe, Dec. 26, 1776, ibid.; Melchor de Echagüe y Andia al virrey, Santa Fe, Feb. 6, 1781, AGN, IX, 4-1-6; Relación de Miguel Gerónimo Venavides corregidor y cacique principal . . . de San Jerónimo al virrey, Monte-

video, n.d. [1781], AGN, IX, 4-1-6; El virrey al teniente de Santa Fe, Buenos Aires, July 11, 1799, AGN, IX, 4-2-3.

78. El cabildo de Santa Fe al virrey, Santa Fe, Oct. 12, 1798, AGN, IX, 4-2-3.

79. Fr. José de Córdoba al virrey, Santa Fe, Nov. 5, 1780, AGN, IX, 4-1-6.

80. Don Damaso Queran also went to see the viceroy, but his lack of sophistication and poor Spanish thwarted his efforts to secure relief for his people; Miguel Benavides al teniente, San Jerónimo, Jan. 26, 1788, AGN, IX, 4-1-7; El virrey al teniente de Santa Fe, Buenos Aires, Feb. 13, 1788, ibid. See also Saeger, "Another View of the Mission," 509–12. Joaquín Maciel al gobernador, Santa Fe, Dec. 2, 1769, AGN, IX, 4-1-3; Francisco Antonio de Vera Múxica al gobernador, Santa Fe, Jan. 25, 1762, AGN, IX, 4-1-2.

81. Fr. Juan Antonio Jorge al comandante, San Jerónimo, June 30, 1799, AGN, IX, 31-7-6; Prudencio María de Gastáñaduy al virrey, ibid.

82. Domingo Nebedanaca al capitán a guerra Juan Francisco de la Riva Herrera, San Javier, Feb. 15, 1773, AGN, IX, 4-1-4.

83. Lazaro de Almirón al gobernador, Corrientes, July 9, 1770, AGN, IX, 3-3-7.

84. Protector de los indios al gobernador intendente, Salta, Feb. 9, 1790, AGN, IX, 23-10-7, exp. 9.

85. By the 1700s cannibalism was not prominent in Guaycuruan society. Paucke, *Hacia allá,* 2:302–13.

86. Prudencio María de Gastañaduy al virrey, Frontera de Santa Fe, Mar. 11, 1803, AGN, IX, 4-2-4.

87. Paucke, *Hacia allá,* 2:212–13; vol. 3, pt. 1, 24–25.

88. Various testimony, Lima, Oct.–Dec. 1766, AGI, BA, leg. 244.

89. Dobrizhoffer, *Account of the Abipones,* 3:139–43.

90. Dobrizhoffer, *Account of the Abipones,* 3:143–56.

91. José Clain [Klein], S.J., al visitador Nicolás Contucci, San Fernando, July 18, 1762, AGN, IX, 6-10-5.

92. Dobrizhoffer, *Account of the Abipones,* 3:165–69.

93. Dobrizhoffer, *Account of the Abipones,* 3:170–73.

94. Nicolás Patrón a Francisco Antonio Vera Múxica, Corrientes, Mar. 23, 1750, AGN, IX, 3-3-6; Antonio Martínez al gobernador, Corrientes, June 25, 1759, ibid.; Nicolás Patrón al gobernador, Corrientes, Feb. 8, 1758, ibid.; Capellán Joseph Clain [Klein], S.J., al gobernador, Corrientes, Nov. 11, 1758, ibid.; Capellán Tomás Arnau, S.J., al gobernador, Corrientes, Sept. 10, 1758; ibid.

95. Joseph Bonifacio Barrenechea al gobernador, Chaco, July 11, 1762, AGN, IX, 3-3-7.

96. Dobrizhoffer, *Account of the Abipones,* 3:170–98, 207–13.

97. Dobrizhoffer, *Account of the Abipones,* 3:230–55; Juan Victorino Martínez de Tineo a los padres Joseph Sánchez, C.J., y Bartolomé Araos, Salta, Jan. 13, 1750, AGN, IX, 6-10-1; Juan Victorino Martínez de Tineo a Joseph de Andonaegi, Salta, Mar. 20, 1753, AGN, IX, 5-6-6.

98. Certificación del Capt. Matheo Lencina, n.p., Mar. 9, 1758, AGN, IX, 6-10-5; Certificación del S. M. Bernardo Garmendia, n.p., Apr. 15, 1765, AGN IX, 6-10-6.

99. Juan Francisco de la Riva Herrera a Juan José de Vértiz, Santa Fe, Mar. 2, 1776; AGN, IX, 4-1-5; Agustín Fernando de Pinedo a Cacique Don José Benavides, Asunción, Aug. 23 and Nov. 5, 1775, ibid.; Riva Herrera al gobernador del Paraguay, Santa Fe, Feb. 17, 1776, ibid.

100. Juan Francisco de la Riva Herrera a Juan José de Vértiz, Santa Fe, Sept. 21, 1775, AGN, IX, 4-1-5.

101. Fr. Blas Brite al virrey, San Jerónimo, Oct. 17, 1781, AGN, IX, 4-1-6; Melchor de Echagüe al virrey, Santa Fe, June 6, 1783, ibid.

102. Florian Paucke, C.J., al visitador Nicolás Contucci, C.J., San Javier, May 16, 1764, AGN, IX, 6-10-5.

103. SLPC, 2:138–51; José Coene al gobernador intendente, Asunción, Aug. 6, 1795, ANA, NE, vol. 71; Queja de don Casimiro Coene, ibid.

104. Joaquín de Alós al virrey, Asunción, Jan. 15, 1793, AGN, IX, 33-8-4.

105. Don Pedro de la Vega, natural de España vecino de Jujuy al gobernador de armas, Jujuy, May 4, 1785, AGN, IX, 5-8-1; José de Gálvez al gobernador Andrés de Mestre, Pardo, Jan. 12, 1782, ibid., 5-7-2.

106. Urbano de Iriondo, "Apuntes," 55–69.

CHAPTER 6. *Religion*

1. This chapter concentrates on changing beliefs of Guaycuruans with some account of behavior, especially ritual. Anthony F. C. Wallace, *Religion,* 53–71, lists thirteen essential categories of religious behavior: prayer, music, physiological exercise, exhortation, reciting the code, simulation, mana, taboo, feasts, sacrifice, congregation, symbolism, and ritual. Insufficient sources ruled out a systematic examination of all categories.

2. Miller, "The Christian Missionary," 14–15.

3. Wilbert and Simoneau, eds., *Folk Literature of the Mocoví Indians,* 13; Wilbert and Simoneau, eds., *Folk Literature of the Caduveo Indians,* 23. Most creation accounts in these and the two volumes of Toba belief narratives (*Folk Literature of the Toba Indians*) are from the twentieth century.

4. Furlong, *Entre los Abipones del Chaco,* 36–38.

5. Dobrizhoffer, *Account of the Abipones* 2:65.

6. Métraux, "Ethnography," 350–53; Métraux, "Religion and Shamanism," 559–60, 564–65; Susnik, *Los aborígenes,* 6:7.

7. Susnik, *Los aborígenes,* 6:8–9, 53; Métraux, "Religion and Shamanism," 566–67.

8. Quotes in Dobrizhoffer, *Account of the Abipones,* 3:355 and Wright, "Dream, Shamanism, and Powers," 150 (see also pp. 149–79).

9. Dobrizhoffer, *Account of the Abipones,* 3:355

10. Métraux, "Religion and Shamanism," 566–67; Susnik, *Los aborígenes,* 6:53–56.

11. Like other spirits, this one had many human characteristics.

12. Susnik, *Los aborígenes,* 6:46–64.

13. Susnik, *El rol de los indígenas,* 2:95–96; Wilbert and Simoneau, *Folk Literature of the Caduveo Indians,* 23.

14. Oberg, *The Terena and the Caduveo,* 64. This account resembles eighteenth-century versions, but a loss of pride in the hunting way of life appeared in Oberg's time.

15. Dobrizhoffer, *Historia de los Abipones,* 2:70 (hereafter abbreviated MDHA). This is the Spanish edition of Dobrizhoffer, *Account of the Abipones.* Both were consulted for this chapter.

16. The priest incorrectly concluded that the role of religion in Abipones' lives was negligible. In fact, Ychoalay's remarks were partly a truthful response and partly a way to change the subject.

17. Furlong, *Entre los Mocobíes de Santa Fe,* 87–88; Susnik, *Los aborígenes,* 6:26; Fr. Antonio Lapa, Diario exacto y fiel de los acaecim.tos sucedidos en la entrada al Gran Chaco Gualamba por años de 1770, diary entry for July 30, AGN, IX, 30-1-7.

18. Furlong, *Entre los Mocobíes de Santa Fe,* 87; Wilbert and Simoneau, *Folk Literature of the Toba Indians,* 39–43.

19. Susnik, *Los aborígenes,* 6:7–9, 12; Wilbert and Simoneau, *Folk Literature of the Caduveos,* 32–34; Wilbert and Simoneau, *Folk Literature of the Mocoví Indians,* 47.

20. Cordeu and Siffredi, *De la algarroba al aldodón,* 14.

21. Susnik, *Los aborígenes,* 6:35, 46–50; SLPC, 1:193–94; Métraux, "Ethnography," 352; Dobrizhoffer, *Account of the Abipones,* 3:355.

22. Oberg, *The Terena and the Caduveo,* 63.

23. Métraux, "Ethnography," 352; Susnik, *Los aborígenes,* 6:35.

24. Wright, "Dream, Shamanism, and Powers," 149–79.

25. Miller, *Harmony and Dissonance,* 11.

26. Miller, *Harmony and Dissonance,* 6; Susnik, *Los aborígenes,* 6:53.

27. Spanish clerics interpreted this activity as the work of the devil. Fr. Antonio Lapa, "Diario . . . advertencias y noticias breves que noté en estas naciones," folio 47v, AGN, IX, 30-1-7.

28. Métraux, "Ethnography," 351–52.

29. Lapa, Diario . . . advertencias y noticias breves de las cosas particulares . . . en estas naciones, folio 47, AGN, IX, 30-1-7.

30. Jesuits ridiculed this personification of death; Paucke, *Hacia allá,* 2:237; SLPC, 2:48.

31. Métraux, "Ethnology," 360; MDHA, 2:78; Tabla estadística del Gran Chaco . . . habitado de tribus independientes en 1777, CMG, Cal. 1320.

32. Jolís, *Ensayo sobre la historia natural del Gran Chaco,* 315–16.

33. Jolís, *Ensayo sobre la historia natural del Gran Chaco,* 263–70; "Carta de Fray Francisco Méndez," in Cortesâo, *Manuscritos de Coleçâo de Angelis,* 7:63.

34. SLPC, 2:31–32, 283.

35. MDHA, 2:78–79.

36. MDHA, 2:103, 109.

37. Dobrizhoffer, *Account of the Abipones,* 2:77.

38. MDHA, 2:82.

39. MDHA, 2:84.

40. Belief in omens once brought an Abipon to Father Martin Dobrizhoffer with a request that his most precious possessions—a bridle with an iron bit and a hatchet—be safeguarded in the chapel because his mother predicted an attack. She learned that enemies were near from a flea bite on the arm. The priest explained the occurrence naturalistically, saying that fleas bit his arms daily without precipitating attacks. MDHA, 2:80–81.

41. Paucke, *Hacia allá,* 2:248–49; Muriel, *Historia del Paraguay,* 231.

42. "Carta de Fray Francisco Méndez," in Cortesâo, *Manuscritos de Coleçâo de Angelis,* 7:60.

43. Paucke, *Hacia allá,* 2:236, 249.

44. MDHA 2:86, 91; "Carta de Fray Francisco Méndez," in Cortesâo, *Manuscritos de Coleçâo de Angelis,* vol. 7.

45. Cardiel, "Carta y relación de las misiones," 193; Métraux, "Ethnography," 353.

46. Métraux denies that Mocobis had true female shamans (see "Ethnography," 361).

47. Furlong, *Entre los Mocobíes de Santa Fe,* 98; Paucke, *Hacia allá,* vol. 2, drawing following p. 236; "Relación de . . . San Xavier," in Cortesâo, *Manuscritos de Coleçâo de Angelis,* 7:19.

48. Miller, "Shamans, Power Symbols, and Change," 481.

49. Wallace, "Revitalization Movements," 267, 269.

50. Ibid., 267.

51. MDHA, 220–21.

52. Lapa, Diario . . . de 1776, entries for June 23 and Sept. 5, AGN, IX, 30-1-7.

53. Tratado de paz de Dn. Etazurín Nazac y el cabildo de la Asunción y los cabos militares, Asunción, June 1, 1776, AGI, BA, leg. 295.

54. Ordenanza para la observancia de indios Tobas y Mocobís reducidos . . . , Cangayé, Gran Chaco, Jan. 26 [1780], AGN, IX, 24-1-1; Padrón de Mocobís de Santiago de Cangayé, Cangayé, Feb. 8, 1780, ibid.

55. Melchor de Echagüe y Andia al virrey, Santa Fe, Apr. 14, 1782, AGN, IX, 4-1-6.

56. Lapa, "Diario . . . de 1776," entries for June 25 and July 8 and 11, AGN, IX, 30-1-7.

57. Young women welcomed Christian marriage, while young males resisted it.

58. Farriss, *Maya Society under Colonial Rule,* 295.

59. This summary was adapted from *Catecismo en la lengua española y aymará del Piru,* the model for all subsequent missionary programs in Spanish South America, including those of the Jesuits. See McNaspy, *Conquistador without a Sword,* 102–3; also see the following articles in the *New Catholic Encyclopedia:* "Catechism," 3:225–31; D. E. Tanck, "Catechisms in Colonial Spanish America," 3:232–34; F. X. Murphy, "Creed," 3:432–38; J. R. Quinn, "Sacraments, Theology of," 12:806–11; I. McGuiness, "Sin, Theology of," 13:241–45; R. L. Richard, "Trinity, Holy," 14:295–306; T. M. de Ferrari, "Baptism (Theology of)," 2:62–68; J. M. Egan, "Matrimony II, Sacrament of," 9:468–72; W. F. Dewan, "Penance, Sacra-

ment of: Dogmatic Aspects," 11:73–78; K. J. Healy, "Prayer (Theology of), 11:672–78. The basic tenets of Catholic faith were taught to Indians in the Americas. Beyond the basics, however, missionaries improvised. Ricard, *Spiritual Conquest of Mexico,* 102.

60. Tanck, "Catechisms in Colonial Spanish America," 232–34; quotation from Ricard, *Spiritual Conquest of Mexico,* 101–2.

61. Muchembled, *Popular Culture and Elite Culture in France,* 222.

62. Cardiel, "Carta y relación de las misiones," 195.

63. Cardiel, "Carta y relación de las misiones," 26–27, 192, 195; Muriel, *Historia del Paraguay,* 237–38.

64. Burkhart, *Slippery Earth,* 11.

65. Muriel, "Breve noticia de las misiones vivas," 176.

66. Furlong, *Entre los Abipones del Chaco,* 36–37.

67. Dobrizhoffer, *Account of the Abipones,* 2:57, 193–94.

68. Furlong, *Entre los Abipones del Chaco,* 117–18.

69. Muriel, "Breve noticia de las misiones vivas," 175–76.

70. Ibid.

71. Relación de Miguel Gerónimo Venavides al virrey, Montevideo, n.d. [1781], AGN, IX, 4-1-6; Fray Juan Antonio Jorge al comandante, San Jerónimo, June 30, 1799, AGN, IX, 31-7-6; Prudencio María de Gastañaduy al virrey, Santa Fe, July 10, 1799, ibid.

72. Dobrizhoffer, *Account of the Abipones,* 3:109–10, 254, 285–86, 300; quotation in 3:285.

73. Muriel, "Breve noticia de las misiones vivas," 162–63; Muriel, *Historia del Paraguay,* 82–83.

74. Axtell, *The Invasion Within,* 93–98, quotation on p. 98; SLPC, 2:31–32.

75. José Brigniel, C.J., al alcalde de primer voto, San Jerónimo, Jan. 22, 1752, AGN, IX, 4-1-2.

76. Farriss, *Maya Society under Colonial Rule,* 75.

77. Francisco Xavier Rodríguez a Rafael Martínez, Santa Fe, Oct. 11, 1800, in Expediente de . . . reducciones de . . . Ispín, AGI, BA, leg. 612.

78. Dobrizhoffer, *Account of the Abipones,* 2:82–83.

79. Dobrizhoffer, *Account of the Abipones,* 2:253, 274.

80. Paucke, *Hacia allá,* 2:236, 249, 254.

81. Axtell, *The Invasion Within,* 101; SLPC, 1:192–93.

82. SLPC, 191–92.

83. Cardiel, "Carta y relación de las misiones," 198.

84. MDHA, 2:87.

85. Oberg, *The Terena and the Caduveo,* 64.

86. MDHA, 2:95.

87. MDHA, 2:91–92.

88. MDHA, 2:89.

89. MDHA, 2:227–30.

90. MDHA, 2:83.

91. Dobrizhoffer, *Account of the Abipones,* 2:74–75.

92. MDHA, 2:89.

93. This denigration of Indian religion was perpetuated by scholars of the first half of the twentieth century. See Weber, "John Francis Bannon," 336–37.

94. MDHA, 2:220–21.

95. Ibid., 2:246, 248–50.

96. MDHA, 2:253; SLPC, 1:190–93, 250.

97. Paucke, 2:235, 250–51; "Carta de Fray Francisco Méndez," in Cortesâo, *Manuscritos de Coleção de Angelis,* 7:63.

98. Cardiel, "Carta y relación de las misiones," 197; Paucke, *Hacia allá,* 2:247–48.

99. Paucke, *Hacia allá,* 2:250–53.

100. Professor Ursula Lamb, personal communication, July 19, 1988.

101. Nutini, *Todos Santos,* 18.

102. ". . . el Padre o es mago, o nacido de madre profética," MDHA, 2:77.

103. MDHA, 2:79.

104. Muriel, "Breve noticia de las misiones vivas," 180–81.

105. Carta del cura de San Pedro al visitador Nicolás Contucci, S.J. (fragment), San Pedro, n.d. [1765], AGN, IX, 7-1-2.

106. La ciudad de Santa Fe al rey, Santa Fe, Mar. 6, 1745, AGPSF, AC, vol. XI; Florian Paucke, C.J., al Visitador Nicolás Contucci, AGN, IX, 6-10-5; Don Domingo Nevedagnac, Cacique, Corregidor y Maestre de Campo, Manuel Antonio Dañagoidín y Esanislao Ytininga, alcaldes ordinarios, al virrey, San Javier, Nov. 1, 1780, AGN, IX, 4-1-6.

107. Certificación del Padre José Clain [Klein], San Fernando, 1766, AGN, IX, 6-10-7.

108. Statistics also corroborate another missionary assertion about the particularity of San Fernando: that the Yaaucanigas there clung to traditional religion more tightly than did the Riikahé Abipones of San Jerónimo.

109. Furlong, *Entre los Abipones del Chaco,* 149–50; "Joseph Klein, S.J., al visitador Nicolás Contucci, S.J., San Fernando, Oct. 10, 1763," in Alumni, *El Chaco,* 95–96.

110. Most examples in this chapter are from the four Abipon missions, the Mocobi settlements of San Javier and San Pedro, and the Mbayá Belén, which Jesuit chronicles describe most extensively. Archival sources from other missions confirm these trends.

111. Alonso de Quesada a Francisco Paula de Sanz, Corrientes, Oct. 26, 1785, AGN, IX, 3-3-7.

112. I am unable to account for the high number of non-Christian girls in this pueblo in 1785, when the number of unbaptized minor females was almost eight times the number of unbaptized minor males (39 to 5). The likeliest explanation is that they were fairly recent captives from another Guaycuruan band, because the years after 1776 were a time of troubles and conflict for the Santa Fe missions.

113. Padrón, Reducción de Santiago en el Fuerte de San Nicolás, June 1, 1793, AGN, IX, 30-5-2; Benito, obispo de Buenos Aires, al virrey, Jan. 10, 1804, ibid.

114. Muriel, "Breve noticia de las misiones vivas," 160–61.

115. Muriel, *Historia del Paraguay*, 82.

116. "Relación . . . de San Xavier," c. 1750 [1753], in Cortesâo, *Manuscritos de Coleçâo de Angelis*, vol. 7.

117. Lázaro de Almirón al gobernador, Corrientes, July 9, 1770, AGN, IX, 3-3-7; Juan Manuel Labarden al gobernador, Corrientes, Nov. 8, 1767, AGN, IX, 3-3-7.

118. Informe del estado actual de las reducciones del alcalde ordinario de Santa Fe al superintendente general, Santa Fe, Oct. 6, 1785; AGN, IX, 4-1-6.

119. Dobrizhoffer, *Account of the Abipones*, 3:300.

120. Ricard, *Spiritual Conquest of Mexico*, 96–96, 108; Muriel *Historia de Paraguay*, 85; Cabildo abierto, Asunción, Sept. 25, 1767; CMG, Cal. 1270; Capítulos del padre provincial de la Compañía de Jesús al gobernador de Tucumán (n.p.), Feb. 17, 1764, AGI, BA, leg. 49.

121. Dr. Matías de Ziburu al gobernador, Pueblo de San Javier, Mar. 9, 1768; AGN, IX, 4-1-3; Joaquín Maciel al gobernador, Santa Fe, Mar. 23, 1768, ibid.; Cacique Corregidor Don Domingo Nebedenaca a Juan Francisco de la Riva Herrera, San Javier, Feb. 15, 1773, AGN, IX, 4-1-4; Juan Francisco de la Riva Herrera al gobernador, Santa Fe, Feb. 22, 1773, ibid.; Riva Herrera al cabildo, Santa Fe, Oct. 3, 1774, AGN, IX, 4-1-5; Riva Herrera al gobernador, Santa Fe, Oct. 4, 1774, ibid.

122. "Relación . . . de San Xavier," c. 1750 [1753], in Cortesâo, *Manuscritos de Coleçâo de Angelis*, 7:20.

123. Beck-Bernard, *Cinco años en la Confederación Argentina*, 226, 250.

124. "Relación . . . de San Xavier," in Cortesâo, *Manuscritos de Coleçâo de Angelis*, 7:17.

125. "Relación . . . de San Xavier," in Cortesâo, *Manuscritos de Coleçâo de Angelis*, 7:22.

126. Ibid.

127. Burkhart, *Slippery Earth*, 144.

128. "Relación . . . de San Xavier," in Cortesâo, *Manuscritos de Coleçâo de Angelis*, 7:19–20.

129. "Relación . . . de San Xavier," in Cortesâo, *Manuscritos de Coleçâo de Angelis*, 7:19–21.

130. Ibid.

131. Exhorto del obispo al gobernador, Córdoba del Tucumán, Aug. 21, 1770, AGI, BA, 200; Certificación de Gabriel Güemes Montero, Jujuy, Aug. 19, 1778, AGI, BA, 37.

132. Burkhart, *Slippery Earth*, 191. Fray Juan Ignacio Ayzpuru al teniente Prudencio María Gastañaduy, San Jerónimo, July 17, 1807, AGN, IX, 4-2-6; Benito Villanueva al teniente coronel Gregorio Tadeo de la Cerda, Villeta, Jan. 20, 1807, ANA, CVRB, cat. 138, n. 35.

133. Comandante de Armas Prudencio María Gastañaduy al virrey, Santa Fe, July 10, 1795, AGN, IX, 30-5-2; Gastañaduy al virrey, Fuerte de Almagro, Sept. 9, 1795, ibid.

134. Benito, obispo de Buenos Aires al virrey, Buenos Aires, Jan. 10, 1804, AGN, IX, 30-5-2.

135. Oberg, *The Terena and the Caduveo,* 64.

136. Fr. Francisco Rodríguez al alcalde ordinario de Corrientes, Pueblo de San Fernando de las Garzas, July 24, 1792, AGN, IX, 31-7-1.

137. Relación de don Miguel Gerónimo Venavides, corregidor y cacique principal al virrey, Montevideo, n.d. [1781], AGN, IX, 4-1-6.

138. Farriss, *Maya Society under Colonial Rule,* 286, 295–96.

CHAPTER 7. *The Nineteenth and Twentieth Centuries*

1. Urbano de Iriondo, "Apuntes"; F. Cervera, "Los blandengues de Santa Fe."

2. Page, *La Plata,* 253.

3. Urbano de Iriondo, "Apuntes," 50.

4. Urbano de Iriondo, "Apuntes," 50–53, 70; Scunio, *La conquista del Chaco,* 108–11, 113–19; F. Cervera, "Las reducciones indígenas," 90–95.

5. Urbano de Iriondo, "Apuntes," 50–51; F. Cervera, "Las reducciones indígenas," 95; Scunio, *La conquista del Chaco,* 113–19.

6. Mantilla, *Crónica histórica de la provincia de Corrientes,* 1:182–83, 202.

7. Letter of Constancio Ferraro de Cavour, in Beck-Bernard, *Cinco años en la confederación argentina,* 228–29; Scunio, *La conquista del Chaco,* 123–30.

8. Urbano de Iriondo, "Apuntes," 71–72.

9. Beck-Bernard, *Cinco años en la confederación argentina,* 228; D'Orbigny, *Viaje a la América meridional,* 270; Scunio, *La conquista del Chaco,* 136–39.

10. Williams, *Rise and Fall,* 44.

11. Susnik, *Los aborígenes,* III/1: 94–97, 100–5; Williams, *Rise and Fall,* 75–76; Wilbert and Simoneau, *Folk Literature of the Caduveo Indians,* 1.

12. Urbano de Iriondo, "Apuntes," 85–89; Gianello, *Historia de Santa Fe,* 243; F. Cervera, "Las reducciones indígenas," 99–100; Alumni, *La ciudad de Resistencia,* 2; Scunio, *La conquista del Chaco,* 133–35; Nellar, *Política seguida con el aborigen,* vol. 2, pt. 2, 466–87.

13. D'Orbigny, *El hombre americano,* 292–94.

14. Nellar, *Política seguida con el aborigen,* vol. 2, pt. 2, 531–38.

15. Susnik, *El indio colonial,* vol. 3, pt. 1, 173–76; Williams, "El Dr. Francia," 139–54; Chaves, *El supremo dictador,* 322–30; Durán Estrago, *Presencia franciscana en el Paraguay,* 182–85.

16. D'Orbigny, *El hombre americano,* 281–82; D'Orbigny, *Viaje a la América meridional,* 277–80; Alemán, "Contribución de Santa Fe," 106.

17. D'Orbigny, *Viaje a la América meridional,* 274–80.

18. F. Cervera, "Las reducciones indígenas," 91–92, 104–5; Urbano de Iriondo, "Apuntes," 95–97.

19. Urbano de Iriondo, "Apuntes," 105; Nellar, *Política seguida con el aborigen,* vol. 2, pt. 2, 511–26, 552–56; Page, *La Plata,* 253; F. Cervera, "Las reducciones indígenas," 95–97.

20. Rossi, "Relación histórica sobre las misiones," 430.

21. F. Cervera, "Las reducciones indígenas," 92–96; Rossi, "Relación histórica sobre las misiones"; Beck-Bernard, *Cinco años en la confederación argentina,* 225.

22. Letter of Constancio Ferrero de Cavour, in Beck-Bernard, *Cinco años en la confederación argentina,* 228–451; Urbano de Iriondo, "Apuntes," 111–12; Rossi, "Relación histórica sobre las misiones," 428–29.

23. Letter of Constancio Ferrero de Cavour, in Beck-Bernard, *Cinco años en la confederación argentina,* 233–34, 239–41.

24. Scunio, *La conquista del Chaco,* 138–46, 159, 171.

25. Rossi, "Relación histórica sobre las misiones," 428; Mantegazza, *Viajes por el Río de la Plata,* 263–70.

26. Mantegazza, *Viajes por el Río de la Plata,* 267.

27. F. Cervera, "Los blandengues de Santa Fe," 76–77; Fontana, *El Gran Chaco,* 132; Scunio, *La conquista del Chaco,* 146–48.

28. F. Cervera, "Las reducciones indígenas," 105.

29. Wilbert and Simoneau, *Folk Literature of the Caduveo Indians,* 1; Maeder, "Estudio preliminar," in Fontana, *Gran Chaco,* 9–10.

30. F. Cervera, "Las reducciones indígenas," 106.

31. Scunio, *La conquista del Chaco,* 151–59, 247–327; Alumni, *La ciudad de Resistencia,* 36–48, 59, 93–115; F. Cervera, "Las reducciones indígenas," 107–8; Serrano, *Los primitivos habitantes del territorio argentino,* 109.

32. Cardús, *Las misiones franciscanas entre los infieles de Bolivia,* 258–66; Nordenskiöld, *Indian Civilizations in South America,* 89.

33. Miller, *Los Tobas argentinos,* 60–65, 77–78, 80, 116–31; Nordenskiöld, *La vie des indiens dans le Chaco,* 18; Campi and Lagos, "Auge azucarero y mercado de trabajo en el noroeste argentino," 179–208; Níklison, *Los Tobas,* 44, 48–50, 89.

34. F. Cervera, "Las reducciones indígenas," 108–10; Hagan, *American Indians,* 129–31; Ubertalli, *Guaycurú,* 51–59.

35. Mendoza and Wright, "Sociocultural and Economic Elements," 245–46.

36. Ibid.; Karsten, *The Toba Indians of the Bolivian Gran Chaco,* 7–13; Níklison, *Los Tobas,* 57–75; Serrano, *Los primitivos habitantes del territorio argentino,* 111–14.

37. Palavecino, "Breve noticia sobre los Mocobíes actuales," xvi–xvii; Reyburn, *The Toba Indians of the Argentine Chaco,* 6–10; Ribeiro, *Kadiwéu,* 24; Oberg, *The Terena and the Caduveo,* 56–60; Lévi Strauss, *Tristes tropiques,* 170–77, 180; Canals Frau, *Las poblaciones indígenas,* 298; Balieff, "The Present-Day Indians of the Gran Chaco," 371–80; Ganson, "The Evueví of Paraguay," 460–88, Susnik, *El indio colonial,* vol. 3, pt. 1, 128–39.

38. Mendoza, "Estrategías adaptivas de migrantes Tobas," 139–44; de la Cruz and Mendoza, "Les Toba de l'ouest de Formosa," 43–51; Wilbert and Simoneau, *Folk Literature of the Toba Indians,* 1; Griva and Stroppa, eds., *Yo, Montiel Romero, de raza Toba,* 20.

39. Wilbert and Simoneau, *Folk Literature of the Mocoví Indians,* 1–2.

40. Translation: "The Indian who perished lives on in the gaucho; the gaucho, who is perishing, survives in the creole of the present, and the three will live in the Argentina of the future." Cardozo Gómez, *Poblar el desierto,* 2:47.

CHAPTER 8. *Conclusion*

1. Page references throughout this chapter are from Sweet, "The Ibero-American Frontier Mission in Native American History." Sweet's is a bold approach to a touchy subject. Many North American historians, in response to criticism from Native Americans, are reluctant to admit that they are taking a native perspective. For example, in *The American Revolution in Indian Country,* Colin G. Calloway claims that he "does not pretend to try and tell the 'Indian side of the story,'" even though that is precisely what much of his book aims to do (p. xvi).

2. Letter of Constancio Ferraro de Cavour to Lina Beck-Bernard, Santa Fe, n.d. [1860?], in Beck-Bernard, *Cinco años en la confederación Argentina,* 240.

3. The ecology of the Chaco has been hostile to archaeological efforts. Thus it is unlikely that any effort similar to Farnsworth and Jackson's "Cultural, Economic, and Demographic Change in the Missions of California," which benefits from recent archaeological findings, will provide much help for investigators of Chaco topics.

4. Melville, *A Plague of Sheep,* 5.

5. Ibid.; see also Crosby, "Virgin Soil Epidemics."

6. Radding, *Wandering Peoples,* 110.

7. The Guarani mission population of 141,182 in 1732 was almost halved owing to disease and the repercussions of the rebellion of the *comuneros* in Paraguay. Guarani men were mostly away from the missions in a state of almost constant mobilization. Consequently, mission crops and livestock suffered. The birth rate fell. The population reached its nadir of 73,910 for the Jesuit period in 1740. It recovered to 104,483 in 1755, but the Guarani War led to another decline in the 1760s; Maeder and Bolsi, "La población de la misiones guaraníes entre 1702–1767." Unfortunately, we have no similarly detailed records from Corrientes, Villa Rica, or Asunción for comparison.

8. Paucke, *Hacia allá,* 2:250–51.

9. Mocobis relied on captive labor less than did Abipones, Mbayás, or the Toba.

10. Most missionaries, who came from societies that saw slavery as normal, thought that Guaycuruan masters normally treated servants and slaves well.

11. In "Missions and the Frontier Economy," Erick Langer identifies "three periods in the life of the mission—establishment, mature functioning, and eventual secularization" (p. 51).

12. See Saeger, "Eighteenth-Century Guaycuruan Missions," 81, n. 38.

13. A large proportion of these people assimilated into Platine communities, but it is doubtful that many made a conscious choice to do so.

14. Deeds, "Rendering unto Caesar," 15–39; Taylor, *Magistrates of the Sacred,* 83–86.

15. Cabildo records of Santa Fe contain numerous references to Mocobi and Abipon prisoners in the local jail. See AGPSF, AC, vols. X–XVII.

16. A generation or a "generational unit" here is understood as a period of fifteen years. See Lewis, *Political Parties and Generations*, 9–11.

17. Métraux, "Revolution of the Ax," 28–30.

18. Naranjay—which Durán Estrago, *Presencia franciscana en el Paraguay*, 184–85, identifies as a separate reduction—may have been either a regional identification of San Antonio or a separate settlement of new bands.

19. Utley, *The Indian Frontier of the American West*, 129–33.

20. Ibid., 219.

21. Ibid., 213–18, 269.

22. Zeitlin, "Ranchers and Indians," 26–27.

BIBLIOGRAPHY

MANUSCRIPT SOURCES AND ABBREVIATIONS

Archivo General de Indias, Seville, Spain (AGI)
  Audiencia de Charcas (Charcas)
  Audiencia de Buenos Aires (BA)

Archivo General de la Nación, Buenos Aires, Argentina (AGN)

Archivo General de la Provincia de Santa Fe (AGPSF)
  Actas Capitulares (Actas del Cabildo) (AC)

Archivo Histórico de Jujuy (AHJ)
  Libros Capitulares (LC)
  Archivo de Tribunales

Archivo Nacional de Asunción (ANA)
  Sección Historia (SH)
  Sección Nueva Encuadernación (NE)
  Coleçâo Visconde Do Rio Branco (CVRB)

Archivo Nacional de Chile (ANC)
  Jesuítas de Argentina (JA)

Manuel Gondra (now Nettie Lee Benson) Collection, University of Texas, Austin (CMG)

PUBLISHED WORKS AND DISSERTATIONS

Acevedo, Edberto Oscar. *La intendencia de Salta del Tucumán en el virreinato del Río de la Plata.* Mendoza, Argentina: Universidad Nacional de Cuyo, 1967.

Aguirre, Juan Francisco. "Diario del Capitán Juan Francisco Aguirre." *Revista de la Biblioteca Nacional* (Buenos Aires), vols. 17–19, nos. 45–48 (1949–1951).

Alden, Dauril. *The Making of an Enterprise: The Society of Jesus in Portugal, Its Empire, and Beyond.* Stanford, Calif.: Stanford University Press, 1996.

Alemán, Bernardo E. "Caciques indígenas de la época colonial Santafecina," Santa Fe, Argentina, n.d. (Reprinted in *Revista de la Junta Provincial de Estudios Históricos de Santa Fe* 48 [1978?]:67–95.)

———. "Contribución de Santa Fe a la conquista del desierto." *Revista de la Junta Provincial de Estudios Históricos de Santa Fe* 51 (1981): 99–114.

———. "El problema del indio en la historia de Santa Fe (1810–1853)," in *Historia de las instituciones de la provincia de Santa Fe*, vol. 3, 37–85. Santa Fe, Argentina: Comisión Redactora de la Historia de las Instituciones de la Provincia de Santa Fe, 1970.

Alumni, Mons. José. *El Chaco: figuras y hechos de su pasado, 1750–1959*. Resistencia, Argentina: n.p., 1951.

———. *La ciudad de Resistencia: apuntes históricos*. Resistencia, Argentina: n.p., 1958.

Andrien, Kenneth J., and Lyman L. Johnson, eds. *The Political Economy of Spanish America in the Age of Revolution, 1750–1850*. Albuquerque: University of New Mexico Press, 1994.

Angelis, Pedro de, ed. *Colección de obras y documentos relativos a la historia antigua y moderna de las provincias del Río de la Plata*. 6 vols. Buenos Aires: Imprenta del Estado, 1835.

Arenales, José Ildefonso Alvarez de. *Noticias históricas y descriptivas sobre el gran pais del Chaco y Río Bermejo*. Buenos Aires: Hallet y Compañía, 1833.

Assadourian, Carlos S., Guillermo Beato, and José Chiaramonte. *Argentina: de la conquista a la independencia*. Buenos Aires: Editorial Paidos, n.d.

Axtell, James. *The Invasion Within: The Contest of Cultures in North America*. New York and Oxford: Oxford University Press, 1985.

Axtell, James, and William C. Sturtevant. "The Unkindest Cut, or Who Invented Scalping." *William and Mary Quarterly*, 3d. ser., no. 3 (1980): 451–472.

Azara, Félix de. *Descripción e historia del Paraguay y del Río de la Plata*. 2 vols. Madrid: Imprenta de Sánchiz, 1847.

———. *Geografía física y esférica de las provincias del Paraguay. . . .* Montevideo: Imprenta Oficiales, 1904.

———. *Memoria sobre el estado rural del Río de la Plata y otros informes*. Buenos Aires: Bajel, 1943.

———. *Viajes por la América meridional*. 2 vols. Madrid: Calpe, 1923.

Balieff, Juan. "The Present-Day Indians of the Gran Chaco." In *Handbook of South American Indians*. Vol. 1, 371–380. Washington, D.C.: Government Printing Office, 1946.

Beck-Bernard, Lina. *Cinco años en la confederación argentina, 1857–1862*. Trans. José Luis Busaniche. Buenos Aires: El Ateneo, 1935.

Benítez, Luis G. *Historia del Paraguay: época colonial*. Asunción: Imprenta Comuneros, 1985.

Bidondo, Emilio A. *Historia de Jujuy, 1535–1950*. Buenos Aires: Editorial Plus Ultra, 1980.

Biedma, José J. *Crónicas militares: antecendentes históricos sobre la campaña contra los indios*. Buenos Aires: Editorial Universitaria Comuneros, 1975.

Biolsi, Thomas. "Ecological and Cultural Factors in Plains Indians Warfare." In *Warfare, Culture, and Environment*. Ed. R. Brian Ferguson, 141–68. Orlando, Fla., 1984.

Biscay, Acarete du. *An Account of a Voyage up the River de la Plata, and Thence Over Land to Peru. With Observations on the Inhabitants . . . the Cities, Commerce, Fertility, and Riches of that Part of America.* London: Samuel Buckley, 1698.

Bischoff, Efrain U. *Historia de Córdoba: cuatro siglos.* Buenos Aires: Editorial Plus Ultra, 1979.

Block, David. *Mission Culture on the Upper Amazon: Native Tradition, Jesuit Enterprise, and Secular Policy in Moxos, 1660–1880.* Lincoln and London: University of Nebraska Press, 1994.

Blujaki, Agustín. *Un gran paraguayo: presbítero Juan Francisco Amancio González y Escobar.* Asunción: Escuela Técnica Silesiana, 1972.

Boggiani, Guido. *Os caduveos.* Trans. Amadeu Amaral Jr. Brazil: Editora da Universidade de Sâo Paulo, 1975.

Bolton, Herbert E. *The Mission as a Frontier Institution in the Spanish-American Colonies.* El Paso: Texas Western College Press, 1962. First published in *American Historical Review* 23, no. 1 (1917): 42–61.

Bowman, Isaiah. *Desert Trails of Atacama.* New York: American Geographical Society, 1924.

Braunstein, José A. *Algunos rasgos de la organización social de los indígenas del Gran Chaco.* Buenos Aires: Universidad de Buenos Aires, 1983.

Brown, Jonathan C. *A Socioeconomic History of Argentina, 1760–1810.* Cambridge: Cambridge University Press, 1979.

Buffalohead, Priscilla K. "Farmers, Warriors, Traders: A Fresh Look at Ojibway Women." *Minnesota History* 48 (Summer 1983): 236–44.

Burkhart, Louise. *The Slippery Earth: Nahua-Christian Moral Dialogue in Sixteenth-Century Mexico.* Tucson: University of Arizona Press, 1989.

Bushnell, Amy Turner. *Situado and Sabana: Spain's Support System for the Presidio and Mission Provinces of Florida.* Athens, Ga.: University of Georgia Press, 1994.

Cabeza de Vaca, Alvar Núñez. "Comentarios." In *Naufragios y Comentarios,* 198–213. Bilbao, Madrid, and Barcelona: Espasa Calpe, 1932.

Calloway, Colin G. *The American Revolution in Indian Country: Crisis and Diversity in Native American Communities.* Cambridge: Cambridge University Press, 1995.

Caloni, Fr. Vicente. *Apuntes históricos sobre la fundación del colegio de San Carlos y sus misiones en la provincia de Santa Fe.* Buenos Aires: Imprenta y Librería de Mayo, 1884.

Campi, Daniel, and Marcelo Lagos. "Auge azucarero y mercado de trabajo en el noroeste argentino, 1850–1930." *Andes: Antropología e Historia* 6 (1994): 179–208.

Canals Frau, Salvador. *Las poblaciones indígenas de la Argentina: su origen—su pasado—su presente.* Buenos Aires: Editorial Sudamérica, 1953.

Caraman, Philip. *Lost Paradise: The Jesuit Republic in South America.* New York: Dorset Press, 1975.

Cardiel, José. "Carta y relación de las misiones de la Provincia del Paraguay." In *José Cardiel, S. J., y su carta relación (1747).* Ed. Guillermo Furlong [Cardiff], 115–213. Buenos Aires: Ediciones Theoría, 1953.

Cardozo, Efraím. *El Chaco y los virreyes: la cuestión paraguaya-boliviana según los archivos de Buenos Aires y Rio de Janeiro.* Asunción: Imprenta Nacional, 1934.

———. *El Paraguay colonial: las raíces de la nacionalidad.* Buenos Aires and Asunción: Ediciones Nizza, 1959.

Cardozo Gómez, Humberto Jesús. *Poblar el desierto: proyecto especial para el congreso argentino pro-integración definitiva con el indio.* 2 vols. Santa Fe, Argentina, 1984–1985.

Cardús, R. P., Fr. José. *Las misiones franciscanas entre los infieles de Bolivia: Descripción de ellas en 1883 y 1884 con una noticia sobre los caminos y tribus salvajes. . . .* Barcelona: Librería de la Inmaculada Concepción, 1886.

Carillo, Joaquín. *Jujuí, provincia federal argentina: apuntes de su historia civil.* 1877. Reprint, Jujuy: Universidad Nacional de Jujuy, 1989.

Catecismo en la lengua española y aymará del Piru. Ordenado por autoridad del Concilio Provicial de Lima, y empreso en año de 1583. Seville: n.p., 1604.

Cervera, Frederico G. "Los Blandengues de Santa Fe." *Revista de la Junta Provincial de Estudios Históricos de Santa Fe* 51 (1981): 61–79.

———. "Las reducciones indígenas en el período independiente." In *Historia de las instituciones de la provincia de Santa Fe: el problema del indio en Santa Fe.* Vol. 3, 87–110. Santa Fe, Argentina: Comisión Redactora de la Historia de las Instituciones de la Provincia de Santa Fe, 1970.

———. "Reseña histórica del período hispanico." In *Historia de las instituciones de la provincia de Santa Fe: el problema del indio en Santa Fe.* Vol. 3, 17–35. Santa Fe, Argentina: Comisión Redactora de la Historia de las Instituciones de la Provincia de Santa Fe, 1970.

Cervera, Manuel M. *Historia de la ciudad y provincia de Santa Fe.* 2 vols. Santa Fe, Argentina: Imprenta "La Unión" de Ramón Ibáñez, 1907.

———. *Poblaciones y curatos: estudio histórico.* Santa Fe, Argentina: Talleres Gráficos Castellvi Hermanos, 1939.

Chaves, Julio César. *El supremo dictador: biografía de José Gaspar de Francia.* 4th ed. Madrid: Ediciones Atlas, 1964.

Clausewitz, Carl von. *On War.* Ed. and trans. Michael Howard and Peter Paret. Princeton, N.J.: Princeton University Press, 1976.

Clendinnen, Inga. *Ambivalent Conquests: Maya and Spaniard in Yucatan, 1517–1570.* Cambridge and New York: Cambridge University Press, 1987.

Cline, S. L. *Colonial Culhuacán, 1580–1600: A Social History of an Aztec Town.* Albuquerque: University of New Mexico Press, 1986.

Comadrán Ruiz, Jorge. *Evolución demográfica argentina durante el período hispano.* Buenos Aires: Editorial Universitaria de Buenos Aires, 1969.

Cooney, Jerry W. *Economía y sociedad en la intendencia del Paraguay.* Asunción: Centro Paraguayo de Estudios Sociológicos, 1990.

Cooney, Jerry W., and Thomas L. Whigham. "Paraguayan Commerce with the Outside World, 1750–1850." In *The Political Economy of Spanish America in the Age of Revolution, 1750–1850.* Ed. Kenneth J. Andrien and Lyman L. Johnson, 215–41. Albuquerque: University of New Mexico Press, 1994.

Cordeu, Edgardo Jorge and Alejandra Siffredi. *De la algarroba al algodón: movimiento mesiánico de los Guaycurú*. Buenos Aires: Juárez Editor, 1971.

Cortesâo, Jaime, ed. *Manuscritos de Coleçâo de Angelis*. Vol. 7, *Do Tratado de Madri á conquista dos sete povos (1750–1802)*. Rio de Janeiro: Biblioteca Nacional, 1969.

Crosby, Alfred. "Virgin Soil Epidemics As a Factor in the Aboriginal Depopulation in America." *William and Mary Quarterly*, 3d ser., 33, no. 2 (1976): 289–99.

Cruz, Luis de la, and Marcela Mendoza. "Les Toba de l' ouest de Formosa et le processus de reconnaisance légal de la propieté communautaire de terres." *Recherches Amérindiennes au Quebec* 19, no. 4 (1989): 43–51.

Cushner, Nicholas P. *Jesuit Ranches and the Agrarian Development of Argentina, 1650–1767*. Albany: State University of New York Press, 1983.

Deeds, Susan McClymont. "Rendering unto Caesar: The Secularization of Jesuit Missions in Mid-Eighteenth-Century Durango." Ph.D. diss. University of Arizona, 1981.

Dobrizhoffer, Martin. *An Account of the Abipones: An Equestrian People of Paraguay*. 3 vols. London: John Murray, 1822. Reprint New York: Johnson Reprint Corp., 1970.

———. *Historia de los Abipones*. 3 vols. Resistencia, Argentina: Universidad Nacional del Nordeste, 1967–68. (Spanish edition of previous work.)

Domínguez Ortiz, Antonio. *The Golden Age of Spain, 1516–1659*. New York: Basic Books, 1971.

Doucet, Gastón Gabriel. "Sobre cautivos de guerra y esclavos indios en el Tucumán: notas en torno a un fichero documental salteño del siglo XVII." *Revista de Historia de Derecho* (Buenos Aires) 16 (1988): 59–152.

Durán Estrago, Margarita. *Presencia franciscana en el Paraguay, 1538–1824*. Asunción: Universidad Católica, 1987.

Edmunds, R. David. "Native Americans: New Voices: American Indian History, 1895–1995." *American Historical Review* 100(June 1995): 717–40.

Ensinck, Oscar Luis. *Historia económica de la provincia de Santa Fe*. Rosario, Argentina: Universidad Nacional de Rosario, 1985.

Farriss, Nancy M. *Maya Society under Colonial Rule: The Collective Enterprise of Survival*. Princeton, N.J.: Princeton University Press, 1984.

Farnsworth, Paul, and Robert H. Jackson. "Cultural, Economic, and Demographic Change in the Missions of California: The Case of Nuestra Señora de la Soledad." In *The New Latin American Mission History*. Ed. Erick Langer and Robert H. Jackson, 109–29. Lincoln and London: University of Nebraska Press, 1995.

Ferguson, R. Brian. *Yanomami Warfare: A Political History*. Seattle: University of Washington Press and School of American Research Press, 1995.

Ferguson, R. Brian, ed. *Warfare, Culture, and Environment*. Orlando, Fla.: Academic Press, 1984.

Figueroa, Fernando R. *Historia y geografía de Salta (tierra gaucho)*. Buenos Aires: Editorial Plus Ultra, 1977.

Fontana, Luis Jorge. *El Gran Chaco.* "Estudio preliminar por Ernesto J. A. Maeder." Buenos Aires: Solar/Hachette, 1977.

Furlong [Cardiff], Guillermo. *Cartografía jesuítica del Río de la Plata.* Buenos Aires: Casa Jacobo Peuser, 1936.

———. *Domingo Muriel y su relación de las misiones (1766).* Buenos Aires: Librería del Plata, 1955.

———. *Entre los Abipones del Chaco: según noticias de los misioneros jesuítas.* . . . Buenos Aires: Talleres Gráficos "San Pablo," 1938.

———. *Entre los Mocobíes de Santa Fe, según noticias de los misioneros jesuítas.* . . . Buenos Aires: Sebastián Amorrortu e Hijos, 1938.

———. *Entre los Vilelas de Salta según las noticias de los misioneros jesuítas. . . .* Buenos Aires: Academia Literaria del Plata, 1939.

———. *Florián Paucke y sus cartas al visitador Contucci (1762–1764).* Buenos Aires: Casa Pardo, 1972.

———. *Francisco de Miranda y su sinopsis (1772).* Buenos Aires: Ediciones Theoría, 1963.

———. *Joaquín Camaño, S.J., y su "noticia del Gran Chaco" (1778).* Buenos Aires: Librería del Plata, 1955.

———. *José Cardiel, S.J., y su carta relación (1747).* Buenos Aires: Ediciones Theoría, 1953.

———. *Manuel Querini, S.J., y sus "informes al rey," 1747–1750.* Buenos Aires: Ediciones Theoría, 1967.

———. *Misiones y sus pueblos de Guaraníes.* Buenos Aires: n.p., 1962.

Ganson, Barbara. "The Evueví of Paraguay: Adaptive Strategies and Responses to Colonialism, 1528–1811.: *The Americas: A Quarterly Journal of Inter-American Cultural History* 45, no. 4 (1989): 460–88.

Garavaglia, Juan Carlos. *Mercado interno y economía colonial.* Mexico, D.F.: Grijalba, 1983.

Gianello, Leoncio. *Historia de Santa Fe.* Buenos Aires: Editorial Plus Ultra, 1978.

Gorham, J. Richard. *Paraguay: Ecological Essays.* Miami, Fla.: Academy of the Arts and Sciences of the Americas, 1973.

Gori, Gastón. *El indio y la colonia esperanza.* Santa Fe, Argentina: Museo de la Colonización, 1972.

Griva, Edelmi E., and María Cecilia Stroppa, eds. *Yo Montiel Romero, de raza Toba: historia de vida de un indio Toba de Chaco argentino.* 2d. ed. Mexicali, Mexico: Editorial Mar de Cortés, 1983.

Groussac, Paul. *Ensayo histórico sobre el Tucumán.* Tucumán, Argentina: Fundación Banco Comercial del Norte, 1981.

Guy, Donna J., and Thomas E. Sheridan, eds. *Contested Ground: Comparative Frontiers on the Northern and Southern Edges of the Spanish Empire.* Tucson: University of Arizona Press, 1998.

Hack, Henk. "Indios y menonitas en el Chaco paraguayo." *Suplemento Antropológico: Universidad Católica: Revista del Centro de Estudios Antropológicos* (Asunción) 14 (1979): 210–48.

Hagan, William T. *American Indians.* Rev. ed. Chicago and London: University of Chicago Press, 1979.

Haring, Clarence H. *The Spanish Empire in America.* rev. ed. New York: Harcourt, Brace and World, 1952.

Harris, Marvin. *Cannibals and Kings: The Origins of Cultures.* New York: Vintage Books, 1977.

———. *Cows, Pigs, Wars and Witches: The Riddles of Culture.* New York: Vintage Books, 1978.

Haskett, Robert. *Indigenous Rulers: An Ethnohistory of Town Government in Colonial Cuernavaca.* Albuquerque: University of New Mexico Press, 1991.

Hemming, John. *Red Gold: The Conquest of the Brazilian Indians.* Cambridge, Mass.: Harvard University Press, 1978.

Historia de las instituciones de la provincia de Santa Fe. Vol. 3, *El problema del indio de Santa Fe.* Santa Fe, Argentina: Comisión Redactora de la Historia de las Instituciones de la Provincia de Santa Fe, 1970.

Humins, John H. "Squanto and Massasoit: A Struggle for Power." *New England Quarterly* 60 (March 1987): 54–70.

Huntington, Samuel P. *Political Order in Changing Societies.* New Haven and London: Yale University Press, 1968.

Ibarra Grasso, Dick Edgar. *Argentina indígena y prehistoria americana.* Buenos Aires: Tipográfica Editora Argentina, 1967.

Jackson, Robert H. *Indian Population Decline: The Missions of Northwestern New Spain, 1687–1840.* Albuquerque: University of Mew Mexico Press, 1994.

Jackson, Robert H., and Edward Castillo. *Indians, Franciscans, and Spanish Colonization: The Impact of the Mission System on California Indians.* Albuquerque: University of New Mexico Press, 1995.

John, Elizabeth A. H. *Storms Brewed in Other Men's Worlds: The Confrontation of Indians, Spanish, and French in the Southwest, 1540–1795.* College Station: Texas A & M Press, 1975.

Jolís, José de. *Ensayo sobre la historia natural del Gran Chaco.* Trans. María Luisa Acuña with "estudio preliminar" by J. A. Maeder. Resistencia, Argentina: Universidad Nacional del Nordeste, 1972.

Jones, Kristine L. "Comparative Raiding Economies: North and South." In *Contested Ground: Comparative Frontiers on the Northern and Southern Edges of the Spanish Empire.* Eds. Donna J. Guy and Thomas E. Sheridan, 97–114. Tucson: University of Arizona Press, 1998.

———. "Conflict and Adaptation on the Argentine Pampas, 1750–1880." Ph.D. diss. University of Chicago, 1984.

Josephy, Alvin M., Jr. *The Indian Heritage of America.* New York: Knopf, 1978.

Karsten, Rafael. *The Toba Indians of the Bolivian Gran Chaco.* Oosterhuit, The Netherlands: Anthropological Publications, 1967.

Keegan, John. *A History of Warfare.* New York: Knopf, 1993.

Kersten, Ludwig. *Las tribus indígenas del Gran Chaco hasta fines del siglo XVII: una contribución a la etnografía histórica de Sudamérica.* Trans. Jorge von

Hauenscheld. Resistencia, Argentina: Universidad Nacional del Nordeste, 1968.

Labougle, Raul. *Historia de San Juan de Vera de las Siete Corrientes.* Buenos Aires: Librería Platero, 1978.

Langer, Erick. "Missions and the Frontier Economy: The Case of the Franciscan Missions among the Chiriguanos, 1845–1830." *The New Latin American Mission History.* Eds. Erick Langer and Robert H. Jackson, 49–76. Lincoln and London: University of Nebraska Press, 1995.

Langer, Erick, and Robert H. Jackson, eds. *The New Latin American Mission History.* Lincoln and London: University of Nebraska Press, 1995.

Levene, Ricardo, ed. *Historia de la nación argentina (desde los orígenes hasta la organización definitiva en 1862).* 10 vols. Buenos Aires: Imprenta de la Universidad, 1936–1950.

Lévi-Strauss, Claude. *Tristes tropiques.* New York: Atheneum, 1974.

Levillier, Roberto. *Historia argentina.* 5 vols. Buenos Aires: Plaza y Janés, 1968–69.

Lewin, Boleslao. *La rebelión de Túpac Amaru y los orígenes de la emancipación americana.* Buenos Aires: Librería Hachette, 1957.

Lewis, Paul. *Political Parties and Generations in Paraguay's Liberal Era, 1869–1940.* Chapel Hill and London: University of North Carolina Press, 1993.

Lizondo Borda, Manuel. *Historia del Tucumán (siglos XVII–XVIII).* Tucumán, Argentina: Universidad Nacional de Tucumán, 1941.

Lockhart, James. *The Nahuas after Conquest: A Social and Cultural History of the Indians of Central Mexico, Sixteenth through Eighteenth Centuries.* Stanford, Calif.: Stanford University Press, 1992.

———. *Nahuas and Spaniards: Post-Conquest Central Mexican History and Philology.* Stanford, Calif.: Stanford University Press, 1991.

Lockhart, James, ed. and trans. *We People Here: Nahuatl Accounts of the Conquest of Mexico.* Berkeley: University of California Press, 1993.

Lowie, Robert H. *The Crow Indians.* New York: Farrar and Rinehart, 1935.

———. "Social and Political Organization of Tropical Forest and Marginal Tribes." *Handbook of South American Indians.* Vol. 5, 313–50. Washington, D.C.: Government Printing Office, 1956.

Lozano, Pedro. *Descripción corográfica del Gran Chaco Gualamba.* Tucumán, Argentina: Instituto de Antropología, 1941.

Lullo, Orestes di. *Caminos y derroteros en Santiago del Estero.* Santiago del Estero, Argentina: n.p., 1959.

———. *Cuatro siglos de historia.* Tucumán, Argentina: Universidad Nacional de Tucumán, 1953.

MacCann, William. *Two Thousand Miles' Ride through the Argentine Provinces: Being an Account of the Natural Products of the Country and Habits of the People; with a Historical Retrospect of the Río de la Plata, Monte Video, and Corrientes.* 2 vols. London, 1853. Reprint, New York: AMS Press, 1971.

McNaspy, C. J. *Conquistador without a Sword: The Life of Roque González, S.J.* New York: Xavier Society for the Blind, 1984.

Maeder, Ernesto J. A. "Documentos sobre la historia del Chaco en la colección de Angelis de la Biblioteca Nacional de Rio de Janeiro." *Folia Histórica del Nordeste* (Resistencia, Argentina) 2 (1976): 180–216.

———. *Historia del Chaco y de sus pueblos, 1862–1930*. Buenos Aires: Librería el Ateneo, 1967.

———. *Historia económica de Corrientes en el período virreinal, 1776–1810*. Buenos Aires: Academia Nacional de Historia, 1981.

———. *Misiones del Paraguay: conflictos y disolución de la sociedad guaraní (1768–1850)*. Madrid: Editorial MAPFRE, 1992.

Maeder, Ernesto J. A., and Alfredo Bolsi. "La población de las misiones guaraníes entre 1702–1767." *Estudios Paraguayos* 2, no. 1 (1974): 111–37.

Mantegazza, Paolo. *Viajes por el Río de la Plata*. Buenos Aires: Coni Hermanos, 1916.

Mantilla, Manuel Florencio. *Crónica histórica de la provincia de Corrientes*. 2 vols. Buenos Aires: Espiasse y Compañía, 1928–1929.

Marfany, Roberto H. "La guerra con los indios nómadas." In *Historia de la nación argentina (Desde las orígenes hasta la organización definitiva en 1862)*. Vol. 6, sec. 2, ed Ricardo Levene, 1041–86. Buenos Aires: Imprenta de la Universidad, 1944.

Martin, Calvin. "Ethnohistory: A Better Way to Write Indian History." *Western Historical Quarterly* 9 (1978): 41–56.

———. "The European Impact on the Culture of a Northeastern Algonquian Tribe: An Ecological Interpretation." *William and Mary Quarterly*, 3d. ser., 31, no. 1 (1974): 3–26.

Meli, Rosa. "La dominación del Chaco." *Investigaciones y ensayos* (Academia Nacional de Historia, Buenos Aires) 4 (1968): 303–43.

Melià, Bartomeu. *El Guarani conquistado y reducido: ensayos de etnohistoria*. 2d. ed. Asunción: Biblioteca Paraguaya de Antropología, 1988.

Melville, Elinor G. K. *A Plague of Sheep: Environmental Consequences of the Conquest of Mexico*. Cambridge: Cambridge University Press, 1994.

Mendoza, Marcela. "Estrategías adaptivas de migrantes Tobas en el Gran Buenos Aires." *Acta Psiquiátrica y Psicológica de América Latina* 35, nos. 3–4 (1989): 139–44.

———. "Politics and Leadership among the Toba of Northwest Argentina." Ph.D diss., University of Iowa, 1998.

Mendoza, Marcela, and Pablo G. Wright. "Sociocultural and Economic Elements of the Adaptation Systems of the Argentine Toba: The Nacilamolek and the Taksek Cases of Formosa Province." In *Archeological Approaches to Cultural Identity*. Ed. Stephen Shennan, 242–57. London: Unwin Hyman 1988.

Merrell, James H. "The Indians' New World: The Catawba Experience." *William and Mary Quarterly*, 3d ser., 41, no. 4 (1984): 537–65.

Metcalf, Richard P. "Who Should Rule at Home? Native American Politics and Indian-White Relations." *Journal of American History* 61 (December 1974): 651–65.

Métraux, Alfred. "Ethnography of the Chaco." In *Handbook of South American Indians.* Vol. 1, 197–370. Washington, D.C.: Government Printing Office, 1946.

———. "Religion and Shamanism." In *Handbook of South American Indians.* Vol. 5, 559–99. Washington, D.C.: Government Printing Office, 1956.

———. "The Revolution of the Ax." *Diogenes* 25 (1959): 28–40.

———. "Warfare, Cannibalism, and Human Trophies." In *Handbook of South American Indians.* Vol. 5, 383–411. Washington, D.C.: Government Printing Office, 1956.

Miller, Christopher L., and George R. Hammell. "A New Perspective on Indian-White Contact: Cultural Symbols and Colonial Trade." *Journal of American History* 73, no. 2 (1986): 311–28.

Miller, Elmer S. "The Christian Missionary: An Agent of Secularization." *Anthropological Quarterly.* 43, no. 1 (1970): 14–22.

———. *A Critically Annotated Bibliography of the Gran Chaco Toba.* 2 vols. New Haven, Conn.: Human Relations Area Files, 1980.

———. *Harmony and Dissonance in Argentine Toba Society.* New Haven, Conn.: Human Relations Area Files, 1980.

———. *Nurturing Doubt: From Mennonite Missionary to Anthropologist in the Argentine Chaco.* Urbana and Chicago: University of Illinois Press, 1995.

———. "Shamans, Power Symbols, and Change in Argentine Toba Culture." *American Ethnologist* 2, no. 3 (1975): 477–96.

———. *Los tobas argentinos: armonía y dissonancia en una sociedad.* Mexico: Siglo Veintiuno, 1979.

Mintz, Sidney W. *Sweetness and Power: The Place of Sugar in Modern History.* New York: Penguin, 1985.

Miranda, Guido. *Tres ciclos chaqueños (crónica histórica regional).* Resistencia, Argentina: Editorial Norte Argentino, 1955.

Monferini, Juan M. "La historia militar durante los siglos XVII y XVIII." In *Historia de la nación argentina (Desde las orígenes hasta la organización definitiva en 1862).* Vol. 4, sec. 2, ed Ricardo Levene, 307–436. Buenos Aires: Imprenta de la Universidad, 1938.

Mörner, Magnus. *Actividades políticas y económicas de los Jesuítas en el Río de la Plata: la era de los Habsburgos.* Buenos Aires: Paidos, 1968.

Muchembled, Robert. *Popular Culture and Elite Culture in France, 1400–1750.* Baton Rouge: Louisiana State University Press, 1985.

Muriel, Domingo. "Breve noticia de las misiones vivas de la Compañía de Jesús en la Provincia del Paraguay. . . . "In *Domingo Muriel y su relación de las misiones (1766).* By Guillermo Furlong [Cardiff], 130–218. Buenos Aires: Librería del Plata, 1955.

———. *Historia del Paraguay desde 1747 hasta 1767.* Trans. P. Pablo Hernández. Madrid: Librería General de Victoriano Suárez, 1918.

Necker, Louis. *Indios guaraníes y chamanes franciscanos: las primeras reducciones del Paraguay (1580–1800).* Asunción: Centro de Estudios Antropológicos, Universidad Católica, 1990.

Neill, Stephen. *A History of Christian Missions.* 2d ed. Rev. by Owen Chadwick. London: Penguin, 1986.

Nellar, Fued G., ed. *Política seguida con el aborigen.* Vol. 1 *(1750–1819)* and vol. 2 in 2 books *(1820–1852).* Buenos Aires: Círculo Militar, 1972–1975.

New Catholic Encyclopedia. 16 vols. New York: McGraw-Hill, 1967.

Nickson, R. Andrew. *Historical Dictionary of Paraguay.* 2d. ed. Metuchen, N.J.: Scarecrow Press, 1993.

Níklison, José Elías, *Los Tobas.* Buenos Aires, 1916. Reprint, Jujuy: Universidad Nacional de Jujuy, 1990.

Nordenskiöld, Erland. *Origin of the Indian Civilizations in South America.* Göteborg: Elanders Boktryckeri Aktiebolag, 1931.

———. *La vie des indiens dans le Chaco (Amérique du Sud).* Paris: Delagrave, 1912.

Nutini, Hugo. *Todos Santos in Rural Tlaxcala: A Syncretic, Expressive, and Symbolic Analysis of the Cult of the Dead.* Princeton, N.J.: Princeton University Press, 1988.

Oberg, Kalervo. *The Terena and the Caduveo of Southern Mato Grosso, Brazil.* Washington, D.C.: Smithsonian Institution, 1948.

D'Orbigny, Alcides. *El hombre americano considerado en sus aspectos fisiológicos y morales.* Buenos Aires: Editorial Futuro, 1944.

———. *Viaje a la América meridional.* Buenos Aires: Editorial Futuro, 1945.

Page, Thomas J. *La Plata, the Argentine Confederation, and Paraguay . . . during the Years 1853, '54, '55, and '56.* New York: Harper and Brothers, 1859.

Palevecino, Enrique. "Breve noticia sobre los Mocobíes actuales." In *Hacia allá y para acá (una estada entre los indios Mocobíes, 1749–1767),* ed. Florian Paucke, vol 3, pt. 1, xvi–xviii. Tucumán and Buenos Aires: Universidad Nacional de Tucumán, 1944.

———. "Las culturas aborígenes del Chaco." In *Historia de la nación argentina (Desde las orígenes hasta la organización definitiva en 1862).* Vol. 1, ed. Ricardo Levene, 429–72. Buenos Aires: Imprenta de la Universidad, 1936.

Pastells, Pablo, ed. *Historia de la Compañía de Jesús en la provincia del Paraguay.* 8 vols. Madrid: Librería General de Victoriano Suárez, 1912–1949.

Pastore, Carlos. *La lucha por la tierra en el Paraguay.* Montevideo: Editorial Antequera, 1972.

Paucke, Florian. *Hacia allá y para acá (una estada entre los indios Mocobíes, 1749–1767).* 4 vols. Tucumán and Buenos Aires: Universidad Nacional de Tucumán, 1942–1944.

Pospisil, Leopold. "Feud." In *International Encyclopedia of the Social Sciences.* Vol. 3, 389–93. New York: Macmillan and The Free Press, 1968.

Radding, Cynthia. *Wandering Peoples: Colonialism, Ethnic Spaces, and Ecological Frontiers in Northern Mexico, 1700–1850.* Durham, N.C.: Duke University Press, 1997.

Ramírez, Susan E., ed. *Indian Religious Relations in Colonial Spanish America.* Syracuse, N.Y.: Maxwell School, Syracuse University, 1989.

Reyburn, William D. *The Toba Indians of the Argentine Chaco: An Interpretive Report.* Elkhart, Ind.: Mennonite Board of Missions and Charities, 1954.

Ribeiro, Darcy. *Kadiwéu: ensayos etnológicos sobre o saber, o azar, e a beleza.* Petropolis, Brazil: Livraria Poliedro, 1980.

Ricard, Robert. *The Spiritual Conquest of Mexico: An Essay on the Apostolate and the Evangelizing Methods of the Mendicant Orders in New Spain, 1523–1572.* Trans. Leslie Byrd Simpson. Berkeley: University of California Press, 1966.

Rock, David. *Argentina, 1516–1987: From Spanish Colonization to Alfonsín.* Rev. ed. Berkeley and Los Angeles: University of California Press, 1987.

Rodrigues, Nemesis J. *Oppression in Argentina: The Mataco Case.* Copenhagen: IWGIA, 1975.

Rossi, Antonio. "Relación histórica sobre las misiones en el Chaco de Santa Fe presentado al gobierno nacional en 27 de julio de 1864 por el prefecto de misiones." In *Poblaciones y curatos: estudio histórico,* by Manuel M. Cervera, 427–30. Santa Fe, Argentina: Talleres Gráficos Castellvi Hermanos, 1939.

Saeger, James Schofield. "Another View of the Mission As a Frontier Institution: The Guaycuruan Reductions of Santa Fe." *Hispanic American Historical Review* 65, no. 3 (1985): 493–517.

———. "Clerical Politics in Eighteenth-Century Peru: The Trial of José de Antequera y Castro." *Journal of Church and State* 17, no. 1 (1975): 81–96.

———. "Eighteenth-Century Guaycuruan Missions in Paraguay." In *Indian-Religious Relations in Colonial Spanish America.* Ed. Susan E. Ramírez, 55–86. Syracuse, N.Y.: Maxwell School, Syracuse University, 1989.

———. "Government Policy and Guaycuruan Missions." Unpublished manuscript.

———. "Priests and Friars in Guaycuruan Missions." Unpublished manuscript.

Sahlins, Marshall. *Stone Age Economics.* Chicago: Aldine-Atherton, 1972.

Salisbury, Neal. "American Indians and American History." In *The American Indian and the Problem of History.* Ed. Calvin Martin, 46–54. New York: Oxford University Press, 1987.

Sánchez Labrador, José, S. J. *El Paraguay Católico.* 3 vols. Buenos Aires: Imprenta de Coni Hermanos, 1910–1917.

Sánchez Quell, H[ipólito]. *Estructura y función del Paraguay colonial.* 5th ed. Asunción: Casa América, 1972.

Schroeder, Susan. *Chimalpahin and the Kingdoms of Chalco.* Tucson: University of Arizona Press, 1991.

Scunio, Alberto D. H. *La conquista del Chaco.* Buenos Aires: Círculo Militar, 1971.

Serrano, Antonio. *Los primitivos habitantes del territorio argentino.* Buenos Aires: J. Roldán & Compañía, 1930.

Silverblatt, Irene. *Moon, Sun, and Witches: Gender Ideologies and Class in Inca and Colonial Peru.* Princeton, N.J.: Princeton University Press, 1987.

Slatta, Richard W. *Cowboys of the Americas.* New Haven and London: Yale University Press, 1990.

Smaby, Beverly P. "The Mormons and the Indians: Conflicting Ecological Systems in the Great Basin." *American Studies* 16 (1975): 35–48.

Socolow, Susan Migden. "Spanish Captives in Indian Societies." *Hispanic American Historical Review* 72, no. 1 (1992): 73–99.

Stern, Peter A. "Social Marginality and Acculturation on the Northern Frontier of New Spain." Ph.D. diss. Berkeley: University of California, 1984.

Steward, Julian H. "The Native Population of South America." In *Handbook of South American Indians.* Vol. 5, 655–68. Washington, D.C.: Government Printing Office, 1956.

Steward, Julian H., ed. *Handbook of South American Indians.* 7 vols. Washington, D.C.: Government Printing Office, 1946–1959.

Susnik, Branislava. *Los aborígenes del Paraguay.* 7 vols. Asunción: Museo Etnográfico Andrés Barbero, 1978–1985.

———. "Dimensiones migratorias y pautas culturales de los pueblos del Gran Chaco (enfoque etnológico)." *Suplemento Antropológico: Universidad Católica* (Asunción, Paraguay) 7, nos. 1–2 (1972): 85–101.

———. *El indio colonial del Paraguay: El Chaqueño.* Vol. 3, pt. 1. Asunción: Museo Etnográfico Andrés Barbero, 1971.

———. *El rol de los indígenas en la formación y en la vivencia del Paraguay.* 2 vols. Asunción: Instituto Paraguayo de Estudios Nacionales, 1982–1983.

Sweet, David. "The Ibero-American Frontier Mission in Native American History." *The New Latin American Mission History.* Eds. Erick Langer and Robert H. Jackson, 1–48. Lincoln and London, 1995.

Tanck, D. E. "Catechisms in Colonial Spanish America." *New Catholic Encyclopedia.* Vol. 3, 232–34. New York: McGraw-Hill, 1967.

Taylor, William B. *Magistrates of the Sacred: Priests and Parishioners in Eighteenth-Century Mexico.* Stanford, Calif.: Stanford University Press, 1996.

TePaske, John J., and Herbert S. Klein. *The Royal Treasuries of the Spanish Empire in America.* Vol. 3, *Chile and the Río de la Plata.* Durham, N.C.: Duke University Press, 1982.

Tommasini, Gabriel. *La civilización cristiana del Chaco: segunda parte (1554–1810),* Buenos Aires: Librería Santa Catalina, 1937.

Toscano, P. Julián. *El primitivo obispado del Tucumán y la iglesia de Salta.* Buenos Aires: Imprenta de M. Biedma e Hijo, 1907.

Ubertalli, Jorge Luis. *Guaycurú: tierra rebelde.* Buenos Aires: Editorial Antarca, 1987.

Urbano de Iriondo, [José]. "Apuntes para la historia de la provincia de Santa Fe." *Revista de la Junta de Estudios Históricos de Santa Fe* (Santa Fe, Argentina) 1 (1935): 38–83, 2 (1936): 83–119.

[Uriburu, Napoleón]. *Memoria del gobernador del Chaco con una exploración del Pilcomayo y decretos del gobierno nacional.* Buenos Aires: n.p., 1875.

Utley, Robert M. *The Indian Frontier of the American West, 1846–1890.* Albuquerque: University of New Mexico Press, 1984.

Vayda, Andrew. "Primitive Warfare." *International Encyclopedia of the Social Sciences.* Vol. 16, 468–72. New York: Macmillan and The Free Press, 1968.

Velásquez, Rafael Eladio. *El Paraguay en 1811.* Asunción: n.p., 1965.

Viola, Blanca Rosa de. *Paraguay, siglo dieciocho: período de transición.* Asunción: Ediciones Comuneros, 1987.

Wallace, Anthony F. C. *Religion: An Anthropological View.* New York: Random House, 1966.

———. "Revitalization Movements." *American Anthropologist* 58, no. 2 (1956): 264–82.

Warren, Harris Gaylord. *Paraguay: An Informal History.* Norman: University of Oklahoma Press, 1949.

Weber, David J. "John Francis Bannon and the Historiography of the Spanish Borderlands: Retrospect and Prospect." *Journal of the Southwest* 29, no. 4 (1987): 331–63.

———. *The Spanish Frontier in North America.* New Haven and London: Yale University Press, 1992.

Whigham, Thomas. *The Politics of River Trade: Tradition and Development in the Upper Plata, 1780–1870.* Albuquerque: University of New Mexico Press, 1991.

Wilbert, Johannes, and Karin Simoneau, eds. *Folk Literature of the Caduveo Indians.* Vol. 1. Los Angeles: UCLA Latin American Center, 1989.

———. *Folk Literature of the Mocoví Indians.* Los Angeles: UCLA Latin American Center, 1988.

———. *Folk Literature of the Toba Indians.* Vol. 1. Los Angeles: UCLA Latin American Center, 1982.

Williams, John Hoyt. "El Dr. Francia y la iglesia paraguaya." *Estudios Paraguayos: Revista de la Universidad Católica* (Asunción, Paraguay) 2, no. 1 (1974): 139–54.

———. *The Rise and Fall of the Paraguayan Republic, 1800–1870.* Austin: University of Texas Press, 1979.

Winckler, Edwin A. "Political Anthropology." *Biennial Review of Anthropology, 1969.* Ed. Bernard J. Siegal. Stanford, Calif.: Stanford University Press, 1970.

Wright, Pablo G. "Dream, Shamanism, and Powers among the Toba of Formosa Province." *Portals of Power: Shamanism in South America.* Eds. E. Jean Matteson and Gerhard Baer, 149–79. Albuquerque: University of New Mexico Press, 1992.

Zapata Gollán, Agustín. *El Chaco Gualamba y la ciudad de Concepción del Bermejo.* Santa Fe, Argentina: Librería y Editorial Castellvi, 1966.

Zeitlin, Judith Francis. "Ranchers and Indians on the Southern Isthmus of Tehuantepec: Economic Change and Survival in Colonial Mexico." *Hispanic American Historical Review* 69, no. 1 (1989): 23–60.

Zubizarreta, Carlos. *Historia de mi ciudad.* Asunción: Editorial EMASA, 1964.

INDEX

ABOUT THE AUTHOR

James Schofield Saeger is professor of history at Lehigh University, where for many years he was co-director of the Gipson Institute for Eighteenth-Century Studies. He received his Ph.D. from The Ohio State University. He is the author and editor of articles and books on rebellion in colonial Spanish America, institutional and administrative issues, labor systems, race relations, film and history, Catholic missions, and other topics. Currently he is at work on a biography of the Paraguayan dictator Francisco Solano López and on a military history of the Viceroyalty of the Río de la Plata.